Tarantula's Web

JOHN HAYWARD, T. S. ELIOT
AND THEIR CIRCLE

Tarantula's Web

JOHN HAYWARD, T. S. ELIOT
AND THEIR CIRCLE

JOHN SMART

MICHAEL RUSSELL

© John Smart 2013

The right of John Smart to be identified
as the author of this book has been asserted by him
in accordance with the Copyright, Designs
and Patents Act, 1988

First published in Great Britain 2013
by Michael Russell (Publishing) Ltd
Wilby Hall, Wilby, Norwich NR16 2JP

Page makeup in Sabon by Waveney Typesetters
Wymondham, Norfolk
Printed in Great Britain by MPG Books Ltd
Bodmin and King's Lynn

ISBN 978–0–85955–324–7

Contents

Acknowledgements

The Hayward family have supported this biography in every way. Dr Henry Oakeley has been a constant helper, provider of information, photocopies, discs and hospitality, along with his father the late Rowland Oakeley. I am especially grateful to them. Major Ian and Gillie Ferguson provided family material as did Mr and Mrs John Rolleston. Mrs Josie Wrangham has generously allowed me to use private letters in her possession. Friends of John Hayward including Dr Ann Baer, Miss Binney, David Bevan, Richard Garnett, Catherine Porteous, Kathleen Raine, the late Humphrey Spender and his sister-in-law Lady (Natasha) Spender and Gwen Watkins all brought him to life for me. Professor A. S. G. Edwards and Adrian Barlow read through the manuscript at an early stage and were most encouraging. Kathryn Hughes gave splendid advice as my mentor on behalf of New Ventures Partnership. I would also like to thank them for financial support and encouragement. Professor John Haffenden was most generous in passing on the materials on Hayward he had gathered together over many years. Anthony Hobson, Jim McCue and Tamsin Morris improved drafts considerably and saved me from many errors. I have benefited from conversations with all of them. D. J. Taylor commented helpfully and encouragingly as did Dr Nick Fisher. John and Amrei Harrison translated the Latin and German texts. Dorothy Bartholomew, John Begg, Steve Benson, David Bowen, the late John Coleridge, Christine Eberhardie, Jane Fairbrother, Hugh Wright, Simon Kinder, the late Dr John Hope Simpson, Dr Richard Maxwell, Dr Nicholas Owens, Richard Peaver, John Rayner, David Sharp, Carolyn and Bill Thomas, Cecil Woolf, David Warnes – all helped with the text in many different ways.

I would also like to thank for their help Dr Rosalind Moad and Patricia MacGuire at the Modern Archives Centre, King's College, Cambridge, Dr Judith Priestman at the Bodleian Library, Oxford, and the librarians of St John's College, Cambridge and of the Harry Ransom Centre at the University of Texas, Dr Leslie A. Morris, Curator

Acknowledgements

of Modern Books and Manuscripts at the Houghton Library, Harvard University, Cambridge MA., Nicholas B. Scheetz, Manuscripts Librarian Special Collections Division, Georgetown University Library, Washington and the librarians at Reading University and at the Wimbledon Historical Society. At Gresham's School the archivist Liz Larby and the librarian Carol Buxton built up the school background and Sue Shaw retyped my work. Kelly Delevan was a superb researcher at the University of Texas

I am very grateful to the late Mrs Valerie Eliot who kindly allowed me to see the correspondence between Eliot and Hayward at King's College, Cambridge and to the generosity of Faber and Faber in allowing me to print extracts from Eliot's writings and papers at King's. Mari Prichard and Kate Trevelyan have allowed me to quote from 'The Pope of Russell Square'. Professor Helen Gardner was a friend of both Hayward and Eliot and her *The Composition of 'Four Quartets'* is the indispensable account of the textual development of the poem. I am also indebted to Dr Lyndall Gordon's work on Eliot, Hayward and Mary Trevelyan, and her insights into their relationship in *T. S. Eliot's New Life*. I have also learnt from Peter Ackroyd's biography of Eliot, Carole Seymour-Jones's work on Vivienne, *Painted Shadow*, and Professor Richard Badenhausen's *T. S. Eliot and the Art of Collaboration*. Professor Edwards's detailed pioneering work recording Hayward's published works has been crucial, as has his essay in *The Book Collector*.[1] Michael Russell has been a 'creative critic' of all aspects of this biography and has saved me from countless errors by his meticulous scrutiny of the text.

Adrian Barlow is the godfather of this book. He first gave me the idea of writing about John Hayward and using the papers at King's that had been embargoed until 2000. Finally, my wife Susan has been tirelessly encouraging in her comments over many years and in patiently looking through all the drafts. All the faults, however, are my own.

I
An Edwardian Childhood

The Haywards were an old Wiltshire family of yeoman farmers, originally from Beechingstoke and North Newton, small villages in the Vale of Pewsey. The surname, according to John Hayward, came from their occupation looking after the hay at the abbey of Shaftesbury. Before the railway came to the Vale many old rural customs flourished just as they had in Elizabethan times. On Whit Monday or 'Club Day' villagers used to process through the villages patrolling the Downs to make sure the children did not pick lilac or laburnum which would mean bad luck for the rest of the year. At Christmas, mummers walked into the houses, wearing strips of wallpaper and long peaked caps crying, 'Wark in. Wark in. I zay ...'² The family's successful careers as landowners there can be seen in the parish records; a whole row of Haywards lie buried in Beechingstoke churchyard, their prosperous table tombs marking the path to the church.

The best-known member of them was John Hayward's great-uncle Abraham.³ There are uncanny parallels between 'wicked old Uncle Abraham' and his great-nephew. In *Vanity Fair* of 1875 Ape's cartoon in the series of 'Men of the Day' shows an elderly grey-haired man, wearing a short tail coat. He has a heavily-lined face, a protuberant lower lip and tired eyes. Thumbs in his pockets, he leans forward as if making a point in some argument and half-looks toward the viewer with raised eyebrows, perhaps world weary, perhaps cynical. It is not a flattering portrait but it is certainly one full of character. Born in 1801 in the village of Wilton, Abraham Hayward became an eminent Victorian, the personification of Samuel Smiles's principle of Self-Help. After Blundell's School in Tiverton he was articled to a solicitor in Somerset but the quiet life of a country solicitor did not suit an ambitious clever young man with literary leanings. He left for London in 1824 and entered himself as a student of the Inner Temple to train as a barrister. Soon he became a well-known figure at the Bar and set up and jointly edited the *Law Magazine*, becoming its sole editor in June 1829. He held the post for the next fifteen years.

Abraham Hayward also began to make his mark at the London Debating Society where he met and argued with the most prominent young liberals and radicals of his day such as John Arthur Roebuck and John Stuart Mill. It was hard, wrote Mill, for them to find Tories to argue with, but Hayward and another barrister, Sergeant Shee, filled the bill excellently. Arguments were fierce and sometimes bitter. It was passionate intellectual theatre, 'a *bataille rangée*',[4] as Mill put it, between the philosophical radicals and the Tory lawyers. Hayward was outspoken and feared no one in debate, but there was little doubt that in Mill he had met his match. It was, said one witness, like watching a ploughshare going over a mouse. Hayward never forgot a slight and the enmity between him and Roebuck and Mill was to echo down the course of his career.

Hayward's reputation began to spread through his network of contacts and friendships. It spanned the literary, political and aristocratic worlds. As a young man he had launched his career in 1833 with a translation of Goethe's *Faust*, hailed by Thomas Carlyle as the best version of its time, and admired by Wordsworth and Southey. He knew or met Wordsworth, Southey, Dickens and Tennyson. Fluent in French and German, he visited the Continent to talk to Alexandre Dumas and the Goethe family. He was friendly with Bulwer Lytton and Macaulay and played whist at the Athenaeum with Anthony Trollope and the Liberal politician W. E. Forster. Throughout his life he wrote prolifically: volumes of political essays, translations from German and French, an account of crossing the Alps, *Short Rules of Modern Whist* – and even volumes of verse. Reputed to be one of the two best-read men of his time (the other was Lord Macaulay), he was also a prodigious writer of letters in an age of prodigious letter writers and a regular contributor to the *Quarterly Review,* the *Edinburgh Review* and newspapers such as *The Times*. His astonishing memory along with an encyclopaedic grasp of detail served him well when he became one of the chief leader writers for the *Morning Chronicle*.

Hayward made close friends but his acerbic tongue and strongly held views also made him many enemies. Some found him 'arrogant, overbearing, loud, insistent, full of strange oaths and often unpardonably coarse'. Or, in a word, 'odious'.[5] Another enemy talked of 'the many-sided yet concentrated malice which supplied the stock in trade of Abraham Hayward'. He was appointed QC in 1845 and the natural next step was to be appointed a Bencher in the Inns of Court. Roebuck, now an MP and a Bencher, immediately blackballed his old opponent. By the rules, one blackball was sufficient and Hayward was refused. He responded with bitter pamphlets and letters but it was to no avail. He decided to give up his legal career and devoted himself to writing and reviewing.

In his bachelor chambers, overlooking the Thames, he gave dinners at which his guests could appreciate the wit of the Reverend Sydney Smith or the political oratory of Lord Macaulay. As a lover of fashionable gossip he developed the reputation of being 'not only a connoisseur of a bill of fare but also of a bill of company'. One of his secrets was always to dilute the male company with two or three ladies. 'Wicked old Uncle Abraham' was throughout his life a ladies' man and a well-known figure at the leading ladies' salons of the day. The Hon. Mrs Caroline Norton was a notorious dark-eyed beauty and a regular guest at his dinner table. Hayward acted as her confidant and legal advisor during a long period of litigation. Her 'cher avocat' became a lifelong friend. He enjoyed friendships too with many of the leading hostesses of his day such as Lady Holland, Lady Waldegrave, and 'the Queen of hostesses', Anna Jameson. 'Hayward amuses me extremely,' she wrote. 'He is clever, well-read, lively, satirical and knows everyone.'[6] He often flirted with younger and prettier ladies in privately printed verse, and collected photographs and *cartes de visite* in a leather album. Fond of the stage, he admired Sarah Bernhardt and the Jersey Lily, Lillie Langtry, whose stage début in 1881 he attended. As he grew older he enjoyed becoming the confidant of many society ladies: 'My charming friends so often make me the recipient of their irregular fancies, that I begin to fear their moral estimate of my moral principles is not so high as it should be.'[7] Yet there was never a suggestion of a romance or of marriage in his life.

Hayward chose not to put himself forward as an MP but grew increasingly involved in the politics of his day, supporting the Peelite cause and a programme of moderate reform. His Temple chambers became 'the scene of great political interest' when the formation of a coalition was preceded by a dinner there. Hayward wrote to his sisters: 'My dinner went off capitally and has done great good by consolidating the Peel party ...'[8] His political friendships included many European statesmen such as Count Cavour in Italy and Adolphe Thiers, President of the Third Republic in France. He was friendly with two prime ministers, Lord Palmerston and William Gladstone;

with Gladstone he corresponded for more than thirty years. He hated Disraeli and infuriated him by detecting plagiarism in his eulogy of the Duke of Wellington. (Disraeli replied by partly basing his envious character St Barbe in *Endymion* on Hayward.) In touch with many leading political figures of his day in England and in Europe and, as a counsellor to politicians and their wives, he had an influence 'surpassing that of a cabinet minister'.[9]

It was a debate over birth control that re-ignited all the hostilities with Mill and Roebuck in 1873 when Hayward wrote Mill's obituary in *The Times*.[10] It was an opportunity, however unsuitable, to settle old scores. The substance of Hayward's accusation was that Mill had got into trouble with the police for distributing copies of pamphlets giving detailed instruction about contraception to maidservants and the poorer classes. Hayward argued that Mill's dangerous advocacy had not just been a folly of youth but a persistent error. Perhaps more unpleasant and personal were the insinuations of his remarks about Mill's personal life: 'When Mill fell in love with a lady (a married woman) he wrote a succession of papers in *The Examiner* against marriage as a binding tie, and in favour of unlimited liberty of divorce.' Raking over these events in *The Times* made Hayward few friends; equally alienating were his strenuous efforts to make sure Mill was not buried in Westminster Abbey.

Throughout his life he had an enormous energy, 'a veritable salamander in the hot forge of hard work'. Even at the age of seventy he was contributing lengthy reviews to each issue of the *Quarterly*. But with advancing years he grew out of sympathy with his age, saying that he had 'outlived everyone he could really look up to'. He fell ill in autumn 1883 and was confined to his rooms in No. 8, St James's Street, where Byron had once lodged. His sister Frances and friends, including Gladstone and the writer and historian A. W. Kinglake, visited. But gradually he faded, and expired 'peacefully and painlessly' on the morning of Saturday 2 February 1884. His last words were: 'I don't know what it is, but I feel it is something grand.'

The funeral cortège was modest. It was 'too quiet and unpretending to attract attention as it passed the clubs', reported *The Times*.[11] The coffin was simply draped in black cloth; no black plumes caught the eye. Only two mourning coaches followed. Leading the mourners was Prime Minister Gladstone who placed on the coffin a basketful of snowdrops fresh from his garden at Hawarden. There were a number of lengthy obituaries and *The Times* incorporated its tribute in its leading article: 'The number must be comparatively small of those who remember a time when Mr Hayward was not a conspicuous ornament of social life. To the present generation he was almost an institution, so unquestioned was his position ... '

On a cold morning in February 1901 Abraham's nephew, Dr John Arthur Hayward, married Rosamond Grace Rolleston at Christ Church, Lancaster Gate, Paddington. According to Agatha Christie the Rollestons were 'one of our oldest families' and could claim descent from Sir Henry de Rolleston who became Lord of Rolleston in 1280.[12] George Rolleston, John's maternal grandfather, was born in 1827. After winning an open scholarship to Pembroke College, Oxford and gaining a first-class degree in Greats in 1850, he decided to follow the increasingly respectable profession of medicine at St Bartholomew's Hospital in London. In 1862 he married into another medical and scientific family. His wife, Grace Davy, was the daughter of Dr John Davy, Inspector of Army Hospitals and the niece of Sir Humphry. George and his family established themselves in professorial comfort – the 1881 census showed five living-in servants – in the solid red-brick house he had built for them in North Oxford, Park Grange in South Parks Road. In 1860 he was appointed as the first Linacre Professor of Anatomy and Physiology at Oxford.

John Hayward's mother, Rosamond Grace Rolleston, was born in 1865, the third child of the family.[13] As a three-year-old 'Rosie' was a bridesmaid at the wedding of the novelist Mrs Humphry Ward, showering the bride with pear blossom. She grew into a lively, friendly girl who enjoyed playing the fashionable sport of lawn tennis, loved dancing and parties and also gave French lessons to a class of girls in the 'Young Women's Association'. 'Our Rosie thoroughly enjoys life here, being so energetic about her work, and being so fond of the society of her fellow creatures,' wrote her mother to her sister-in-law in New Zealand. The picture is of a devoted family thriving in mid-Victorian comfort at the centre of the social world of Oxford. But the days of prosperity and tennis parties were soon to come to an end. In October 1881 Professor Rolleston was brought back from Paris suffering from Bright's disease. Three days later he died, aged fifty-four, and left seven children to be looked after. His wife Grace slowly recovered, only to suffer from the first of a series of clinical depressions which were to dog her for the rest of her life. The world of childhood security was over: Grace's sister was drafted in to act as a surrogate mother to the two youngest boys.

Rosie had left her home in Oxford to train as a nurse at St Bartholomew's in London. Adventurous and independent, she had gone to South Africa to the Boer War to tend the wounded and returned to Bart's as a hospital sister. It was there that she had met the ambitious Dr Hayward. They were not a young couple – he was thirty-four and she was a year older. They had already decided to move to fast-expanding Wimbledon after living in London. The London and South Western Railway had come there in 1838 and the population had grown dramatically, from just over 2,000 to nearly 55,000, bringing demands for new villas and terraced housing – and a need for more doctors. The Haywards set up home on Lingfield Road where they lived in modest upper-middle-class style: the census of 1901 showed that they kept two servants. Their first child, George, was born there two years later. Able and very hard-working, Dr Hayward soon built up a large and lucrative practice and, unusually, continued to take exams that qualified him as a surgeon. It was not long before he and his family moved up the hill to a larger house on the edge of Wimbledon Common.

23, The Grange was built of solid yellowish London brick in 1889, part of a late Victorian development in which a grand eighteenth-century house was demolished and its land split up and sold for build-ing twenty-three large villas. The inhabitants of The Grange, mainly wealthy widows, army officers and professional men, could look down from its height on the smaller houses of 'new' Wimbledon below them. Number 23 had 'a light and cheerful basement' with range, scullery and 'capital butler's pantry, larder, and a wine and coal cellar'.[14] A lift helped the servants carry food upstairs to the dining room. There was a large hall and dining room facing the road and the floors were of fash-ionable pitch pine. The main living rooms overlooked the garden which Mrs Hayward loved to tend. There was a greenhouse in which she care-fully stored fruit and vegetables for her family. Dr Hayward expanded the plot and later added a conservatory and then a 'motor house'. The servants' accommodation of hall, bathroom and windowless bedrooms was up in the attic so that they could not overlook the family at play in the garden.

John Davy Hayward, the second child of the marriage, was born at The Grange on 2 February 1905. From his mother he inherited big eyes, long doll-like eyelashes and full sensual lips. 'I always think of him as he was between 2 and 7 – John with the innocent noble little face and later with the unruly hair and dirty hands,' wrote his father from the trenches of 1918. One morning as John was being wheeled in his pram on the Common a long-haired figure stooped to kiss him. It was the ageing poet, Algernon Swinburne, a serial baby kisser, on his daily pilgrimage from his drab semi-detached villa to the Rose and Crown and a glass of beer. Some years later, as a schoolboy who hoped to be a famous poet, Hayward felt that this was a benediction. Robert Graves had received the same blessing a few years earlier but when John's elder brother George had also been approached the nursemaid had flourished an angry umbrella and beaten Swinburne off.

It was natural for the young John Hayward to dream of becoming a man of letters for he came from two families of writers and loved to complete long lists of their books.

> When I was a little boy I used to play at being a man of letters. This engrossing game of make-believe kept me quiet for years on end in an attic at the top of my parents' home. Hidden on three sides by piles of books, borrowed from the nursery and heaped upon a solid foundation of gold bound volumes of *Punch*, I would sit smugly behind this breastwork and, with bottles of coloured inks, pencils, rubbers, paper-clips, scissors and paste to stimulate my fancy, would dream of literary fame in the years to come.[15]

On the Hayward side were all great-uncle Abraham's works and his father Joseph's learned treatises on *The Science of Agriculture* and *The Science of Horticulture*. On the maternal Rolleston side there were two eccentric volumes from the eighteenth-century Reverend William Rolleston: *On Places of Retirement* and *A Dissertation on Barley Wine*. The three family Fellows of The Royal Society – John's grandfather, Professor George Rolleston, and great-uncles Dr John and Sir Humphry Davy, the inventor of the miner's lamp – all wrote copiously on scientific and philosophical topics. George Rolleston was an amateur antiquarian and Dr Davy published on angling, the interior of Ceylon and the Ionian islands; Sir Humphry started his writing with a volume of poems and ended it in 1828 with *Salmonia*, a book on fly fishing.

The two boys were followed by two girls, Rose Mary in 1906 and Diana in spring 1908. George, two years older than 'Jonnie', as the family called him, did not get on easily with either his younger brother or his father. By contrast, the sisters were very close. Rose Mary trained at the Royal Deaf School in Manchester and planned to work at an Indian mission, but died suddenly aged twenty-three in 1931 of double pneumonia. John kept in close contact with Diana until his death, and their letters show their lifelong affection.

The Grange and its garden seemed enormous to the young John. He remembered it as 'set handsomely in seven acres of grounds'. He could easily lose himself among its dark corridors and remote rooms. There was a cellar that flooded like a lake and an attic that was to become his literary den.[16] Hanging in the loft was a pair of angler's waders stuffed with newspapers that looked like the severed trunk of a giant. Underneath them lay his father's ancient 'elephant gun'. The Grange was large and mysterious but it lacked comfort. It was, as he recalled later, 'a mansion replete with every ancient inconvenience from an immense penumbral lodgement to remote attics', with a household that comprised 'nine elderly housemaids, a gouty butler and an apoplectic mistress'.[17] In the nursery John had his first taste of poetry as he was read Kipling's rhymes and stories. Religion played a large part in this conventional upper-middle-class home. After breakfast every morning family and servants assembled in the drawing room for hymns and the reading of the collect for the day. On Sundays Dr and Mrs Hayward and their children did a two-mile walk to church; in the evening there were more hymns and prayers at home. As cleanliness was next to godliness John's nanny insisted without much success that her grubby charge should always wash and dry carefully between his toes so that, in the event of an accident, he would be recognised in hospital as a well-brought-up child.

Very close to home, just off the Common at 9 Ridgeway Place, was Oakhill School, run by two elderly spinsters. There in 1909 four-year-old John had his first taste of education. His report showed that he 'sings very heartily' and he was already marked out as having some ability for recitation: 'He remembers the words well and recites with expression.' All in all, summed up the headmistress, John was 'a very earnest worker'. It was pleasant to fantasise, he wrote many years later, that for those born between 1900 and 1910 'a sunset of a Golden Age gilded their perambulators and time was measured by the shadows of patrician cedars falling across the immaculate lawns of stately homes'.[18] The Grange was certainly not a stately home and no cedars shaded its

Wimbledon lawns, but he did look back on his Edwardian childhood as the happiest of times.

His father liked to take John to the West Country where they toured around by car as whim took them. Bath was a favourite resting-place but the heart of these jaunts was the visit to Dr Hayward's birthplace, Beechingstoke, on the Wiltshire Downs. It was, his son recalled, an idyllic spot sheltered in a warm valley by two clumps of beeches from which the village took its name. Here the young boy plucked the 'great yellow globes of the marsh marigolds and picked handfuls of fresh mint' and visited the scenes of his father's youth; his old home with its shrubbery, smelling of dead pine needles and laurel leaves, its walled garden, and paddock all 'invested with some of the romance of a life which I have never shared'.[19] He enjoyed hearing his father's old tales of familiar landmarks, of the field where a pig had been chased to death after a long hunt and of the day when the family cow wandered into the garden and exploded after eating too much new-mown grass.

When he was given his first tricycle at the age of eight, he set off from home, without his parents' knowledge, to fulfil his ambition to visit the newly built Lots Road Power Station. This meant an epic and danger-ous journey through busy traffic, from Wimbledon, across Putney Bridge then through Hurlingham and on across Wandsworth Bridge Road. He presented himself at the main door and demanded, success-fully, to be shown round. Then he tricycled all the way back 'to face the hue and cry' from his angry parents.[20] His tricycle also featured when he recalled in mock-heroic vein family holidays in Wales, the Black Mountains and the Brecon Beacons. Poignantly, he linked his boyhood with images of fast movement and activity:

> ...the small fellow on the tricycle,
> Speeding with whirling feet concentrical,
> To Sunday service in far Kingston's vale;
> And the egregious schoolboy, quick to scale
> Plynlymmon, or Black Bredon's swarthy slopes,
> (The grubby Darling of a Father's hopes!) ... [21]

2

Wartime

The Hayward family took regular summer holidays in Dorset and Devon. On 1 July 1914 they packed their belongings as usual for the journey westwards. They rented Monastery Farm at East Lulworth, in Dorset. It was a beautiful and remote place for the children, who enjoyed playing on the sands and sea bathing for a month, unaware that the world outside was beginning to close in on their holiday. On 4 August 1914, after a hot day on the beach, they all went happily to bed, tired by the sun and sea air. A sudden loud rapping on the door woke Dr Hayward. 'On the same night when you were all fast asleep,' wrote Mrs Hayward in the history that she wrote for her children, 'the lonely farm by the chalky Dorset cliffs was aroused by two telegrams for your father, one to take up Red Cross Duties and one to take up duty as a doctor in the East Surrey Regiment, the latter being intended for another doctor but reached Daddy by mistake. The next day your father left for Wimbledon and duty and had no more holiday that year.'[22] The telegram that awoke the sleeping Dr Hayward was from the regional director of the Red Cross. The summons read: 'ENGLAND AT WAR. MOBILIZING. RETURN FOR RED X DUTY. LONGSTAFF.' Immediately, Mrs Hayward felt 'a deep gloom coloured everything and formed a heavy background to all attempts at holiday life'. Mother and children stayed on after Dr Hayward had left, but for Mrs Hayward too the holiday was over. The children's German-Swiss governess had to be hurried off home to Bonn. Steel-grey battleships appeared in the bay and khaki uniforms were everywhere. Mrs Hayward felt the contrast between the innocent lives that her children continued to lead and the bleak news from France and Belgium. She wrote in her history: 'The devastation of Belgium, the sack of Louvain, the terrible retreat of our army at Mons, all took place while you and I were bathing, paddling, picnicking, sketching and blackberrying.'

In early September the family returned to Wimbledon. For both boys it was time to go back to preparatory school for the autumn term. John began his first term at Hillside, a small school of about fifty boys set on the edge of the Surrey countryside at Farncombe, near Godalming. There he followed in the footsteps of the brothers Julian and Aldous Huxley into 'a strange, rough and often brutal world'.[23] The school was a ramshackle house built on a very steep incline. The elderly headmaster used to interview boys sitting in a low basket chair wearing ancient leather bedroom slippers in 'a funny little study reeking of tobacco and Harris tweed'; photographs of former pupils in elaborately-carved picture frames looked down from the walls with pipe racks and university shields hanging above their heads.[24] There were endless flights of wooden stairs to climb and long dark stone passages to walk down. Facing the house were the playing field and a cricket pavilion surrounded by six poplars that the boys used to listen to at night rustling and tossing in the wind.

To the eight-year-old John Gielgud, who had arrived as a new boy in 1913, Hillside was Dotheboys Hall: 'an altogether ghastly place; a good deal of bullying went on ... and between lunch and the next morning's breakfast all we ever got were three chunks of bread, thinly buttered with a scraping of jam'.[25] Visits to the outdoor lavatories were frightening as shafts of light through the corrugated iron roof cast 'enormous and appalling shadows as the cisterns dripped and gurgled in the distance'. It was alarming to hear footsteps from behind – at any moment a bully might leap out from the shadows. There were initiation ceremonies in which the new boy had to swing hand over hand along the iron girders of the dormitory as the elder boys pelted him with sponges and flicked him with wet towels. Snobbery was taken for granted. Corporal punishment was common, even for breaking such minor rules as reading in the dormitory. Aldous Huxley later painted a picture of the casual brutalities of Hillside, thinly disguised as 'Bulstrode', in *Eyeless in Gaza*.

Gielgud was immediately struck by John Hayward's looks – 'an ugly boy with a big sloppy mouth' – but soon found him very funny and very likeable; he became Gielgud's 'first chum'. The two had plenty in common. John Hayward sat in his Wimbledon attic imagining himself as a writer while Gielgud was playing with his pillared and elaborately-gilded toy theatre in his parents' home in South Kensington. Both boys took little part in sports at school: Gielgud was 'delicate' and 'a funk at games' and Hayward was already having problems with his knees. But both loved acting, sketching and drawing, and sang together in the school choir. In the school holidays John Gielgud soon became a visitor to The Grange. He was alarmed by how mother and son looked so similar, sharing 'the same loose mouth and spikily-prominent eyelashes like the mask of a ventriloquist's doll'.[26]

Hayward's letters home showed him to have been busy in a boyish way. Deeply into a train craze, he wrote to his parents from 'The Railway Club'. A drawing of the front of an engine heads the page: 'I have got most of my railway pictures above my bed in my dormitory,' he added. In the holidays he loved to be taken to Victoria Station to watch the Continental expresses. When visiting his wealthy cousins in Scotland, the Smith Sligos, he spent whole days at Glasgow Central Station where the London expresses drawing out of the station and those 'dazzling blue locomotives of the old Caledonian' thrilled him. He was struck too by the 'southbound trains threading through the towering cantilevers of the Forth Bridge which would fill me with unutterable heart-ache'.[27] (The romance of the train never left him; a party piece in later life was a vigorous full-voiced imitation of steam engines.) He was chatty about the ordinary life of the prep school boy, noting his disappointing position in Greek and mathematics, commenting on Sports Day and how much he had enjoyed a 'very nice tea'. A friend (probably John Gielgud) requested him to stay with his family in the holidays and he enthusiastically asked his mother's permission – already showing a precocious sense of style when he signed himself floridly:

Your affect.
Son
John D H

At Hillside he devoured the early science fiction novels of H. G. Wells, especially *The Time Machine*, *The War of the Worlds* and *The First Men in the Moon*. Inspired by them, he loved to devise and draw 'the most elaborate rocket machines for flying into inter-stellar space or amphibious craft for exploring the secrets of the submarine world'. Like his father, he took a keen interest in the world of nature and flowers. A favourite holiday visit was to the Natural History Museum; all his life he remembered the exhibition of nature's smallest and biggest animals there – an Indian elephant towering above a tiny shrew mouse. At school he enjoyed cultivating a small garden. 'My aubriceas [*sic*] are flowering beautifully and one of my roses is in full bloom,' he wrote to his parents, adding proudly that he had won a prize for his nasturtiums.

Even at this age he was a passionate collector. The butterflies, moths and postcards of famous expresses at speed of his boyhood would become the books of his maturity.

At school there were problems with his knees. At first the doctor prescribed Iodex and all exercise was forbidden. John was then allowed to play cricket in the nets and to swim as his knees got a little better. But he could still run at only a 'moderately fast pace' and on Sports Day was relegated to giving out the programmes. He became that last refuge of the unsporty – the cricket scorer. Dr Hayward was concerned. He had noticed something very unusual: from babyhood John had always slept with his eyes wide open. Could these problems be connected? It was time to consult a specialist. The worst was confirmed: the growing loss of muscular control that had begun with the eyelid was a sign of creeping paralysis, or muscular dystrophy as it had recently been scientifically classified. There was no alleviating cure and no treatment for this wasting and fatal illness. It is now clear that he suffered from a particular kind of 'facio-humero-scapular muscular dystrophy … the synonymous eponym of the limb-girdle muscular dystrophy of Landouzy-Dejerine'.[28] Although this was not as severe or fast-developing as the more common Duchenne's, the young boy faced the bleakest of futures. Little was known about the disease at the time and the likely rate of its progress, but the outline was all too clear. Paralysis would first affect shoulders, neck and facial muscles. Walking would become more and more difficult until it became impossible. No one could say how much the disease would shorten John Hayward's life. His father took him for more visits to specialists and even organised a week of prayer from the nuns at the local Ursuline convent in Wimbledon. But it was to no avail.

When the two brothers returned to school for the autumn term of 1914 they found that the war had already changed Hillside; some of the staff had enlisted and others were on their way to the Front. Surrey itself was directly in the path of German bombing raids to London; searchlights beamed through the night skies and began to play over the roof of the school and the surrounding hills. The onset of war also altered their parents' lives drastically. Dr Hayward was now in charge of organising the local Red Cross Aid Detachment and training a force of 100 women and 50 men. He had volunteered as assistant-surgeon to the big new British Red Cross hospital at Netley which was purpose-built to receive casualties from the Front. Mrs Hayward began to undertake war work and, as an experienced nurse, was offered the post of Commander of the Wimbledon Red Cross Detachment – a post she had to turn down because of her responsibilities to her children: she did, however, become the Assistant Commander in August 1914. The war hit the family personally when a second cousin of Mrs Hayward, the young George Smith Sligo, with whom John had watched trains in Glasgow, died in September 1914, fighting with the Cameron Highlanders. It was to be the first of many family losses. Already Mrs Hayward reported that more than half of her friends were mourning a loved one: both of her Wimbledon neighbours had already lost sons at the Front. The favourite tune of the Tommies at the time was 'It's a Long Way to Tipperary' – but Mrs Hayward found it hard to listen to 'a tune with a great swing to it which has become the saddest and most tragic of all tunes'.

When the boys returned home for their Christmas holidays in 1914 everything had changed. They had to decamp to Bursledon, two miles from Netley, so that they could see something of their father, whose work did not allow him the chance to come home for Christmas. Mrs Hayward organised her children into a concert party to entertain the wounded. There were songs, choruses and popular tunes on the gramophone. George wore a pirate's costume and sang a patriotic song; John looked imposing as a king in glittering robes and recited 'There was a boy whose name was Jim', one of Hilaire Belloc's cautionary tales he remembered from the nursery. The real stars, however, were the two young sisters: Rose Mary was dressed as a Red Indian squaw and Diana, who stole the show, wore the miniature uniform of an Army sister. The performance was such a success that it had to be repeated on New Year's Eve and Mrs Hayward received many letters from the men thanking her and 'the dear children' for their efforts.

After Christmas the boys went back to their schools and their parents continued their war work. In May 1915 Dr Hayward was appointed as medical officer to the new Queen Alexandra Hospital at Roehampton which had been set up to look after officers and men who had lost limbs. Mrs Hayward helped him by organising the staff, by marking the linen and forming 'a ladies needlework auxiliary party'. She and the Red Cross Commandant, Miss Gosling, greeted King George and Queen Mary when they paid their first visit to the hospital on 1 July 1915. She also helped in the newly set up War Depot for Wimbledon where women prepared all kinds of splints, swabs and surgical dressings. Every Saturday morning she dispensed tea, buns and good humour at the Church Army canteen. She met batches of wounded soldiers as they arrived by train at Victoria Station, and sometimes acted as a stretcher-bearer and took casualties to hospital by ambulance. She also looked after the Belgian refugees who were accommodated nearby at a big house near Wimbledon Common. As summer approached, the Common became an armed camp and fighter squadrons were stationed there with their planes lined up ready to defend London from attack. Wimbledon was full of bandaged and convalescent soldiers recuperating in the sunlight. The endless summer parties and 'the strawberry ices eaten off wicker chairs in sunny gardens'[29] of the Edwardian childhood John Hayward so fondly remembered now seemed worlds away.

The routine of the traditional Hayward summer holiday also fell victim to the war. Lack of petrol made the family try to find somewhere much closer than Devon or Dorset. So in August 1915 they stayed at Elstead Vicarage, in the countryside just outside Godalming, and not far from John's prep school at Farncombe. Even here it was impossible to forget the war. Big camps of troops surrounded the village. The roads were cut up by heavy lorries and provision vans and choked by military vehicles. It made travelling very difficult: 'We never went out without meeting long trains of artillery and gun carriages,' wrote Mrs Hayward in her history. One hot August morning there came a surprise. As the family enjoyed the shade of the rectory garden they were told a rumour that the King and Queen were expected to drive through the village. The children rushed to the roadside and outside the gate of the rectory found two immaculately-groomed black horses, one for the King and one for Princess Mary. Soon a large car drew up – and immediately out stepped the King, Queen and the Princess. The King and Princess mounted their horses and Queen Mary got into a car behind. The boys were playing at soldiers and gave a respectful military salute that was 'kindly acknowledged' by the King.

At the outbreak of war the family chauffeur Frank Sanderson had volunteered for Kitchener's army and Mrs Hayward regularly sent him letters, clothes and food parcels. On 30 September she packaged up a shirt and wrote that she and her husband were wondering 'whether he had taken part in that great and glorious and splendid onslaught that has cheered us up in England greatly'. In October she received a letter in handwriting she did not know.

Dear Madam,

I am writing a few lines as I thought you would like to hear the news of Mr. Sanderson. I am the girl to whom he was engaged. I am sorry to tell you he was killed in action on the morning of the 25th September, I have often heard him speak of how good you were to him and I take this opportunity of thanking you very much for your kindness to my sweetheart. Although his death is hard to bear I am proud to know he did his duty,

Yours sincerely,
Ellen Coates[30]

When George and John returned home after the autumn term of 1915 for their second wartime Christmas they were told the sad news. They found a household firmly on a war footing. The ten-year-old John voiced his disappointment at his holiday in a poem he wrote at Hillside, 'Christmas in Wartime'. It was printed in *The Doddite*, the school literary magazine, produced on an ancient 'jelligraph' machine:

> No Christmas tree in the Hall doth stand,
> No children dance around hand in hand,
> No crackers bright with toys inside
> Await their blue and eager eyes.
>
> Why not this usual gay surprise?
> Why not those blue and eager eyes?
> A war is on their parents say,
> No Christmas tree for you today.
>
> Care not for books that you may read,
> Which from your friends you have received,
> But try and think of our soldiers brave
> And how our country they will save.[31]

Mrs Hayward recorded the poem in her history, but added, a little defensively, 'we did not indeed have a tree but a very nice bran pie'.

1916 brought more problems. John had to be brought home from school suffering from influenza which developed into jaundice. On the Sunday night of 2 April at 11.30 the boy scouts came around to The Grange to report the dramatic news that 'the enemy is attacking in force'. Six Zeppelins were bombing the south-east of England. The sick boy asleep in his mother's bed was violently woken as he 'got the full benefit of the electric night bell overhead and the warning message up the speaking tube'. Three more nights of Zeppelin raids and alerts followed. Often, after an alarm given by the boy scouts, Mrs Hayward would don her VAD uniform and make her way through darkened streets to wait for her orders at Red Cross Headquarters. According to her history, the winter of 1916–17 was the coldest since 1877. Certainly in Wimbledon Arctic conditions prevailed over Christmas and lasted until March. The boys learnt how to skate and the girls tobogganed merrily on the slopes of the Common. The bad weather, however, combined with the sinking of ships by German submarines, led to an increasing food shortage and, as prices rose, Mrs Hayward noted that by November 1916 there was no meat for dinner and even potatoes had become a rarity, to be replaced by soup, macaroni and apples from the garden. Public eating was by law reduced to two courses at lunchtime and three in the evening. Her son contributed another poem to the *The Doddite*. His mother wrote with some pride: 'It deserves preserving here as a school boy's twelve year old form of expression on a burning topic of the day.'

'Two Course Lunches'
(by one who suffers)

Before this aggravating war
When courses numbered four or more
I always liked my lunch to start
Not 'Table d'Hôte' but 'à la carte'.

The very first thing that I bought
Would be a cooling glass of port:
Some soup, some fish, some game, some meat
Would be the next thing I would eat.

Then puddings, ices, biscuits, cheese –
Good walking Dutch to make one sneeze –
And last of all some luscious fruit
And coffee of far-famed repute.

But now – my courses are but two;
That is a thing I really rue:
Besides last Tuesday, if you please,
I could not get my dish of cheese.

And now I must my poor lunch start
With 'Table d'Hôte' not 'à la carte'!
No biscuits now can I procure
For even that's against the law.

So now, fair Reader, be aware
Of greed, that all enticing snare,
For soon of food you'll want much more,
And get still less, thanks to the War.[32]

The centrepiece of the table in the drawing room of The Grange for Christmas 1916 was a Father Christmas snowman, clutching in one arm a Union Jack and in his other an envelope containing a sad appeal for Belgium's starving children. This 'formed an object lesson for the children gathering around and we all put in what we could, including our good maids at their dinner,' wrote Mrs Hayward in her Victorian style. This year too there was no turkey, no fruit, and no expensive luxuries. Typically, she entertained some less fortunate children to help enjoy the bran pie and play Christmas games with the family. All in all, she wrote, 'John's poem was not quite verified'.

Spring passed and at Hillside during the hot summer afternoons of 1917 John and 'Master Jack Gielgud' lazed on rugs set on the grass, ate cherries and whispered smutty jokes together while watching cricket. It was Gielgud's final year: he was Head Boy and they shared the duties of scoring as he learnt his lines for the next school production of *Julius Caesar*. Hayward looked back on these summer afternoons with nostalgia, recalling in almost photographic detail the cricket matches played in blazing June sunshine against Priorsfield, the local girls' school. The girls always won by bowling 'sneaks' along the ground. At tea the young cricketers paired off to hammocks slung cosily under shady trees, where they were served bowls of strawberries and cream by the younger girls. Then two horse-drawn charabancs arrived at the front door to pick up the Hillside boys. 'The tender farewells were completed by the girls' high-piping cheers as the charabancs crunched over the gravel to take the boys back to school for 6 o'clock prep.'[33]

It was not always so peaceful: even at Hillside the casualty lists of old boys had to be read out every few days. In the summer of 1917 Zeppelin raids began to disrupt lessons. A treat for boys who had gained more than 70% in their exams was a full holiday to visit a bomb crater made by a Zeppelin just outside Guildford: 'It was about the size a moderately large dog might make in a frenzied effort to recover a lost bone,' remembered Hayward.[34] Eating jam puffs, Gielgud and Hayward stared at the hole and hoped to find bomb fragments as trophies. Their trip ended in disappointment, as Gielgud recorded in schoolboy style in 'The Zeppelin Raid on Guildford':

> Back to Hillside went we sad
> Not a bit of bomb we had
> But we saw some houses had
> Had some bombs inside 'em.

The two boys shared a love of acting and, from the age of eight, performed together in school plays. A raised platform at the end of the dining hall made a good stage. Gielgud was, naturally, already the lead player, with a rendition of the song of the Mock Turtle, 'Soup of the Evening', from *Alice's Adventures in Wonderland* which made some of the parents in the audience cry. Surprisingly, the school had a strong dramatic tradition: 'We were encouraged to think of Shakespeare in terms of theatre,' Gielgud's elder brother Val recalled.[35] At the age of ten, Hayward had played the part of the Duke in *The Merchant of Venice* to Gielgud's Shylock, both plastered with make-up. Later, in 1917, in their final school play together, Hayward was Trebonius in *Julius Caesar* and Gielgud Mark Antony; Gielgud also managed the production and designed all the sets. Hayward's lifelong love of theatre started with his friendship with one of the most famous actors of his age.

The hot summer of 1917 brought some relief from food shortages. Nationally the harvest was good. Mrs Hayward gathered record crops of peaches and pears from her garden and pickled all the fruit so that she had a store of gooseberries, cherries, plums, walnuts, beans and crab apple jelly ready for winter. Hundreds of eggs were laid in water-glass to preserve them. The news from the Western Front also gave hope. In November she felt that, finally, there was the prospect of an end to the war. Douglas Haig had achieved 'a great victory', reclaiming five miles of French territory, nearly reaching Cambrai and taking 10,000 German prisoners. On Friday 23 November the bells of St Paul's and the churches of the City of London rang for the first time after three years and three months of silence to celebrate the victories. On this mild and sunny day Mrs Hayward joined the mass of people in the churchyard to rejoice in the first public – and premature – celebration of victory for the Allies. When the bells stopped the whole crowd burst into cheers and sang 'God Save the King'. There was good news too from the Middle East, where in December the British army under General Allenby took Jerusalem and ejected the Turks. She described this, as she described the whole course of the war, as a crusade. 'The city welcomed the British occupation, thankful to be freed from Turkish misrule – after 673 years the Holy City was freed from the Infidel.'

This final Christmas of the war witnessed her more hopeful mood. At last all the family could enjoy a dinner of roast beef and a plum pudding in good conscience – it 'was economical in the first place and delicious in the second'. Afterwards they went to join in the celebrations at the local hospital where crackers, music and decorations brightened the wards. 'Co-operative tea parties' followed Christmas Day, with each guest bringing some share of the meal. There were theatricals, dancing and games for the young; their parents brought potted-meat sandwiches, buns, scones and cakes. The evening finished with jellies and lime juice. Despite the lack of luxuries, the children all voted it a most successful Christmas. 'So we defied the Germans and their U Boats from spoiling the children's happiness,' wrote Mrs Hayward proudly. New Year, however, brought disappointments and reversals. Paris was bombarded, air-raids continued and the German Spring Offensive broke through at St Quentin with enormous loss of life.

Despite all the medical work he was doing in and around Wimbledon, Dr Hayward fretted, longing to get to the Front. On Good Friday 20 March, there came a telegram to The Grange: 'Very urgent need for Medical Officers in France who have already served. It is hoped you will volunteer.' At last he had got his chance.[36] Immediately he went to the War Office to sign on for six months. 'In response to a personal appeal from the authorities I have decided that it is my duty to volunteer for service in the RAMC in France during the emergency,' he wrote in a letter to all his patients. Events now moved very quickly. He received his marching orders on 13 April and four days later Mrs Hayward went to London to stay with him at the Grosvenor Hotel on the night before he embarked. At 7.35 she saw him off on the officers' train that left Victoria Station. Whatever fears the stoical Mrs Hayward might have felt about her husband's departure she kept to herself and wrote only in her history, 'He crossed the same day to Boulogne and began his interesting new life.'

'Full of enthusiasm and with no little pride and satisfaction to my family and myself', Dr Hayward set out to explore the port of Boulogne and bought presents of wax pigs for his daughters and 'a sweet little miniature wee dolls' morning-tea-set for Mary'.[37] Tea at the officers' club was followed by a trip to the huge basilica church of Notre Dame whose fine dome could be seen from the sea. There he noted how sad it was to see so many widows in black with little children. A large body of soldiers in full uniform marched past, the breezy sound of the military band mixing with the boom of the distant guns. It was all very strange to him: the town crowded with soldiers; the constant saluting he received; the picturesque streets with dug-outs and shelters made of sandbags. He was something of an oddity himself – at fifty-one he was one of the oldest volunteers and felt 'rather like a grandpa among so many young men'. He considered buying a wig from the coiffeur.

Before he could get used to life in Boulogne, however, Dr Hayward learnt that he had been posted to the large base hospital at Trouville on the Normandy coast where he had holidayed with his wife before the war. After the exciting novelty of a ten-mile trip aboard a minesweeper he arrived at the watering place. There, high on a plateau overlooking the sea, three 2,000-bed hospitals had been built. He was disappointed not to be closer to the fighting. The operating theatre had not been completed, so, frustratingly, there was little work to do. He was allocated a spartan room that was a divided off apartment in a hut that could hold ten men, with bare boards, a bedstead, a mattress and a wicker stand, but no table or chair. It made a stark contrast to the comfort of The Grange, but he never complained to his wife. Gradually he made his room more homely; the carpenter built him a table. He bought a small kettle and lamp so that he could make himself tea, a carpet and some curtains from the big store in the town. Soon the walls were covered with drawings that his children sent him and photos of home that he carefully mounted in brown paper frames. Just like his son at Hillside he enjoyed creating a garden. He asked Rosie for some Webbs' lettuce seeds to put under the frames one of his fellow officers had made. He also requested some rock plants and established a little border round his hut where he planted these and some of the wild flowers he found on his walks. Two months later, in June, there were gardens growing around the huts and the lettuce was ready for transplanting. Mrs Hayward kept him in close touch with how her garden was doing in Wimbledon and the state of the peach, pear and apple trees. He replied with letters that gave detailed advice about watering and planting. This constant concern for growing plants was no doubt a therapeutic contrast to the world of destruction that war had bought.

Apart from the war the theme that dominated his letters home was his concern for his family. He kept on buying little presents to send home for the children and wrote copiously to them. Cheered by any kind of photograph or letter that brought them back to mind, he chatted about their caged birds – Bully the bullfinch and Roly the redpoll (which he was sure was a linnet) and asked for copies of the 'Golliwog Gazette' the girls wrote. He enjoyed George's letters and always wrote affectionately of 'dear old John' who wrote long chatty letters illustrated with coloured sketches. 'John's letter was brimming with affection … as good as the best pommery and his drawings of my supposed debauches at the mess table were excellent,' Dr Hayward wrote proudly. 'It makes me so happy to have such dear children.' His letters also show his devotion to his wife, who regularly sent parcels of all kinds including seeds and plants, woollen vests and pants, pyjamas, torch refills, pencils, 'strawberry jam (Tiptree)', lavender soap ('a real taste and smell of dear old home'), home-made cakes and books on surgery and botany. 'Really people in Wimbledon seem to look upon you as a tower of strength,' he wrote – and so, of course, did he.

Meanwhile at Hillside the summer term of 1918 went on as usual. John was made captain of the school shooting team and twice won the prize for the best shot – a success he afterwards attributed to shooting with his eyes shut. There were regular trips to the seemingly vast school swimming pool at nearby Charterhouse. Ominously, he wrote to his parents: 'This term is very nice only I wish my knee would get better so I could play games and swim.'[38] As it was his last term there naturally came the question of where he should go next. The family hoped that he might win a scholarship to a public school and so in early June 1918 Dr Hayward wrote a long letter to his son to encourage him in his exams. On 14 June he received some excellent news – John had won the Fishmongers' Scholarship to Gresham's School in Holt in North Norfolk. This was the school's top award, given by the governors, the Fishmongers' Company of London, worth £30 a year, renewable until he left, subject to good performance. As he read the letter over a late tea in the mess room, Dr Hayward was so delighted that he danced a hornpipe – much to the amusement of the senior nurses. Immediately he wrote to his wife, 'Dear old John. I felt sure he would come out one of these days, and I am sure he never worked hard for it. I am so awfully pleased and have lumps in the throat, and giggly gulps while I am writing.' He decided that his son deserved a really good present for his success and suggested a bicycle. Soon afterwards he was proud to hear that his wife had visited Hillside and seen John's name in gilt letters on the school's Honours Board.

Dr Hayward became more and more frustrated at being away from the main action. On 15 June as the guns fired night and day he heard that the Germans were nearing Paris: 'I do want to get nearer the centre of things,' he wrote. Life at the base camp was too 'safe and soft and sound for war time'. In his powerful letter to Rosie on 30 June he wrote about leaving Trouville:

> I shall miss the lively country and my beloved expeditions, but I have that feeling that I must get nearer to the Maelstrom and see and feel what others felt and saw. I have no fear except that of not being able to do the work adequately and that can be got over by determination. The summer goes on apace, the woods and valleys are bathed in a summer haze, berries begin to show, spirea smelling in the fields and elder in the hedges, and with it all the guns go on booming, and far off beyond the haze and beyond the woods the appalling slaughter goes on and the wrecks come back here to be turned back again to face it. You can understand why I must go.[39]

Finally in July 1918, to his delight, he found himself posted as a surgeon to 47 Casualty Clearing Station at Crouay, near Amiens. If the war had disappointed Dr – now Captain – Hayward so far by its form-filling bureaucracy and its remoteness, he had now got into the thick of it. The station itself consisted of a number of canvas tents pitched in the middle of the countryside. At the Front he was amazed at the rapid advances in surgery: 'The most extraordinary recoveries take place by operating on some of the bad cases at once and unheard of things are done successfully ... some cases I have seen are real miracles.' He was astonished that now the whole wound and damaged muscles were cut away before infection took hold. 'Dozens are saved in this way ... who would otherwise die of gas gangrene,' he wrote.

Back in England, there was no summer holiday together for the family in 1918. George was employed doing land work and John went with his mother to Belmont, near Hereford, where together they bicycled around the lanes and explored the windings of the River Wye. Even on holiday, Mrs Hayward worried about the future. Although air-raids had become much less frequent, and less effective, there were prospects of a dark and cold winter ahead; the Fuel and Lighting Order was a 'a grim spectre' facing households. Rationing had become still more severe. More seriously, a deadly 'flu epidemic was beginning to take hold of the country.

While his family were on their summer holidays August and September became the most hectic months for Captain Hayward as 47 Clearing Station followed the 4th Army's advance eastwards towards the Hindenburg Line. By 12 August he was doing as many as ten to twelve operations a day and sometimes working for thirty-six hours without sleep. Processions of ambulances and trains continued to arrive every three hours, disgorging more of the wounded for treatment. The teams of surgeons could not keep pace with the arrivals; dozens of patients had to lie on the grass night and day on stretchers; it needed the pen of a Zola to describe the sheer horror of the scenes outside the casualty clearing stations, wrote Hayward. He was now confidently in control of the nurses and attendants but his authoritarian manner and sharp tongue earned him the nickname the 'little Pharaoh'.

By October 1918 he had nearly served his six months at the Front and wondered what lay ahead. He was fascinated by the state of the war as it reached a crisis point, but he desperately wanted to see his wife and children again. 'It will be difficult to leave in the midst of all that is happening ... It will be lovely to be at home – but you can also imagine that I shall have many regrets at leaving the centre of these extraordinary happenings, at this particular time ... I could not leave with the tents full of men waiting for help.' It was duty that held him, but also excitement at having finally reached the centre of the 'Maelstrom'. Cheered by a sense of the approaching final victory, he felt he was now approaching the war's climax: 'The great thing is we are on top of the Hun and everybody is in great spirits and bucked up.' And just at this moment his time ran out. There could be no extension. On 16 October Mrs Hayward received a telegram that read, 'ARRIVE VICTORIA ABOUT 8 TONIGHT. JACK.' Captain Hayward's war was over.

He returned home to resume practising medicine from The Grange. His was, as was common at the time, a single-doctor practice. He also had some beds in the local hospital, and was unusual in that he was not only a qualified doctor but also, thanks to his war service, an experienced surgeon. Hayward was to recall to Eliot his father's female patients as Victorian 'old trouts' from another age.[40] There was the spinster who had above her bed for forty years the text 'OCCUPY TILL I COME' and the lady who would not allow her four daughters in their late sixties to venture out unchaperoned. He remembered Mrs Davidson, bitten in the navel by her favourite chow, and the 30-guinea operation on Mrs Boodle who had to have a broken hypodermic syringe extracted from her ample backside. 'Like looking for a needle in a haystack,' Dr Hayward said to his son. One patient had such confidence in his skills that she brought in her off-colour chameleon in a cardboard box. Another reported that her son had been successfully cured of bed-wetting by eating a brown mouse correctly dressed and cooked. All these – and many more – came to the surgery at The Grange and formed the basis of a very successful practice, allowing Dr Hayward to pay for the education of his children. That he was a popular and conscientious doctor is shown by the large number of letters of gratitude from patients – letters he carefully tied up in pink ribbon and kept.

When John Hayward came to recall his wartime childhood the picture was a mixed one: 'a confused memory of darkened windows, margarine and fearful visions in the pages of *The Illustrated London News*; of fathers and elder brothers returning on leave with bits of shrapnel and pressed wild flowers; of drawing-rooms littered with cretonne bags and skeins of wool'.[41] The elder brother back home from leave is a fiction, but the strange dislocation of the time, the margarine, his mother's knitting littering the house, the darkened windows and images of his father, back from the Front, surrounded by war souvenirs and natural history specimens, are all drawn from life.

3
Gresham's, Holt, and France

At the age of thirteen, in Michaelmas Term 1918, John followed in George's footsteps as Fishmongers' Scholar not only to Gresham's, but also to Woodlands House, a fine eighteenth-century building of white stone on the Cromer Road. Governed since Tudor times by the Fishmongers' Company, the school had been re-founded in 1900. The appointment of a new headmaster, G. W. S. Howson, lent it the kind of shaping vision that great headmasters such as Thring of Uppingham and Sanderson of Oundle had given their schools. In the prospectus Gresham's announced itself as a different kind of school, a 'Public School on Modern Lines', with a large science laboratory, an emphasis on practical work and the use of the direct (oral) method of teaching French. German was an alternative to Latin – and Latin itself not taught in the two lowest forms. It was also noted for a gentler régime than many other boarding schools and a relative lack of interest in games. Beating was replaced (at least in theory) by a system which put every boy on his honour to behave well. Bedales and Gresham's were the two best known 'modern' schools to survive the war, and were very popular amongst thoughtful middle-class professional parents who wanted to break away from the old traditions of the public school that had led to the slaughter of so many young soldiers.[42] Robert Medley, the painter and theatre designer, who was a contemporary of Hayward's, noted 'the social homogeneity of our cultural backgrounds' arising from the fact that 'no parent sent his children to either school out of tradition, and certainly not for snobbish reasons'.[43] As a man of science, Dr Hayward must have liked the look of the curriculum and perhaps too, after being beaten at Marlborough College himself, was looking for a gentler education for his boys – especially since John's health was in question.

John's housemaster was J. R. Eccles, who became headmaster after the death of George Howson in January 1919. Eccles was quite a contrast to the predecessor he revered. A prim bachelor, he decreed that all boys, apart from prefects, should have their trouser pockets sewn up to prevent 'personal abuse'. What he lacked in charisma he made up for in energy and his presence was felt everywhere in the school. Auden was later to gain enormous pleasure out of mimicking him and parodied Eccles's earnest manner of speech, his frequent use of questions and repetitions, and tone of breathless naïveté: 'Commemoration. Commemoration. What does it mean? What does it mean? Not what does it mean to them, there, then. What does it mean to us here now? It's a facer, isn't it boys?'[44] Few Old Greshamians who read these lines had any doubt who the target was. The sophisticated young Hayward viewed his housemaster with the same amusement. He did not find his brother George easy to get on with either and soon after his arrival managed to infuriate him. During the argument in George's study John angrily threw a pocket book at his brother's head. It hit him hard in the eye. The result was the shattering of a 'much-valued monocle' given to George as a love-token from his favourite cousin, Winnie:

> He seized me by the throat and banged my head against the hot-water pipes. I can smell now the stifling odour of hot dust, as I heard through the singing of blood in my ears the hysterical shouts of the boys rushing past the window crying 'The War's over! The War's over! Hurray! Hurray! Hurray!'[45]

So John Hayward remembered Armistice Day, 11 November 1918, in his first term at Gresham's School.

When peace was declared Mrs Hayward could not immediately share in the general rejoicing. Her Scottish cousin, Winifred Smith Sligo, had been shot dead in the last month of the war as she was driving an ambulance in France. Mrs Hayward attended the military funeral at Aldershot, but when she returned home via Waterloo Station she was caught up in the excitement of crowds singing patriotic songs, waving flags and cheering wildly. On the following day she and her husband drove around the streets of the city, now lit up for the first time since war began. The West End was *en fête*, draped with flags and bunting; crowds of men and women thronged the pavements and climbed on every kind of vehicle. Sirens shrieked and the cheering and shouting reminded her of the wildly enthusiastic scenes at the beginning of the war. Now, at last, she felt she could round off her history on a note of hope: 'The lights began to shine out again in the streets, the search lights disappeared, white bread re-appeared and every day the load and pressure and inconvenience of war were lifting gradually – and this strange eventful history I have endeavoured to record for you may come to an end.'

At Gresham's John Hayward was seen as a delicate boy, immediately marked out as different. He walked with an awkward dog-paddle gait and could not fully control his open thick lips. There was evidently something very wrong with him, but no one was clear about exactly what it was. Although he was not bullied, his contemporary Edward Blanshard Stamp recalled him as an outsider, 'an odd boy' who cut a pathetic and lonely figure. His school record, however, tells another story. His disability ensured that he could not play games – he was allowed to ride a horse for exercise – but otherwise he played a full part in school life. He sang in the choir, developing a strong resonant bass voice; he enjoyed the debating society and was able to be in the Officers' Training Corps; he sat on the library committee and edited the school magazine. The activity that gave him most pleasure was acting. He was lucky to find that Gresham's, like Hillside, had a strong dramatic tradition. There were annual house plays and every summer a Shakespeare production in the outdoor theatre in the school woods. He relished playing broad comic character parts: Tony Lumpkin in *She Stoops to Conquer* and the butler in Sydney Grundy's Victorian farce, *A Pair of Spectacles*. In the Woodlands House play of 1919, *The Rivals*, he took the role of the neurotic suitor, Faulkland, and George took the smaller part of David. He acted too with W. H. Auden, who was three years junior to him, in *Much Ado About Nothing* in July 1921. Sebastian Shaw, later to become a leading Shakespearean actor, was Claudio. The young Auden made a 'charming' Ursula, the waiting maid, and the watchmen, of whom Hayward was one, were singled out for the reviewer's praise in the school magazine, *The Gresham*: 'The watch, quaint in their looks, queer in their manner, supremely energetic in their arrest, all delighted us …'

With him to Gresham's Hayward brought four volumes of Swinburne's poetry, bound in blue morocco leather. He had paid more for them than he could afford but he prized them as he had never prized a book before 'as a passport to emotional maturity'.[46] In a notebook, dated 1921 but evidently started before, he wrote in strong black capitals PRIVATE on the inside cover and followed this warning with another in blacked capitals: THE CONTENTS OF THIS BOOK ARE OF A PERSONAL NATURE AND ARE THEREFORE OF A STRICTLY PRIVATE CHARACTER. Inside was a collection of poems, imaginative prose essays, doodles (Hayward was an expert doodler all his life) and drawings. On the right-hand side of the page he wrote his first drafts and, on the left-hand side, in ink, he gave the final 'reworked' version. In boyish untidy pencil the first poem begins: 'The columbine's the daintiest flower / That's ever graced an earthly bower.' 'Surrey Hills' develops in the same manner:

> I know a Surrey hillside
> Where the grass is soft and green,
> Where North, South and far and wide
> A perfect view is seen.
>
> Right straight across the valley
> Majestic Leith Hills lie
> Where pine trees closely rally
> And shade me from the sky.

Much of this early verse has an adolescent dreaminess, escapism clothed in self-conscious poetic language. The sun sheds 'golden beams'; the summer air has a 'melting beauty'; streams 'ripple' and unnumbered waves thunder beneath faint moonbeams. Some of the poems explicitly treat this theme of escape. 'Imaginations' begins:

> Give me the fruits of Old Cathay,
> And laden I will sail away,
> To furthest shores of golden land
> so happy.
>
> Give me the smiles of Princesses
> Of Dream Land and in recesses
> Of my boat I'll hide them all
> so quietly.

Their titles – 'Sea', 'The Tides', 'Pacific Dreams', 'For the Sunset' – indicate the late romantic style and themes that attracted the young Hayward. 'I especially love Rupert Brooke's poems,' he wrote and Brooke's influence is clear in the sonnet 'English Heaven': 'All this was theirs: but they have given all / To England that her beauty may not die.' He was extremely fond, too, of Walter de la Mare, James Elroy Flecker and Alfred Noyes. John Masefield was an especial favourite. His 'England' was the first poem quoted, opening with lines which ten years on Hayward would have scorned: 'Oh beautiful is love and to be free is beautiful / And beautiful are friends.' Much later, writing to Eliot, Hayward laughed off the poetry of his youth as a kind of illness: 'an acute attack of Rupertbrookeitis with symptoms of Flecker's syndrome'.[47] This later dismissal does not quite do himself justice: his own verse was developing as he took on broader themes of love, loneliness and death within the control of the sonnet:

> We cannot tell the primal source.
> Closed is the beauty of a face
> Of loveliness that has no course
> Nor knows nor time nor space.

Many poems show how deeply the First World War affected him. Above the lines from Milton's *Samson Agonistes*:

> Nothing is here for tears, nothing to wail
> Or knock the breast, no weakness, no contempt,
> Dispraise, or blame, nothing but well and fair ...

to commemorate his dead cousin he wrote, 'Lancelot Rolleston's death Flanders 1915'. His youthful patriotism was linked to a deep sense of a pastoral England and found its expression in another line he quoted from Rupert Brooke: 'In Avons of the heart her rivers run.' Noyes's 'Victorious Dead' was in a similar vein – 'Now for our sake our lands grew lovelier / Through the visible radiance of their memory' – as were Binyon's 'For the Fallen' and John of Gaunt's 'Sceptred Isle' speech from *Richard II*. In his own poem 'Night', however, he moved closer in style and subject matter to the later war poets Owen and Sassoon:

> A bitter night, dense fog hangs like cloud
> Over the river. Rain washes the streets
> Mud, darkness, misery visibly evident
> Poison the air where foulness broods
> Like some Devil's slut on holiday.
> Faintly the gas flare flickers.

Perhaps he was also recalling his father's wartime experiences. The words 'Amor vincit omnia' stood emphatically on their own as did the verse from Isaiah that his mother had written into his Bible: 'In quietness and confidence shall be your strength.'

In another small black notebook[48] Hayward confided his most secret

[30]

ambitions. He entitled it 'Quotations and Sayings of Famous Men collected by Me beginning of 1921 year'. Opposite the title page he proclaimed his purpose in ringing and romantic terms:

> I keep this record as I hope one day to be a poet but more than anything I keep these remembrances in honour of the muse who first inspired me with the emotions of love, joy, peace, sorrow and the many, many things that come and make clear the soul's better understanding. 1921 is a birth year of my hope for everything pure, good, true and lovely.

He included passages from Isaiah, the Apocrypha and Ecclesiastes, together with classical authors such as Plato, Aristotle and Martial along with verse from Chaucer, Daniel, Milton, Pope, Wordsworth and Shelley. There was a wide range of prose too, including Carlyle, Richter, Hazlitt, Oscar Wilde and A. C. Benson, Already, at the age of sixteen, Hayward was compiling his first anthology. Both that and his poetic notebook show him beginning to break free from the influence of late romantic poets such as Swinburne and Brooke, yet still tied very much to them. They also reveal a passionate, serious young man full of hope and idealism.

In August 1921 the Hayward family returned to the West Country for their summer holiday as they had done before the war. They stayed at Lee, near Ilfracombe, on the North Devon coast. Twenty years later Hayward could still remember the long yellow stretches of Saunton Sands, 'the smell of puffballs and sun-warmed samphire, cold apple-pie and clotted cream, and the underwater touch of sea anemones'.[49] It was not only the beauty of the Devon coast that marked out his holiday. He also fell for a fifteen-and-a-half-year-old Swedish friend of his sisters, Dagmar Erhardt. In the back of the poetic notebook he painted a sketch of her sitting in an elegant white dress with bouffant brown hair and a Cupid's bow mouth in vivid red lipstick. On her knee is some material she is busy 'knotting', a craze of the time. All morning he prowled along the cliff top, a melancholy lovelorn figure, carrying his notebook and copy of Rupert Brooke's poems bound in limp suede. In the evening he dressed up in his father's white spats to impress Dagmar at the local dances. Ever literary, he wrote sonnet sequences to attract 'the Cruel Fair' and, for a while, she acted as his Muse. 'The New Moon's Purity' is dated 27 August 1921:

> The purple coverings of the heaven part
> And you are there crowned with the ecstasies
> Of love new born in loveliness; and power
> Has gone and each pale shadow dies.

Full of the thrill of his romance, Hayward returned to Gresham's School for the Michaelmas term and in September 1921 he completed 'To Dagmar' in his notebook:

> Sweet child, the spotless gift I offer here,
> Accept: and in return give me one smile,
> One corner of your throbbing heart and there
> My love shall grow and we shall sleep awhile,
> Till the last morning break and we shall find
> The sorrows of our childhood left behind.

After this, however, all did not go well between them – his intense feelings and throbbing heart were not reciprocated – and, shortly after this outpouring, 'Desire' takes on a more Byronic world-weary and cynical tone:

> I know the vainness of desire,
> The flower that yields its soul and scent
> Leaves little trace; and our love's fire
> No more astonishment.
>
> Around this neck thine arms are wrapt
> In idle dreams – frail links of clay
> That hardly joined, must soon be snapt
> And soon be cast away.
>
> We are deceived when we caress
> 'Tis with no purpose we're caressed.
> How shall we stay our weariness
> Upon a woman's breast.

Nevertheless, some forty-five years later, after his death, in a drawer of his desk John Hayward's executors found a faded daguerreotype of a toothy, smiling young girl. It was signed in the corner: 'Daggie'.

Hayward remained troubled by thoughts of Daggie and sex and had some hope that the religion he was beginning to doubt might help him to resolve them. One rite of passage at Gresham's was Confirmation –

he noted that like the Officers' Training Corps it was pretty well compulsory. As a conscientious objector both could be avoided, but in this conventional world no one dared to be different. There was still 'a faint spark among the dying embers when promised the sevenfold gifts of the Holy Ghost which I presumed would solve the pains of adolescence and the problems of sex'.[50] But one misty cold November afternoon in the school chapel at the Confirmation Service the Bishop of Norwich 'cleansed with clammy hands' all his thoughts of religion. That was the end of God for Hayward.

Hayward's closest friend at school was a schoolmaster. Armand Trèves, who had come to Gresham's just after the war in 1919. With his youth, his long hair and perfect bilingualism, Trèves stood out from the rest of the staff. According to a contemporary, not only was he French and 'delicate', living with his wife in a bungalow in Sheringham, when most of the staff were bachelors living in Holt, but he also 'held not merely left-wing but revolutionary views'.[51] Robert Medley remembered him as 'a mystery whom some credited with being an extreme left-wing political exile',[52] a Communist who had a tremendous impact upon the political thinking of the school. As a teacher of French he joined the very different Colonel Foster who, the boys said, had learnt the language in the trenches of the First World War. They liked to repeat the story of an infuriated Foster telling off an idle pupil with the words: 'Il faut que you really must buck up and try to fait an effort.' Acerbic and witty, Trèves's lessons echoed with laughter, but it was as a fiery speaker and debater that he made his mark.

'The Great Debate' – as it came to be known – was held on a Saturday night in November 1919. The main speaker, J. A. Spender, Stephen's uncle, the distinguished journalist and editor of the *Westminster Gazette*, proposed the topical motion that 'This House is opposed to Direct Action' – strikes and demonstrations. A full house of pupils and parents, together with the headmaster, listened as he failed to catch the mood of his audience. Trèves took the floor and declared how fitting it was that a Frenchman – and a poor one at that – should oppose the motion. 'Personally,' he said, he was 'not afraid of being called a Bolshevik'. He resented the argument that the pupils were going to be leaders of men. On the contrary they could all learn from mixing with working men. He sincerely hoped they would do away with the existing order of society. For twenty years he had been in close touch with the Socialists, Syndicalists, Bolsheviks – even Anarchists –

in fact with all the revolutionary movements in Western Europe. All had one purpose – the greatest good of all.[53] When he sat down to a loud burst of applause everyone realised that the House was behind him, and the motion in danger. The debate stirred up passions that the Society had never before known. Speakers could not make themselves heard amidst the din as he made his final appeal to the House. 'Does the House really want a social revolution?' he asked dramatically. From the fervour and the delight with which the vote was received it looked very much as if the House did: twenty-three for the motion and thirty-five against. Trèves had triumphed. As the fifteen-year-old Hayward was a keen member of the Debating Society, Trèves's victory must have added to his respect for the 'charismatic outsider with the acid tongue'.[54] What is remarkable is that such an intellectual and radical political thinker as Trèves, with all his close contacts with revolutionary European political groups, should have turned up in a public school in North Norfolk – and manage not to get sacked.

When the League of Nations Union was founded at the school in November 1920 Trèves was the natural choice to represent the Staff. No doubt it was his influence that led Hayward to become Secretary of the Gresham's branch in May 1922. In his October editorial of *The Gresham* he showed how much he had learned from his master, beginning by calling on the idealism of Shelley and Wordsworth. England was, as he saw it after the First World War, 'in the throes of the mill race of riot and revolution … passing through the darkest period of the eclipse of her prestige,' he wrote grimly.[55] However there was no reason to despair. Hayward and Trèves advocated a new determination to rebuild society. What was needed was, 'Courage then, to put off the old man and take a fresh plunge; to risk a league of nations and not another war … in short, to keep before us Shelley's revolutionary ideals – and not to funk.' This was the authentic voice of Trèves speaking through the schoolboy argot of his young disciple.

Somehow Trèves managed to contrive an 'off-licence' to take Hayward to his hospitable bungalow in Sheringham in school hours, with Hayward riding pillion on the back of his motorbike. There was also the occasional jaunt to Norwich 'where my special tuition was continued (in French) over dinner in a restaurant'.[56] During one of these escapades Trèves spoke of his admiration for the neglected seventeenth-century French writer Saint Evrémond, 'a sceptic after his own heart'. They then decided on a trip to Westminster Abbey in search of his monument. Under the suspicious eye of a verger, Hayward climbed a ladder and transcribed the inscription for his teacher. More than thirty years later he recalled the episode:

Few, if any, of the visitors to the poet's corner in Westminster Abbey now spare his monument a glance of curiosity and wonder for a moment whom it commemorates and why it is there. The lapidary inscription below the animated bust provides answers to these questions in marmoreal Latin worthy of one who

PHILOSOPHIAM ET HUMANIORES LITTERAS

FELICITER EXCOLVIT

GALLICAM LINGUAM

EXPOLIVIT ADORNAVIT LOCUPLETAVIT

But the lettering has become dim with the passage of time and its testimony cannot compete for attraction with the surrounding memorials to more celebrated literary figures. Nevertheless, for one youthful visitor, more than thirty years ago, the task of deciphering and copying it for his French tutor marked the beginning of a lifelong interest in Saint Evrémond and his writings and of an unending search for the scarce early editions of his work.[57]

Trèves was a complete contrast to Dr Hayward – radical in thought, sophisticated and witty – all qualities of course that made him much more attractive to the Wimbledon schoolboy. Their friendship continued after Hayward left school. Ten years later he carefully inscribed Trèves's name in his visitors' book for 1933. 'A wonderful man,' Hayward wrote of him, 'encyclopaedic in English and French Literature, an excellent advanced mathematician, and a philosopher, he has taught me how to mould my ideas and given me ideals on which to set my mind. He was an extraordinary strange person, full of sympathy and exquisitely gentle ... a brilliant and unorthodox teacher from whom I learnt more about life and letters than I did from all my other masters in as many years.'[58]

In his final year at school Hayward seemed to his fag, James Richards, 'an intellectually somewhat arrogant boy, given to sarcasm but not unkind'.[59] (Many years afterwards when they met on a Chelsea street, Richards, now an international authority on planning and architecture, expected the cry 'Fag' to ring out with a peremptory demand to push his old fag master ...) House photographs show Hayward, arms akimbo, in a challenging almost truculent pose. Certainly, according to his contemporary G. Evelyn Hutchinson, he did not bow down easily to the authority of his housemaster and headmaster J. R. Eccles.

> The only person I remember standing up to him was John D Hayward, who was asked to remove his most cherished possession, a signed photograph of Karsavina, from his study wall, on the grounds that the great dancer's costume was inadequate. Hayward snapped back, 'Madame Karsavina, Sir, is a very beautiful woman,' but the photograph was removed.[60]

Hayward was a keen supporter of the newly-founded Literature Society and read a 'most interesting paper' on Modern Poetry to it in summer 1922. He was already reading the periodical *The Bookman* and being commended for epigrams he submitted for its competition. With so many literary interests, he was an obvious choice to edit *The Gresham*. He immediately used his editorial to appeal for some more poetry: 'From our point of view the school is sadly lacking in budding poets,' he wrote – ironically enough since the young Auden had just arrived at Gresham's – 'The Editor is never inundated with manuscripts, but we hope that the near future will produce a much larger mass of matter sent in to *The Gresham* for publication.'[61]

The artist and designer Robert Medley had come to Gresham's in 1919, a year after Hayward. He had first got to know Auden when they went together in March 1922 on one of the Sociological Society's outings to visit a boot and shoe factory and the Great Eastern Railway works in Norwich. (It was, of course, Armand Trèves who led the trip.) On the following Sunday the two boys took a walk and Medley asked Auden whether he wrote poetry, 'confessing by way of exchange that I did. I was a little surprised that he had not tried and suggested he might do so.'[62] As Auden was to record later, this was for him the decisive moment:

> Kicking a little stone he turned to me
> And said, 'Do you write poetry?'
> I never had, and said so, but I knew
> That very moment what I wished to do.[63]

Very soon afterwards Hayward was printing the verse of 'this precocious puffy little boy with colourless hair'[64] in the columns of *The Gresham*. The first poem he published was 'A Moment'. Auden was just fifteen at the time.

Behold the sky
That once was one great glowing sapphire
Begins to die,
And now is but a glinting opal fire,
Smould'ring to a faded scarlet,
O'er the embers of the sunset.

And lo, a soft gossamer-like cloud,
That round the crescent moon, enveils
Its vaprous shroud,
And passing on its way reveals
Her, trembling, silvery, rainbow-clad,
Silent, fraily sad.[65]

Beneath the poem Hayward appended the note: 'We publish this in
spite of technical errors. Considering the age of the author it shows
great promise – Ed.'[66] He had picked out Auden's originality beneath
the conventional poetic diction of the poem's opening. Later, in December 1922, he published two, or possibly three other unsigned Auden
poems in the last edition of *The Gresham* he edited before leaving
school. In her edition of Auden's *Juvenilia* Katherine Bucknell noted
that there was also a lost poem, 'Sunset from Primrose Hill', contemporary with 'Dawn', and published in a school literary magazine edited
by two of Auden's friends at Gresham's, James Richards and William
Rivière, but added, 'All copies are now lost.'[67] In fact this poem, or a
version of it, immediately preceded 'Dawn' and the two poems were
printed as an obvious pair. It is entitled 'Evening and Night on Primrose Hill'.

Splendid to be on Primrose Hill
At evening when the world is still!
And City men, in bowler hats, return now day is done,
Rejoicing in the embers of the sun.

The City men they come, they go, some quick, some slow.
Then silence; the twinkling lights are lit upon the hill,
The moon stands over Primrose Hill.[68]

Hayward clearly enjoyed his time at Gresham's but increasingly felt
that he was cut off from the literary world to which he already aspired.
Later he remarked that at school he had not heard of T. S. Eliot, 'but

the names of the Sitwells – Edith, Osbert and Sacheverell – had pene-
trated the prison wall that isolates an English public schoolboy for
three-quarters of every year'.[69] When he was awarded the A. C. Benson
Prize for English Literature in 1922 he deliberately chose the latest
number of Edith Sitwell's avant-garde verse anthology *Wheels* to shock
the more conventional taste of his teachers. It succeeded. 'My choice
was grudgingly approved by the authorities on condition that the
customary impression of the school arms in gilt should not appear on
the highly unconventional "expressionist" cover.'[70] This was a sure sign
to him that it was time to leave the land of 'Philistia' and move on.

The obvious next step for the Fishmongers' Scholar was Oxford or
Cambridge. George had already gone up to Oxford with a scholarship.
In the autumn of 1922 Hayward duly applied to King's College,
Cambridge. No doubt it was largely due to Trèves's unusual 'special
tuition' that Hayward decided to choose modern languages, rather
than history. After writing his exam papers at King's he managed to
cycle to Grantchester, so 'weak-kneed that I could scarcely turn the
pedals', to be interviewed by the Professor of Spanish who lay in bed
with a streaming cold as Hayward read bits of *Don Quixote* to him.
On his return home he was delighted to receive a telegram announcing
that he had won an Exhibition. So it was perhaps with surprise that he
read the letter from Dr Chapman of King's that was sent the next day: 'I
was very glad to be able to wire you last night. Frankly I think you were
lucky. Your actual French and Spanish performance was not really
good – only about 46% or so. But you did an excellent English literature paper and your general work was some of the best sent in. So we
are, as we say, gambling on you in the belief that you are a fellow of
intelligence …'[71]

The question of how to make best use of his son's time before he
went up to Cambridge occupied Dr Hayward's mind; both parents felt
that they could not face the prospect of their precociously clever
offspring idle at home for nine months. They decided that a spell in
France learning more of its language and literature would help. But,
before leaving Wimbledon and England, Hayward had some personal
affairs to deal with. He felt himself already 'fairly experienced' in
matters of love and sex. Sylvia Pearman was his childhood sweetheart.[72] He often stayed with her and her elder sister Barbara at Epsom.
At the age of fourteen he was 'madly in love with her' and he imagined

that he had been in love with her 'since infancy'. At the end of January 1923 she told him that she had got engaged, but confided that she was unsure and unhappy about her future. To him she seemed caught like a bird in a net: 'Poor child! She has my sympathy.' More feelingly, he wrote in his diary: 'A long day with Sylvia – had to stay for dinner. She nearly broke my heart and I had to restrain myself. She was most kind ...' They bet each other a guinea that he would never marry. 'I think I melted her heart a little,' he added.

Less than a week after the long day with Sylvia, Hayward embarked at Newhaven for Dieppe. It was the first time he had left England. 'Everything is v. strange and new,' he wrote in his diary.[73] After sharing a train carriage with a *poilu* and an Algerian missionary he arrived in Paris. He was full of the excitement of 'tearing across Paris in a minute taxi' and the 'glorious places' of the city before he took the train to the Loire valley and Tours. On 1 February he arrived at the small village of la Monnaie, just north of Tours, and then a winding track led him up through leafless birch and chestnut trees to the château of le Mortier, where he was to spend the next six months. It was a fine Italianate building of cream and red brick set on the crest of a small hill in park-land with its own lake and Japanese bridge. Here he stayed *en pension* with a small group of English students under the supervision of their host, M. Bricoyne, who ran an establishment that was both a hotel and a kind of language school for young Englishmen on their way to university.

Straightaway Hayward found the contrast between France and England an exciting novelty, noting the 'many queer ill-dressed mechanics speaking very pure Touraine French'. He was delighted too by the glories of the old town and the brilliance of the 'exquisite' medieval stained glass in the cathedral. Surprised at French hospitality and the way that complete strangers greeted him in the street and shook him by the hand, he was even more struck by the egalitarian way that masters raised their hats to their servants. 'LIBERTÉ EGALITÉ FRATER-NITÉ' he summed up in his diary. But if the manners of the citizens of Tours came as a pleasant surprise, the lycée itself was a disappointment. Part of the intention was for him to attend the evening classes, but on the Monday after his arrival he noted: 'A collection of old maiden ladies and young brainless idiots turned up. Appallingly duff lecture on Napoleon in a dirty classroom, covered with maps and v stuffy.' By Friday, after some novels had been slowly and tediously explained to an impatient and insulted Hayward, he decided never to go again and duly found an aged private tutor. However, he quickly shocked him by writing an essay proving that the earth was flat, which led to 'a furious almost painful discussion'. John Hayward was never going to be an easy student.

A daily routine was quickly established. Mornings were spent studying. His diary detailed a varied diet of reading: *Madame Bovary, L'Ile de Pingouins, Les Dieux Ont Soif, La Révolte des Anges, Le Chanson de Roland* and the poetry of Alfred de Vigny. In the afternoon he often paid 60 centimes for a bus into Tours where he visited the bookshops and explored the narrow streets of the medieval town clustered around its gothic cathedral. He would take tea and enjoy some patisserie with English friends at a café. Sometimes he would share coffee and uneasy adolescent laughter with his companions as they gazed at the garishly dressed 'filles de joie'. They then returned to le Mortier, where they had supper and played cricket in the garden, and the evenings generally ended with a game of bridge or chess.

Spring came early to le Mortier with cowslips along the tracks and chestnut buds in the woods. As summer approached, Hayward began to relish the intense heat of the Loire valley – on 1 May the temperature rose to 26c degrees in the shade. Asparagus appeared at the table and long drowsy afternoons were spent reading under the chestnut trees, admiring the wisteria and the green vines around the château. He especially loved the sunsets which he described lyrically in his notebook: 'Sky gold and green and pink with a white moon and on the horizon heavy clouds ... and a big strawberry sun.' Some trips and events interrupted these languorous days. He took High Mass in the cathedral, which he found 'awe-inspiring' – despite the fact he was by now a convinced atheist – and visited some of the châteaux of the Loire. Azay le Rideau was 'exquisite' – his favourite tourist word at the time. At Blois he had lunch with the Marquis where he drank in some Vouvray along with 'the atmosphere of the old French aristocracy'. A welcome surprise was a glimpse of the grand old man of French literature, Anatole France, in Tours. With his gentle expression and grey beard 'he had the exact face I imagined him to have'. There was also the excitement of a motor race on the circuit near le Mortier where he patriotically cheered on the Sunbeams in their British racing green colours as they fought off and beat the bright red Italian Fiats and the blue French Delarges. He watched a gala performance from the Comédie Française and was entranced by the beauty of the leading actress, but, the next day, was repulsed by the 'practically naked tattooed woman' at the fair that visited Tours. 'This was disgusting and I was glad to get outside,' he wrote. One incident stood out from the diary:

> Today opposite the Café de Commerce I saw the bright sparkling girl who washes up knocked down by a motor. The accident has had a great effect on me. It was not serious but to see the white face, the tears, the childlike cries of someone who an hour previously I had seen from Massie's window pass like a gay sparrow along the pavement ... I admire the control of the doctor ... I think perhaps there is no greater profession than that of a healer of men's bodies.

The girl's combination of beauty and weakness was powerfully appealing. The final phrase reveals an admiration for his father. Perhaps, too, John Hayward was thinking of his own, unhealable, body.

On 6 July Hayward's time at le Mortier finally came to an end. He shook M. Bricoyne by the hand and took the train to Paris. There he enjoyed the revue *Toutes les Femmes* – 'a very fine spectacle of nakedness' – before heading off to join his respectable father and brother for the last part of his Grand Tour. Two days later he met them in Berne and marvelled at the view of the Jungfrau. Travelling with them on the railway was pure pleasure for Hayward the train lover, as the engine negotiated the spectacular viaducts, loops and tunnels through the mountains. It was, however, no easy companionship. Dr Hayward seemed determined to conquer the heights in his own energetic style, but his son could not follow him. The diary entry after a day of climbing – 'Daddy went higher' – leaving his son behind on his own is a sad commentary on their relationship. On the 12th he was exhausted by 'a hideous walk of five hours'. By contrast the next day he enjoyed sketching the Matterhorn and there followed more relaxing days taking the funicular to see spectacular views and collect alpine roses. But very soon he became tired of the mountains, and descended 'humbly like Don Quichote or Napoleon on a mule'. As he parted from his father and brother he was overcome by homesickness: 'I nearly wept as I said goodbye to them ... I loathed everything except home at that moment.' He had had enough. On 24 August he boarded the night express to Paris. The final entry was written on the train: 'At last my long exile is over. Eight months! Mon Dieu it has been a long time.'

4
Cambridge

Four years after the end of the war Bunny Garnett, who had just won the Hawthornden Prize with his first novel, *Lady into Fox,* and his friend the poet and writer Francis 'Frankie' Birrell, set up a bookshop near the British Museum at 19 Taviton Street, a stone's throw from Gordon Square where Virginia and Vanessa Bell had lived. Both men were part of the younger Bloomsbury set. Their bookshop was more like a club than a shop and often became as busy as a pub at closing time. Frankie, sitting on the big sofa that dominated the room, was the fashionable centre of conversation and argument, but neither man was a natural bookseller: Frankie felt that selling anything for more than the price paid for it was immoral, and Bunny was more interested in his own writing. The shelves were stacked with volumes from the Hogarth Press; Roger Fry's Omega Workshop provided the tables and Duncan Grant designed the first catalogue. Patronised by customers such as Lytton Strachey, E. M. Forster, Ottoline Morrell and Joseph Conrad, the bookshop became a Bloomsbury success. When it moved to Gerrard Street in 1922 Francis Meynell decided to take on the basement to start a new publishing venture. A few weeks later Francis and his partner Vera Mendel (soon to become Vera Meynell) invited Bunny to take on the role of their business partner and the Nonesuch Press was born. Meynell aimed to bring clear lettering in line with advances in typesetting and printing. Books were first designed on a hand press in the traditional way but then farmed out for printing on mechanised presses. As Hayward wrote later, 'The Press effected a revolution in typography: they have destroyed the idea that a book can be a thing of beauty only if set by hand.'[74]

Just before he went up to King's in 1923 Hayward's ambition to be part of the metropolitan literary world led him to visit Meynell at the bookshop.

John Hayward was 18 when I first met him. I have to force my mind to remember that he was already somewhat affected by the disability which later so controlled his physical (but not his mental) life. One's easy and dominant memory is of his purposeful gaiety, of his delight in exactitude, (and in the exposure of sloppiness), of the impressive head and bright eyes, of the comic imitations of people and puffing trains.[75]

Meynell introduced him to Bunny whom Hayward already admired as 'the greatest living master of natural description'. Bunny was also taken by the young Hayward:

> There is more than a touch of the Ancient Mariner about him. That is to say his large eye dwells on the person he is talking to in a dubious expressionless manner, and he hesitates, gripping the arm of his chair so hard that you are glad it's not your arm: and then the pearls of wit, the delightful, personally visualised anecdotes come out spasmodically, like jets of water expelled from the tap when there is air in the pipes.[76]

They were soon to become the closest of friends. Frankie seemed to Hayward a reincarnation of the best of early Bloomsbury: 'With his wild curly hair, his tie caught round his neck, he had such an easy, shy charm that "buttonless and unbraced" he could melt the hearts of stiff shirts.'[77] He was 'a highbrow in the best sense of the word'.

Hayward was full of enthusiasm about possible projects for the Nonesuch Press and suggested that he ought to try the riskiest of them all – Lord Rochester, notorious for his rakish life and obscene poetry. Meynell, impressed by Hayward's knowledge and self-confidence, asked Garnett for his opinion; he was quick to say yes. It was extraordinarily brave to take on an unknown eighteen-year-old editor – and perhaps even braver to risk prosecution by publishing work with such a scandalous reputation. As was to become apparent, they had also chosen Hayward against another obvious and well-established editor. Hayward never forgot the trust that Meynell had vested in him and the risk he had taken. When an album to celebrate Meynell's seventieth birthday was assembled, Hayward drew, 'with infinite care', a coloured picture of a hand, a foot and a ladder. He inscribed it: 'Francis Meynell placing John Hayward's foot on the first rung of the literary ladder, 1923.' The colours soaked through the paper and Hayward wrote above them, 'Look, we have come through / Francis, thanks to you.'[78]

The Revd Alphonsus Joseph-Mary Augustus Montague Summers

was one of Nonesuch's first editors. Summers had an extensive knowledge of Restoration Drama and bawdry and enjoyed a reputation as a 'prodigiously learned and prolific man of letters ... and a leading influence on the English theatre during the 1920s and 1930s'.[79] To some he seemed nothing less than a saint; to others a charlatan. He had trained for the Anglican ministry but, after being charged with pederasty, had to leave his curacy 'to flee into the arms of the Roman Catholic Church'.[80] Although probably defrocked, he carried on as if nothing had happened, keeping his clerical title and wearing a dog collar and cassock. Later he devoted himself to pornography and witchcraft, publishing editions of the *Malleus Maleficarum*, and studies of black magic. When he visited the British Museum dressed in black soutane, cloak, silver buckled shoes of patent leather and carrying a file labelled 'Vampires' in blood-red ink, he himself seemed to be part of the world of the occult that fascinated him. Short and fat, with greying greasy hair hanging in curls over the back of his dog collar, yellow teeth, cheeks 'smooth as bladders of lard' and 'small, cruel and shark-like lips', he filled Francis and Vera with repulsion.[81] His character matched his looks – 'opinionated, cantankerous and thoroughly devious'.[82] Summers often browsed the shelves and borrowed materials on which to base his texts from the bookshop at 30 Gerrard Street – but as he never paid for his unreturned books he became unwelcome there too. As they disliked him so intensely, it was left to Bunny to look after him at the Nonesuch Press.

It was the success of his edition of Congreve for the Press that had inspired Meynell and Garnett to think of a series on Restoration writers. Summers was already signed up to do an edition of the dramatist William Wycherley. Ever since 1910 he had been collecting material for an edition of Rochester. His old friend 'the famous bibliographer' T. J. Wise – later to be exposed as a fraud and a faker – had lent him 'a perhaps unique copy' of Rochester's tragedy *Valentinian*. In a letter to *The Observer* of 19 February 1922 Summers had confirmed that he was about to issue the first complete and annotated edition of Rochester.[83] No doubt he was confident that as a Rochester expert, a friend of Francis Meynell and 'Nonesuch's principal editor', he would be the Press's first choice. Summers was therefore stunned when Francis Meynell wrote to him out of the blue, introducing 'a Mr John Hayward who is doing a Rochester for us'. Not only had he been deprived of a project he had already marked as his own, but to be beaten to the line by 'this young cock crowing on his dunghill' – as Bunny observed – was a crowning insult. The rivalry was to have its consequences.

On 10 October 1923 Hayward arrived at King's to start his first Michaelmas term. He was very impressed by the efficiency of the taxi drivers and the porters; everything had been scrupulously organised for him, his trunk and all his packages already stored in his rooms and a fire arranged in the grate. The sitting room itself was excellent, with two wing-chairs and a sofa, but 'in a vile situation'. As yet there were no curtains and, as he immediately noticed, little book space. He made himself known to the others on the staircase and did the things an undergraduate did: he had his first dinner in Hall; bought himself a waste-paper basket; joined the musical club; and started a grocery account. But he was clearly different from his fellows. As other under-graduates pedalled furiously, bare-headed in bright college scarves, to lectures, college sports grounds, the ADC Theatre or the Rex cinema, Hayward cut 'an arresting and unmistakeable figure, walking painfully along King's Parade with that pitiable uncoordinated movement of his legs and flapping feet'.[84]

The contrast between the worlds of Wimbledon and Norfolk and the intellectually and socially sophisticated world of King's College was a stark one. King's had formed the nucleus of the Bloomsbury set in Cambridge and the intellectual tone when Hayward went up was still, he felt, dominated by it. 'From the early years of the century until the close of the 1920s it was almost impossible for an intelligent and impressionable undergraduate of King's or Trinity colleges to remain unaffected by the prevailing climate of "Bloomsbury" thought and sensibility.'[85] He was introduced to many of the 'Bloomsberries' by Frankie Birrell: E. M. Forster was at King's, as was the economist Maynard Keynes and the pacifist historian 'Goldie' Lowes Dickinson; the philosopher of Bloomsbury, G. E. Moore, was at Trinity. Virginia and Leonard Woolf visited Cambridge regularly as did the art critic Clive Bell, and the literary critics Desmond MacCarthy and Raymond Mortimer. Hayward sat at the feet of Roger Fry, 'the oracle of the intel-lectuals of Bloomsbury', and was entranced by 'the irresistible wit and charm of his conversation'.[86] He met Lytton Strachey at a dinner party in Maynard Keynes's rooms. 'What a strange and original figure he was!' wrote Hayward, remembering a fancy dress party in Gordon Square in which Bunny and Leonard Woolf did a performing 'moke' and Lytton, dressed in pork pie hat and sailor's blue jersey, spoke in his 'intensely witty yet grave manner'.

> Lytton, in a sense, created Bloomsbury and the intellectual society it represents. It dates back, I suppose, to Cambridge. Lytton belonged to a great generation there; and it was that group to which he belonged that helped to make Cambridge an influence of paramount importance on contemporary thought ... Lytton was not only a representative of ideas, but also an example – and perhaps a supreme example – a representative of the society from which those ideas sprung. He was in fact a social event.[87]

So before Hayward was nineteen he had met many of old Bloomsbury's leading figures. Although he belonged to a younger generation, he still felt its effects as 'the blast of the cold, intellectual east wind of Cambridge'. Through the King's research student George 'Dadie' Rylands he quickly got to know some of the younger figures of the group too, such as Julian Bell and Julia Strachey. It was, of course, 'exhilarating and flattering' for one who felt himself so young and provincial to meet the great names, but, pleased though he was by their attention, Hayward's attitude was always tinged with doubt. He was later to write a powerful critique of Bloomsbury and all it came to represent in his eyes: arrogance; sterility; selfishness and 'an assumed blindness and contempt for the world at large'.

A handsome Old Etonian, Dadie Rylands was at the centre of the younger Bloomsbury set, part of the fashionable 'homintern'[88] of King's. Dora Carrington described him as having 'hair the colour of a canary bird and the most heavenly blue eyes'. His rooms were like a stage-set, lavishly decorated with elaborate bows around the mantelpiece and painted in rich colours. Here it was that Virginia Woolf ate the memorable lunch she described in *A Room of One's Own*, which 'began with soles, sunk in a deep dish, over which the college cook had spread a counterpane of the whitest cream, save that it was branded here and there with brown spots like the spots on the flanks of a doe ...'[89] Already a leading figure in the dramatic scene in Cambridge, Rylands acted and directed plays that attracted the attention of the national press, who dubbed him, as Hayward loved to repeat, 'the least donnish of dons'. It was through acting that they had first got to know each other. Rylands recalled Hayward's performance in the Marlowe Dramatic Society's trail-blazing production of *The Duchess of Malfi* in which he himself had played the Duchess and Hayward 'ye Mad Doctor':

> At the primitive ADC in March 1925 John played Fourth Madman with enormous relish. His grievous physical affliction was still at an early stage. The performance was at once comical and macabre (as it should be). In after years when we foregathered he delighted to roll out the grotesque fantasies of *all* the Madmen. They seem, as it were, to have sounded a *mot d'ordre* for his wit, future studies and predilections. I can hear him now: 'Shall my pothecary out-go me because I am a Cuckold? I have found out his roguery: he makes allom out of his wives urin, and sells it to Puritains, that have sore throats with over-strayning ...'[90]

Hayward acted 'with all the zest of an inebriated gorilla'. From behind the scenes his voice could be heard as he single-handedly played the part of a body of prisoners under torture and 'produced some of the most blood-curdling Grand Guignol noises ever heard in Cambridge'. But after the performance the defiant lines spoken by the Duchess stuck obstinately in Hayward's mind and refused to go away:

> Though in our miseries Fortune has a part
> ... Yet in our noble sufferings she hath none.
> Contempt of pain, that we may call our own.

Not only did Hayward act for the Marlowe Society, he also designed programmes and sat on the committee, and eventually was elected as Secretary. By his second year he was writing jokes for the Christmas revue at the ADC Theatre and devising sketches for the Footlights. He used his fine singing voice in Cambridge musical societies. His 'Rabelaisian wit' enlivened festivities at his first Founder's Feast at King's and shocked some of his elders.[91] After many glasses of claret he staggered to his feet and sang an impromptu verse in honour of Maynard Keynes and as a tribute to his fellow guest, the painter Duncan Grant:

> Here's a very good health to my friend Mr Grant,
> So Vive la Compagnie.
> He'd paint like Bougereau – but he can't,
> So Vive la Compagnie.[92]

It was through Dadie that Hayward had first got to know Victor

Rothschild, an extraordinarily rich, able and flamboyant young man, superficially living the life of the *jeunesse dorée,* driving a Bugatti, throwing lavish parties and taking his English tutor, Dadie, for a holiday to Monte Carlo. In fact, he was a serious and dedicated scientist. Most at home in the laboratory working as a research chemist, his work on the sexual behaviour of the sea urchin earned him a prize fellowship at Trinity College. It was Rylands who first gave Rothschild his passion for book collecting: 'In those days he talked of books with all the enthusiasm of a schoolboy who had suddenly discovered stamps or cigarette cards,' he recalled.[93] Like Hayward, Rothschild started by buying books on 'Old David's' stall on Cambridge market, but soon began dealing with the leading booksellers in London and New York. In the slump at the end of the 1920s the book market fell dramatically and he was able to buy wisely and at good prices, aided by the enormous Rothschild wealth – at one time he owned one seventh of all the pre-1800 gold in the world. Hayward exaggerated when he credited him with reviving the fortunes of the bookselling world, but he was certainly an important figure in that revival. Rothschild collected only the best. Within twelve years he had assembled the finest collection of eighteenth-century books in private hands. From this shared love of books their friendship had sprung.

After a year away at Princeton University, a rather conventional Old Etonian undergraduate, Denys King-Farlow, returned to King's in October 1924 to complete his degree. As he gazed from his first floor rooms across the immaculately tended expanse of lawn towards its statue of Henry VI, with the familiar prospect of the Chapel ahead of him, and the eighteenth-century frontage of the Gibbs' building to his left, he was disturbed by something quite out of keeping:

Along the gravel path, there appeared, parading itself slowly, before my gaze, an exhibitionist nightmare, flamboyant under an exceptionally broad brimmed hat, the head and shoulders thrust back and, for no apparent good reason, the stomach distastefully thrust forward. The lower lip of this portent was of a quite extraordinarily brilliant red. Could the colour be artificial? The lip jutted straight out from the face, striking, perhaps intentionally, a somehow grand guinol [*sic*] note. His right hand was languidly twirling a thick, pale walking stick, while the left caressed an outsize green bow tie.[94]

Outraged by this dandyish apparition, King-Farlow turned to his friend Dick Wood to ask him who this 'disgrace to the college' was. 'That', replied Wood, 'is John Hayward, charming, and brilliant <u>and</u> the most erudite bibliomane in King's bar none, Maynard Keynes included.' King-Farlow agreed to come round to his friend's rooms after Hall that evening to meet the nightmare. He found him just as charming and learned as promised and the two became close friends.

Hayward was appointed treasurer of the Heretics, a humanist Cambridge discussion society – a more open and less famous version of the Apostles. Membership was conditional on 'a willingness to reject all appeal to authority on the discussion of religious questions'. Invited speakers included Bertrand Russell, G. E. Moore, Roger Fry and Virginia Woolf. (Russell told the society that the Ten Commandments were like an examination paper and should bear the instruction: 'Only six need to be attempted.')[95] Hayward gave a lecture to the society, 'Gradus ad Parnassum', in which he analysed the cultural state of the times. Through the Heretics he first met the poet and critic William 'Bill' Empson, whom he saw as one of the brains of his generation. Empson became, as he recalled, the next President of the Heretics but one or two. In 1925 Hayward asked Eliot to give a talk to the society – an invitation which was turned down because he argued that to address such a distinguished gathering would involve him in too much preparation, 'knowing the reputation of your Society for merciless criticism of your speakers' weaknesses'.[96] In 1926 Hayward invited D. H. Lawrence – and was again turned down. The choices were significant ones: Hayward's membership of the Heretics shows him as a radical-thinking young man anxious to question authority on all matters of sex and religion, keen to reject the stuffiness of his Wimbledon childhood and wanting to get in touch with the leading and most controversial writers of his day.

Cambridge nourished Hayward's growing love of parties. Typical was the one in his rooms in honour of the fashionable young French surrealist writer and painter René Crével. Collector-like, in his Private Journal Hayward carefully listed the names of all the famous or interesting people he had attracted round him. 'The party lasted till midnight and nothing but French was spoken ... Quite the most exotic gathering of people I have gathered in my room.' Yet as soon as the guests left he felt a desperate loneliness. And this alternation of moods puzzled him: 'I wish I could refuse invitations but I cannot; I am

everlastingly tempted to accept with the same hopes of finding someone or something interesting in the end.'

University contemporaries 'regarded him with awe', partly because
he seemed so brilliantly learned, and partly because his illness
surrounded him with mystery.[97] By some it was whispered that 'he had
not long to live', while others hoped that the obscure trouble with his
spine would be cured within a few months. Whatever was the matter,
all agreed he bore his pain with remarkable bravery and gaiety. Already
he found the stone flights of steps of King's difficult and needed help
from friends to get up them; he walked with the aid of his rubber-toed
stick and began to go around Cambridge in his wheelchair, but once
behind the wheel of 'Oxley', his baby Austin, he drove with a flair and
a speed that, in every sense, shook his passengers. He soon gathered
round him a coterie who admired the precocious, pale-faced undergraduate who was already editing an edition of the works of Rochester.
The daring of producing an unexpurgated edition of works that had
not been published for over a hundred years because of their obscenity
added to Hayward's prestige – and the excitingly dangerous possibility
of prosecution hung over him when it came out in 1926.[98]

'The Earl of Rochester's work has never been edited,' began Hayward's Prefatory Note.[99] It was partially the challenge that led him to
defy the advice of his elders who had tried to warn him off. No doubt
too their cautions smacked of Victorian prudery and only spurred him
on. The text presented exactly the kind of difficulty, and therefore
fascination, which would continue to occupy him for much of the rest
of his life. Rochester had shown aristocratic disdain about the fate of
his poetry after it had been circulated around the court. Collating and
dating all the different editions was a very difficult and complicated
task. They also had to be treated with caution because many imitators
used the notoriety of Rochester's name to sell their own work. So the
task of the editor was also to exclude all the material that had been
fathered onto him, including, for example, the obscene drama *Sodom*.
'My aim has been to choose a text which, after a careful comparison
with that of other editions, seems to be least corrupt and most likely to
be Rochester's,' wrote Hayward.[100]

The Restoration seemed to Hayward a heady, intoxicating period –
and Rochester was its representative figure. It was a post-war moment
when 'the experience of the older generation was no longer of use to
men who had to make a new set of values for every occasion in their

lives',[101] a foreshadowing of the Roaring Twenties, of the Bright Young People, and the world of Evelyn Waugh's *Vile Bodies*. The end of the seventeenth century was nothing less than the 'beginning of a new, the so-called modern world. Into this changing world, Lord Rochester, a singularly modern character, was born.'[102] He and his young editor were both part of this new world, questioning authority, discarding religion, and rejecting the morals of their parents' generation. Sharing a taste for wit and satire, they both loved women and frankly enjoyed pornographic and erotic verse. The disillusion and romantic melancholy of Rochester's poetry also had a strong appeal. Hayward held up the final stanza of 'Love and Life' as an example of 'one of the swan-songs of the love poetry which had been one of the treasures of the Renaissance in England':

> Then talk not of Inconstancy
> False *Hearts* and broken *Vows*;
> If I, by *Miracle* can be
> This live-long *Minute* true to thee,
> 'Tis all that *Heav'n* allows.[103]

As he had just fallen seriously in love for the first time, he must have found this irresistible.

The *Collected Works of John Wilmot Earl of Rochester* finally appeared in 1926 and, after all the effort and its editor's hopes, turned out to be a damp squib. 'It was received with no acclamations and some disgust,' Hayward wrote in his Journal. Montague Summers took his revenge by renaming it 'Rochester and Others' since it contained so many poems he claimed were by Rochester's contemporaries. Francis Meynell commented: 'The critics didn't know how to take Rochester ...so they had nothing to say about John as editor.'[104] Dr Hayward hid the book from prying eyes in a locked trunk at home in Wimbledon. 'So much for the work that might have made a reputation for me,' wrote his deeply disappointed son. Mixed with disappointment, however, there was also a sense of a satisfaction: 'Now that it is done with, I can think with a mixture of bitterness and pride that my name is written for ever (?) in the catalogue of the British Museum, the last resting place of ignominious, ignorant and soon forgotten editing.'[105] There was one public exception to the general indifference. Sir Edmund Gosse in the *Sunday Times* called Hayward 'the best, and in fact, the only competent editor of Rochester'.[106] Privately, Bunny sent him the 'kindliest letter I have ever had', full of praise and encouragement. Not only did Hayward claim that this was the first time Rochester's work had been properly edited but also that it was the largest collection of his poems and letters that had appeared in print. The growth of Rochester's reputation as one of the central voices of the Restoration owes its beginnings to this remarkable work of scholarship from a twenty-one-year-old undergraduate.

It was Rochester who brought Hayward and Graham Greene together. Hayward was one year older than Greene and had already established the beginnings of a literary reputation. The recently married Greene, on the other hand, had written three novels and a thriller that had all failed, and needed money. Deciding to try a new tack, he turned to biography – and to Rochester. He wrote asking the young editor for advice and in October 1931 he brought the manuscript of what was to become *Lord Rochester's Monkey* for Hayward's comments. Heinemann had already rejected the book because of fear of prosecution. Hayward felt that any possible legal action might well bring the law down on his own head – it was after all his own edition of the poems that would be quoted – and he therefore advised Greene against publication. At first meeting neither wanted to own up to an interest in Rochester's erotic verse, although in fact both shared a fascination with erotica and pornography. So it was some time before they realised that they had in common a taste for 'human beings *sans culottes,* undignified and loveable'.[107] This was the beginning of a forty-year friendship. Greene always remained grateful to the scholar who encouraged him at the beginning of his career who 'received me generously and gave up his time to me without the slightest hint of patronage'.[108]

From childhood Hayward had always loved books, but it was in Cambridge that he became a passionate collector. 'The atmosphere in Cambridge in the mid-twenties was fatally congenial to anyone with a budding taste for book collecting,' wrote John Carter.[109] From the early decades of the century King's had led the way and now Carter, Maynard Keynes, Victor Rothschild and Alan Clutton-Brock maintained the tradition. Hayward's first acquisition had been a miserable object – 'a badly stained, closely cropped, hideously rebound copy of Jacob Tonson's edition of Rochester's *Poems* (1691)',[110] which he bought from 'Old David'. This was the beginning of Hayward's lifelong devotion to book collecting, that led much later to his putting together the finest collection of Rochester's works in private hands, including three extremely rare editions printed in London, but carrying the imprint 'Antwerp' to evade censorship laws. ('It is hardly decent that you have three. I don't think Bodley has any,' wrote Colonel Wilkinson, the librarian of Worcester College, Oxford.)

'Old David' himself was a Cambridge institution, half-smoked brown cigarette stub permanently glued to his lower lip, as he shuffled about behind the book-laden tables in an enormous shabby overcoat, presiding over the chaos of a musty gas-lit shop in St Edward's Passage as every Friday evening a consignment of books arrived from Bond Street and Chancery Lane.[111] His stall in the market place became a centre for all the bibliophiles of the university. On Saturday mornings he took his stock to Peas Hill and it was there that Hayward had first met Lytton Strachey browsing the shelves. 'Old David' could be found discussing his wares with an eclectic mix of customers ranging from masters of colleges and undergraduates to housewives and tramps sheltering from the icy winds of a Cambridge winter ... 'I can see him now, buttoned up against the cold, a marvel of slovenliness apart from a well-curled Stetson, muttering an imprecation or a welcome in the same breath,' wrote Hayward ten years later, adding that David's bookstall had left him with a more lasting love of books than all his teachers and lecturers put together.

More significant to Hayward than the world of Bloomsbury was first reading the poetry of Eliot. The publication of *The Waste Land* in 1922, just before Hayward went up, had made Eliot a subject for 'frenzied discussion' in Cambridge. Partisan positions were immediately taken up and fiercely held. To John Hayward and his contemporaries it seemed the essence of modernity and summed up 'the postwar ragtime world, the world of 1920, restless, aimless, hectic, fearful, futile, neurotic'.[112] They relished the 'great knockout up-to-date quality' of the poem with its disillusion, its urban settings and 'jazz' rhythms. Hayward noted how Eliot made his classical allusions modern, for example, by substituting a suburban 'Dog' for Baudelaire's wolf and by transforming a Spenserian bridal party into a modern 'petting party' leaving behind a sordid detritus of cardboard boxes, cigarette ends and contraceptives. Many of Hayward's elders, however, like the Georgian poet and critic J. C. Squire, found the poem incomprehensible. His own tutor, F. L. ('Peter') Lucas, was an inveterate and articulate opponent and refused to allow any of Eliot's works into the College library. Meanwhile his tutee was already writing reviews in which he contrasted the exciting new world of Eliot's poetry with that of Squire, who represented the dead past, using a lifeless language and mummified figures of speech: 'The language of poetry is dying if it is not nourished with new expressions ... In Europe we are beginning to understand that if poetry is to be kept alive, it must be brought in contact with a world that has been changed ...'[113] Hayward did, however, have some reservations about the new poetry. As a young romantic he found Eliot's theory of poetry bloodless and later wrote: 'Mr Eliot will hardly admit that there are people with *strong* desires who find in poetry a *catharsis*, which they are unable to induce in themselves. He requires of those who read poetry an asceticism which is easier to admire than to emulate.'[114]

It was not, however, the publication of *The Waste Land* which had been the decisive moment for Hayward, but rather 'The Love Song of J. Alfred Prufrock', published in the summer of 1915. When he was asked to do a broadcast on the BBC Third Programme in August 1948 to celebrate Eliot's sixtieth birthday, Hayward recalled how that poem was nothing less than 'a revolutionary break-away from the century old tyranny of the Romantic tradition'.[115] There were few people at the time, however, who were sharp enough to listen properly to the 'strange, uncompromising and somewhat harsh notes of the new poet'. Ever the bibliophile, he noted 'its unpromising arrival into the world as part of a drab little volume printed on a kind of stiff blotting-paper and cased in stiff buff paper wrappings ... modestly priced at a shilling; but even at this price it failed to sell.' But, despite its appearance, 'Prufrock' was, like Wordsworth's *Lyrical Ballads*, a poetic watershed. Savaged in the columns of *The Times Literary Supplement* where it was left to die in the 'morgue' section at the back of the magazine, it met hostile reviews as it came as an utter shock to all those 'who were attuned to the native wood-notes wild of Rupert Brooke and Flecker and Edward Thomas' – precisely, in fact, Hayward's own favourite poets as a boy. 'If that small volume may be called, as I think it is entitled to be, epoch-making, it is because it effected a re-orientation of English poetry.' He concluded that 'It is as if meandering or merely stagnating in the local water-meadows, the tributary waters of English poetry had been turned back again into the mainstream of the European tradition.' Just as in his criticism Eliot had reviewed the past of our literature and 'set the poets and the poems in a new order',[116] so 'Prufrock' changed the face of poetry for Hayward and his generation.

It was on Wednesday 17 March 1926 that Hayward and Eliot first met. Eliot was then thirty-seven years old and Hayward twenty-one. Eliot had been chosen, in the teeth of strong opposition, to give the Clark Lectures at Cambridge University for the Lent term on 'The Metaphysical Poets of the Seventeenth Century', for which he received a much-needed £200. As was the custom, six of the most promising undergraduates were selected for the honour of breakfasting with the visiting lecturer. Expectantly at 9.30 the young men gathered around the table; Bill Empson was there, as was John Hayward who sat, pale-faced, rubber-toed stick at his side. After Eliot arrived there followed a full minute of embarrassed silence, broken at last by Hayward's asking: 'Mr Eliot, have you read the last volume of Proust?' 'No, I'm afraid I have not,' he replied. Silence resumed.[117] But, according to Empson, by the following week when a newcomer to the group raised the question of Scott Moncrieff's translation of Proust, Eliot delivered 'a very weighty, and rather long, tribute to that work'.[118]

'Is there honey still for tea?' Hayward called his article in *The Cambridge Review* remembering his undergraduate years.[119] 'There was in those days,' he replied to his own question – and went on to describe a Cambridge social life in the 1920s that tried to rival the Oxford of Harold Acton, Evelyn Waugh and Brian Howard. Differences in dress reflected differences of attitude between the two universities, as Hayward noted later in the *New York Sun*: the dandyish love of the finely creased trouser meant that many Oxford men 'could never sit down at all unless they are first allowed to take their trousers off' – whereas at Cambridge there were 'only a dozen or so' men who found themselves with that problem. Oxford wore high-necked jumpers in shades of eau de nil; Cambridge heavy ill-cut clothes, lightened only by a rare patch of colour. Cambridge men looked gloomier too, thought Hayward: 'The over-wrought faces remind us that here also Ibsen has been studied.' By contrast to the gaiety of aesthetic Oxford Cambridge felt drably Scandinavian; sartorially Hayward was at the wrong university.

So far the twentieth century had done little to change the appearance of Cambridge: streets were quiet and traffic light. Hayward noted that as yet there were no 'snack bars' to modernise the centre of the city. Undergraduate life was leisured and comfortable. Sherry and aperitifs were no part of the fashionable undergraduate's ritual but tea, or 'The Five o' Clock Circle', as it was known, was. There were pastries in the flowery rooms on Bridge Street of the St John's undergraduate Cecil

('Cecilia') Beaton, or tea in King's drunk from delicate porcelain cups served by a dazzling young man in sky-blue plus-fours – Dadie Rylands. In the evening Cambridge dinner parties tried to rival those held by the Oxford sophisticates of the day. A quick spin down to London and lunch at the Café Royal could be followed by supper in hall and dinner at the Pitt Club. Although it was 'as hard to smuggle a single woman student into college as it was to smuggle a single bottle of vermouth into Newnham', Hayward relished the game of outwitting the University proctors and described the pleasures of an *omelette flambé au rhum* in Girton and fashionable mixed-bathing 'à la mode Tsarko Selo' (nude) in the water meadows beyond Harston. A cultural centre was the Old Vic cinema in the Market Place where the best seats cost 1s 6d. Hayward recalled the tawdry crimson velvet hangings and the stained oil-cloth on the floor as he waited for the violinist and a pianist to strike up at five o'clock. More important European films were on elsewhere, but Hayward preferred the sound of the two-piece orchestra thundering out the overture to *Coriolanus* as the screen swarmed with mounted sheriffs, cowboys and Indians.

5
Elaine: Before the Fall

Though I am handicapped physically, I have enjoyed life and had many memorable experiences, many friends and many acquaintances. Many things are closed to me, but their absence has not spoiled my pleasure in other directions. Simply I take no notice of my disability and in this I am helped by those who know me for they are all marvellously kind to me. ...

So begins John Hayward's 'Private Journal' of 1926 which reveals his most intimate thoughts about his last years at Cambridge. Academic life was beginning to weary him as he felt time and his youth slipping away As he cut the pages of yet another book of modern verse he had the urge to 'pluck dès aujourd'hui the roses of youth'. In the 'Scholar Complains in Spring' he expressed his frustration.

> Spring, said the scholar, must pass unnoticed ...
> All the day long and when night has fallen
> Chained to the rock of sorrow and learning,
> I number the words in the ranks of instructions
> Marshal the army of books at my side.
>
> Eyes that once traced the smiles of a mistress
> Through nights of high passion when grief passed me by,
> Are sealed with a dust of grey knowledge.
> The lips that kissed in the shadow now are dry.
> We cannot return to the old lands of pleasure,
> Rediscover again the lost isles of delight.

Just at this point Elaine Finlay came into his life. He had first met her at children's Christmas parties in Wimbledon. She was the daughter of a Scottish doctor who had moved south to establish a practice there and the two medical families knew each other quite well. Even as a small boy he was struck by her good looks and flattered by the interest she showed in his conversation. He continued to see her occasionally in school holidays and, as a young adolescent, confided to his

Commonplace Book that he was beginning to find her very attractive. Looking for consolation after Sylvia had got engaged he had written an anguished letter to Elaine from Woodlands House. He was full of trepidation: 'I only remember the anxiety, a kind of longing as strong today as it was then, with which I awaited a reply.' When it came it gave him some comfort and strengthened his feeling for her. 'You are a sensitive soul who has necessarily to suffer in love,' she wrote. 'This is the story of romance, seeing that by nature I am a romantic,' Hayward began his Journal.

After this they continued to meet as friends when Hayward returned from Cambridge to The Grange for his holidays. In his second year at university he had an affair with a mysterious woman he calls in his Commonplace Book 'M' – perhaps a foreign student. Their affair lasted a year before she had to return home. He recorded its progress in a series of anguished poems, fragments of recorded conversation and diary entries, often quoting from the letters of another unhappily parted pair of lovers – Abelard and Héloïse. One summer morning before M left, they bicycled out of Cambridge to beyond the small village of Marston where they lay down together on the banks of the Cam. Suddenly M stood up, flung off her clothes and walked into the river. He watched her as she bathed.

Their last meeting came a little later in London when on 16 June they went to Stravinsky's *Les Noces*. After the performance was over they said their goodbyes in Piccadilly Circus. M turned to wave as she walked away. Hayward was shocked by the brutal finality of their farewell. 'Goodbye M. Goodbye John. Voilà tout!' he wrote. Next morning he rang her. 'Don't forget me,' he implored. 'I promise you that, John,' she said.

After M's departure Hayward's thoughts turned back once more to Elaine. She had grown into a pretty young woman with light-brown hair, blue eyes and a fashionably slender figure, but it was the gentle kindness of her features that was most appealing. Knowing his parents were away, Hayward invited her to tea at The Grange. Elaine started to talk about her feelings and her engagement that had recently been broken off; then Hayward told her how much as a boy he had felt for her. 'I suppose all that has ended now,' she said very quietly, and Hayward replied, 'Tell me what I have to do to keep you here.' Elaine said nothing. 'Whatever is the matter?' he asked. She burst into tears. 'You don't know how to treat me.' He persuaded her to meet for lunch the following day. This time he carefully arranged the chairs in his room so that no prying eyes might intrude on them. 'The rest of the story needs no recording ... we all make love as cooks make cakes,' he noted ungallantly.

Although Hayward enjoyed all the stratagems by which his parents could be outwitted, it was difficult to conduct an affair under their watchful eyes and so he hatched a plan. He had already organised a touring holiday in France and, by coincidence, Elaine had agreed to visit relatives in Switzerland at the same time. He therefore proposed that she should accompany him and his friend to Lucerne and finish her journey to Chamonix by train. Elaine's mother was horrified by the idea. A fierce row followed; she paraded the conventional arguments against a young unmarried couple making the trip together and Hayward countered by saying how worthwhile it would be. In the end, to his disgust, she forbade her daughter from going away with him. It seemed an exact re-run of the tedious conversations he had with his own parents. Worse followed as Mrs Finlay questioned her daughter until she broke down and admitted having an affair. Hayward was told that he was unwelcome in the house. He began to doubt Elaine: then a letter from her further disturbed him: 'You must not make love to me so much another time ... It is not that I don't like it – I do very much. I can't stop you doing it when you are there, but I feel I ought not to let you.' When they next met he threw her words angrily back at her. She countered tearfully, 'Ever since I saw you on the street in Cambridge you have been my one interest. I think of nothing in the world except you. It's not my fault if I am not passionate.' With that she fell into his arms and told him to forget the letter. She seems then to have persuaded her mother to change her mind about the French trip. Mrs Finlay agreed to Elaine going, provided that Hayward told his parents what he was doing and that he received their blessing – neither of which, of course, he did.

They took the boat train to Paris. France was a country he had always associated with romance and now, almost to his own disbelief, he found himself there with Elaine. They drove through the Paris suburbs until they reached the town of Mélun on the banks of the Seine. There an old friend from le Mortier, Crompton Johnson, and his male companion, joined them. The first night with Elaine in France was a disappointment to the ardent Hayward. They dined with the others and he looked forward impatiently to being alone with her. After dinner he went to her room, but she was 'tired and unwilling' and told him to leave. Later he tiptoed back along the hotel corridor, only to find her bedroom door was locked. He wondered how he might have offended her.

The next morning, however, resolved all his fears. Elaine, in green silk jumper and cream skirt, was as charming and alluring to him as before, and the travellers started their journey south-westwards to Avallon. Anxious to avoid the events of the previous night, Hayward asked Elaine if he might come to talk to her before she went to sleep. Shyly she agreed. 'That night we lit our candle in Heaven ... I comprehended a new form of happiness, the responsibility for another's innocence.' They continued on their journey motoring through Burgundy, staying the night at Bourg. At dinner he suddenly felt sick and had to go back to his room. There Elaine joined him and sat in a chair by his bed embroidering. He told his diary, a little over-lyrically, that 'the reading light made her hair a bright halo against the surrounding shadows of the room'. He wondered if he had ever been so happy.

The following day, 5 August, they had to part. The journey from Bourg to Aix-les-Bains on the shores of lac Bourget was a short one. Seeing the lake made famous by the nineteenth-century poet Lamartine's 'Le Lac', Hayward was immediately transported back to his schooldays when, gazing onto the North Sea from the cliffs of Sheringham, he had learnt the words by heart. The view reminded him too of the trip he had made with his father when he had first seen the mountains of Jura. Past and present fused as he stood now beside Elaine. Like Lamartine, he wanted time to stand still:

> O temps! suspends ton vol, et vous, heures propices!
> Suspendez votre cours:
> Laissez-nous savorer les rapides délices
> Des plus beaux de nos jours!

Elaine and he stared at the chameleon surface of the lake, hands clasped. When they returned to their hotel, Hayward watched Elaine begin to pack. Suddenly, to his enormous surprise, she came towards him and covered his face with kisses. It was the first time she had done such a thing, enough to 'cram me once again with happiness'. What she next said in her shy manner took him even more by surprise. 'Though I should like to marry you, I think we'd better not. We might become impatient with each other.' Marriage had not been mentioned before and was far from Hayward's thoughts. 'True our relations grew deeper and deeper as time passed but I had no wish to marry, neither had I the right to.' The statement that he had 'no right to marry' is the first indication of his feeling that he could not have children for fear of their inheriting his disability. Her remarks 'almost frightened' him; he described the moment as a 'crystallisation' of their relationship as he became aware of a 'certain responsibility in my attitude'.

Parting the next morning led him to cry in Elaine's arms. 'This then was the end of our holiday in the pale morning light, the romance quite gone, only the cold crumpled bed clothes, the half-unpacked valise and our two speechless bodies.' They drove to the station at Chambéry where she caught the train for Chamonix. He returned immediately to his room and wrote a long love letter and a poem for Elaine:

> Out of night's troubled cup the pale dawn flows
> But comes unwelcome to his tired eyes
> And unacknowledged by his form that lies
> Caring not what the daybreak shall disclose.
> Time in the end, he thought, will bring repose:
> Just as an infant in the night that cries
> But ends in sleeping as its terror dies –
> So love outlives the memory of love's woes.
> He rose as one who triumphs in debate.
> 'All will be well,' he cried, 'Nor Time nor Fate
> Can love's invulnerable spirit kill!'
> But as he turned he saw her stand and wait
> To say Farewell and his worst fears fulfil.[120]

Now the holiday had lost all its point and he wondered whether to carry on. But then Crompton Johnson received an urgent message summoning him home and the trip had to be abandoned anyway. They returned via le Mortier where, by chance, Evelyn Waugh was staying with M. Bricoyne in the old house Hayward remembered so well. It was now inhabited by 'some rather awful English students', whom Waugh disliked intensely. Hayward, on the other hand, he found 'charming and incredibly learned', and rather like the elegant Brian Howard to look at.[121] Suddenly Hayward thought of an unexpected possibility: he had just time to rush to Paris and intercept Elaine on her way back from Switzerland. He telegrammed her and at first she seemed very keen. Then she sent a stark message that filled him with dismay: 'WILL NOT STAY IN PARIS. WILL TRAVEL ALONE.'

Not one to be put off so easily, Hayward checked her train and decided to get to Paris and wait for her at the Gare de Lyon. 'This indeed was an adventure packed with romantic possibilities,' he wrote. Ticketless, he played the role of the secret lover, hiding behind pillars and piles of luggage on the cavernous station platform. A train drew into the station and the passengers disgorged; he watched as the platform emptied. No sign of Elaine. He was desperate with anxiety – but then realised he had been waiting for the wrong train. Elaine was due on the next one. Once again, he waited nervously on the platform until the train drew up, once again he searched anxiously amongst the crowds. Suddenly he saw the familiar elegant toque and hurried towards her. She was totally surprised, but her first words were, 'Let's stay in Paris.' And so the holiday continued for three more days. They shared an apartment and walked together through the Tuileries Gardens and strolled by the Seine. As a love token he gave her an intaglio ring he had chosen at a Florentine goldsmith's.

From Boulogne they boarded a boat back home. 'In all our experiences,' Hayward wrote, 'there had been a rich flavour of romance that sometimes made me doubt its reality. Now that the reality has fled, the romance of it all seems all the more vivid.'[122] Back in Wimbledon, he took advantage of his parents' absence and invited Elaine to stay with him at The Grange. Now, as he confided to his Journal, 'each of us became aware of some new quality of love'. In bed she seemed much more at ease, 'tenderly surrendering herself completely to me'.

In October 1926 it was time for him to return to Cambridge to begin his fourth year and the pair once more went through agonies of separation. Elaine burst into tears and Hayward wrote a poem, 'Valediction'. Underneath it he inscribed: 'Before parting. For E. October 8th 1926.' Beside the draft, in his tiniest writing, he pencilled, 'I can't bear it.' Not that their separation was by any means complete. As Elaine worked in London they could meet at weekends either in Wimbledon or Cambridge, but weekly partings made Hayward feel that his time in Cambridge was over. He felt ecstatic when he was with her and desperate when she left him for London after a weekend. He was overcome by her beauty and his notebooks contain nude sketches he drew of her. As he gazed upon her in his rooms

Afternoon passed into evening unperceived until through my tall windows and across the stone balcony outside moonlight burst ... It was an astonishing sight, unearthly it seemed beyond all belief romantic. Its rays fell straight upon Elaine's body so that her beauty became fixed like a statue in the silver-grey of its blanching light ... and so we sat when love had wearied us both, side by side before the fire as we had been Adam and Eve before the Fall, happy that in the absence of desire, the communion of two minds was more easily and gently possible.

He was running a huge risk in having her to stay at King's. Three years later, in 1929, a woman was found in the Magdalene College rooms of his friend the critic and poet William Empson. He suffered Draconian punishments: he was sent down and lost his fellowship; his name was removed from all college lists as if he had never existed, and he was forbidden to live in Cambridge. Luckily, Hayward was not caught.

After Elaine had to go back to London Hayward hosted a large party in his rooms and was struck by the contrasts of his experience – at one moment he was totally absorbed with Elaine and at the next he could almost forget her in a noisy party. Was his time with her merely a fleeting moment of no significance? What did it all mean? He answered his own questions by the assurance of some verses which he rewrote in bold capitals and underlined for extra emphasis: 'BY BRIEFEST MEETING SOMETHING SURE IS WON ...' Under the quotation he wrote: 'I saw clearly that whatever followed the days I had spent with Elaine would not lose in value at the hands of a benign or cruel fortune. That she could not forget what had passed between the warm radiance of the fire and the cold rays of the moon one short November day in her lover's arms in Cambridge.' He added eight lines of senti-mental verse in which he placed their affair: 'Amid the spheres / As part of sick life's antidote'. When discussing his love for Elaine he often used images of disease and health; he felt a sense of well-being when with her, and ill as soon as she left. Her love gave him, for a moment, a feeling of freedom and release.

Hayward returned to Wimbledon for the Christmas holidays desper-ate to see Elaine again and visited her at home, only to find, to his irri-tation, an American visitor occupying her time and attention. He tried to eclipse him by 'talking as brilliantly as I could', and soon, beaten down, the American left. Almost the first thing Elaine said was, 'I'll come to your room tonight if you want me.' Hayward was thrilled: 'She might have said we shall never be separated again – I could not have been more carried away with desire and happiness. Her mood was deeply passionate due (as I was aware) to the oncoming of her illness.' The lovers had dinner with the family impatiently. When they were alone together afterwards Elaine confided to him that she was nervous that her 'illness' might prevent their love making and how frightened she was because of the risks that she was taking. 'I can't resist the temptation,' she added. Perhaps the tryst had an extra frisson from the danger of discovery – Elaine's father slept in the room opposite. John Hayward and Elaine had adjoining rooms. He retired to bed and waited nervously, listening to the snoring from across the corridor, wondering if she would come. At last he heard a light step outside his door and Elaine, 'lovely and naked', crept into bed beside him. On another occasion she 'suddenly elected to take all her clothes off' in the drawing room of her father's house – 'Had we been disturbed there would have been no escape.' Once, to avoid detection, he had to creep 'Casanova-like' from her bedroom into the garden. He enjoyed picturing himself as the lover of a French romance, or perhaps his hero Rochester, eluding the clutches of aged parents and dashing off with the girl, but he also felt that these were the most significant moments of his life. Aware as he was that he did not have time on his side, Elaine's physical love for him had the force of a vindication. He *could*, after all, lead a sexual life and find an attractive woman to share his life with. 'I feel deeply alive and serene,' he wrote.

As he reviewed 1926 in his Private Journal Hayward had no doubt that it had been a splendid year. Gazing from the window of his parents' home, where he was staying for Christmas, he looked out on a bright late-December morning:

> This indeed is the first intimation of Spring in Winter such as the old poets loved. The sunlight is pale and dusty, the shadows of bare trees on the slate roof soft and barely defined; the air too is soft, full of moisture as if it contained all the sap from the sleeping branches ... Tomorrow the sun may be lost again in cold fog and snow clouds, for the season is unsettled. It is the year's ending: the close of one of the best years of my life, the last year of seclusion at college before I am pressed into the service of the world.

But behind the rapture of the relationship with Elaine there lay always the shadow of his disability. Hayward felt guilty and responsible if all he could offer was a childless marriage. The issue surfaced once more before he returned to Cambridge. Was he standing in her light, he asked her?

> I went as far as to offer her complete freedom if she wished it, for I knew it would be easier to leave her then ... compelled as I was to return to Cambridge ... than at any other time. I explained to her how I was prepared to learn that my physical disability was a barrier to her loving me completely. She said that only a superficial vanity compelled her occasionally to be shy of being seen with me; or rather I said so for her, since she was troubled with the explanation and with the tears our conversation had evoked.

The underlying anxiety that is rarely mentioned even in the Private Journal is of course the pace and progress of the creeping paralysis. After a long, emotional discussion the couple began to discuss getting engaged. Hayward wrote that he had begun to consider 'with unusual seriousness the question of marriage' and added, 'I cannot imagine a life without her.' He himself was resolved, but realised that there were many difficulties:

> I should marry her if I could afford to and if she would agree to without children; but I have no money and she wants children, though she is simple enough to believe that anyone can make children for her, but I alone can love her and be loved by her. And yet she wants me for ever. I am troubled by all this ... And yet, the happiest situation, that of living illegally together, that has made us so happy hitherto, is a heavy responsibility for me. Elaine's future is very much in my hands.

It seemed that the moment was right to raise the matter with his mother – a task made more difficult because they were not close – he described her to Eliot as the 'apoplectic' mistress of The Grange and called her 'brisk'. Over lunch at home on 21 March Hayward began to talk about Elaine. He got a very hostile reception: his mother told him that his father was extremely concerned about the possibility of an engagement. Apparently Dr Hayward disliked Elaine and was worried about the chastity of the couple. 'Are you sure she's not engaged to someone else?' his mother asked. 'I don't think so or she would, I suppose, have told me,' he replied. He felt that his parents were dense and distant not to have understood their relationship. 'What ignorance was there! How little they knew of my life. For an instant I saw more clearly than ever before that impenetrable barrier that lies between us and those with whom we live most intimately ... Sex to them is a fearful bogey.' Seeing himself as the emancipated voice of a younger generation confronting the prejudice of his parents' Victorian attitudes, he had to conceal from them that Elaine was his mistress – and then he blamed them for their ignorance.

There followed a tremendous family row. Mother and son were bitterly at odds. Hayward's cutting tongue added to the hurt. Dr Hayward finally decided that he could no longer put up with his son's rudeness and his loose behaviour. This dispute became the 'quarrel of considerable magnitude' that led him to offer his son an allowance of £30 every two months on condition that he did not return home. The argument crystallised John Hayward's attitudes to his father and mother. Despite being very angry with his father he still felt that he was on his side: 'although he is often impatient with me he is devoted to the task of helping me ... I am very fond of him and grateful for all he has done for me.' The case of his mother was very different. 'My mother is not sympathetic to me: she is over-impetuous. I feel that she is not very interested in me.' George had already been estranged from his parents for two years. Furious with his father, he had decided to change his name to Rolleston; it seemed Hayward was beginning to follow in his brother's footsteps.

Under the influence of Dadie Rylands and Peter Lucas, Hayward had changed from Modern Languages to the recently-founded school of English for the second part of his Cambridge degree. In 1927 he took a second class degree in the final part of the tripos. His failure to gain a First was a disappointment and a surprise. With a First he would surely have been offered and accepted a university post. Not only was he intellectually suited to the life of the don, but the security of the college would have allowed him to have lived a comfortable life with his domestic needs organised for him. After all, he was 'already gravely crippled by the progressively paralysing disease which he was to defy with such gallantry for the rest of his life'.[123] The second class degree uncomfortably opened up the question of his future. Dr Hayward was 'gloomy and impatient', constantly asking his son what he was going to do. 'Let me know if you hear of a vacant crossing I could sweep,' Hayward wrote to

Bunny.[124] Meanwhile Virginia Woolf's husband, Leonard, sent him a pile of novels to review in the *Nation*, which for the moment kept him busy – and his father from the door. Hayward paid what he thought was to be one last visit to Cambridge, and already felt that in the depth of the Long Vacation it was 'like the city of the dead', as dead as his future there, as his Journal entry for 28 August shows:

> One thing however was certain: there had been fulfilment, something complete and finished, beautiful also. There had been preparation and completion: nothing was left to mourn over. Perhaps I knew then that Cambridge is too complete in itself, too much in miniature – the perfect doll's house – to be prolonged indefinitely in time … the security it offers is given at the risk of mental paralysis. A quicksand, a home that too closely resembles a prison.

But after what appeared to be a final farewell to Cambridge the next paragraph surprisingly reveals the news that he had suddenly been offered and had accepted a postgraduate studentship at King's, a studentship normally awarded only to those with Firsts. After the disappointment of his degree he now felt that the wound to his *amour propre* had been at least partially healed.

In the summer of 1927 Hayward repeated the previous year's French trip. On 26 July, after another clandestine escape from The Grange in his father's car, with the chauffeur's collusion, he set out for Victoria Station, going by a roundabout route to pick up Elaine. At Victoria the couple met Crompton Johnson, crossed to France at Boulogne and followed the road to Montreuil. They drank coffee in the courtyard of the Hôtel de France and then moved on to Hesdin to see Elaine's parents, who evidently had fewer reservations about the couple's relationship than Dr and Mrs Hayward. Elaine's father was dangerously ill but her mother persuaded her not to abandon her holiday.

The journey, fewer than ten years after the end of the First World War, took them through the battle-scarred landscape of Northern France and Hayward was able to retrace the course of the war through the places where his father had served in Northern France: Arras, Cambrai, Bapaume, Vimy Ridge and along the Hindenburg Line:

> I was profoundly moved by the spectacle of the great waste area over which the war had passed, and by the vivid contrast between

the awful loneliness of the land, the absence of all trees, even houses, and the beauty of the acres of corn and roots, golden and green, stretching over hill and hollow further than the eye could reach.

He was struck by the scale and the simplicity of the recently-built cemeteries, the red roses at every corner, the well-clipped lawns and the inscriptions on the white altars: 'Their Name Liveth for Evermore'. From Cambrai the travellers moved on to Charleville-Mezières and the Belgian frontier. Looking over the prospect towards Germany from the Col de Saverne, Crompton Johnson suddenly burst out that he disapproved of Hayward's immoral behaviour with Elaine. Hayward, furious, said nothing. Worse was to come when, back in the hotel in Strasbourg, Elaine said how much she hated the idea of living in sin.

> Naturally I felt that as far as love was concerned all was over between us. I broke down and left the room. For some time I felt absolutely lost; then slowly I began to feel the pain through my numbness. Elaine came to me, weeping hysterically, begging me to forget those words she had uttered thoughtlessly. At first I found it hard to free myself from a bitter feeling of disillusionment. I just sat, dry mouthed, with E clinging to me. Finally however her tears reassured me and after the storm a wonderful and sudden calm fell on us.

So they sat together and made up their quarrel over a pot of tea, 'accusing each other of every imaginable virtue'. When Crompton Johnson turned up to apologise and Hayward understood that he had thought he had seduced Elaine and feared that he would be an accessory to an unwanted pregnancy, Hayward forgave his companion and ordered champagne for dinner.

Hayward felt that his relationship with Elaine was no longer 'experimental' as it had been a year before, but tested and secure. It was the 'wonderful and sudden calm', not the squalls, that Hayward recalled when on 5 August 1927 he wrote 'The Balcony' from the Grand Hotel in Lausanne. Beside the title, in tiny letters, he wrote, 'For Elaine'. The most intense experience that he could imagine was this moment of love's harmony, which he described in words echoing the poem he had just been editing in England – Donne's 'The Extasie':

Elaine: Before the Fall

Noon passed and evening and night came
Over far hills and closed about us twain
Together standing and the lake beneath
Under a world of stars lay still as death.

The quiet crowning of a day much loved
Prepared our bodies and our minds to rest.
We spoke no words and neither of us moved –
The hour itself two single lives expressed.

Things that hurt us once had there their ending
And our two minds as our two hearts were one.
Love there was reconciled with hate – the blending
Of the dark midnight and the noonday sun.

6

The Editor

Away from the noonday sun, Hayward returned to face the question of where to live and what to do after he left Cambridge. Wimbledon was clearly out of the question. He toyed with the idea of applying for the job of Pepys Librarian at Magdalene College, but nothing came of it. University posts seemed closed because of his second-class degree. Involved in this decision was the question of how quickly his muscular dystrophy would spread and how he could manage to cope as a disabled man. He could not possibly live on his father's allowance. So he decided to become an editor and critic, picking up work as and when it came and feeling that the future for an ambitious young writer had to be in London. One Cambridge contact came immediately to mind. T. S. Eliot had impressed Hayward so much in his lectures and at their breakfasts that he wrote from his parents' home to remind him of their meetings. Could Eliot recall him, he wondered. He asked if he might do a review for *The Criterion*, the very influential quarterly magazine Eliot had set up in 1922. This contained a mixture of original work – *The Waste Land* had appeared in its first issue – and critical articles which aimed to place British literature within a European context. 'Of course I remember you very well and I should be glad to have some reviews from you,' Eliot replied, and invited him to tea.[125] So Hayward duly did a piece on Horace Walpole which appeared in January 1928. Its scholarship appealed to Eliot, who wrote that he was only sorry that it was not longer; he asked Hayward to do another about the metaphysical poet Abraham Cowley. These were followed by articles on Sir Walter Raleigh and Restoration Tragedy. Hayward began to lend Eliot books and Eliot invited his young contributor to lunch at Faber's and to tea with his wife Vivienne. So began a friendship that was to last nearly thirty years and have an immense impact on both their lives

While he looked for a more permanent base Hayward stayed fretfully with his parents in Wimbledon. Elaine's mother, Jane Finlay, now widowed, offered him accommodation in the flat she owned at 125 Queen's Gate, Kensington. Hayward sat for hours dreading the thought of packing and worrying about his bookshelves and where he should sleep. It was like having a baby, he reported to his Cambridge friend Lyn Irvine.[126] What would happen if labour started at 9.00? – 'I don't get up before 9.15'. As he waited anxiously he sent her his version of 'The Hollow Men'. Eliot's emaciated figures become burly removal men in white overalls, not full of straw themselves, but using it to pack away Hayward's possessions and his beloved books.

> Teach me to be patient and to be patient
> and not to understand –
> What? to understand
> what those men in white
> The men in white who stuff with straw
> The far-from hollow men desire –
> Teach me to be a good dog
> Teach me to gnaw my bone.

'My dear Lyn your old and affectionate friend John is going off his head,' he ended.

In June 1930, much to his parents' horror, he settled down with Elaine in his new flat. They lived a cosy domestic existence together – the only time in life that he did so. In the morning Elaine went out to work leaving him at his desk. When she returned in the evening, he loved to tell her all the details of the day's events – just like a newly married couple. Weekend trips were often spent with Bunny at his beautiful seventeenth-century house, Hilton Hall, near Huntingdon, where in summer they enjoyed picnics under the elms in the shady garden. Their host was a hypnotic story teller.

Denys King-Farlow was surprised that when he came to visit Hayward the door was opened by a very attractive young woman, whom he took for the maid, who showed him to the study.[127] Astonished – and gratified – that she apparently knew his name and all about him, he ribbed Hayward about having such a 'gorgeous creature to minister to his every need'. Then the two men discussed Hayward's work on Donne and the planned letters of St Evrémond. They began to laugh together about a 'Rabelaisian romance' King-Farlow had enjoyed on his six-day boat trip back to England. There followed a great deal of 'ribald jocularity'.

> Suddenly John amazed me, in fact he appalled me, by saying that he'd fallen deeply in love, head-over-heels in love with this girl

we'd been talking about. She was his (widowed) landlady's daughter. More serious yet, that overpowering love for her was now fully reciprocated, and she, a really strong-minded young woman, was determined that they should marry very soon.

Hayward was only hoping, he told his friend, that she loved him despite his 'terrible physical condition and not in a masochistic way, because of it'. Ignorant to the last, King-Farlow did not dare to ask the question that he most wanted to: 'How was all this flaming passion going to be consummated?' Badly shaken, he left the flat.

Top of Hayward's list of tasks was the completion of his edition of Donne. After years of relative neglect Donne had become a spokesman for Hayward's postwar generation. 'Donne was our poet: Webster our playwright,' said Dadie Rylands. 'It is not difficult to draw a parallel between Donne's spiritual difficulties and those of a generation that was growing up at the outbreak of war,'[128] wrote Hayward who agreed with Eliot that Donne reflected the 'underlying current of uncertainty' of an age which tried to grapple with the problem of reconciling new philosophy with the dogmas of the past. Hayward's *John Donne, Dean of St Paul's: Complete Poetry and Selected Prose* was finally published by the Nonesuch Press in 1929. In his Introduction he noted the crucial part that Sir Herbert Grierson's edition of 1912 had played in determining his text because 'it is well-nigh impossible to improve on his recension'. The ever-scrupulous editor added that he had 're-collated' the text using all previous editions and most manuscript collections. This scrutiny had however only confirmed Grierson's readings. The number of sources and helpers that Hayward gratefully acknowledged indicated the heaviness of his task. Sir Edmund Gosse lent him 'two valuable MSS'; the Earl of Powis gave him permission to print an unpublished letter; Sotheby's a MS of poems from Lord Leconfield's library – and so on. It was to the surgeon and book collector Geoffrey Keynes (whose edition of Donne's sermons had also been published by Nonesuch) that he owed the most. Keynes had allowed him to borrow volumes from his collection of Donne – 'probably the finest in existence'. This would have been a help to any editor, but to the immobile Hayward, it must have been a godsend. 'Anyone who has suffered the inconveniences of collating texts in public places will understand how much time and labour is saved by being able to work how, where, and when one chooses.'[129]

The volume provided one of the first generally accessible editions of Donne's poetry, but its real originality lay in linking this with his much less well known prose. Jack Donne, the daring love poet, was one and the same man as the Dean of St Paul's. Hayward pointed out for example that *Paradoxes and Problemes*, written in the 1590s at a time when Donne was at his most brilliant and witty, could shed light on the early love poetry. Grierson had already noted how useful the prose could be in understanding some of the poems' scholastic arguments, but it was the Nonesuch edition that gave the general reader a chance to test the assertion. In it he could examine not only the sermons but also a selection of letters, and even the obscure *Ignatius His Conclave*, printed for the first time since 1625.

The plaudits that greeted *Donne* went some way to making up for the lack of interest that *Rochester* had received. The *Morning Post* called Hayward, 'a most judicious and learned critic' and the *Criterion* reviewer praised the selection of sermons. It was 'the last word in Donne editing … and the next step can only be to select six verse and six prose aphorisms, bind them in limp leather, and capture the Christmas trade.'[130] Hayward was also pleased to receive a very satisfactory fee of £75 from Francis Meynell for his work. But the verdict that mattered most came from Eliot who wrote, with a touch of irony, to congratulate him on a book that 'does credit to the Press – it is very cheap at eight and six – and to the Editor'.[131] He asked for a copy of the limited edition and told Hayward that it would also be very useful for his own work as he prepared to revamp his Donne lectures.

After Hayward had become a regular reviewer for *The Criterion*, invitations from Eliot to lunch and supper soon followed. Hayward was the first to praise Eliot's essay 'Dante' when it had appeared in 1929, the same year as his own *Donne*. Eliot was delighted and reassured: 'I cannot try to tell you how much pleasure your letter gave me. It is the first opinion that I have had. I cannot take it as indicative of what the world will think – you know me too well to be at all representative of that – but at all events what you say seems to indicate that the book has been to you what I hoped it might be to persons like yourself. I put a good deal of blood, if little scholarship into it.'[132] He signed the letter 'Ever gratefully'. When *Ash-Wednesday* was published in spring of the following year Eliot was again delighted by his friend's enthusiastic letter: 'I do not expect to receive many like it; not many people will really like that sort of verses.'[133] Hayward wrote asking about the symbolism of the yew in the poem, but the reply came that it might not mean as much as he supposed: it was merely an image from a dream he had had two or three times. Already Hayward was beginning to act as a friendly but questioning commentator. 'It is always a pleasure to send you the little things I write because your acknowledgements are so particularly satisfying,' wrote Eliot.[134] He had found his ideal reader.

Hayward's next task was to finish his edition of the letters of Saint Evrémond. His interest in that seventeenth-century Frenchman went back to schooldays and had been sharpened by his study of Saint Evrémond's friend and contemporary Rochester. *The Letters of Saint Evrémond*[135] was prepared with Hayward's usual scrupulous attention to detail, after a careful examination of sources. In his Introduction he painted a picture of a nobleman who spent most of his life as an exile in the English court, a man of letters who led a tempered epicurean life amongst the debauchery of the Restoration. The attraction of this obscure courtier was not only to do with a sweetness of character which Hayward found charming and civilised. Writing to a gentleman who could not endure or understand the idea that the eighty-year-old Earl of St Albans could be in love, Saint Evrémond developed his theme:

> The greatest pleasure that old Men have left them, is to live; and nothing secures their Life so effectually as Love. *I think, therefore I am*, is the conclusion upon which the whole Philosophy of *Descartes* turns; but 'tis cold and languishing for an old Man. *I love, therefore I am,* is a consequence that has all life and spirit in it ... What are we the better for Life, if we are not sensible we are alive? We surely owe our life to our love ...[136]

'I love, therefore I am,' was exactly the key to Hayward's own romantic philosophy. He described Saint Evrémond as 'one of those men who are incapable for some subtle psychological or perhaps physiological reason, of enjoying a passionate love affair, but who nevertheless remain, all through their lives, devoted admirers and obedient servants of several women'.[137] After the death of the woman he loved, the beautiful Duchess Mazarin, Saint Evrémond fell into a melancholy decline: 'He struggled on for another two years, until his health, which all his life had worried him, began to fail. It became impossible for him to go abroad as much as he wished and he was reduced to staying indoors where he was a prey to his own regrets.'[138] It is hard to read these passages and not think of Hayward himself, in love with Elaine, still only twenty-five years old, and beginning not to be able to walk. As he wrote this account from his wheelchair, did he see this as his own bleak future?

On Wednesday 16 December 1931 there came a sudden crisis in Elaine's health.[139] Dangerously ill, she was admitted to hospital at 6.30 in the evening. The meticulous Hayward was in so anxious a state that he put the wrong date on his calendar entry and had to strike it out. On Thursday evening Elaine had to undergo an emergency operation. The following day he pencilled into his calendar '9.00 pm 24 hours' and then '48 hours' as he waited powerlessly for news and cancelled all his appointments. The only person he saw for this critical period was Bunny, who called on his friend just after the operation to give him some company and reassurance. After 72 hours the doctor's son wrote 'T 90.6 P 88' in the margin of the calendar – a low temperature and a high pulse – but Elaine had survived. It is not clear what had been wrong but, whatever it was, it nearly proved fatal: Elaine herself described it later as 'a close-run thing', and said the operation just saved her. Hayward's complete absence from her bedside may suggest that she was in a women's ward and the silence about the nature of her condition might point to something gynaecological, possibly an ectopic pregnancy, but it is impossible to be sure. She remained in hospital for six weeks and Hayward showered her by post with 'delicate foods and mild temptations'. Although he did not (could not?) visit her, he wrote once, or often twice, a day, describing his activities and planning their future together. 'Her illness and your devotion have emphasised what I knew before: that love and friendship are the two things in life most worth fighting for,' he told Bunny. Meanwhile Lytton Strachey was also in hospital, fighting the stomach cancer that was to kill him in January. Under his last entry in his December calendar after a lonely, anxious Christmas Hayward wrote: 'Thus ends a year of sorrows.'

The task of making a living was always a crucial one for Hayward: money was vital if he was to maintain the independent way of life he prized so highly. Once he was established in London it became imperative. There was a modest allowance from his father every two months, but no other private means. For these reasons he had turned with such energy to reviewing and journalism after leaving Cambridge: increasingly they gave him a regular income. He kept the records in his account book. It provides a detailed picture of the earnings of the reviewer in the 1930s.[140] In 1930 he earned a total of £89 from 34 articles. By 1932 his output had increased dramatically: 155 pieces gave him £388 and in 1933 177 brought in £394. In other words, in two years he had written over 300 reviews, at the rate of one every two days. His financial circumstances later were considerably improved when in 1935 Francis Birrell died and left him the interest from £4,000 during his lifetime. It was a very generous sum, based on the assumption that its recipient had no more than five years to live.

Hayward contributed reviews regularly to *The Times Literary Supplement, The Times*, the *Daily Mirror,* the *New Statesman, The Spectator, The Observer* and to *Life and Letters,* run by Desmond MacCarthy. Faced by the need to make a living, his output became more wide-ranging; he began to review the newly popular genre of crime fiction for *The Times* and received 5s apiece for brief notices on books with titles such as *Plain Murder, The Eel Pie Mystery, Ghost's High Noon, Murder at University*, and *Naked Truth*. A quick reader, he took the book to bed, finished it and did the piece the next morning. As, like Eliot, he was an addict of detective fiction this was a welcome relief from more academic journalism. He soon became a prolific journeyman. In June 1932, for example, he reviewed three thrillers for *The Times*, and wrote articles for the *Daily Mirror* on topics which ranged from Sicily to the state of Russia and Germany, and from the English landscape to the welfare of the infant. As 'Autolycus' he wrote weekly titbits of gossip for the *Sunday Times*. For a brief while he became the broadcasting correspondent of Graham Greene's *Night and Day*. Soon he added foreign journalism, becoming the London Correspondent of the *New York Daily Sun* from 1934 to 1938. The sheer quantity of his work is staggering: between 1929 and 1937 he contributed more than 200 pieces to *The Times Literary Supplement* alone.[141] The pace slowed a little after this but journalism remained a steady source of income until the war severed nearly all his contacts.

Hayward's scholarly reviews were those of the textual critic. From his family medical background he inherited skills of diagnosis and analysis of evidence. No detail was too small for his notice. He described his own practice with heartfelt accuracy in the remarks that he made on Agnes Latham's edition of the poems of Sir Walter Raleigh:

Miss Latham has performed a very difficult task very well ... she has, at least established a canon, and a text, based upon a wide collation of available sources that will not easily be surpassed. This should be some consolation for the long hours of laborious comparisons of texts, the often fruitless examination of books and manuscripts, that are seldom referred to by the critic, or appreciated by the general reader. With admiration, mingled with disappointment, one examines the slender progeny of mice engendered by such a mountain of research.[142]

By contrast, Hayward was a devastating critic of lazy, incompetent or pretentious editors.

When Montague Summers turned aside from his interest in the occult to edit the dramatic works of Dryden in 1932, Hayward was given the task of reviewing the book in *The Criterion*. It was an opportunity not to be missed and one of the only reviews in which he showed personal bias. He worked with his friends Richard Jennings and Percy Dobell to collect evidence of Summers's 'wicked habits' in order to present his 'fearful attack'. Noting how Summers swept away all his editorial predecessors, 'withered in his indiscriminating sarcasm', Hayward began his own demolition with a modest disclaimer: 'After the fate of Ker and Sargeaunt, I certainly do not feel myself qualified for the task of criticising Mr Summers, but, since I have undertaken it, I will try to describe what a careful scrutiny has revealed to my bat-like vision.'[143] He then proceeded to show how Summers's editorial practice, which was to follow the later folio, was at odds with his professed aim to follow the first quartos. Hayward told his readers he had to give up the task, having found sixty unauthorised or false readings in the first four pages. The book's editorial claims 'are mere eye-wash to deceive an innocent reader into believing that Mr Summers has weighed the merits of every variation', Hayward concluded. What, then, could account for this travesty of a text? Either the writer could not make sense of Dryden's works or he had hired 'some well-meaning but incompetent hack'. Now Hayward had his victim lined up and there is no mistaking the note of delighted malice with which he concluded:

There is one other possible explanation ... It may account for Mr Summers' treatment of the text, it may also explain why he has quoted as his own the annotations of previous editors; it may also be responsible for the virulence of his attacks upon their work, even when he has benefited from it. 'Some evil spirit,' Mr Sargeaunt wrote in the preface to his edition of the poems, 'seems to have dogged the steps of Dryden's editors.' Since Mr Summers also appears to have been affected by this baleful influence, it is a pity that his recognised familiarity with the powers of darkness did not help him to exorcise it.[144]

After this Summers edited no more Restoration texts.

As joint-founder of the Nonesuch Press Bunny felt responsible, as he had hired Summers in the first place. He was hurt and infuriated by Hayward's review. On 6 June 1932 they had a dramatic row in which Bunny accused his friend of malice and vindictiveness. Who was Hayward, whose whole career as a writer had been started and nourished by the Press, to turn on one of its authors in such a vicious way? And what about the betrayal of friendship, and all the hospitality that Elaine and he had enjoyed at Hilton? 'I cannot believe that you really meant all the horrible things you said about me this morning,' wrote Hayward angrily immediately after Bunny had left. 'Your bitter remarks about my character have only intensified the unhappiness of the last month'[145] – but he stuck by every word of his attack. The friendship, it seemed, was over.

Later on in 1932 Hayward also reviewed a very dissimilar work in *The Criterion – The Orators* – an experimental collection of verse and prose written by his friend from schooldays, W. H. Auden.[146] Like many critics he found the book 'exceedingly hard to understand', and he criticised its author for his obscurity and a fatal fondness for the private joke: 'Auden expects far too much of the uninitiated; he expects them to understand the incomprehensible.' His style could be compared with the decadent metaphysical poets, who relied on the ingenuity rather than the truth of their conceits.

> The ordinary reader cannot relate them to his experience of the external world, and I still believe, old-fashioned as it may seem, that it is the poet's business to interpret this world in terms that educated people can understand and to give us the emotional and intellectual experience of sharing what our own feeble gifts of sensibility and intelligence cannot provide on their own account.[147]

This emphasis on communication, understanding and clarity aligned Hayward with that school of criticism that has Dr Johnson as its source. Despite all his reservations, Hayward had the confidence to recognise the quality of Auden's work which he declared in ringing tones:

> I have no doubt that it is the most valuable contribution to English poetry since *The Waste Land*. The last ten years have been singularly unfruitful; the next ten years will show whether the promise, contained in *The Orators* and in Mr. Auden's first volume of poems, published eighteen months ago, is fulfilled, as I believe it will be.[148]

Another critic took a very different view. The young Cambridge lecturer Dr Leavis wrote a scathing piece in *The Listener* denouncing the book for its smug 'satisfaction in undergraduate cleverness' and its 'boyish romanticism'.[149] This was the beginning of the long vendetta waged by Leavis, and later by *Scrutiny*, the influential critical magazine he edited, against Auden who 'became the whipping boy for *Scrutiny*'s profound antipathy to Oxford, Bloomsbury and the academic and literary establishments which had, he thought, made Auden fashionable. He achieved a kind of mythical status as culture villain.[150] Not for the last time Hayward and Leavis were diametrically opposed in print. From this moment one can trace their mutual hostility.

After six weeks in hospital Elaine came home on 30 January 1932. Hayward had longed to see her again and was full of hopes for their future together. He had bought her an expensive Louis XV chair, which he could not afford, upholstered in old rose silk 'to sit and sew in' and had planned a holiday by the sea and weekends touring round friends' houses. Meanwhile he took her for sunlight treatment to Hampstead and cancelled all his appointments. His relief was expressed in the dedication he composed to his 1932 anthology *Nineteenth Century Poetry*:

> To Elaine:
> Tu quoniam mea lux magno periculo dismissa[151]

She was indeed his light, saved from great danger, and his undated 'Hymn to Proserpine' reflects his joy at her recovery. The poem owes a considerable debt to *The Waste Land* in its setting, and its insistent repetitive rhythms, but in transforming the desert imagery into a garden of birdsong and flowers, offers a vision of hope, rather than despair.

Where there was sand only
Swept into smooth hills
By familiar winds;
There where the calcined rock
Crumbled parched crystals
Over the dry land –
There now is water.

There all was still before
And only the wind's voice
Creeping around the dust-hills
Whispered inaudible comments.
There was no music
No murmur of pity or compassion –
There now a bird is calling.

In this dead place, this dune-land
Beyond the last flowers and the lost grasses,
No shelter, nor shade of tree
Welcomed the strayed wanderer.
But where the bird flew
And where the water flows now –
The wilderness has become a flowering place.

Where there was once thought only
Thought devoid of any hope,
And answer none to any supplication,
There is one voice now
And one walking in the garden.
The solitary place is now an habitation.

In this bleached valley of resignation
Wells up pure mountain water;
Where there was only sand and mute air
There are flowers and the shadow of wings;
Where there was once no dwelling,
Where only a broken wall stood –
Stands wide an open casement.[152]

Elaine's recovery was, however, not to be as speedy as they both had hoped. In March 1932 she fell ill once again and, seven weeks after her return, was immediately readmitted into hospital. This time she stayed for ten days, returning to Queen's Gate on 1 April to convalesce in bed for five days. Hayward tried to look after her as best he could and do the 'horrible spring cleaning' that had to be done. But as Elaine's health began slowly to improve, so their relationship fell apart. On 22 May he noted in his calendar that he had been to look at more lodgings. A week later in the entry for Saturday 28 May, two months after her return, he pencilled in the one word: 'Notice'. In July he sold 'Oxley', the baby Austin that taken them out for so many weekend trips, and went again to search for somewhere to live in Kensington. The entry for 3 August is heavily underlined: 'Elaine leaves for good.'

Whatever had gone wrong? 'It could not go on for ever; she married someone else,' was Bill Empson's terse summary.[153] King-Farlow reported, in a version he had evidently heard from Hayward, that 'Mamma whose suspicions had been building up, had suddenly put her foot down and this was the end of the episode that John felt so deeply had transformed him into a completely new and completely better human being'.[154] (Clearly he did not know that Elaine had been Hayward's mistress since Cambridge days and that at that time Mrs Finlay had accepted it.) He believed that events came to a head in May when Elaine told Hayward she could no longer live with him. At this point, according to King-Farlow, he had a kind of mental breakdown.

But the story may not be so simple. Elaine was a strong-willed woman, not the puppet of King-Farlow's account. No doubt Mrs Finlay had the chance to influence her daughter during the six weeks when Elaine was in hospital and Hayward was in his flat – but even so Elaine must have been a willing partner in the decision to end the affair. If she were really determined she could have persuaded her mother as she had done before. Peter Quennell recalled Hayward's attitude to Elaine as proprietary and dominating. When he asked her to find a book which he could not reach himself and she found the wrong volume he would 'scold her harshly'. On holiday at the seaside he sat on a camp stool at the waves' edge 'like a fantastic King Canute' watching her as she swam. From his seat he commanded her 'either to retreat or advance, and show her graceful outline to full advantage'.[155] He was beginning to show signs of becoming what the nurse called his father, a 'little Pharaoh'. It was this attitude that Quennell felt led to the break-up: 'At last, I believe, his possessiveness tired her out; she resolved to snap her chain and reluctantly deserted him.'

There was another factor. Hayward's physical condition had worsened disturbingly fast since he had fallen in love in Cambridge in 1925. Then he was a handsome young man who had reminded Evelyn Waugh of the dangerously attractive Brian Howard. Although 'gravely afflicted', he had dashed around in Oxley and used a rubber-toed stick for walking. But by 1932 he was often in his 'pram' and the car had had to be sold. It was one thing to marry someone with a disability, but quite another to look after a man who was wheelchair-bound for the rest of his life.

Whatever the reason, Elaine's desertion came as a most terrible blow. 'From this time John's character never completely recovered. He was left a different person, embittered and, from that time on, inclined to do and say the most wounding and malicious things – whenever the spirit moved him – which was not seldom,' wrote King-Farlow.[156] More than twenty years later Bunny Garnett's son Richard was visiting Hayward in his Chelsea flat and remarked that by chance he had just met Elaine in the street and they had had tea together. 'At once I realised that I had caused him great pain, and if I had tried to be cruel I could not have been more unkind. I was sorrier for John in that moment than ever I was for his disability. It was the only time that he ever seemed helpless.'[157]

Within a month Hayward seemed to have lost both his mistress and his best male friend. In his calendar Hayward drew another firm line under Sunday 7 August and the next day announced his move to a nearby Kensington flat at 15 Bolton Square Gardens. Five days after Elaine's departure Hayward left Queen's Gate to begin his 'rather lonely new life', which he pictured to Lyn Irvine:

> The calm and emptiness of evenings by the fire, cats purring, coal clicking, dogs barking in the garden – a kind of enchantment, but, like all of them, so momentary. One seems to live on, or by, such moments and dies, slowly, for the rest of time.[158]

Eliot's marriage was also disintegrating as Vivienne moved ever closer to a mental breakdown. In a most uncharacteristically open letter to Hayward he discussed physical and mental suffering. 'I am sure you know much of both,' he wrote, confiding that he knew little of physical suffering but adding, 'I have had considerable mental agony at one time or another.' At times he had felt close to 'imbecility' and even 'insanity' – which was a very different state of mind. He went on to suggest that, finally, a pattern emerged from suffering from which one might learn.

This was a kind of intimate self-revelation that he shared with very few. The letter was signed, 'Yours affectionately, T.S.E.'[159] In January 1932 while Elaine was in hospital they lunched together. Eliot told Hayward that he had decided to accept the Charles Eliot Norton lectureship at his old university of Harvard in order to escape for a while from the impossible situation with Vivienne – and also to make some money. Hayward, always shrewd on financial matters, was very impressed by the $10,000 – £2,700 according to his calculations – that his friend was to receive for seven months' work. He was surprised and pleased when Eliot began to take him into his confidence about his family and his American roots. Eliot recounted how his great-grandfather had gone to St Louis in the 1830s to preach the gospel, of 'a very peculiar American brand', and talked of his three sisters and his deaf brother who wrote detective stories under a pseudonym, having been implored by an old aunt not to disgrace the family.[160]

Eliot assured Vivienne that he would return in May 1933 – but, in fact, he had already made the decision to abandon her permanently. On Saturday 17 September she went with her husband to Southampton and together they walked the deck of the Cunard liner SS *Ausonia*. Then, along with her brother Maurice and his wife, she waved a tearful goodbye from the dockside. They were seen only once in company again. As the liner sailed in dense fog through the straits of Belle Isle towards Montreal, Hayward wired his good wishes. 'It was the only missive I got, and revived my already sinking spirits,' Eliot replied on Michaelmas Day 1932. Meanwhile his wife had rung Hayward to ask him round to dinner at a few hours' notice. He could not go and so she had decided to pay him a visit in her new motor car which she could not drive. 'And she insists on coming alone. What will happen?' Hayward wrote anxiously to Ottoline Morrell. Anything was possible as she was now 'mad, quite mad'.

Hayward kept up the correspondence with his friend, sending him Christmas greetings, and perhaps news of Vivienne. 'God Bless you for your Christmas message, which was cheering – the only one I got by cable,' Eliot replied.[161] His life had reached a nadir of loneliness and frustration and as he prepared the legal papers for his separation he was beginning to rely more and more on Hayward's loyal friendship. From now on they were constant correspondents through letters (Hayward and Eliot) telephone calls (Hayward) and postcards (Eliot). Back in England, Vivienne patiently and pathetically awaited her husband's return. She had their flat painted ready for him and threw parties where the guests toasted his health. She confessed to friends that she had scarcely changed her clothes since his departure. Just as Eliot was asking his London solicitor to prepare a deed of separation and getting ready for a clandestine return, he received a letter from her to ask if she could join him in America – a request which, he wrote to Hayward, had on him all the effect of an electric shock.

7
Bina Gardens

On Thursday 23 March 1933 John Hayward moved into 22 Bina Gardens. Set in a quiet part of South Kensington, his flat was part of a late Victorian four-storey mansion. The whole area seemed to breathe genteel decay and was populated by 'the relicts of empire builders and civil servants clinging to the fading splendours of the past in respectable boarding-house and mansion flats'.[162] He told Eliot that Kensington stood for 'the decaying rentier, frayed respectability and the keeping up of outmoded conventions'. He was happy, however, with his choice and proud to have achieved a move within three weeks of having been given notice to quit Bolton Gardens. He soon had the walls of what he called his 'Etruscan-Tudor bed-sitting room' painted. It had a large bay window overlooking a small garden where he could sit in the summer. He installed his desk in front of it and surrounded himself with books. As the window faced south-west he could enjoy the afternoon sunshine – he hated cold weather and loved to feel the warmth of the sun. In a letter to Ottoline Morrell he drew a sketch of himself at his desk, smiling smugly at the world, looking out from his new home.

An unsympathetic Virginia Woolf gave a sharp vignette of the house and its occupant's unhealthy and antiseptically ordered mind.

> He sits askew in a three-cornered chair. Can't get up. His room is an uncreative room: spick and span: too tidy. Carrington painted him a bookcase: the books all ranged in sizes. Two glass horses on the Victorian mahogany table: flowers separately springing: a dish of carefully-arranged fruit.[163]

Hayward's taste was clearly not that of Bloomsbury: the two glass horses, the Victorian table, the neatly-arranged books and the regimented appearance of the room were all far too conventional – Dora Carrington had to step in to add something of the real Bloomsbury touch by painting his bookcases light green. When she had first met 'the paralyzed man' at King's in 1925 Virginia Woolf noted he even talked in a 'jerky, angular way'. She noticed his 'great thick soft red lip: frozen green eyes; and angular attitudes like a monkey on a string'.[164] The muscular dystrophy that had deprived him of movement was beginning now to distort his features. Everything about him seemed to be made up of sharp edges. In 1934 he had horrified her by losing his balance and taking a clattering fall at one of her parties. It was such an unnerving spectacle that she told her husband Leonard that they could never let him come again. Hayward never understood why the invitations dried up.

As soon as he had settled in, Hayward began to record his visitors' names in an exercise book. At the top of his list, surprisingly, was Elaine, accompanied by his sister Diana. Soon after the dramatic end of their affair, she had gradually become his closest companion, often visiting at weekends and taking him for a walk in his chair. After the two women came Hayward's male friends and colleagues: Bunny, with whom he was now reconciled, Francis Birrell, the poet and novelist 'little' Bryan Guinness, and Richard Jennings, the editor of the *Daily Mirror*, a famously fastidious and morose bibliophile. (A country bookseller visited Jennings and picked out a volume from the shelves and said in reproving tones, 'Oh, Mr Jennings, you've been reading this one.')[165] In April Hayward received and recorded more than forty visits and Bina Gardens became a focus for scholars, critics, aristocrats, journalists and writers. The entries read like a social and literary *Who's Who* of the time: Eliot, John Betjeman, W. H. Auden, Anthony Powell, Brian Howard, Cyril Connolly, James Thurber, Arthur Symons and William Empson signed the book. Arthur Waley, the sinologist and poet; Peter Lucas; the Duchesse de la Rochefoucauld; the Marx brothers; Maurice Richardson, the critic; James Laver, the historian of fashion from the Victoria and Albert Museum; Geoffrey Faber; Bruce Richmond, the editor of *The Times Literary Supplement*; the bibliographer Simon Nowell-Smith; the historian Carew Hunt; the harmonica player Larry Adler; the poet Paul Valéry; the cartoonist David M. Low; the film critic Dilys Powell – all these, and many more, made their way to Bina Gardens. 'Tarantula' was beginning to spin his web. Rather incongruously amongst the list of names Hayward wrote: 'R. G. Hayward (Mummy)' and 'J. A. Hayward (Daddy)'. Even they had to book a time to see their son.

One important visitor was 'that great salonière', as Hayward called her, Lady Ottoline Morrell, half-sister to the Duke of Portland. Now more than sixty, she was no longer Bloomsbury's châtelaine at Garsington Manor. Her dyed-red hair had greyed and long gone were the ostrich plumes that had made her look like 'a baroque flamingo'. In 1928 she had been diagnosed as having necrosis of the jaw: the major operation that followed nearly killed her and resulted in her losing all her lower teeth. Half-deaf, she had to use a large black ear-trumpet. In autumn 1932 she had seized eagerly on Hayward at a party in Croydon Park and monopolised his attention. 'I rather threw myself at you,' she wrote apologetically. They had shared sympathetic glances at one of Eliot's poetry readings where the audience sat uncomfortably in church-like rows as he quietly intoned his verse while a maddened Vivienne could be heard baying outside in the street, her voice 'frantic with rage'.[166] Ottoline Morrell never lost her trust in friendship and when she made a new young friend such as John Hayward she believed that here at last 'in this new mind lay the tramontane land which her spirit had been seeking unavailingly'.[167] For his part Hayward was always ready to be impressed by aristocratic old Bloomsbury and by the kindness of a Lady.

Letters between them began on a formal note. He addressed her as 'Lady Ottoline' and signed himself 'John Hayward', but she soon became 'Dearest Lady Ottoline' and he, 'John'. They had met again at Eliot's 'peculiar' and tense farewell party on 15 September two days before he embarked to the USA. Despite the considerable age gap of thirty-two years, they quickly became friends and confidants as the increasing number and frequency of letters shows. By November 1932 she was asking him to read and help to edit her private memoirs. Shortly afterwards she listed the Christmas presents she would give him if she were rich, which included a 'lovely little Fiat car, a charming agile man to fetch and carry for you ... An adorable little house like the ones I envy on Highgate Hill ... with sash bayed windows and lovely doors.'[168] She wished she could ride in London so that 'she could come galloping up to your Door'.[169] Soon she was sending him photographs of the red-lacquered walls of her room at Garsington in its heyday and personal letters from Virginia Woolf, Bertrand Russell and Lytton Strachey. Her arrival at Hayward's dingy flat – 'all pink veils and glossy black and frilly sunshade, like an Edwardian Duchess'[170] – must have been quite a shock to the residents of Bina Gardens.

Ottoline began to confide in her new young friend about how miserable and lonely her marriage to the Liberal MP Philip Morrell was. 'The centre of everyone's life must go on alone but it is very very hard to be alone in the other Chambers of one's Life,' she wrote.[171] It was a feature of Hayward's life to attract confidences – especially from women. 'I am sure no man in London in his day was a repository of more intimate confessions,' wrote Graham Greene.[172] His habit of keeping friends in separate compartments encouraged this, but it was a sense of his physical vulnerability that led Ottoline Morrell to trust her secrets to him.

> I admire you so very much for the way you do regulate your Life – the one thing you perhaps gain in – is that people *are* very fond of you – and if you were strong and well you might not get to know people as you do now ... or have such heart to heart contact with them.[173]

She felt enormously sympathetic to her gracious-mannered, adoring young suitor, wooed by offerings of gifts of a pomander, roses, white carnations and fat bunches of violets – and above all by his letters. No one, she wrote, had ever written to her in such a way. Hayward would often embellish envelopes and postcards with witty drawings and advice to the postman and inside would draw telling sketches or cartoons. The contents themselves were written in small perfectly-formed letters. It was a hand that he developed after he left Cambridge; a style that owed something to his love of the eighteenth century. Ottoline and many of his friends described it as 'mandarin' because of its precise calligraphy, decorative flourishes and curlicues. It echoed his taste in typography which, according to his printer friend John Dreyfus, showed 'classical refinement, enlivened by love of ornament discreetly used'[174] – it was also characteristic of the man, just as Ottoline's almost impenetrably ornate arabesques were of her.

He knew chivalrous old-fashioned ways to please her. On 23 December 1932 his letter was 'a most lovely Christmas present' and made her feel very happy. In turn she gave him gifts of cologne, handkerchiefs, soap, flowers and a salmon for Christmas. He was touched by the presents and the kindness they implied, and flattered by the attentions of 'my dear kind patroness'. 'You see, no-one has ever taken such trouble with me before,' he wrote. Her letters were full of tenderness and admiration for the way he led his life: 'I should love to come and see you again ... I do admire you so much ... but you have this wonderful quality I imagine of friendship – & the gift of intimacy and that is great richs [*sic*].'[175] She even remembered his birthday. Ottoline's understanding showed too in the way she treated his disability. He told her he had to turn down her invitation to the theatre, owning up to how insecure he felt in strange places and amongst crowds, even when he was in his chair. It was the kind of confession he could never have made to his parents. The problem was, he confided, their inability to accept how difficult it was for him do some things. It was as if they refused to acknowledge his condition; Ottoline on the other hand was always aware of his limitations.

Without Elaine the cold winter of 1933 was a lonely one: 'There are moments when I would rather feel that I was wearing my heart out for one person than just giving it away vicariously in sympathy to others,' Hayward wrote to Ottoline. He insisted to her that 'one should have an anchor to one's life at all costs'. He was just beginning to doubt his own future as a writer – his reviews were successful and paid the rent, but he had not aspired to be a mere reviewer. She revived for a moment his dreams. 'Your encouragement lasted only a few hours: I dreamed placidly of writing works of incomparable splendour; and then – I remembered that I was only a *squalid* journalist, with nothing very much to say … Sometimes I feel as if I had a tiny flame inside me, but I think it is like the flame of a night light incapable of being blown up into a fire.'[177]

As they both knew Eliot it was natural for them to gossip about him: both found that he could be a peculiarly enigmatic friend. 'Did you know that Tom had an armorial bookplate?' asked Hayward disingenuously. They shared a sense that there was something exaggerated, almost comic, about his worship of tradition. When Ottoline quoted Bertrand Russell's remark that 'Tom had the manners of an Etonian', Hayward replied that he lacked self-possession, or 'a kind of ease'. The trouble was that 'America is always breaking in'. He continued that as Americans lacked 'a general background of culture and tradition' they went in for too much 'window-dressing' – parading their learning almost as self-defence. It was this cultural difference which led Eliot, Hayward thought, to an obsession with the European tradition and love of formality – 'bowler hats, stiff collars, Royalism, old port, Classicism etc'.[178] As an illustration Hayward told the story of how when Eliot had met his old friend Bonamy Dobrée in a London street he solemnly raised his hat in formal salute. Ottoline agreed there was a sense of chilly reserve and repression about 'the Undertaker' as she nicknamed him – she confided that she could never dare to attempt any kind of joke in his company. When Eliot published his essay on Dryden whilst he was in America, Hayward wrote to her with a frankness he rarely dared to show in print:

> He's too dry in his prose: no passion, scarcely any feeling at all. It's odd because his poetry is quite otherwise. Sometimes he makes me feel that he is frightened of giving himself away, or giving something away – I don't know what. I have felt as much in his conversation. Has Vivien killed him, do you suppose?[179]

However much he may have hated the thought of being a mere journalist Hayward kept on writing. In the *New York Sun* he wrote a sneering attack on 'the extraordinary antics of a certain Mr and Mrs Leavis who have decided that a little paper they edit called *Scrutiny* is the last defence between the literary elect and the mammon of unrighteousness, viz best sellers, vulgar journalism, e.g. "London Letters" to *The Sun*'. Later, he reported a row that had shaken Cambridge.[180] In May 1933 the septuagenarian – and apparently 'dry as a bone' – A. E. Housman gave the Leslie Stephen lecture on 'The Name and Nature of Poetry'. It was eagerly awaited as it was the first time that the great classical scholar had lectured on modern English poetry. The English faculty was there in force. It was still in its infancy and there was fierce debate about the nature of the subject. Two of the most important twentieth-century critics were in the audience: I. A. Richards, one of the faculty's founders, who, in works such as *Practical Criticism*, demonstrated a close-reading approach to literature that shaped the attitudes of a whole generation of readers, and F. R. Leavis who founded the magazine *Scrutiny* as a deliberate challenge to the literary journals of the 1930s.

On that late May afternoon, much to his audience's surprise, Housman found some of the poetry he read so moving that his voice trembled with emotion. 'No one will forget the exalted way he recited passages,' recalled Hayward. The definition of poetry Housman put forward was as romantic as the way he read it: the mark of true poetry, he said, was that it drew tears to his eyes or made his hairs bristle as he was shaving. Poetry came more from a passive than an active process; the Ancients described it as possession by the Muse. Housman's view clashed with the 'advanced' critical mood in Cambridge and aroused a storm of argument and dissent. Richards was reported to have said, 'It will take us experts ten years to repair the damage that he has done.' Dr Leavis and his wife Queenie were also angry and upset. Peter Lucas, who had previously been one of their supporters, now changed sides and wrote a slashing attack on them in *Cambridge University Studies*.[181] With wry amusement Hayward reported the controversy and naturally weighed in on Housman's side.[182] He considered that Leavis's criticism was based on a desiccated intellectualism, and contrasted him as a critic unfavourably with Housman. His idea of literature was based on the premise that 'I feel therefore I think', whereas Leavis's was based on the opposite – 'I think therefore I feel'. However severe and Augustan he appeared in later life, Hayward was a romantic at heart. With some relish he told his American readers that he had no doubt that 'a particularly poisonous counter-attack is in active preparation under the Neo-Gothic shadow of Girton, the ladies' college where the Leavises have established their last outpost of culture'.

As part of their 'Great Lives' series Hayward was commissioned by Duckworth's to write *Charles II*; it was published in 1933 for two shillings. Here he was in territory that he knew best – the Restoration. He wrote throughout as a Royalist. Under Cromwell England had slipped into a military dictatorship, 'a system above all others repugnant to a people who detested any form of tyranny'.[183] The tone of the history can be caught in the description of the execution of Charles I: 'On the 30th of January of the New Year – one of the coldest and saddest mornings in English history – Charles I was beheaded at the window of his own palace of Whitehall.'[184] The major interest of *Charles II* was, naturally, the portrait of the King himself – a portrait which, in many ways, is uncomfortably close to Hayward's own character. He saw Charles as the victim of an unhappy and lonely childhood whose mother, Henrietta Maria, was ashamed of his ugliness. Her formidable presence cast a chill over his youth: 'His mother, indeed, exasperated him, and it was probably her domineering temperament which accounted for his breaking away from her and ever afterwards resenting the advice of the older generation.'[185] This maternal coldness led to Charles's attitude to women, whom he tended to value only as creatures to be used for pleasure. His love of mistresses, of company, and his sociability were masks to cover an essential unhappiness. 'Fear of loneliness and its corollary, an excessive craving for society, are the common symptoms of an unquiet, unhappy mind, and there can be little doubt that Charles – the "Merry Monarch" by tradition – was actually the victim of some intermittent form of melancholy.'[186]

In the same year Hayward received £50 for a long essay on Benjamin Disraeli, as part of Hector Bolitho's *Twelve Jews*.[187] Written in the style of Lytton Strachey's *Eminent Victorians,* full of visual detail and anecdote, his essay pictured Disraeli as a Jew and a romantic outsider. Hayward described the young Disraeli's dandy-like appearance, 'dressed in a blue surtout and light blue trousers, his gloved and beringed fingers, and raven-black curls artfully disposed',[188] and compared this carefully prepared persona to the brilliant surface of Disraeli's conversation. Both elaborate dress and wordplay concealed his inner self from the Gradgrinds of Victorian life: 'His hyper-sensitive nature could not face the world unprotected; but this protective armour ... never wholly concealed the ardour of a profoundly romantic temperament.' In his success lay the seeds of failure. Disraeli had finally got to the top of the greasy pole, only to find neither acceptance nor love, becoming finally a sad ghost-like figure, rather like Hayward's great-uncle Abraham.

> In society, which clamoured still for his company, he withdrew further and further into himself and his own dreams. Silent, brooding and impassive, he seemed deaf to its siren voice, oblivious to its charms. The world he knew was changing; the influence and renown of the aristocracy, which had once meant so much to him, were slowly waning. With failing eyes, he watched – aloof, mysterious, sphinx-like – the passing of the old order of things. In the House of Lords, as in his later days in the Commons, he became fixed in a kind of Ozymandian immobility from which even the taunts of his opponents failed to rouse him.[189]

All the figures Hayward wrote about in the early 1930s – Saint Evrémond, Charles II, Disraeli and, finally, Swift – were, as he saw them, aliens in their own worlds. Saint Evrémond was exiled in London for most of his life; Charles was cut off from Restoration society by his melancholy and Disraeli set apart as a Jew. Swift's misanthropy and illness set him apart from common humanity. How they coped was the theme of all these works. It was a theme that had a clear resonance with his own wheelchair-bound life: each of his subjects had to develop strategies to make good in a hostile and difficult world – and, ominously, they all ended their days as lonely, isolated old men.

In early March Hayward could see from his window the beginnings of spring, the green tips of lilac and 'one almond tree already pink though still very pale and virginal'. The neighbourhood cats kept him awake at night with their noisy love-making. Each day the milder air cheered him: 'I am beginning to admit, with discretion, certain agreeable feelings of hope ... whatever for?' Perhaps there would, after all, be someone to anchor his own life. On 22 June 1933 he went to meet old friends from his Cambridge days, Dick and Minette Wood who had settled in America. He invited them to dinner at Bina Gardens on Saturday 1 July and they brought with them Joséfa Shiras from New York. Married with three children, she was visiting Europe to try to escape an unhappy marriage. Hayward was immediately captivated by her Hispanic looks, black hair, big curving lips and an expression that was a little fearful and startled. Her 'dark tragic eyes would melt me like a flame', Hayward said. 'Our first strange and fatal interview,' he called it later. All her life Joséfa had the kind of magnetism that made her the centre of attraction, surrounded by male admirers. Later, Jake Carter and the writer Sinclair Lewis were among the many who were to fall under her spell. Hayward immediately invited her to come for tea at Bina Gardens.

This story of this secret love affair can be read in his letters to Joséfa and to Ottoline Morrell and the desk diary he kept. In it he recorded a five-week-long affair. He carefully noted his invitations to 'Mrs Shiras' for tea and dinner three times in the first half of July. The entry for 21 July is totally different to the rest of the plain business-like entries. It reads, 'Fepha to dine', and is then followed by three XXXs and a pointer – clearly marking a crucial romantic moment. From now on they met almost every day until 9 August and sometimes the calendar records their meeting twice or three times a day, for 'lunch' or 'to dine' or simply 'evening'. He embellished these days in red crayon, as they were indeed red-letter days in his life. Ever the sentimentalist, he drew a heart pierced by an arrow with 'J. S.' beside it.

She gave Hayward the admiration he craved, telling him how much she liked his English elegance, his crisp white shirts and his silk bow ties. She praised his sensitive fingers; Hayward knew that his nose was ugly, his lips too big, his hair thinning, but felt himself attractive through her eyes. He contrasted their time together with the the bitter end of his affair with Elaine: 'I don't want to think ever of the misery she caused me,' he confided. He remembered this time as a series of romantic scenes: a picnic in Cadogan Gardens; reading love poetry from his latest anthology; an evening when she arrived all in white like an angel; hot summer nights at Bina Gardens with open windows and curtains blowing. 'You gave me something I can never wholly repay,' he wrote.

Joséfa and he went down together to Leamington Spa in Warwickshire for a long weekend for the first holiday Hayward had had in two years. A brief postcard to Ottoline followed on 30 July saying how much he hoped to see her and, tantalisingly, 'Il y a des experiences à raconter!' He asked her to forgive his short note as 'I am so preoccupied ... ' For him this was 'a time of transcendent sunshine, and while it lasted, supreme happiness'. But a fragment from a torn letter found among Hayward's papers tells another story. It is from from 31 Lowndes Street, Belgrave Square and reads: 'Dear Mr Hayward, Shiras has instructe ...' Joséfa's husband Winfield was becoming aware of what was going on and thinking of legal proceedings. He decided to follow her to Europe. She rang him in America begging him not to come, but received no answer. She began to express doubts to Hayward about continuing their relationship. The last weekend they spent together was brilliant and sunny. On Saturday 5 August they enjoyed an afternoon in the garden and had dinner together. The next day they spent the afternoon at Cadogan Square before Joséfa called around to Bina Gardens at 11.30 to say farewell.

She left for Switzerland on 9 August. Hayward's entry was brief: 'F leaves for ever.' He was in a desperate state. Ottoline was one of the very few people he could face. He described his anguish to her: 'I had a perfect letter from Joséfa ... only the future seems without hope of any kind.' He buried himself in work but 'the intensity of repression' hurt him every time he lifted his eyes from his desk. Feeling utterly lost and wretched, Hayward wrote to her that he could bear almost everything except his lonely meals and getting into bed at night. He sent letter after letter with no reply. He even rang her in Switzerland only to receive an icy rebuff.

On 29 August there came a sad and passionate letter 'containing a slender hope that she might return to London and say good bye – I suppose for ever'. Now Hayward was in his most despairing of moods: 'I know I must resign myself and my longing ... the bright day is done and we are for the dark. And yet how splendid the day has been ...' Ottoline replied immediately, holding out the hope that Joséfa would reject her husband because of his cruel treatment of her. He was not necessarily a reformed character. The case was not so hopeless, she suggested. 'Don't blow out the lights ... or cast too dull a shadow on the lovely, lovely gift of her love. Whatever comes this has been such a marvellous gift. Radiating and glorifying ... and it may stretch on and on.'[190] He replied briefly, thanking her for her consolation when he was 'dim and bemused'.

In her next letter, however, Joséfa confirmed all Hayward's fears. Despite all her pleas Winfield had decided to follow her: 'I am *crushed* ... I can bear no more.' She insisted that this had to be the end of their relationship. 'I can only wait: I do not hope, seeing now how hopelessly slender the chances are. It has been a splendid, a supreme moment in my life ...' Hayward wrote.[191] Another 'agonizing' message from Joséfa finally announced her husband's arrival in Switzerland. Ottoline still tried to offer hope. It did not follow that she would actually *like* her husband when he arrived or that he had become a reformed character. But at last the telegram which Hayward had dreaded arrived: 'Sailing for home Saturday. Heartbroken not to see you. All is well. Better so, my love. Writing. Féfa.'[192] For her it was a holiday romance that was over: he could not let go of her so easily. Part of him knew that it was better that she should slip back into her former life with husband and children, but the phrase, 'All is well, better so', in its insouciant finality, numbed him. His heart rose up against the detachment that told him it was all for the best. On Saturday 16 September Joséfa and her husband sailed back to the United States.

The news was, Ottoline wrote, 'shattering. I am most dreadfully sorry. How agonizing to have the curtain brought down so suddenly and finally. I cannot tell you how much I sympathize.'[193] She sent violets and carnations with her message. 'O Dearest John I am so unhappy for you about this & you are *so brave and wonderful*.'[194] He tried to comfort himself. Joséfa had sent a loving letter from on board her liner, which he quoted to Ottoline: 'I am sick and heart-broken at the pain I have caused you, my Darling, but I don't regret any of it, do you?' Even in the midst of grief he agreed that he was a stronger person as a result of his affair, as he explained:

You know what I mean. Your life has been shot through with griefs and disappointments; without them life would be less remarkable, less noble. The great thing, I am sure, is to be able to feel: deeply, passionately. The pain in the end seems valuable – cleansing, purifying, strengthening. But like iodine on a wound it is hard to bear at first – I won't tell you how much your thoughts and sympathy means to me – you must know.[195]

He feared he might have overburdened Ottoline, but was intensely grateful for all her kindness: 'I come to you as into the shadow of a great rock in a weary land.' There was still part of him that clung to the slender hope Joséfa might return even after she arrived back in New York on 23 September. Time, he remarked, was not the great healer it was purported to be. By mid-November there was still no news. 'I wait and long for a message,' he wrote. But there was no message.

The affair had been as short-lived as it was intense. Soon after Joséfa left, Hayward finally gave up the effort of walking with his stick and took to his chair. The end of the affair marked that point in his life when his disability irrevocably shaped his future. He was not only distraught about the parting, but also by the knowledge that there could be little chance of love or happiness of the kind he had known: there would never be another Joséfa. He was, after all, only twenty-eight years old. He did one more thing in her memory, as he had done for Elaine. He dedicated his next work – his edition of Swift – to her:

J. S.
TOTO ORBE DIVISAE
AMICITIAE MEMOR
QUAE FUIT
J. H.[196]

[In memory of a past friendship, divided by the whole world.]

He shared his grief with no one else apart from Ottoline. Eccentric and self-indulgent though she could be, it was to her that he found it easiest to pour out his secrets. She took a motherly and protective role in trying to expand his circle of friends by directing 'some very interesting & delightful and lovely creature to your door'. She even found Barbara, the daughter of Frieda Weekley, the wife of D. H. Lawrence, and attempted to pair them off – but it did not work. She also kept up the distraction of a regular stream of invitations to her tea parties on Thursday afternoons to her small Georgian house in Gower Street. But, although there was no one to replace Elaine or Joséfa in Hayward's affections, this did not mean that there were no more girlfriends or relationships. He was a man of passion and matters of sex always intrigued him. His notebooks are full of pencil studies of nude women and he loved to shock by retelling his 'contes scabreux'. When two young and attractive students from the Chelsea College of Art came to paint his bookshelves for some pocket money he entertained them to tea. He began by mentioning disingenuously 'the many letters to Agony Aunts in the Press from barely literate girls wanting advice on whether they should sleep with their boyfriends or not'. Apparently he was gratified by their liberal attitude. A young nephew was greeted by his uncle with the breezy question, 'Do you masturbate? I never do.' It is more difficult to answer the question of what exactly he did do.

After the success of *Donne*, Francis Meynell had asked Hayward if he would follow it up with an edition of Jonathan Swift, offering the same terms as had been agreed before of £100 and £30 for each reprint. By now Hayward had become more used to bargaining for his services and demanded 30 guineas rather than £30. Meynell was quick to write back to praise his 'careful and researchful treatment' and accepted the terms in gentlemanly fashion: 'Agreed. You are certainly worth guineas rather than pounds.' Editing Swift was a task bristling with difficulties and challenges, detailed in Hayward's introduction to his Nonesuch edition. He felt that his main purpose was to rescue the text of *Gulliver* from careless editors. The problem of establishing the copy text stemmed from Swift's eccentric methods of publishing his works. The manuscript of *Gulliver's Travels*, for example, was delivered to the publisher, Motte, through an intermediary 'by the odd expedient of dropping it at his door from the window of a hackney coach'. Because of Motte's 'timidity', according to Hayward, 'words and whole passages in the MS were altered or omitted without the author's knowl-edge'. Most of these errors were incorporated in Motte's fourth edition of *Gulliver* but it was left to Swift's Irish publisher, George Faulkner, to restore the original text in the first collected edition of his works in 1735. Before Hayward's edition it had been customary to use Motte's revised text. His decision to use Faulkner as his copy text for *Gulliver* was therefore a major change. 'The result, I venture to believe, is a more exact and reliable text than any that has been published in the last two hundred years,'[197] Hayward promised.

As a critic Hayward constantly wrote of the mutilation of the text as if it were tissue mangled by an incompetent surgeon. His belief in its absolute integrity and the duty of scholars to identify it and to restore it to its readers was one of the unswerving passions of his life.

If an author is to be read at all, he should be read in a text which resembles as closely as possible his original manuscript. With very few exceptions ... Swift has been denied this right. The main purpose, therefore, of the collations in this volume is to justify the attempted restoration and rehabilitation of the text itself, and at the same time possibly to encourage a more scholarly treatment of Swift's text in the future.[198]

When the Nonesuch *Swift* finally emerged, Meynell was delighted. He wrote that it remained only 'to gloat over' the finished product and promised to bring the first copy to Hayward personally. The press, too, were very enthusiastic. *The Spectator*'s reviewer wrote that *Gulliver's Travels* had to be read in this edition. *The Times Literary Supplement* stated that 'to make a tolerable text of *Gulliver* generally available is sufficient justification for Mr Hayward's volume, but he has done much more ... whatever he has selected he has edited with scrupulous care.'[199]

In the summer of 1933 Hayward had been putting the finishing touches to *Swift* when the affair with Joséfa had been at its most intense. His subject's life hauntingly reflected his own. For many years Swift had written intimate letters to 'Stella', whom he had known as a girl and taught. The sudden arrival in his life of the attractive young 'Vanessa', who fell passionately for him, and the tumult of feelings he felt as he was caught between the two, started many echoes in Hayward's mind. Vanessa was Joséfa, a dangerously attractive new arrival who had come to England in 1933, disturbing his long-standing relationship with faithful Elaine. Hayward took an ambivalent view of Swift's character: 'There is something hard and chilling about the old man that repels. I admire it, or should I say respect it. I think Swift has had a salutary influence – a kind of disciplinary effect – upon me.' After Joséfa had deserted him, Hayward was overwhelmed by feelings of despair: 'Because I feel much more than I think (sentio ergo sum) I need always to keep a watch on my feelings, dreading the pain they can inflict as much as I treasure the happiness they sometimes bring.' Swift was therefore a kind of antidote to the violence of Hayward's romantic side – but also a warning. He dealt with his love by killing part of himself: 'I think Swift understood the meaning of loneliness ... he crushed in himself the need for love.' No wonder Hayward found him a sobering study.

After his Harvard lectures Eliot finally set out for England on 24 June 1933. He stayed overnight at the Oxford and Cambridge Club before fleeing to live near his friend and fellow director at Faber's, Frank Morley, at Pikes Farm in Surrey. His main purpose was to keep his whereabouts secret from Vivienne until she was able to accept the separation from him – his Anglo-Catholic principles ruled out divorce. As he did not have the courage to tell his wife face to face that he considered their separation final, he was in constant flight from her. The misled, self-deluding Vivienne could not believe that her husband wanted to leave her and so began to think that he must have been taken from her against his will, kidnapped or captured. She left the door of their flat unlocked at night and for the next two years tirelessly and pathetically searched though London for him. Eliot, for his part, was determined to leave no tracks by which he might be traced.

Hayward was frustrated that for many months his letters to Eliot had gone unanswered. His old friend seemed determined to keep away and he could not understand why. On 9 July 1933 Eliot finally replied to a letter accusing him of neglect: 'You have been constantly in my thoughts. I am at present in the country. As soon as I am in town again I shall write or ring up & am anxious to see you.' Four months later, in November, still no visit had been paid and Hayward was feeling angry and forgotten. It was now more than a year since they had last met. Not only had Eliot failed to visit, he had also not sent copies 'for the archives' of the lectures he had delivered in America. Eliot's letter on 6 November indicates how hurt Hayward felt. Eliot began by giving him a stern talking to: 'Don't be so silly. You have been constantly in my mind. I have been in London very rarely and only for the day.' As for the lectures that had not been sent, he went on, they were lacking in structure and purpose and definitely not worth preserving.

On the morning of 17 November there was a surprise visitor to Bina Gardens. It was Eliot, looking much healthier and happier than when he had left England. He appeared as from nowhere, invited himself to lunch and stayed all afternoon. A delighted Hayward reported that all was now well between them. He did not ask Eliot about his plans, but another visit was promised in ten days' time. Both men had had to endure the bitterness of broken relationships and now, in autumn 1933, they retreated into the familiar safe world of male camaraderie. Eliot began to have supper or dinner at least once a week at Bina Gardens. A typical note thanked Hayward for the 'kind entertainment – generous table – superb cognac – delightful conversation – fireworks music'.[200] Eliot often apologised for staying too late, or tiring his host out with reminiscences or bawdy jingles. Often too, the next morning he regretted the whisky or the cognac. 'Brandy and Beethoven together are too much, anyway,' he wrote after a late session.[201] 'Sorry I Kept you Up so late, but I was Enjoying Myself.' Both men loved literary jokes of all kinds, crosswords and wordplay and shared a taste for pedantry. They liked to lay traps for the unwary, as when Eliot gave Hayward a spoof presentation copy of *Prufrock*, dated 1917 – when in fact they did not meet until 1926. They enjoyed playing a parlour game in which Hayward had to identify the master's blurbs from Faber's list – Eliot was a prolific, witty blurbist and prided himself on the skill. After dinner the two might play chess together or listen to music on the wireless. They enjoyed concerts from the Berlin Philharmonic under its conductor, Furtwangler. (Hayward saw himself as one of the few 'highbrows' who enjoyed listening to the wireless.) When Eliot went down with one of his frequent chest infections, Hayward was always sympathetic and sent copies of the *New Yorker*, daffodils, oranges, peaches and tins of Lusty's turtle soup – which became an unlikely kind of talisman of their friendship. 'Back & head be full of aches / Chest be full of croup, / But Belly see thou have store enough / Of jolly good turtle soup,' he rhymed his thank-you.[202] Their relationship now had the casual intimacy of old friends. Eliot might drop in as he passed by from his nearby lodgings in Grenville Place to recite 'a Poem about the Pig' that he had just finished – or just for drink and conversation. Sunday evenings around Hayward's electric fire became a regular winter fixture.

In October 1934 Eliot asked if he could bring 'a very old friend from America' to tea in Bina Gardens. Emily Hale's name was duly inscribed in the visitors' book for 9 November. Eliot had known her since his Harvard days; he had acted with her in amateur theatricals, sent her roses and, before he left the United States for Europe, declared his love, but did not feel that his feelings were reciprocated. In 1927, after a long silence, she had written to him and their friendship and an intimate correspondence resumed. Between 1934 and 1938 she paid annual visits to England. There can be little doubt that Emily Hale hoped to marry him once he was free. Such apparently was Eliot's promise; indeed they behaved like such old friends that they were often thought to be already engaged.[203] At first Hayward felt pleased to be treated as one of Eliot's intimates when he was introduced to her. But soon, like

Virginia Woolf and Ottoline Morrell, he took against 'that awful American Woman' and her 'sergeant major manner'. He particularly disliked the way she seemed to boss Eliot about. She was a 'grim, prim, schoolma'amish female who takes a dreadful proprietary interest in poor Tom,' he wrote to Ottoline Morrell.

Eliot and Hayward shared a highly-developed sense of the ridiculous and a love of parody. Eliot suggested a modern version of common errors based on Sir Thomas Browne's seventeenth-century *Pseudodoxia Epidemica*. Modern errors might include: 'All Policemen have big feet', or 'A fart, strained through bath water, loses both odour and inflammability,' or 'A cigarette, smoked before breakfast, is sovereign against costiveness.'[204] He told Hayward how disappointed he was in the French translation of *Murder in the Cathedral*, and included his own pastiche and a footnote to appeal to the scholarly editor:

> That bird wych in the dark times of the yeerë
> Sitteth in the dudgeon (1) on the aspen bouwë
> And cryeth arsehole, arsehole lhoude and clearë ...

1. The word does not appear in this sense till 1573.[205]

Both men found Scots dialect intrinsically funny. Eliot sent Hayward his Yule Tide Greeting 'HOOCH and MERRY WHOOPEE' from the Moffat House Hotel in Dumfriesshire. He signed his card with three pseudonyms: Hugh Macdonald, F. Valéry and Dorinda, 'with a drappie in the ee, John!' He gave Hayward the typescript of 'When Cam Ye Fra the Kirk?' or 'The Lass Wha Wrapt Me in her Plaidie' or 'The Bonnie Bonnie Braes of Glengoofie' or 'A Porpoise Sang by Tam o' Elliot'. Letters were studded with all kinds of cuttings from newspapers, headlines, verses and indeed anything that struck Eliot's sense of irony. Adverts for a 'Men's Beauty Parlour at MARY STUART' of South Wardour Street and the JUNGLE CLUB, 'A Rendezous for East Africans and Others Home from Abroad' in Wardour Street, along with a matchbox label, HAYWARD'S MILITARY PICKLE SAFETY MATCHES, were duly pasted on postcards and sent, along with an Easter card showing two west highland white terriers, one wearing a pink bow tie the other in blue, nose to nose with a red rose between them. The card read: 'Easter Easter in the Air / Easter Easter Everywhere!' Inside the message was: 'May yours be bright / May yours be gay / May yours be perfect Easter Day.' Eliot signed it in pencil T P.[206] He also cut out headlines such as: CURATE GAOLED FOR STEALING HAT ... HE KNOWS THE CAT SLAYER and WAKE UP YOUR LIVER BILE. Drawn to the names 'Firo and Farts' in a newspaper advertisement, he suggested a *New Statesman* competition to provide the most succinct *Who's Who* entries for the two. This kind of comic collage is the same technique Eliot used for serious purposes in *The Waste Land*.

As 'a satirical wit ... a connoisseur of the ridiculous, an ironical commentator on human folly' – as Hayward called him[207] – Eliot was ever-alert to any ironic, comic, or telling detail he read or picked up in conversation. When, for example, Hayward told him the story of his youthful infatuation with Dagmar and how he had carefully chosen a pair of his father's white spats to impress her, these became fixed in Eliot's imagination. 'Mr Eliot's book of Pollicle Dogs and Jellicle Cats as Recited to Him by the Man in White Spats' was illustrated by Eliot's pencil drawing of two men sitting at a bar. One was bearded, wearing a bowler hat and plus fours and the other, bespectacled in top hat, tails – and of course the spats – was pointing as if to dictate the verse. Hayward became the 'only begetter' of the fashionable Mayfair cat Bustopher Jones in *Old Possum's Book of Practical Cats*: 'It must and shall be Spring in Pall Mall, / While Bustopher Jones wears white spats.' His interest in railway trains also fathered Skimbleshanks the Railway Cat. Both Eliot and Hayward liked doodling and showed each other their drawings for the cover. ''Ere. I didn't know you was such an accomplished Illustrater,'[208] Eliot wrote when Hayward sent him his cat sketches. (In fact Hayward was very disappointed when they were turned down for the dust-jacket, signing himself, 'l'homme aux guêtres blancs'.) Eliot's own design pictured two heavily bearded and bespectacled dancing men on roller-skates. The leader was wearing country tweeds and pointed ahead with his umbrella to show the way to his top-hatted companion. Behind them was a row of eight dancing cats. 'The villainous figure with the beard represents Eliot himself; the other figure is John Hayward in customary evening dress, but mobile as he had not been for years'[209] – and, naturally, wearing spats. Eliot dedicated the book to 'The Man in White Spats'.

Frequently communication took the form of light verse. In December, Eliot sent 'The Country Walk', dedicated to Emily Hale, which he subtitled: 'An Epistle, to John Hayward, suggested by certain experiences of the Author in the Countryside of the West of England, and set down after parting from Canon Tissington Tatlow, at the corner of Lime Street and Fenchurch Street.' (While walking with Emily Hale,

Eliot had been chased by a cow.) Following this spoof eighteenth-century title, the poem begins:

> Of all the beasts that God allows
> In England's green and pleasant land
> I most of all dislike the cows.
> Their ways I do not understand.

In similar vein Hayward replied, 'There is something really rather lâche / In what you feel about a vache.' He replied with a poem of his own: 'The Cowlover's Retort ... A Pindarycke':

> Your letter makes it clear, dear Tom,
> That when you wander out of town ...
> Your urban poise that can annul
> The terrors of a papal bull
> Instantly vanishes before
> The friendly moo and placid roar
> Of Nature's masterpiece the cow ... [210]

In the margin, next to 'Dear Tom', Eliot pencilled some mock-serious corrections: 'Do you mean Pissington Patlow?' he asked. 'It would be hard to over-emphasize the triviality of this',[211] but the exchange shows that in Hayward's company Eliot showed a relish for absurdity and laughter and shed that dark-suited clerical propriety which he often presented to the world.

Hayward's taste was more schoolboy-like. He had always enjoyed and shared with friends such as Eddie Sackville-West the double-entendres of Thackeray's 'At the Church Gate': 'The organ 'gins to swell: / She's coming! She's coming! / My lady comes at last.' He was especially fond of lavatorial humour and carefully inscribed from the Victorian *History of Europe* Archibald Alison's statement, 'The Austrians held the Po, while the Italians slowly evacuated.' This side of Hayward is represented by 'Captain Marganser':

> O Tell me the story of Captain Marganser,
> O Tell me, Muvver, do!
> Did he drop a Brick at the Church Bonanza,
> Or pinch a pair of Miss Goosecurd's pants? Ah
> Tell me the story of Captain Marganser,
> Oh, Tell me, Muvver, do.[212]

The speaker is a young girl lamenting her pregnancy: 'If only I'd learnt from my friend Miss Trelliot ... I'd not have a big belly yet ...'

Hayward's frankness about sex gave Eliot licence to express, in private, his own buried taste for crudity which was quite at odds with his strict Unitarian background. The taste for obscenity shown in the 'King Bolo' verses of Eliot's Harvard days could once again be enjoyed in Hayward's unshockable company. Eliot invented a 'Fragment of *Macbeth* in which Macbeth met Banquo on "Hayward's Blasted Heath"' and the dialogue between the witches which was entirely composed of coarse anagrams of Thomas Stearns Eliot:

First Witch
Shit! Master a'nt loose.

Second Witch
Harlot's note is steam.

Third Witch
Arsehole stations MT.[213]

Not long after settling in Bina Gardens Hayward suggested to Eliot that they should share a flat together. At the time Eliot was living with Father Eric Cheetham, the vicar of St Stephen's, Kensington, in accommodation shared with some of his curates at the presbytery. Eliot liked and admired his host, a flamboyantly eccentric clergyman who designed religious pageants and loved dressmaking. 'No pageant will ever surpass that designed and produced by Fr Cheetham at the Albert Hall for the Mothers' Union Annual Festival.'[214] After being received into the Anglican Church in 1927, Eliot had become a regular worshipper at St Stephen's. In this Gothic Revival church, with its Lady Chapel, its statue of the Virgin, and its shrine to Our Lady of Walsingham, six tall candles lit dimly the Edwardian green and gold furnishings. The reserved sacrament was denoted by a red lamp. Here the rituals of the Anglo-Catholic liturgy were followed in an incense-laden atmosphere – St Stephen's was so 'high' that in the 1930s it became the target of demonstrations from evangelicals waving 'No Popery' placards. Eliot found much comfort in the words of the Prayer Book and the drama of church ceremonial there. Father Cheetham made him vicar's warden, the highest office for a layman in the parish.

Unsure about the idea of moving in with Hayward, Eliot was at a crossroads, caught between the worldliness of Bina Gardens and the ascetic Christianity of the vicarage. On 2 May 1935 he wrote that he was 'torn with indecision'. On the one hand there would be 'the satisfaction of your proximity': on the other he did not want to let down Father Cheetham. He would also have to buy furniture, as he only possessed a couple of bookcases. Another, and certainly stronger, argument against moving into Bina Gardens was the proximity of the danger Eliot feared most: Vivienne. 'I have not got over the feeling of being hunted.' He wrote of pursuit by a nameless enemy – 'They know who I am, they know my circumstances' – and his terror of being 'tracked down and molested'. These fears might be unfounded, but they were 'something plus fort que moi, of the nature of nightmare, and I have to give way to it'. Like Harry, Lord Monchensey, the hero of *The Family Reunion*, he felt himself relentlessly stalked by the Furies even when he had fled to his own home. 'In my sleep I am pursued like Orestes, though I feel with less reason than that hero. Where I am I feel relatively *safe*,' he wrote to Hayward.[215] Eliot therefore decided to turn down the offer, adding that he was sorry that he might have to miss a unique opportunity of sharing with him, but left things open for the future: 'In another year none of these reasons may survive. I hope they won't. But at the moment they are all powerful.'

Letters between Hayward and Eliot at this time form a tapestry of allusion to a writer whose work they both loved, and Eliot could quote by heart: Arthur Conan Doyle. They both relished the world of detectives and of aliases – Hayward was Jean-Baptiste Aillevard, Jonny Heywald, Miss Eleanor Gellielax, Headmistress of St Winifred's School, Eastbourne, or Tarantula; Eliot, Shorlock Holmes, J. Hussein B.A. (Calcutta), Tom Possum – and so on. The correspondence is full of references to disguises, mysterious plots, and letters written on plain pages in case they fell into the wrong hands: 'P.S. I sign in this way, as this letter may be intercepted,' Eliot warned Hayward.[216] Their correspondence was a comic version of the real persecution that Eliot felt so frightened of. 'W. L. Janes late of B Division' features strongly and sounds like part of the stream of comic invention. In fact he was a real life ex-detective who acted as a servant to the Eliots. Vivienne tried to make use of him to find out her husband's whereabouts but in the best le Carré tradition he had been 'turned' and reported back to Eliot all he knew. So when Eliot ended a letter to Hayward with a blank, followed by 'PS I think it is better not to sign my name', it is hard to be sure whether he was joking or not. In Eliot's nightmare world, fantasy and paranoia cannot easily be separated from fact, or comedy from Greek tragedy. Less ambiguously, the letters also allude to the works of P. G. Wodehouse – which both men loved. Eliot told Hayward that he had woken from his 'ethereal sleep' shouting vehemently 'No!!! No!!! My dear John!' in the middle of an argument with him about Bertie Wooster.[217]

At 3.30 in the afternoon of 18 November 1935 the meeting with his wife that Eliot had dreaded did in fact happen. Vivienne had found out that he was to deliver a speech at the *Sunday Times* book exhibition at Dorland Hall. It was the moment that she had been waiting for. She carefully dressed in her 'fascist' uniform of black beret and large black mackintosh and took with her their dog Polly:

> I turned a face to him of such joy that no-one in that great crowd could have had one moment's doubt. I just said Oh *Tom,* & he seized my hand, and said how do you *do* in quite a loud voice. He walked straight on to the platform then and gave a most remark-ably *clever,* well thought out lecture ... I stood the whole time holding Polly *up* high in my arms. Polly was very excited and wild. I kept my eyes on Tom's face the whole time, & I kept nodding my head at him and making encouraging signs. He looked a *little* older, more mature and smart, *much thinner & not* well or robust or rumbustious at *all.* No sign of a woman's *care* about him. No cosy evenings with dogs and gramophones I should say.[218]

As soon as the lecture ended Vivienne let Polly off the lead and strode up to the platform. The dog barked with wild excitement around Eliot's heels as, leaning over the desk, she quietly asked, 'Will you come back with me?' 'I cannot talk to you now,' he replied. He signed three copies of his work for her and left.[219] After this he took even more care to avoid her and wrote to Hayward about having a horror of Regent's Park where Elizabeth Bowen lived and a 'real fear of it in daytime'[220] because of its closeness to his wife. Settling in Bina Gardens was now quite out of the question.

Separation from his wife meant an ever-closer relationship with his male friends and Eliot took to the bachelor life readily. Now the all-male festivity at Bina Gardens became a regular part of Hayward's and Eliot's lives. One side of Eliot turned personal tragedy into practical jokes and laughter. He brought fireworks and chocolates made from soap to take to a party given by Hayward for the Herbert Reads.

Behind the sedate façade of the offices of Faber's, he set whoopee cushions for the Chairman, Geoffrey Faber, and bought a giant cracker to celebrate his return from the grouse moors. As the large chocolate cake iced with WELCOME CHIEF was being cut, the firework exploded with a loud bang beneath the Chairman's feet, festooning him and the chandeliers with coloured ribbons. The next firecracker, 'Snake-in-the-grass', filled the room with smoke and, alarmingly, set fire to the ribbons. The secretaries had to scurry round with pails of water, mopping up: 'A Thot for your next Party,'[221] wrote Eliot encouragingly to Hayward. A more disturbing practical joke was a parcel sent to Geoffrey and Enid Faber containing a frighteningly realistic pair of human ears.

When Father Cheetham moved to a new flat in March 1937 Hayward's invitation to share accommodation was turned down again. Eliot reserved his position: 'Six months hence I may feel more like setting up for myself.'[222] In terms of the running Sherlock Holmes allusions the question of where Eliot was to live became 'The Problem of the Resident Patient'. Eliot's practical kindness was shown by his suggestion that he should buy as a birthday present a new 'more solid and pneumatic' wheelchair to replace Hayward's rather shabby antique – that issue became 'The Problem of the Pocket Pram'. It must have taken some bravery even to mention such an issue. Hayward ignored all matters to do with his disability and liked others to do the same. He replied that the matter was more complicated than Eliot might think since the chair had to go at racing speed, be able to go upstairs and fold up as small as possible. All in all, he added, his 'old pram', although not elegant, fulfilled requirements. Nevertheless he would be pleased to discuss the matter further. No one had ever had the 'pleasant idea' of suggesting an improvement before and he was delighted by such a warmhearted gesture.[223]

8

London Letters

Hayward had taken over as London correspondent of the daily newspaper, the *New York Sun* from his friend Peter Quennell in 1934 and maintained a fortnightly column in the paper, 'London Letter', until 1938, recording the latest news and gossip – his social life and his journalism were always inextricably linked. He dashed off his piece in a couple of hours on Monday morning for the Friday or Saturday edition and was paid $8 for each one. It was very much a personal column; reviewing gave him freedom to write as he wished on any subject that took his fancy. A favourite theme was the destruction of great houses. Discussion of Defoe's *A Tour through London*,[224] for example, provided a good opportunity to comment on how London was changing in the 1930s, lamenting the passing of such elegant landmarks as Devonshire House, Lansdowne House, Norfolk House and Clifford's Inn: 'The age of great private houses is over, and in their place a commercial age has erected monstrous blocks of offices and flats. And not single houses only, but whole streets of them have been engulfed in the sweeping tide of democracy.'[225] Bruton Street, Portland Place had already gone and the Adelphi was about to be swallowed up by the new Charing Cross Bridge. In short, London had altered 'so dramatically that our grandfathers would not recognize it'.

A visit to Cliveden Court in Somerset had struck Hayward powerfully.[226] Beside his bed was the desk on which Thackeray wrote *Esmond* and Hayward wrote to his friend Lyn Irvine on a huge table on which Henry VIII was 'said to have supported his vast bulk'. He looked out over the magnificent terraces and parterres and inside the house at

the pictures, the silver, the dressing for dinner, the intolerable and ignorant guests, the galleries of powder closets, and state bedrooms, the flowerets and sprigged repeater watches and Albert's face in the minstrels' gallery and the rooks & O my God, the elms, they're all there, the whole *catalogus mundanitatis*. It is so lovely and yet in a way so oppressive; tradition hangs about the house like a thundercloud, doors bang in the distance and the aged baronet bursts into loud baronial laughter disturbing a cloud of dust in the chapel ...

It was a fragile idyll of a lost England – but it was also like living in an enormous antique shop. As Hayward grew older he became more and more attracted to the world of the country house and less and less enamoured with modern suburban development. Ipsden House in Oxfordshire became another haven from 'the hideous features – bungalows, by-passes and pylons that are slowly disfiguring the countryside within 50 miles of London'.[227] Similarly Hayward saw the turrets of Renishaw Hall, embattled against the growing industrialisation of the surrounding Derbyshire countryside between Sheffield and Chesterfield, as a symbol of a gracious and doomed way of life. Hayward felt that Edith Sitwell's brother Osbert's autobiography *Left Hand! Right Hand!* with its accounts of the house and his eccentric aristocratic father represented 'the last chapter of the domestic history of patrician England', destroyed by the redistribution of incomes, begun at the end of the First World War and continuing throughout the 1930s. The country houses of England were falling down or being turned into 'scholarly institutions, mental homes and branch offices of bureaucracy'.[228] Their decline and that of the countryside around them were powerful symbols of the wider social changes of the time.

Another favourite topic was the decline of private libraries and book collecting. Heavy death duties and increased tax had spelt the end of 'wealth, leisure and opportunity' and therefore 'the end of collecting in the grand manner'. Great libraries were becoming things of the past, their collections broken up in the saleroom. Many were destined to go to university libraries in the USA. 'I envied, admired, regretted,' he wrote as he watched a flood of manuscripts and books disappear abroad. So what was the future in England, he asked in one of his most personal 'Letters':

> The trend in book collecting in recent years has been in an opposite direction; the emphasis is on collecting, not accumulating. The present state of bibliophily in England is best observed in the small, intensely personal and covetable collections of men like Michael Sadleir, Richard Jennings and Geoffrey Keynes whose love of literature, scholarship and pure bibliography is apparent in every book they possess. [229]

Modestly he did not mention his own, small – but very covetable – collections of St Evrémond and Rochester. He still hoped, however, that treasures from a remote country house library would be unearthed. After all, some of Rochester's poems had just turned up at Welbeck Abbey in Nottinghamshire, and a Malory manuscript had emerged from the archives of Winchester College. Hidden away somewhere, he was sure, there might be a manuscript of Shakespeare's sonnets just waiting to be discovered ...

Sometimes Hayward drew a picture of life in the capital as seen from the windows of Bina Gardens. In November he noted winter's approach: 'It is perishingly cold in this comfortless, unwarmed city. The muffin man, one of the relics of old London, has just passed, his face the colour of opal, jangling his bell.'[230] The cries of the wood-seller and the coal merchant rang out during the day as they had done in Dickensian days, but now Hayward saw unemployed men standing on every street-corner stamping their feet on the icy pavements; at night the drone of manoeuvring aircraft overhead kept him uneasily awake.

Hayward's friendship with the poet and writer Edith Sitwell provided a rich source of literary gossip for his articles. In the 1930s she was at the height of her prestige. With pale oval face, flaxen hair, elaborate costume and long, slender medieval fingers heavy with rings, she seemed as if she had come from another age: 'a high altar on the move'.[231] She had edited and contributed to all six numbers of *Wheels*, which became the official opposition to *Georgian Poetry*; she had published highly-praised collections of her own verse and had enjoyed the notoriety of her musical collaboration with William Walton, *Façade*, in which she declaimed verse through a megaphone. When his anthology *Nineteenth Century English Poetry* was published in 1934, Hayward had immediately sent her a copy. She thanked him for the book and its 'delights' and assured him that on her travels she would need to take it along with her own 'to be rich in all the beauties that I need'. In return she promised to send him her latest anthology. Soon there followed invitations to dinners and theatre visits in London. Hayward found the Sitwells' brand of aristocratic Bohemianism absolutely to his taste.

On 15 November 1934 Edith Sitwell published *Aspects of Modern Poetry,* and was plunged into what was 'arguably the most damaging controversy of her career'.[232] The book began, in a chapter called 'Pastors and Masters', with attacks on many of her traditional targets, such as Leavis, Geoffrey Grigson ('the Griglet'), the editor of *New Verse*, and the iconoclastic painter and writer Wyndham Lewis. Like Hayward, she felt that Leavis led a school of critics 'who shared a semi-puritanical dislike of beauty in poetry'.[233] His criticism was 'graciously antiseptic', reminding her of 'a tenderly-ruthless white coated young dentist' – even her use of the title 'Dr' suggested something improperly scientific about the man. She saw him playing a comical and blundering Watson to Eliot's Holmes. (Her tone was scarcely surprising in view of Leavis's attack in *New Bearings in English Poetry* where he had claimed that she belonged to 'the history of publicity rather than that of poetry'.)[234] After these opening salvoes she discussed her own literary heroes – Gerard Manley Hopkins, Eliot and Pound. With a total lack of discretion she included a chapter on her brother Sacheverell's poetry and sandwiched it between Eliot and Pound. 'Mr Sitwell's' poetry was lavishly praised and, as further provocation, she added a comparison with Auden to show how inferior he was to her brother.

Naturally her critics had a field-day. Not only did they find the praise of Sacheverell absurdly misplaced, they also pounced on inaccuracies and the apparent plagiarisms. The *New Statesman* critic G. W. Stonier noticed that, even when attacking Leavis, she used arguments remarkably similar to Leavis's own. Further articles in the *New Statesman* stoked the fires by providing more examples of borrowings. Grigson added his voice to the condemnation, as did Wyndham Lewis. The Sitwells were as embattled as Renishaw Hall itself. Both Edith and Osbert wrote to deny the charges, as did the academic lawyer John Sparrow in his favourable review in the columns of *The Times Literary Supplement*.[235] No doubt Edith hoped that her friend John Hayward would loyally follow Sparrow's example and support her in the press. If so, she was disappointed. Always fanatical about accuracy, he wrote a piece in the *New York Sun* mocking her.[236] 'The Sitwell Volcano, so long dormant, is in active eruption!' he began melodramatically. He roundly declared that her book was 'riddled with misquotations', but, more damagingly, that the charge of plagiarism was justified in nineteen instances. To be a plagiarist was bad enough, but to be a plagiarist of works written by someone she had publicly ridiculed was doubly humiliating. Her defence was 'frivolous and unconvincing'. Not content with this, Hayward added that Osbert was about to explode over an attack on him by the First World War poet Robert Nichols in his satire *Fisbo*.[237] 'The pity is', Hayward concluded, 'that the Sitwells should lend themselves to this irresponsible clowning.' He added that their behaviour was not inappropriate because it was, after all, the panto season.

The article may have been justified, but it was not the act of a friend. Edith felt totally betrayed. Osbert threatened to sue – but decided not to, as Hayward had no money. Incensed, on 30 March 1935 Edith wrote a withering letter to him:

> I am sorry for your sake that you have done such a cheap and unworthy thing. It is obvious from your article that you have either not read my book, or not read that of Dr. Leavis, and in writing as you have, you descended to gossip-column levels. You should not have attacked my brother. I think you do not know him, and he has certainly never done you any harm. Consequently your affront to him is as wantonly malicious as your statement about him is untrue. I must ask you not to answer this letter: there is no apology that you can make to me, consequently there is no excuse for you to write to me.[238]

He did not reply – indeed there was little he could add. After this, there followed ten years of silence. The friendship that had begun with a literary gesture apparently had ended with one too.

Two years after the Housman controversy Hayward reviewed Leavis's volume of essays, *Revaluation* (1936), in the *New York Sun*[239] and *The Observer*.[240] He immediately dubbed the volume 'Devaluations'; Leavis's criticism, he felt, was all too often merely destructive. He was well aware of all the faults that led Leavis's followers to be disliked so intensely: 'a little group clustered around Leavis, inveighing against vaguely identified opponents and persecutors, indulging in rather heavy invective and assuming an intellectually arrogant pose'. They were a revolutionary minority in the Cambridge English faculty; Eliot had been unwillingly conscripted as their Marx. Despite disliking Leavis's acolytes – and his own personal distaste for the man – Hayward could not help but respect the freshness of the criticism, commenting that *Revaluation* would not set the world alight, but might set the Cam on fire. Surprisingly generously, he concluded that the Leavis school of criticism was 'as lively as an eel' and '... seriously concerned to improve the debased standard of present-day criticism'. But when he came to review the volume in *The Observer* later his tone had become more critical. The cold east wind of 'new criticism' was aimed not so much to persuade one to read poetry and enjoy it as 'to indicate how difficult it is to understand and how dangerous it is to attempt to enjoy it without taking elaborate precautions'. At the centre of the disputes was Hayward's belief that literature should give pleasure. He liked to echo Dryden: 'The chief, if not the only, end of poetry is to delight.' By contrast, Dr Leavis's 'dry scientific method of exposition' destroyed all the pleasure of reading. More criticism followed: *Revaluation* was more like a series of essays than a developed argument; it was derivative – its arguments 'could be tracked everywhere in Eliot's snow'. There was also an absence of charm and lack of intellectual humility in Leavis's desire to find faults; his lecture-room style alienated any sympathy the reader might have. With the exception of the assassination of Montague Summers, it was as hostile a review as any that Hayward ever wrote and the attack was as much personal as literary. He must have expected an angry reply – but it was some years before he got it.

From his prep school days to the end of his life, when Graham Greene kept a box reserved for him in the West End at his latest play, Hayward loved theatre. One of the major themes of his 'London Letter' is his account of the progress of the 'minority theatre' in the 1930s. Through Auden, Eliot and Robert Medley he was closely involved in the innovative Group Theatre. Like the more overtly political 'Unity' it set itself apart from the commercial taste of the West End. From a tiny stage in an attic room in Great Newport Street, just round the corner from Leicester Square, it began its mission. Headed by Rupert Doone, it was avant-garde, experimental, and a touch amateurish. Doone's partner, Robert Medley, was the designer and Benjamin Britten composed for it. It aimed to be a collaborative venture using movement (Doone was a ballet dancer by training), mime and verse, and played a pioneering role in encouraging verse drama. Although mainly associated with the left-wing plays of Auden, Isherwood and Spender, the Group Theatre also produced Eliot's *Sweeney Agonistes* and *The Rock*, both in 1934, and *The Family Reunion* in 1939.

Although Hayward was not directly involved, he knew all its leading lights intimately. Eliot was his closest friend; he had been at school with Robert Medley and with Auden; he also knew Stephen Spender and Rupert Doone well. His advice was sought and his views canvassed by all of them. Despite some reservations, he watched the progress of this theatrical revolution with sympathy. In May 1934 he read *The Rock*, and promised that it would 'surprise and delight'. In June he was impressed by a performance at Sadler's Wells: 'The choruses themselves and their skilful delivery certainly bring the possibility of a revival of poetic drama nearer fulfilment.'[241] The play 'dished', he was pleased to note, all the rumours that Eliot had dried up. In November Eliot telephoned Hayward his account of the first English staging of *Sweeney Agonistes* at Great Newport Street. Eliot sat next to Virginia Woolf and the thirty spectators included Ottoline Morrell and Aldous Huxley.[242] There was no stage and the masked actors wove through the audience making them feel directly involved in the drama. Sometimes the tempo slowed to add more suspense but the experimental performance still lasted only thirty minutes. Eliot himself told Hayward that he was 'satisfied' – even though it was not as he had imagined: 'Apeneck' Sweeney, he said, looked like Dr Crippen.[243] (Strangely enough, Virginia Woolf thought it was Eliot himself who was 'a kind of Crippen in a mask'.[244])

Eliot was already working on a full-length play whose first two scenes Hayward read.[245] In April 1935 he proudly announced a scoop: 'STOP PRESS: Eliot's play is about St Thomas à Becket, provisionally called "Fear is the Key".' Hayward was more enthusiastic about what became *Murder in the Cathedral* than he had been about any of Auden's work. Two months later, on 15 June, he sat in the front row with his sister Diana to watch its first performance in the Chapter House of Canterbury Cathedral. He was particularly struck by the powerful verse of the chorus of women just before the Archbishop's death: 'There is an intensity of terror and foreboding unsurpassed in my opinion by anything Eliot has written.'[246] Its immediate success delighted him. Later in June he read Auden and Isherwood's *The Dog beneath the Skin* and thought it was Auden's best work so far, a 'fantastic entertainment, extravaganza and political satire'[247] rolled into one. Ever practical, he was, however, concerned about the management of a large cast of fifty on such a small stage and was going to discuss the problem with Rupert Doone over lunch ... The success of these two plays allowed the Group Theatre to embark on a West End season in the autumn of 1935 that Hayward felt was a triumph. It had fought for its ideals against the vested interests of the London stage: 'If it succeeds it will do more than anything since the war to revive a serious interest in drama.'

Another 'SCOOP' followed in February 1936: Hayward was the first to make public that Auden had agreed to write a play for the new group. This was not the only encouraging sign: he had read Auden's *The Ascent of F6* and found it gave a hard look at 'the terrifying and pitiful contemporary world'. He told his American readers that 'Auden may not be great poet – yet. But he speaks for his generation and no-one, I imagine, would dispute his right to the first place among his contemporaries.'[248] His enthusiasm was, however, always tempered with some doubt. He enjoyed discussions with the actress Vera Russell about the Group Theatre but she felt he was unimpressed by the Auden/Isherwood plays and that his judgement was 'often swayed by the criterion of worldly success'. Later, however, when she invited him to see her in a production of an experimental version of the Bible story *Judith*, he was thrilled, proclaiming loudly to all around: '*This* is worth any effort to come and see. *This* is the stuff that dreams are made of!' Generously forgetting all his views on the advantages of the West End, he turned to her and said, 'You were right to leave the commercial theatre for this. I thought it was an emotional impulse, but it wasn't. You were right.'[249] Meanwhile *Murder in the Cathedral* was enjoying extraordinary success: by January 1937 it reached 300 performances and was broadcast on the radio. More than 50 performances of the *Ascent of F6* had taken place at the Mercury Theatre, Notting Hill. The Group Theatre moved from its tiny premises to the Westminster Theatre, close to Buckingham Palace, and the London Theatre Studio had established new headquarters in Islington in an auditorium that could hold 150, with a permanent company of actors and John Gielgud and Tyrone Guthrie among the directors. So by April Hayward was finally becoming convinced about the 'flourishing and progressive state' of the avant-garde theatre and foresaw a bright future for it: it was to drama what the little review and the small publisher were to literature – a custodian of artistic standards, an encourager of new, vital work and a bulwark against commercialism.

If he was getting more enthusiastic about the state of drama in the late 1930s, Hayward was growing more pessimistic about poetry. Although he had admired the promise of Auden's early work he now began to feel that the 'gang' of Auden, Spender and Day Lewis was going in a wrong direction, less like individual poets and more like a political group. Hayward began to attack 'les boys' for their hypocrisy: 'They are incessantly pre-occupied with the tragedy of machine-made unemployment and the anarchy and brutality of the contemporary scene though they seek for inspiration in Austria when there is enough misery and need for reconstruction to inspire a thousand poets and reformers in our Industrial North.' Coming from comfortable middle-class homes in the South of England, they simply 'have no idea of what is going on in Jarrow ... Central Europe is a romantic lure ... Risurgimento, like Charity, should begin at home.'[250] Poets were now more interested in politics than aesthetics, it seemed to him, and preferred ideology to ideas. Berlin had taken the place of Paris. The Left Bank had given way to the Left Wing. When the Spanish Civil War broke out in 1937, there was a further swing to the left. To Hayward's amazement even the sybarite Cyril Connolly left for Barcelona. His departure was a sign of the times: 'Ten years ago we puffed on our pipes and talked psychology: now it is all politics. Even the babes and sucklings prattle about ideologies.'[251] Their political conscience was international and it seemed to Hayward that they were ready to lose their own country to save the world. 'They are ready, at least in theory. Action is another matter.' Unlike many English writers both he and Eliot distanced themselves from the conflict in Spain and refused to take up partisan positions.

Hayward was also becoming a sought-after but exacting editor. In his mock-elegy on the journalist and writer Peter Quennell, Cyril Connolly imagined all the tasks to be done in his memory. Geoffrey Faber would publish his works, Bill Empson would take over his reviewing, the philanderer Kit Hobhouse (Oswald Mosley) would have his wife – and Hayward would edit his work:

> Who'll correct his proofs?
> 'I,' said John Hayward.
> 'His syntax was wayward,
> I'll correct his proofs.'[252]

In his journalism for the *New York Sun* and the 'Autolycus' column in the *Sunday Times* Hayward turned his friendships into good copy. After he entertained the distinguished French poet Paul Valéry at Bina Gardens, Hayward devoted his piece in the *New York Sun* to an account of his conversation and anecdotes. He introduced his readers to the young author Rosamond Lehmann – 'photos do no justice to her dark beauty' – and asked his readers to imagine her Cordelia-like 'soft, gentle and low' voice. Elizabeth Bowen, George Barker, Goldsworthy

Lowes Dickinson, Stephen Spender, W. H. Auden, Edith Sitwell, John Lehmann, Cyril Connolly, Virginia Woolf and Dylan Thomas all featured in Hayward's accounts. It was Eliot, however, who was the star of Hayward's journalism. Hayward loved to offer enticing titbits of information about him to his readers. For example, Eliot had confided to him that 'Louis MacNeice was the only educated poet among the moderns'.[253] In 1936 Hayward revealed that Eliot was a 'winter author', distracted by short nights and the busy engagement calendar of summer. And of course he lost no opportunity to publicise Eliot's work in America. When they were published in 1936, he reviewed Eliot's *Collected Poems* in the most flattering terms, contrasting the voice of the master with the 'twitterings of the fledgling poets' and adding, 'This is no dross lightly sprinkled with gold, but the ore itself.'[254]

When 'London Letters' came to an end Hayward was asked to become broadcasting (wireless) correspondent for a newly founded magazine which enjoyed a brief flowering in 1937. Graham Greene was the editor of *Night and Day* which aimed to rival *Punch* and become an English version of the *New Yorker*. It aspired to be witty and cosmopolitan with an unusual take on the issues of the day. A. J. A. Symons covered the impact that the Spanish Civil War was making on the supply of sherry, Evelyn Waugh wrote on mathematics and Cyril Connolly a diary as a young middle-class woman, Felicity Arquebus. Hayward attended the grand launch on 30 June in the Dorchester Hotel. Eight hundred guests enjoyed champagne and complimentary copies of the first issue. Sales however proved disappointing and the magazine collapsed only a few months after it had been founded.

More journalism came Hayward's way when in 1938 he wrote a quarterly article for the Swedish literary publication, *Bonniers Litterara Magasin*. 'Letter from London', as it was re-christened, earned a handsome, and very welcome, £10 an article. Similar in style to his American letters, his pieces were a mixture of pen-sketch, gossip and acute commentary, but they were tailored for an intellectual readership, more developed in argument and about five times as long. Here he recommended new books and put together the latest news of the book world he could glean. (Ironically, when most of these letters were written their author was in fact living in virtual isolation in Cambridge.) Nevertheless the fact that he maintained his stream of articles till 1954 shows how popular and successful they were.

The piece on Graham Greene is a good example of Hayward's magazine style, beginning invitingly: 'If you cross the Thames at Chelsea by the new suspension bridge and keep on for a mile or two, you will presently come to the pleasant open space of Clapham Common.' Amongst the 'relentlessly suburban' houses there are the remains of some of the finest Georgian houses in London. The most beautiful of these was No. 14, where Lord Macaulay had lived as a boy. This was now the home of Graham Greene. (Hayward loved to place his literary heroes in their settings – the Sitwells at Renishaw, Ottoline Morrell at Garsington Manor, Elizabeth Bowen at her eighteenth-century Irish manor house, Bowen's Court, Maurice Bowra at Wadham College and so on.) He then put himself in the picture by describing the delightful parties he had enjoyed there, given by his pretty, smiling (and soon to be deserted) hostess, Vivien Greene. He described how he had first met Greene, then a young man suffering from writer's block and desperate for money, who had come to see him about the possibility of a biography of Rochester.[255] At the centre of the article is his portrait of the writer:

> At the age of 36, Graham Greene is a tall, somewhat loosely-built figure; slim, slightly stooping and with a deceptively frail air, he does not immediately suggest the traveller who made the arduous journeys through Liberia and Mexico described by him in *Journeys without Maps* (1936) and *The Lawless Roads* (1939) ... His face, indeed, is seldom free from a strained, almost anguished look and his eyes reveal an inner weariness and at moments a suggestion of spiritual pain ...

The 'Letter from London' then invited its readers to share in some characteristically chatty gossip: 'In passing it may amuse you to know that Greene's recent thriller *The Confidential Agent* was written, so he tells me, "in six weeks to get cash against a war and was intended to be published under the name Hilary Trench".' Hayward went on to recount a conversation between himself and Somerset Maugham about whether there was something sinister about Greene's view of the world. Here he developed his main point about the novels: they succeeded in conveying a real sense of evil. 'It seems to me to be a powerful and intense source of inspiration to him.' Greene's understanding of the darkness of the human heart was the link between the picture of the man and the strength of his writing. So, finally, Hayward recommended

The Power and the Glory as 'his latest and, to my mind, incomparably his best novel'.

Hayward invited Eliot to lunch at his club in August 1939. At the last minute Eliot asked if he could bring Joyce with him, perhaps because he needed Hayward's friendly support in dealing with a man whom he found difficult. It was Joyce's last trip to London and Hayward was quick to tell his American readers about it:

> He wore opaque black spectacles and indeed looked and, by an occasional fumbling of the hand and an anxious hesitation in his gait, behaved as if he was almost blind ... He seemed extraordinarily remote and subdued in the corner of that sunny dining-room; and yet, when he spoke in his soft melodious voice which had been trained in his youth for grand opera, his personality became imposing and intelligible. Joyce, like many Irishmen, had an incisive witty tongue and a broad sense of humour. I have met people who knew him in Paris when he was in the mood for verbal sparring and sharp repartee. But on this occasion he spoke quietly and gently of books and friends ... I am always reminded of his voice, as I heard it then, when I listen to the gramophone recording he made of the concluding passage, read or rather chanted by himself, of the fragment of 'Finnegans Wake' called 'Anna Livia Plurabelle'.[256]

Hayward went on to link Joyce's lack of sight – he had just had a serious operation on his eyes – with his dependence on the word rather than the visual image. The complex structure and rhythm of his sentences, the elaborate puns and the wordplay, all appealed more to the ear than the eye; this aural quality was the key to understanding Joyce's writing; his later work ought never to have been printed at all, but issued as gramophone records. Hayward developed the image of Joyce's blindness further to suggest spiritual myopia. Surrounded by the adoration of his American acolytes he had, it seemed to Hayward, lost all contact with the real world. The incoherence of his last novel, *Finnegans Wake*, was the expression of this disconnectedness. Every detail of the portrait played its part in creating an image of the man, and what Hayward saw as his weakness.

Although always ready to remind his readers that he was at the heart of the world he guided them through, Hayward did not push himself or his views forward and stand in the way of his subjects. Readers were flattered to feel, thanks to the gossipy conversational tone and the eye for telling detail, that they were almost present at parties in Clapham with Graham Greene, chatting with E. M. Forster at King's, or buying practical jokes and false beards with Eliot at his favourite little joke shop near the British Museum. With Hayward as their guide they could imagine visiting Lady Ottoline Morrell at Garsington Manor or the Sitwells at Renishaw Hall; they could watch 'the absurd gambols' of H. G. Wells at tennis parties and even meet the bard-like grey-bearded figure of W. B. Yeats.

9
Noctes Binanianae

In England in the 1930s there was nothing to resemble the clubs and coffee houses of the eighteenth century, or French *salons* where intellectuals met to discuss serious issues.[257] English writers, unlike the French, Hayward felt, had no taste for arranging culture on a social basis – no doubt he would have relished the clubbishness of Dr Johnson's London. He described the scholar Bonamy Dobrée as an eighteenth-century man of letters in terms that suited him just as well: 'A companionable man like Addison, a lover of good conversation, good company and good cheer.'[258] There were, however, plenty of informal parties where artists of all kinds went not to talk shop but 'to meet fellow scribblers in convenient and agreeable surroundings'. Literary and political hostesses held sway in the 1930s. Hayward enjoyed the larger fashionable parties given by two leading society hostesses of the day, Lady Cunard and Lady Colefax ('La Coalbox'), who vied for pride of place, competing for the greatest prize of all – the guest appearance of the iconic Prince of Wales. Lady Cunard, originally Maud Burke from San Francisco, metamorphosed into the glamorous, less Victorian 'Emerald' – 'a bunch of red cherries on a black straw hat', according to Virginia Woolf. Cecil Beaton thought he had never seen 'a more amusing-looking little parakeet in her pastel-coloured plumage'. Lady Colefax was a Canadian who combined the role of society hostess with a very successful interior design business: she was the most energetic of socialites, often scribbling and sending off sixty postcards in the early post. Their styles of entertaining were very different. Evelyn Waugh wondered whether to spend his evening at 'Emerald's oven or Sybil's Frigidaire'. In the end Hayward threw in his lot with Lady Colefax because she was 'perhaps the best, certainly the cleverest hostess in London at the present time'. But he still found that there was far too much noise and hubbub at her parties for her to be considered a proper *salonnière*.

Quieter parties were held by Lady Aberconway, whose King's Road salon showed off her startlingly fashionable onyx staircase; by the artist

Ethel Sands in her drawing room in the Vale at Chelsea where Henry James had held court, and by Somerset Maugham's wife, the interior decorator Syrie, where 'unearthly white rooms were furnished with lavish white sofas'.[259] Ottoline Morrell had a weekly Thursday afternoon tea party at her small Georgian house in Gower Street. Dressed in black satin, she 'moved like a tall ghost clanking silver tea pots and tea kettle instead of chains'.[260] Yeats, Wells, Eliot and the young Spender might be found there. Edith Sitwell entertained more theatrically on Saturday afternoons in her dingy Bayswater flat in Pembridge Mansions. 'After an interminable climb up a dozen flights of damp, stone stairs' there was Edith, 'dressed like an Italian portrait of the cinquecento, in a long spreading gown, her wrists and neck crusted with fantastic jewels'.[261] She greeted her guests with strong Indian tea, doughnuts and a performance that was 'an odd mixture of the theatre and the lecture room'. Hayward was a regular there along with the MP Tom Driberg, the poet Roy Campbell and the ubiquitous Stephen Spender.

Hayward began to organise a smaller, informal and all-male salon of his own which met on Sunday evenings at Bina Gardens. Despite Eliot's turning down his invitations to share a flat, the friendship between Hayward and Eliot was central to the Sunday evenings' festivities. The nucleus who met regularly for literary gossip, claret, practical jokes and laughter were the three directors of Faber's – Geoffrey Faber, Eliot, and Frank Morley – along with Hayward himself. Geoffrey Faber, the oldest of the four, was a veteran of the First World War, Fellow and Bursar of All Souls College, Oxford, a scholar and a poet as well as being the Chairman of Faber and Faber. (He was in fact the only Faber; the second was a fiction to add weight to the firm's name.) He loved shooting, the grouse moors and the role of country squire, a surprisingly establishment background for the chief publisher of the modernist movement in England. Frank Morley, one of three able brothers, was a large, generous-spirited American, a Rhodes Scholar at Oxford, who had worked as London manager for the well-established Century Company of New York before Faber invited him to be a founder director of his firm. Hayward was, as he dubbed himself, Eliot's 'très loyal serviteur'. Lyndall Gordon, Eliot's biographer, wrote: 'What was happening at the flat in Bina Gardens was nothing less than 'the formation of a court circle round Eliot.'[262] None of them, according to Eliot's friend Robert Sencourt, was what might be called a 'nice' man.

Many others enjoyed the hospitality of Bina Gardens including John Betjeman and Graham Greene, James Thurber and the Marx brothers. The poet and critic William 'Bill' Empson was a regular: eccentric, untidy, dirty-finger-nailed, witty and erudite, he was always good company, and often drank too much. Eliot's letter apologising for staying so late gives a flavour of these evenings together:

> I would like you to understand that I would of left earlier as I had intended and would have been most convenient to me having just arrived but I said to myself that would not be fair to John because Bill would certainly stay to All Hours in that case and if Bill is left to himself he will certainly stay until the whisky is gone and Bill wd. think nothing of walking all the way to Marchmont Street rather than miss any of the whisky. Now don't think I'm being malicious because I value Bill and am concerned about Him was he or was he not tight when he arrived I may have been mistaken and hoping I am but my heart sank it did when I saw the stealthy surbreptitious way he dived at the whisky without so much as having been introduced and then also if Bill had not been present I wd not of drunk so much whisky which is not good for me especially after being with my family so long and being dishabituated to anything but Grade A milk and chocolate ice cream but I could not stand the sight of Bill darting at that whisky and seeing that he was not appreciating the difference between 12. 6d and 13s. 9d but to him it was just so much firewater you might say so I staid later and drunk more whisky than I intended ...[263]

One surprising visitor was 'the most difficult and most renowned of contemporary French poets', Paul Valéry. Relaxed after an evening of wine and gossip, he told anecdotes about himself and the symbolist poet Mallarmé. He laughed heartily with Richard Jennings and the attractive wife of the First Secretary at the French Embassy, Jennie de Margerie ('the Margarine'). Valéry was most impressed by Hayward and later asked him to translate his version of Faust. He found at Bina Gardens a centre of civilisation: 'on a tant de besoin de voir des visages humains dans cette époque des barbares'. Afterwards he confided to Cyril Connolly, 'Croyez-moi je n'oublierai jamais Bina Gardens.' 'Rather touching that he should remember the name of that melancholy street,' commented Hayward.[264]

The festivities were very important to Eliot as well. When he left on a lecture tour in August 1936 Hayward organised a farewell dinner with close friends such as Bunny and Peter Quennell and his wife. The party, the excellent cognac, and Handel's Fireworks Music lasted till the small hours. Afterwards Eliot wrote to thank his host and urged him to rest and 'go to bed early during my absence'. He went on to say how much he looked forward to his return to the 'Kensington Kulture Klub' – as Ezra Pound might have called it – and its autumn hospitality: 'Et quand Octobre souffle, émondeur des vieux arbres ... I look forward to many evenings ... illuminés par l'ardeur électrique ...' He signed himself, '*Ton dévoué, what!*'[265]

All four – Hayward, Eliot, Morley and Faber – relished Sunday evenings gossiping, singing and drinking claret around the electric fire and decided to commemorate them in a privately-printed volume of twenty-five copies. On Eliot's suggestion, it was called *Noctes Binanianae*.[266] The title itself, like the contents, was a scholarly joke, harking back to 'Noctes Ambrosianae', a popular feature of *Blackwood's Magazine* in Victorian times, based on a series of imaginary conversations in Ambrose's Tavern in Edinburgh. *Noctes* is a playful, sometimes scurrilous, collection of occasional verse and prose, full of personal jokes and allusions, a mixture of parody and mutual teasing, a *pot pourri* of languages and styles. Eliot wrote contributions in French and German and Faber in Latin. There are sonnets, a 'Pindarick' Ode, a fragment of a soliloquy, an 'Album Leaflet in Prose', a Nigger Minstrel Chorus and a popular ballad. The poems are loosely linked by the animal fable pattern of *Old Possum's Book of Practical Cats*, but here each member of the quartet took on the character of his animal counterpart. Faber was the Coot because of his baldness; Morley the Whale because he had in fact been a whaler and written a book about whales, and also because of his large size. Eliot was either the Possum, as he had been nicknamed by Ezra Pound, because he could escape trouble by playing dead, or the Elephant, because the elephant never forgot and perhaps, as his Sunday-night circle pointed out, because his ears stuck out. At the centre of the web, Hayward himself took as his nickname 'Tarantula'. It was an exact and appropriate name – if one forgets for a moment that tarantulas, unlike other spiders, do not in fact spin webs (*pace* our title!). Not only could a tarantula entice victims to its parlour, it could also give a venomous bite – Hayward's cutting tongue earned him the reputation of being 'the most malicious man in London'.

Eliot's elaborate suggestions of how the title page should look stressed that he saw the volume as a collaboration of the group of friends:

> Wherein are contained such Voluntary and Satyrical Compliments and Verses as were lately Exchanged between some of the *Choicest Wits* and *Most Profound Deipnosophists of the* AGE.

> (Ornament or Emblem of a Coot,
> or other Absurd Bird) or Figure
> in which is tapester'd an Elephant,
> upon whose back capers a Whale, upon
> whose head a Coot with wings extended,
> holding in his mouth and above all a *Vesperal Spider* suspended,
> which spinneth his Web about all.[267]

The word *deipnosophist*, or 'table philosopher', is a reminder that these were verses intended as part of the eating and drinking that made up the evenings at Bina Gardens. It is also an example of the pleasure both Eliot and Hayward took in digging up an exactly correct word of remarkable obscurity and producing it with the aplomb of a conjuror producing a rabbit from a hat. Hayward shortened Eliot's elaborate heading and added at the bottom of the title page, 'Collected with the greatest care and now printed without castration after the most correct copies'.

Music and singing played a major part in the festivities. Faber gave a pastiche of grand opera in his fable 'The Whale, The Elephant, the Coot, and the Spider', with its invocation, 'Conversing with you sprightly Boys / Was once the best of nightly joys'.[268] It was made up of a largo, a transformation scene and an air, and ended with a chorus of 'nigger minstrels', impersonated by Spider and Elephant, singing lustily. Another of Faber's poems, 'Nobody knows how I feel about You', was to be performed as sung by the fashionable black duo of the time, Layton and Johnstone. And his rollicking 'Poema Latina', 'Tarantula Tarantulae', combining jokey references to the inner circle of friends with a jazz rhythm and chorus of 'Tzing boom', was loudly sung or declaimed as the evening wore on and more drink passed around. It was the noisy revelry of these evenings that Faber recalled during the war when he wrote to Hayward describing how he looked back constantly and nostalgically 'on those nights where our extemporisations ravished the ears of the neighbours in Bina Gardens'.[269] Their host, Tarantula, caught them all within his evening web.

The first poem is Eliot's self-portrait 'How to Pick a Possum', in the style of what Hayward called 'the Cat Book'. When at home he wears ecclesiastical dress, 'A mitre / And a cope, or a cape and a cowl'; skilful at solitaire patience, 'he never reads poetry at all'. The eccentricity continues:

> When he walks, he is quite perpendicular
> Although rather weak in the knees;
> His diet's extremely peculiar,
> For he eats almost nothing but cheese. [270]

His ears are 'almost symmetrical, / And of use when the wind is behind', his lips are small, his teeth beautiful – and false – and his large pinky nose turns blue in winter. The playful self-mockery sets the tone for the volume; poem is set against poem as part of a witty conversation or dispute; a battle of friendly and not so friendly insults. Geoffrey Faber in 'An Answer to the Foregoing Poem', remembering Eliot's love of the sailors and sailing, suggested that water not trees was the natural habitat of the Possum. After a reply, 'The O'Possum Strikes Back', Eliot turned on Frank Morley and in his fable 'The Whale and the Elephant' berated him as a callow thirty-eight-year-old, always off travelling by sea. In reply Morley teased Eliot about his extreme age (49): 'Yet Elephant, while he is lively / Is good as dead, comparatively ...'[271]

Hayward mocked Faber's eccentricity in his ode to his North London home 'Frognal' – his craze for sunbathing, his drunken habits in Oxford, his taste for Turkish baths and new-fangled electric razors and his fondness for the Café Royal, most fashionable of restaurants and nightclubs. In his 'Ode to a Roman Coot' Eliot celebrated the Coot as an unlikely nightingale: 'Thou wast not born for death, Immortal Coot!' and 'My head aches, and a drowsy numbness pains / My sense, as though of White Horse I had drunk'. ('White Horse' was a brand of whisky 'whose vile flavour could be recognised by a man blind-fold', according to Hayward's handwritten notes on the King's College copy.) Eliot composed three sonnets picturing Faber capering to the rhythm 'known as "swing"', 'crooning like a Harlem coon, / A blackface Ruth amid the alien corn / Upon the cob ...' He was dancing to the 'lubricious saxophone' while masticating Wrigley's pepsin gum which he 'Expectoratest in the loud spittoon'.[272] Faber cuts an absurd figure of an Englishman pretending to be an American – Eliot in reverse. Morley's 'Fragment of a Soliloquy' portrays him as 'a nigger minstrel':

> Who dat Man?
> At the Café Royal
> Who dat Man?
> Jest watch his feet
> See them roll and see them go
> See
> Them
> Ro-holl
> And see them
> GO.[273]

The point of this horseplay was, of course, to deflate the self-importance of Geoffrey Faber, bursar, chairman and poet, all rolled into one. He is the chief target of the mutual teasing that is the heart of *Noctes* – one of the sub-texts is that of the two directors getting their own back on the boss. Hayward's, 'A Fig for a Foolish One', subtitled 'Faber in a Firkin', listed the kinds of practical jokes that Eliot and he loved to devise to upset the gravity of a board meeting.

> A pineapple that whistles,
> Bananas, too, that squeak,
> Brooms with explosive bristles,
> A match that merely sizzles,
> And coffee cups that leak.[274]

Perhaps Hayward, who did not have to face the other three at Faber's on the following Monday, could afford to be ruder and more direct than his companions about his aim

> To hoist on high with his petard
> The versifying squire,
> And make life infinitely more hard
> For the poor struggling booby bard
> And his pretentious lyre.

Not surprisingly, Faber, faced with attacks from all sides, subtitled his 'Fragment of a Soliloquy' 'Alone in the Jungle' or 'One Against Too Many', and attacked Eliot in images that became close to sadistically sexual in his 'Expostulatory Epistle of a Coot to a Self-styled Whale and a Soi-disant Elephant':

> When Possum responds to the challenge, and can't
> Refrain from changing his shape, elegant
> Hitherto, into that of Tom Elephant,
> And a tusker at that, the biggest extant,
> Imagine the terror this must implant,
> In the shivering soul of the Coot.[275]

He made even more explicit Eliot's secretive double-nature; his life in the clergy house with blameless Father Cheetham was his cover for illegal, nameless, acts:

> There is, also, a room somewhere in the South West region of
>   London,
> denominated a Vestry,
> Where pious Jekyll purloins letter-paper,
> That Hyde may cut a rogue Elephant's caper,
> Trusting to an ecclesiastical alibi, till
> Chief Inspector French ensures crime's requital.
> Where, Coot may ask, has the gospel business got to?[276]

The last three poems in *Noctes*, in French, Latin and German, were written later, in autumn 1938 and take on a darker tone. Eliot's 'Vers pour La Foulque' (Verses for the Coot) gives a picture of Bina Gardens and its inhabitants in a suburban wasteland, beginning with an invitation:

> Allons nous promener, si tu veux
> Nous allons diriger vos pas
> Du côté de chez Bina
> Cherchez le numero vingt-deux ...[277]

The poem ends with surprising crudeness: 'Nous allons nous donner la peine / De chier sur seuil. Sonnez! Laissez nos culs se ventiler / En attendant la *Madeleine*.' ('We are going to crap on the doorstep. Ring the bell! Let our arses break wind ...'). Hayward added another explicatory note: 'One Magdalen, a rude skivvy at No. 22. Afterwards in a convent but was removed.' Eliot had second thoughts about these lines, as beside them, in the draft at King's College, there is the pencilled note: 'Perhaps better omitted.' It is indeed omitted in the prose version that followed: the Album Leaflet. Eliot also had second thoughts about the draft sent to Hayward which read:

> You notice beyond doubt that this landscape with its tarnished herbaceous borders is queer enough. It is a land of trash. Nothing could be less Picturesque … It is a quarter of bad and low jokes! in which from Willett porticoes, rude skivvies keep an eye on you hoping that you will pay court to them … it is a waste and desolate piece of ground … one observes syphilitic cats, and even now and then a superannuated prostitute … but, in the frame of a huge window, and behind some water lilies: listen! There are rare whispers and lunatic laughter. It is it. It is the disgusting creature. It is the vesperal spider with complex eyes and deadly poison, who, with an immodest look, makes a gesture which is cancelled by his strabismus … we are going to walk straight to these picayune gardens of Bina. Let us search No. 22.

In the printed version 'syphilitic cats' became 'damaged cats' and the 'superannuated prostitute' was replaced by 'a great coarse woman'. Despite Eliot's watering down, the picture of Bina Gardens is sordid, the tone full of nausea and the spider-host 'repulsive and sinister' – and so enfeebled that he is unable even to control his venomous glare. In 'Album Leaflet No. 2' – the Chairman finally reasserted his authority over the rebellious board:

> Wherefrom take warning, sons and daughters of little Tarantula, and keep your mouths shut, while the Man himself, the supreme Triumvir, emits sonorous voices and takes the nocturnal hours captive. So and only so may you have licence for these your worthless burblings, because to FABER is given power over the scabrous. Ye have heard a clear word. Now is the scuttling time for all Tarantulas.[278]

The last poem, Eliot's 'Abschied zur Bina', is a comic-elegiac farewell to 'Binagarten' before Hayward had to leave in November 1938 and all the parties came to an end:

> Im schonen Binagarten
> Der sommer ist vorbei.
> Ich ire langsam uns allein
> Mir bricht das Herz entzwei.[279]

['In lovely Bina Gardens / The summertime is gone / I wander slowly
and alone / With broken heart.']

Noctes has divided critics: the Hayward scholar Professor A. S. G.
Edwards thought that 'the collection as a whole conveys the impression
of middle-aged chaps who are too clever by half and have too much
time on their hands'.[280] Peter Ackroyd found that with the passage of
time it did not make 'particularly amusing reading', but Professor
Haffenden enjoyed this 'narcissistic but immensely entertaining set of
verses'.[281] Vivienne Eliot's biographer Carole Seymour-Jones, stressing
the strongly sexual references, argued that the poems reflected Eliot's
homosexuality and Geoffrey Faber's bisexuality.[282] The American critic
Richard Badenhausen saw the collection as a reassertion of a Renaissance ideal in which drafts are 'performative scripts that become the
occasion for conversational commerce', an important collaborative
exercise for Eliot in which, beneath the masks and the nicknames, he
and his friends could achieve 'a carnivalesque release'.[283] It is certainly
true that on holiday Sundays the three directors of Faber's and
Hayward could stand on level terms of mockery and self-mockery.
Eliot's protruding ears and long nose, Morley's baldness and fatness,
Faber's egotism and poor golf and Hayward's squinting gaze were all
fair targets in the contest of wits. But in the end it was Faber who gave
them all their scuttling orders.

It is very hard to put these verses in their context, to judge their tone
and recapture exactly what they meant to the participants. How far is
'Vers pour La Foulque', for example, an exercise in humorous pastiche,
in the style of Isherwood's Berlin novels? How far does it express that
sense of disgust and decadence associated with *The Waste Land*? At
what point does teasing become a wounding attack? It would be wrong
to take all the sexual allusions too literally; they are part of a witty
competition characterised by exaggeration and style. But beneath the
surface, tensions can still be seen and sometimes, especially in Eliot's
last two poems, the tone predictably becomes far from playful. What is
clear is that all the Bina Gardens regulars relished the game of compet-
itive insults and parody as much as they did the generous supply of
drink Hayward provided. This is shown by their wish to publish a
small volume celebrating memorable Sunday evenings. Hayward
masterminded the whole thing: not only was he the host, he also put
together the poems, organised their printing and select distribution. (He
took six copies; the others had four apiece.) With the advent of war

Noctes Binanianae became a memento of happier days for all of them: 'In the Old Days we should be being thankful for the Autumn, and looking forward to Sunday evenings, the bright electric fire and interesting claret,' Eliot remembered.[284]

Another kind of collaboration between Hayward and Eliot was occurring at the same time as the Sunday night revelry. *The Family Reunion* was taking shape in Eliot's mind in 1938 and being revised in numerous drafts. He went through the usual procedure when a new work was coming into being of asking his friends for advice and encouragement. The chief dramatic adviser for all his plays was E. Martin Browne, an experienced actor who had been appointed as Director of Religious Drama for Chichester, but it was to Hayward that Eliot turned for points of language, manners and general comments. Eliot sent him the first draft for 'very drastic revision'. Hayward made detailed verbal changes. When Harry, Lord Monchensey, returns to his ancestral home after seven years away, Eliot wrote for the parlour maid the line: 'His Lordship is here, my Lady.' 'A trifle weak after seven years,' commented Hayward. He also noted that 'His Lordship has arrived, my Lady' would be 'more likely'. The policeman, Sergeant Winchell, he suggested, should adopt a more formal 'your Ladyship'. Hayward was alert to phrasing that caught the English ear wrongly. When Eliot wrote 'You are unused to our foggy nights / On the moorland country ... '[285] Hayward suggested 'on the moor' or 'in the country'. Although his role was chiefly to look at language, he began to comment on the dramatic structure of the play and Eliot's use of blackouts and curtains. He thought that the long speech by Harry at the beginning of Act 2 Scene ii made for 'a rather heavy opening' and suggested bringing in another character, Agatha, to lighten it. Eliot followed the advice. Hayward saw, and discussed, every draft of *The Family Reunion*. Even Martin Browne, who came to dislike him so strongly that he could not bear to hear his name mentioned, paid tribute to his fellow-collaborator through gritted teeth: 'Hayward was an astute observer of manners, and acutely conscious of social niceties. He also suggested re-ascription of speeches; and all these, together with his exact sense of sound and the meaning of words, were much-valued aids.'[286]

The real originality of *The Family Reunion*, Hayward felt, lay in its forging of a kind of flexible dramatic language which could convey different levels of intensity. 'The new form of stressed verse allowed characters to pass from the level of plain statement to poetic utterance,' he told his American readers.[287] This was essential he felt if the new drama was to succeed. He called *The Family Reunion* Eliot's most ambitious essay into verse drama and summarised the plot: 'Harry arrives, a haunted *hunted* creature obsessed by the memory of his wife's mysterious death ... for whom he holds himself at least morally responsible. For his crime he has been hunted down to the very drawing room of Wishwood.'[288] The unspoken parallels of Eliot's own experiences with Vivienne underlie Hayward's account. Lord Monchensey even described himself as Orestes – just as Eliot had when declining the flat-sharing offer, fleeing from the implacable and lost Vivienne.

'I am glad that you are a collector, because it makes it easier to give you my odd volumes. I don't know anyone else who would both "collect" and read,' wrote Eliot to Hayward on Shrove Tuesday 1936. Less than two years later, on 15 February 1938, Eliot made a proposal that was to have a huge influence on both their lives: he asked Hayward to be his literary executor. 'I don't know anyone else besides yourself whom I should altogether trust in that capacity,' he wrote. He made it clear that the function would be 'chiefly negative'. The executor's task was to dismiss the 'junk' he had written for periodicals – 'F. & F. might be tempted, and your job would be to say no.' Anything not published by the time of his death was not worth publishing. Everything that had not been included in his collected essays should remain uncollected. 'And I don't want any biography written, or any letters printed that I wrote prior to 1933 ... or any letters at all of any intimacy to anybody. In fact, I have a mania for posthumous privacy ... your job ... is to suppress everything suppressible.'[289] (1933 was the year that he had parted from Vivienne; she was to be erased from the record.) Eliot promised not to press Hayward in any way. If he 'felt disinclined for any reason' he would never to refer to the matter again.

In fact Hayward was surprised, flattered and delighted. Nothing could have suited him better, but in his eyes the task became much less one of paring down, and much more of responsibility to preserve Eliot's papers, to create an archive and, later, to become his 'creating critick'. Eliot sent a typescript of 'Burnt Norton' to his executor with his own instructions and corrections. On it he had written '"Burnt Norton" / printer's copy. / from the T. S. Eliot bequest / to John Hayward Esq.'[290] The letter acknowledged Hayward's position as 'Keeper of the Archive'. Hayward promptly had the manuscript handsomely bound and waited impatiently for the next instalment for what he came to call 'le très riche cabinet'.[291] He began to collect everything Eliot had written, drafts of poems and plays, speeches and letters, together with books, photographs, postcards, invitations, programmes, notes and jottings. For the next twenty years Hayward acted as archivist, collector, and editor, putting together a matchless record of Eliot's life and writing. If there was to be no biography Hayward would be the loyal guardian of his reputation.

At weekends Hayward had a very busy social calendar and was an inveterate diner-out for the rest of the week. He relished lunch parties, and then often entertained to tea before going out for dinner. Before the dinner party came inevitably '*l'heure enchantée du cocktail*', in the 'horrible *chi-chi* phrase' he coined with his friend Christopher Sykes. It was an expression which Eliot reluctantly came to use 'and never without a shudder'.[292] (Hayward was still inviting his guests to share 'l'heure enchantée' with him in the 1960s, and the cocktail hour remained a feature of his daily timetable until his death.) Dinners at the Garrick Club involved the publisher Rupert Hart-Davis and friends from the book world such as Tim Munby. In 1931 Michael Sadleir had invited nine fellow book lovers to dinner to try to pressurise *The Times Literary Supplement* to take more notice of their interests. This became an informal dining club, christened 'The Biblioboys' by Richard Jennings. Never more than fifteen in number, the Biblios carried on meeting once a month. Hayward was in his element in a club for those 'who had a real interest in bibliography and book collecting, a considerable measure of enterprise and a tolerance for slander, scandal and hard words ... '[293] Ottoline Morrell often sent a car to pick him up from Bina Gardens and he was a regular and favoured guest at Graham Greene's house in Clapham. There were frequent lunches and dinners with Eliot. There were parties too, of all sorts: embassy parties; parties in Bina Gardens to view Walt Disney cartoons or the latest Charlie Chaplin film; parties where a conjuror of gigantic stature, 'The Greatest Thing in Magic', would entertain; fireworks parties with the Herbert Reads, and with Auden and Eliot; parties where Eliot supplied sugar lumps that became little fish when immersed, bought from his favourite joke shop.[294]

Getting around in his wheelchair was no easy matter, although Hayward made light of the task. He was well known to cabbies and doormen who heaved it and its increasingly heavy occupant into the luggage compartment at the back of the cab. With their help, he gallantly rocketed all over London. '"Let me drop you," he would say, and we would sit in the cab, with the chair sliding back and forth, he talking with animation and no apparent concern ... He made it all seem perfectly natural, indeed easy and even gay: "Tip me back, head first, don't be alarmed, driver", he would say as the chair was pushed into a cab.'[295] Although he was now comfortable in his wheelchair, its weight put strains on his friends: Rupert Hart-Davis recalled how Tim Munby and he would lug the 'pram' up the steps to the Garrick Club. Another time he remembered how he and Auden 'almost ruptured themselves' getting the chair down Lady Colefax's narrow twisting staircase in Lord North Street whilst they listened to 'sharp and peremptory orders' coming from its owner above. There were several Mayfair blocks of flats and embassies where the doormen, familiar with Hayward, took on the challenge and liked to show off their strength and skill in dextrously manoeuvring the chair out of the cab and up the steps to its destination. On one occasion outside Burlington Gardens, Hayward, in voluminous cloak and large ecclesiastical hat, summoned a taxi and reassured its driver: 'It's all right, cabby. I know I'll fit in with your help and my friends.' 'Don't worry, Mr 'Ayward. I knows you. There ain't two like you,' came the reply.

After the Munich crisis Hayward's landlady in Bina Gardens delivered her own ultimatum to him: if war did in fact break out – 'as it damn well nearly did' – she would be unable to look after him or provide any meals. In November therefore he was forced to move once more, this time to a seventh-floor flat in Chelsea at 115 Swan Court. This rabbit warren of a building was presided over by an 'old crone' who did the washing and cooking. From his sitting-room window, as the events of 1939 began to unfold, Hayward gazed eastwards towards 'the direction that the bombers will take if they decide to come'. By the late summer many friends were preparing to leave the country – and some had already left. The departure of Auden and Isherwood had been marked with a farewell party under the auspices of the Group Theatre at Durham Wharf, a studio in Chiswick owned by the painter Julian Trevelyan. His only rule was that the bedroom area was out of bounds. The party guests included Auden's friends from many different worlds: Hayward and Eliot, Geoffrey Grigson, Rose Macaulay, E. M. Forster, Stephen Spender, Brian Howard, Cyril Connolly and Benjamin

Britten.[296] It was an uneasy and edgy event; there was dancing to an accordion and the well-known Group Theatre performer Hedli Anderson sang the blues number from *The Ascent of F6* to Benjamin Britten's accompaniment on piano. Auden's words exactly caught the mood of the moment:

> The stars are not wanted now: put out every one,
> Pack up the moon and dismantle the sun;
> Pour away the ocean and sweep up the wood;
> For nothing now can come to any good.

When Brian Howard and Eddie Gathorne-Hardy took over the bedroom and their infuriated host found them, Howard said he would not have his best friend insulted by the worst painter in London.[297] After they were evicted the party ended with a drunken fight in the courtyard. Early the next morning, on 19 January 1939, Auden and Isherwood, to the flashing of numerous press cameras, set off via China to America and a new life.

More upsetting for Hayward than the departure of Auden was the loss of Frank Morley, who had been appointed editorial director of the New York publishing house, Harcourt, Brace and Co. On his farewell visit, marked by the inevitable party at Bina Gardens, Morley's wife, Christina, left behind her a cheap powder-box on a table. The sentimental Hayward did not have the heart to move it and left it just where it lay 'as a symbol of the frailty and pathos of one's personal possessions'. In July 1939 the Morleys sailed from Glasgow. Even the choice of a port so far away from London seemed to underline 'the melancholy and irrevocability of his departure'. Despite the darkening mood, the pace of Hayward's social life continued unrelentingly. He described a typical week's engagements in July 1939:

> Dinner with Mr. Jenkins, poetry dinner (I told you, I think) with Francis Meynell, week-end with Tom Brown at Rugby; visit to Great Tew & Little Tew ... dinner with Chatto and Windus, dinner with Charlotte Bonham Carter ... dinner with with Vere and Honor Pilkington (and harpsichord music); Elsa Lanchester (off to Hollywood) to tea; Lindsey Hadow (Virginian wife of F.O. Secretary) to tea; German refugee to tea; Thalia Gage to tea (to show her pomes in English and French); Papa to lunch; syncopated pianiste to dinner; bibliographer to sherry; Elizabeth Bowen and

Kirk Askew to whiskybo; Cyril Connolly to lemon squash and this week-end with the Vans. Next week it all starts again ...[298]

It is hard to see how Hayward found a moment to write.

As Europe moved towards war and that 'low dishonest decade' of the thirties was coming to its natural end, in his 'Letter from London' Hayward charted two serious losses. The first was the death of Yeats in January. Hayward thought him the outstanding poet of the twentieth century. He was personally struck by his 'magnificent presence':

> It was my good fortune to meet him several times in the last years of his life at the house of his great friend, Lady Ottoline Morrell. I have never met anyone whose genius was so clearly, one might almost say theatrically, revealed in his speech and his appearance. The massive, leonine head, crowned with billowy white hair, broad shoulders that stooped a little, strong arms and hands that moved rhythmically to the rich intonations of an Irish brogue, which gave even to ordinary conversation the quality of an unaccompanied song, remote and dreamy blue eyes that seemed to reflect vision and reality at one and the same time, the careless distinction of dress – all alike proclaimed the poet.[299]

His death marked for Hayward the ending of the Celtic world of the imagination in which poetry had a lyricism that looked back to the Elizabethan past. It was the death of magic. But, despite the bardic appearance and the brilliance of his late work, Hayward felt that, after the early romantic lyrics, Yeats had had little influence on English poetry. The younger poets, he believed, had followed another master – Eliot. Hayward had no doubt that Eliot had been the dominant influence in the inter-war years from the publication of *The Waste Land* in 1922 to 1939.

The second loss was the end of *The Criterion*, after fifteen years of life. The final issue came out in the same month as Yeats's death. Hayward thought it the most influential and authoritative literary magazine in its day. It was a nursery ground for young poets and critics and 'a focal forum for international thought'.[300] But in its internationalism and its attempt to reflect a European culture, it was swimming against the tide of history in the late 1930s. Both Eliot and Hayward watched with a sense of foreboding the rise of Hitler and the Nazi Party in Germany: 'In a world where the freedom of the human spirit has been shackled and even ruthlessly crushed in the name of militant nationalism, the continuity of culture may have to be maintained by a very small number of people indeed,' wrote Hayward to his Swedish readers. The end of *The Criterion* marked the end of the literary and political idealism of the 1930s.

There was one last celebration. For Hayward P. G. Wodehouse's novels evoked a powerful nostalgia for the safe Edwardian world of his childhood. Bertie Wooster offered relief from the grim international prospects of 1939, picturing an England where 'perpetual summer reigns and virtue finds its reward ... where sex never rears its ugly head or poverty endures for more than a season' – and, of course, war never breaks out.

> Blessed with every thing that moralists have not considered essential to the happy or virtuous life, taking their privileges and unearned incomes for granted, and enjoying them to the full, they inherited the earth just before the deluge which Beach the butler gloomily foretold in the Steward's Hall at Blandings. The Woosters and the Emsworths lived and loved in the setting of a perpetual Edwardian garden party ... feudal without the feuds, they belong to a great social hierarchy whose glory has vanished like so many other things in the last twenty years.[301]

Hayward had already written in *The Spectator* praising Wodehouse as a master of English prose. Now, having collected a complete set of first editions in the finest condition, he made notes towards a 'full-dress critical bibliography'. He looked forward to writing about the Wodehousian butler, Blandings Castle, the stately homes of Wodehouse's England and its peerage. There was also an enticing prospect of 'numerous appendices' detailing elaborate genealogical trees of the Wodehousian peerage ... Hayward was therefore delighted to accept an invitation to Oxford University's Encaenia, the culminating event of the summer term 1939, to see 'the Master' invested with the honorary degree of Doctor of Letters. For Hayward it was nothing less than 'the outstanding literary event of the year'. The day was etched so vividly in his mind that he could describe every detail in the last Commentary he wrote for *The Book Collector*, published after his death.[302] In bright sunshine he joined the group of honorands as he was pushed along the High Street through crowds of cheering onlookers. He listened to the University Orator address Wodehouse as 'vir lepidissime, venustissime, jocosissime, ridibundissime' and heard him translate Gussie Fink-Nottle ingeniously into Latin. Wodehouse was hailed as the Martial of his age. Hayward recalled the velvet-capped Chancellor of Oxford University in robes of black and gold, the scarlet and dove-grey of the doctors; the salmon and limp lettuce of the lunch after the ceremony in the Codrington Library of All Souls and the taking of coffee in the quad as the band of the Oxford and Buckinghamshire Light Infantry struck up. At the centre of the celebration was the somewhat bemused figure of the novelist himself: 'with his bland genial face and eyes that twinkle through his horn-rimmed spectacles, he looks for all the world like the ideal uncle of fiction'. To Hayward he looked as if he had never known what trouble was. The bright memory was all the more poignant for the dark times that were to follow this day of Blandings sunshine. 'But the magic did not work, the lights duly went out all over Britain as well as Europe, the great work was abandoned and the first editions sold as a lot not subject to return.' Little more than a year later, Hayward had fled from wartime London to exile in Cambridge and Wodehouse was imprisoned in France by the Nazis and denounced as a traitor in his home country.

10
Merton Hall

Merton Hall is a substantial and beautiful Elizabethan house overlooking the Backs, the oldest non-collegiate medieval hall in Cambridge, set in the grounds of St John's College. It was owned, incongruously, by Merton College, Oxford. In autumn 1939 Victor Rothschild decided to rent it as a safe haven for his family. Just afterwards, when he found Hayward alone and vulnerable in Swan Court, he invited him to stay at the Hall for the weekend and then suggested that he should remain for as long as the threat of war lasted – a seventh-floor flat in London was no place for someone in a wheelchair. So on 25 August 1939 John Hayward joined the 6,000 evacuees heading from London to the relative security of Cambridge. Neither he nor Victor imagined for a moment that the arrangement would last for the next six years.

Hayward was given a ground-floor room overlooking the garden in what was the old nursery at the back of the Hall. In return for his lodging, he became a general factotum, organising the daily running of the house, interviewing gardeners, housekeepers and cooks and keeping an instructive eye on the Rothschild children, when they stayed at the Hall. As 'Custodian of Ancient Monuments' he was in charge of repairs to the fabric of the building. He was also to act as librarian, looking after and cataloguing Lord Rothschild's acquisitions and helping to convey them to a place of more safety at Rushbrooke Hall in Suffolk which Rothschild had recently bought. So Hayward was now in the uneasy position of being both a friend and a refugee. He had brought with him the few possessions he managed to rescue from Swan Court and, most precious of all, Eliot's papers, letters, manuscripts and drafts of poems that he had been collecting and having bound for inclusion in what he came to call 'the Archives'. Here, isolated from the literary world and metropolitan life, he was to pass the war years; the busy round of parties, literary dinners, concerts, theatre trips, and the soirées at Bina Gardens all belonged to the past: 'Dragged out of my groove and separated from all the people and objects and activities that made up my old life, I feel horribly helpless and burdensome.'[303] He told Graham Greene that he felt like an unwanted child.

Life at the Hall was quiet. Rothschild himself was rarely there as he spent most of his time in London working for MI5. His last years were to be shadowed by unsubstantiated rumours that he had been one of the notorious 'Ring of Five' Cambridge wartime spies. Barbara, his first wife, and the children, Sarah, Jacob and, later in 1940, Miranda, visited only occasionally for the weekend. Barbara was the daughter of Mary Hutchinson, the cousin and confidante of Lytton Strachey, mistress of the critic Clive Bell and a satellite member of the Bloomsbury group.

In September, soon after arriving at Merton, Hayward was taken by Rothschild to Rushbrooke Hall, his large Tudor red-brick property near Bury St Edmunds, surrounded by a moat and set in 300 acres of parkland. Barbara thought it 'a heavenly house' and began to redecorate it; French artists had started painting the chandeliers and 600 bottles of wine had just been put in the cellar when war broke out. Now all but the west wing was requisitioned to be converted into a hospital. Gardeners were still at work restoring the grounds as workers inside were busy installing beds and medical equipment. Not far from Rushbooke was another fine house, Ickworth, property of the fourth Marquess of Bristol, which Hayward described as 'a cross between the Albert Hall and Kensington Gas Works in the classical mode'.[304] Both Hayward and Rothschild were immediately struck by the contrast of the building's neglect and the beauty of its grounds. The omens didn't look good: Victor Hervey, later to become sixth Marquess, had been declared bankrupt at the age of twenty-one; Hayward gossiped that the most 'Dishon. Mr Victor Hervey is now in the Clink for drugging a rich lady from Mayfair in a shady night-club'. But, anyway, nothing could save the house from the depredations of progress: 'It is doomed in any case. The deer will be killed for venison, the cropped turf ploughed under for allotments and bungalows built among the bracken.' The decay of Ickworth seemed to him, like that of Powerscourt and Bowen's Court, to represent the end of a tradition. Ironically, it was Rushbrooke that fell into decay after the war. It was about to be demolished when it was completely destroyed by fire in 1961.

Later, Hayward came to see Evelyn Waugh's *Brideshead Revisited* as the most eloquent expression of this process of country house decline. As the novel begins, Captain Ryder returns to find Brideshead already requisitioned.

The great house was empty and the once warm life departed – a gaunt barrack, desolate and decayed, useful only for the billeting of troops. 'Brideshead' looms out from its once lovely, ordered security, as a symbol of the transience of sublunary things in general and the end in particular of a tradition of civilized living. To Captain Ryder's contemporaries, who were born in time to see the first cracks in its smooth surface opening to the shock of the war of 1914–18, and who grew up in the years of suspense that followed, this symbolism must seem profoundly moving … B is, within its limits, a biography of Charles Ryder's generation.[305]

It was the novel of Waugh's he most admired – and indeed it was the one he said he would have most liked to have written himself.

The beginning of the war had an unreality about it. The expected raids did not happen, although Eliot wrote to Hayward that Kensington swarmed with air-raid wardens and shrieking police whistles. Eliot heard his first warning siren in early September and descended into the coal-cellars under Faber's. No. 6 cellar, he reported, was the most fashionable, containing himself, his assistant Miss Bradby and Geoffrey Faber, the Chairman. In Cambridge an uneasy quiet prevailed in the darkened streets. Hayward called this period the 'Bluff Krieg' – but soon Merton Hall began to feel its effects. Rothschild had a shelter built under the Hall, lined with two feet of steel and concrete and complete with two bedrooms (one for family, one for staff). Hayward had to begin to plumb its 'Cimmerian depths', well aware of the comic ironies of the situation as, watched by giggling maids, he descended, with a bottle of brandy, gas mask, whistle, smelling salts, the *Times* crossword puzzle and some boiled sweets. In the corner of the shelter was a sinister-looking chemical closet. He was met by the 'the Admirable Crichton', the head butler Wagstaff, wearing steel helmet and dressing gown, who produced tea and copies of the illustrated London papers as if it were the drawing room of a London club. On emerging, Hayward – 'a refugee in clover' as he called himself – was greeted by Wagstaff with a reviving something on a silver salver. It certainly was hardship in style. Although it could not have been easy to manhandle a wheelchair into the shelter, soon the 'stuffy windowless night-club' of a shelter became Hayward's regular night-time resting-place

Hayward wrote fortnightly letters to Eliot in a correspondence he maintained until the end of the war, often embellishing the envelopes with topical slogans such as HELP ON THE KITCHEN FRONT or DIG FOR VICTORY. The gossipy tone, the satiric wit and constant use of nicknames are a continuation of the kind of talk that they had both so much enjoyed. 'The best letters are tokens of friendship. We exchange them with people when we can't talk to them. What we try to do is to establish the same kind of intimacy in a letter as we do in conversation,' Hayward had written.[306] In more than 150 lengthy and closely-typed sheets, he gave details of his daily routine at Merton: 'walks' he had taken, visitors seen, daily trials to sharpen his razor, the weather and the presence or absence of his hosts and the tasks of running the Hall. Constantly worried about Eliot, he asked regularly about his bronchitis, his long-lasting colds, his dental problems and his exhaustion. If Eliot did not reply, Hayward was so anxious about what might have happened to him that, after listening to the nine o'clock news, he often asked for a brief note confirming that he was safe. The detail and regularity of Hayward's correspondence show just how vital the contact was to him at this time: 'It is the greatest pleasure of my exile writing to you and hearing from you,' he wrote on 1 December 1939. Eliot's replies were much more infrequent, much shorter and often designed to amuse. He told Hayward that he had just seen some flappers, 'dressed in beach trousers, smoking gaspers', driving a genuine 1905 hotel station bus the wrong way down Gower Street. On the windscreen an official notice read CITIZENS' ADVICE BUREAU.

Pinned to the letters was a sequence of invitation cards with printed Cambridge college crests in the corners. 'Admit John Hayward to visit the Collection of Stuffed Birds' at Christ's was followed by an endless stream of comic invention in which he was invited to the view of King's College from the 'Rears', an exhibition of jujitsu from the Provost, the Lunacy Commissioners at Gonville and Caius, the Hugh Walpole Memorial at Emmanuel, the Possum Memorial Stained Glass Window at Magdalene, the Yuletide Cabaret with Ocharina Octette conducted by 'Sykey Davies' at St John's, to 'Goodness knows what for' at Selwyn – and so on. 'Let me impress upon you – as a Newcomer to Cambridge – the importance of not ignoring these invitations,' urged Eliot. Other letters arrived with the easily-obtained compliments slip, 'From the Vicar and the Churchwardens'.

Hayward loved to tell his own sexual autobiography. His first experience, he told Eliot, was as a schoolboy at Hillside when he was incarcerated in the sanatorium with measles. In a moment that reminded the older Hayward of a lurid extract from the sexologist Havelock Ellis, the attractive young night-nurse undid her dress and 'bared her not-so-chaste-bosom' to the young boy's parched lips. After hearing his friend's 'fascinating recollections' of his youthful fumblings in Wimbledon, Eliot wrote: 'My own infancy, by comparison with yours, seems to have been remarkably protected from, at least, such sexual precocity.'[307] But as a result of Hayward's openness Eliot overcame his 'mania' for privacy and found that he could discuss his own troubled sexual experiences, adding that he was looking forward to a monastic life. The only deprivation that he would feel, he wrote, would be of French tobacco. If Eliot was a volunteer ascetic, Hayward was a conscript, tied to a body that could not readily fulfil his desires. Hayward wrote that he did not expect or hope for too much from life. Eliot replied that this chimed in with his own sense of failure: 'I have no family, no career and nothing to look forward to particularly in this world ... Am I frittering away my life? And are the beignets, or are they not, tasty? I don't know.'[308] Was he, Prufrock-like, measuring out his life with coffee spoons? But, he went on to reassure Hayward, the point was to 'tirer avantage from one's disabilities'. The detachment they brought would allow his friend to write his 'permanent document' about society between the wars. It was small recompense.

Hayward's other chief correspondent was Frank Morley. Before he had left for the United States Morley had agreed that his friend should send useful information about the literary scene in England for which Harcourt, Brace and Co. would pay a fee. So from August 1939 till August 1942 Hayward duly wrote a bi-monthly letter and once again received rather less regular replies. He christened it 'Tarantula's Special News-Service', and in fifty-seven densely typed missives he outlined the progress of the war, preached the need for the USA to join it, related as much literary gossip as he could unearth, and wrote of his own rustication in Cambridge. The letters are full of the old familiar nicknames of Bina Gardens days. Tarantula himself never tired of spinning webs and signing himself all kinds of 'Arachnid' from 'L'Araignée' to 'Tarentâle'; the Whale was 'Leviathan', 'Great Cetacean', 'balleine', and so on; Eliot was 'The Possum', 'The Elephant' or 'The Bard'. For Hayward and his friends nicknames reinforced a sense of companionship and excluded those outside the magic circle. Underneath the banter, these letters gave Hayward a sense of continuity in what he always referred to as his 'exile'. With increasing desperation he suggested titles that

Morley might be interested in publishing. Indeed he had one scoop – the then little-known crime novels of Georges Simenon – but literary information was a scarce commodity in wartime Cambridge. After only a few months it became obvious that he was out of touch and had no news worth sending. He called himself 'a broken reed', but Morley kept on reassuring him of the value of despatches. From the start the arrangement was more an act of kindness than of business. Morley discreetly paid the monthly fee of £6 19s 2d from his own purse: 'Both for my morale and Hayward's morale it was important to keep up the correspondence,' he wrote later.[309]

The first months of Hayward's stay in Cambridge were hard to bear. He found it difficult to understand why his life had changed so much. 'One hardly expects to be a refugee in one of the most comfortable & luxurious houses in the kingdom. But I do feel uprooted and, though amongst friends, am secretly homesick for my old rut in Chelsea. I've got my typewriter & fountain pen and that's about all,'[310] he confided to Morley in August and, as winter closed in and the days grew ever shorter, and the blackout cut off contact with the outside world, he felt lost and abandoned. The old world had 'whirled away like a comet' and the new world had cut him off from everything he was familiar with. In November he wrote: 'We march on, as well as we can, breast-forward into the gathering darkness.' Eliot completely shared his gloom and, faced with a problem that resembled a giant jigsaw puzzle with the wrong pieces, had given up reading or listening to the news. 'My dear John,' he had replied, 'we have no more to look forward to in this world than St Augustine had, and rather less. So what am I to do next?'[311] There was, however, a stoic side to Hayward's character that did not allow him to become too despairing: he had no family or dependents or prospects to be concerned about. 'In a way, I have less cause for discontent and complaint than most people because I never expected or hoped for very much since I took to my chair, and although I live *in* the world and enjoy doing so, I often feel that I am out of touch with the world – in other words experiencing it vicariously.'[312] These remarks struck an immediate chord with Eliot: he too, he replied, had 'no family, no career, and nothing particular to look forward to in this world. I doubt the permanent value of anything I have ever written.'[313]

On one of his despatches to Morley Hayward drew a cartoon of a specially black and venomous-looking hairy-legged spider, with fierce green eyes, supporting on its back the Union flag. Beneath it he wrote,

'Monsieur Tarentâle Patriote.' Despite feeling that the war might be some kind of humiliating trap, he supported it and was reassured by confidence in Winston Churchill, who 'knows what war is and what war demands and how it should be prosecuted'. Like Eliot he was scathing about those 'left-wing intellectuals bewildered by the sudden substitution of positive action for academic debate who have apparently apostatised'.[314] 'I feel deeply and bitterly about their action,' he wrote.[315] Eliot replied that he too felt somewhat shocked by Auden's decision to take American citizenship – although he marked the information 'Private confidential' on his letter. Hayward agreed with Maynard Keynes that in the end it was left to the Colonel Blimps rather than the intellectuals to fight fascism. Auden and Isherwood, now living in New York and California ('Parsnip and Pimpernel' in Evelyn Waugh's *Put Out More Flags*), had recently published *Journey to a War*. Hayward suggested that *Journey from a War* would be a better title. Their commitment was fatally compromised by their desertion of England. 'Here lie the defenders of Madrid and Barcelona,' he punned. Aldous Huxley was near the top of the blacklist after he had flown to Hollywood: 'Certainly the sermon preached by Huxley on his Californian mount was not easy to attend to, on the occasion of its delivery, and was even a little resented by those who in the zone of war were less comfortably and securely placed than he for the calm and detached contemplation of the eternal verities.'[316] Even his friend Stephen Spender came in for criticism, as he seemed to have retreated to his own ivory tower to edit books.

The Rothschilds' way of life was being inexorably changed. Rushbrooke Hall had to be boarded up. Hayward spent the Christmas of 1939 there looking after the mothballing of all the family possessions and treasures and the safe transport of the library. The first heavy snow of the winter found him moat-bound with Rothschild retainers to keep him company: two nurses, a butler, a footman, 'a man who always wears a white apron', a French chef, two nursemaids, a kitchen-maid, an electrician, a bailiff, a carpenter, a bricklayer and 'our old friend, the Partridge in a Pear Tree'.[317] In trainspotting mode, he counted 449 table napkins as they were put away, and marvelled at the gargantuan size of the ice moulds in the kitchen. As he watched the splendours of the country house being packed up and the regiment of servants disbanded, he almost seemed to have his notebook in hand. He told Eliot: 'I'm a fascinated spectator in the strange world in which I live.'[318] His gloom was apparent in the last words of the letter: 'I wish you such happiness and peace as the dreadful New Year will allow.' In the same mood, on the last day of December he wished Morley happiness after the 'Annus Horribilis et Mirabilis' of 1939, lamenting his own lack of literary news and lonely state: 'I lead a solitary life, seeing very few people and hibernating with my thoughts.' He even planned a trip to the United States – a trip that was still theoretically possible. He drew for Morley a touchingly sentimental coloured sketch of a little boat flying the Union flag crossing the Atlantic in brilliant yellow sunshine. Nearing the Statue of Liberty, a cheerful-looking whale spouted in front of the skyscrapers. In a scroll underneath Hayward wrote 'Le Réunion'. The reality was somewhat different. As he gazed out from the study with its six gothic windows, and its three Cézannes on the walls, across the frozen moat onto the expanse of snow-covered parkland, he mused that for him, as for many, civilisation seemed to be coming to an end.

The first winter of the war was brutal. In London the Thames froze, villages were completely cut off and cars buried in snowdrifts; 1,500 miles of railway track were blocked. The coldest January and February for forty-five years added to Hayward's sense of isolation. After Christmas at Rushbrooke, he managed to get back to Merton Hall where the household was cut off for a fortnight. Eliot wrote that he too felt 'marooned' in London without the company of old friends. A thick sheet of ice covered the lawn of the Hall till mid-February. A one-bar electric fire was placed beneath his chair and ran off the socket, giving out less heat than a light bulb; the chimney smoked continuously and Hayward sat for hours, legs covered in a rug, feet in a muff. Muscular dystrophy meant that he suffered extremely from the cold. 'I should have written befaw / But I was waiting for a thaw,' he rhymed to Eliot.[319] A walk in the snow with Rothschild's head butler through Trinity Gardens, carrying a special permit from the Vice Master headed 'Bath Chairs in the Paddocks', was the only variation to the monotony. 'Tomorrow, being the Feast of Candlemas, I commemorate the 35th anniversary of my birth. Talk about selva obscura,' he wrote on 1 February. His calendar, which normally recorded a welter of engagements for lunch, dinner, tea, drinks and visits, was a white blank for these days, but he remarked stoically that 'I continue to lead a quiet life which suits me very well …'[320]

No wonder Hayward continued to value so much his correspondence with Eliot and his 'Prince of Friends across the Water': 'In these short days and long, blacked-out evenings under the Frozen Bear, you seem almost infinitely remote.'[321] One clear virtue of the isolation, however, was that it gave Hayward the opportunity to work on what he hoped would be his *magnum opus*. For some years he had been gathering material for a novel that was to be a re-creation of the social and literary world of London in the thirties; it would do for London what Baudelaire had done for Paris and give 'a sense of the time-kept city's life, pulsing in blood and stone'. As an admirer of Proust he sometimes called his scheme – ambitiously or ironically – 'mon recherche du temps perdu'. The similarity between himself and the invalid Proust must have struck Hayward forcibly. The novel, to be called *Beechingstoke*, was to be based on many familiar characters and friends; he was already choosing some of the more colourful ones for their parts. Robert Sencourt had clearly booked his role in the cast list. Two other likely candidates were the politician Robert Boothby ('booming Boothby') who stayed at the Hall in February and took over Rothschild's bedroom – 'an entertaining cad, with all the interests of a successful failure – and all the malice';[322] and Gerald Wellesley (later nicknamed 'The Iron Duchess') whom Hayward reported as inseparable from a bust of his ancestor which he carried with him everywhere and even installed beside his bed in hotel rooms. Eliot hoped that his own sister would have a part in the novel. Apart from Frank Morley, he was the only person who knew of the project and acted as an encouraging but impatient taskmaster: 'I am happy to think that the Recherche du temps perdu is stirring in your mind. You ought to begin taking notes ... Anyway, get on with it. Forgotten epochs, l'entre deux guerres. I value highly all your reports and observations.[323] He suggested that extracts from the work in progress could be sent to him in the form of letters and constantly spurred his friend on, just as two years later Hayward was to urge him on to complete *Four Quartets*.

Just occasionally Hayward was still able to view the war with comic detachment. In January he wrote that it seemed to have descended into 'a photographic competition swapping aerial snaps of Dagenham with our views of Munster'.[324] On the Home Front he described his father as Colonel Blimp, digging out his ancient rifle, charging his sporting guns with buckshot and scrounging barbed-wire and harrows to block remote bridleways in deepest Oxfordshire. As for the war in Cambridge, 'the Enemy struck at the heart of the English educational system, dropping three bombs on the University cricket pitch.' As spring came he at last began to be able to escape from the confines of the Hall and to think about the future. He told Graham Greene that he clung to the 'small hope that I shall see peace and my friends again in my time'.[325] Just as his father had enjoyed the flowers in the wartime trenches, so his son enjoyed the 'beauty of this peerless first day of spring in Cambridge'.[326] Trinity Fellows' Garden was bright with snowdrops and aconites, he told Frank Morley in March. The first punt appeared in the Backs, piloted inevitably, he noted, by a Japanese student. Crocuses popped up in the long grass and the treetops turned a misty purple. The scene was almost beautiful enough, he wrote, to half persuade him that all was right in the world.

It was in March 1940 that Victor Rothschild drove Hayward away in his camouflaged Mercedes to Rushbrooke Hall for the weekend. On a wet Sunday morning Hayward decided to go to the library to have a look at Rothschild's first edition of *Tom Jones* to check a small point for his book-dealing friend John Carter. It was the only one known in original boards, uncut, and in immaculate condition. The famous dealer A. S. W. Rosenbach had paid what seemed then the astounding sum of $29,000 for it in 1929. Even counting his splendid collection of Swift, Rothschild felt that it was 'one of the most important treasures I possessed'.[327] Rothschild had been offered it in a joint-lot, together with a manuscript of Pope, by the reputed antiquarian bookshop of Gabriel Wells in New York. Rothschild agreed a figure of £3,500 for the pair of items.

No sooner had Hayward begun to look at it than he felt something was wrong:

> While I was casually turning over the leaves of one of the volumes I was suddenly aware of a slight difference in the feel (between thumb and forefinger) and (to an eye familiar with the type and paper of that period) the appearance of one of the leaves. A doubt immediately entered my mind as to the authenticity of the leaf in question and consequently of the whole set of volumes.[328]

There were other features that looked suspicious: the surprisingly pristine cleanness of the boards; the gathering of the book done with a modern, not an eighteenth-century stitch; the thread itself looked modern. Even the glue seemed wrong to his professional eye. Hayward's decided that twelve leaves in all had been inserted from another copy.[329] Pains had been taken to match the paper with the rest of the leaves and to 'fake age marks etc'. Hayward concluded that it was not what it purported to be. *Tom Jones* had recently been through the hands of 'a very clever faker' who had added leaves to make good the missing ones and then presented this as a perfect copy. In short, Lord Rothschild had been sold a pup.

Rothschild was naturally horrified when he was told the news. He was upset at the apparent loss of one of the stars of his collection, but also angry about what appeared to be a fraudulent sale from a well-established dealer whom he had trusted. He immediately asked for his money back. Wells refused and so the case went to court in New York. It was a high-profile trial, in which reputations were at stake, a drama involving an English peer and a top American book dealer. Both sides briefed leading barristers: Lord Diplock appeared for Wells, and Gerald Gardiner, later to be Lord Chancellor, for Rothschild. Hayward was the first expert witness to be called. He began his written statement, 'I am an author and bibliographer', and then went on to describe his relationship with Rothschild and the events that surrounded his discovery of the impostor *Tom Jones* at Rushbrooke Hall. Rothschild appeared in person at the trial to give evidence. After hearing testimony from all the participants, Wells settled out of court for $14,000 rather than allow the firm's reputation to suffer further damage. Hayward's detective skills and understanding were vindicated. Rothschild was triumphant and delighted with 'my faithful and patient mentor', John Hayward. They had taken on the New York book trade and won. Rothschild preserved the account in the privately-printed memoir, *The History of Tom Jones, a Changeling*, as a warning to innocent book buyers of the perils they could run into. On the frontispiece he inscribed 'Caveat Emptor'. In the foreword he drew two morals from the story. One was that the law was so complicated that if you try to understand it 'you will never buy a barrel of glue, a stallion or an old book ever again'. The second was: 'If you are a collector and people like John Hayward or John Carter are your friends, you are bound to have some unpleasant surprises when they "have a look at" your library.'[330]

In early 1940 Eliot signed up as an air-raid warden and was at first responsible for a patch in Kensington, then Russell Square and the rooftop of Faber's. This meant a difficult climb and long nights staring over the London skyline, where he was comforted in his lonely vigil by the companionship of the Faber cat, Cat Morgan. As the cold winter continued Hayward worried about his friend's health and the dangers of his duties. He was also concerned about Eliot's poetry – or the lack of it. Had he finally dried up, as rumour had it? Hayward tried tactfully to sound him out, but the Possum was, as always, too elusive for him. Then, out of the blue in February 1940, Eliot wrote with the news that Hayward had been looking forward to so much:

> I am relieved to hear that Tom has picked up his tablets again after all these months – almost a year – of silence ... He now writes to say that he is making a little progress with a new poem in succession to 'Burnt Norton' – the second of three quatuors – provisionally entitled 'East Coker', of which he has drafted the first two out of five sections. 'It may be quite worthless', he adds, 'because most of it looks to me like an imitation of myself ...'[331]

From then on events proceeded apace. A draft arrived at Merton Hall on 21 February. Eliot did not know 'whether it was worth tinkering with', but asked Hayward to return it with his 'usual neat faint pencil marks' in the s.a.e. he had provided.[332] The poem looked back to Eliot's ancestor Andrew, who in 1667 had left the Somerset village of East Coker to emigrate to America. Hayward was immediately struck by the parallel of their two West Country origins and wrote: 'Your "East Coker" is my Beechingstoke – not so many miles away.'[333]

Eliot valued Hayward's advice on detailed points of English grammar and spelling but as they worked closely together he began increasingly to rely on Hayward's judgement on the poetry itself. 'Tom depended greatly on John as his literary critic and seldom felt quite at ease in his mind about anything he had written unless John approved,' wrote Mary Trevelyan.[334] As they wrestled with the text the relationship between the two became essentially collaborative.[335] Hayward underlined the original word 'aresse', suggesting 'arras?' in the margin. (Frank Morley noted that Faber, who was another trusted 'reader', also objected to 'aresse'. Eliot's reluctance to change this came from the fact that the Tudor spelling recalled his ancestor Sir Thomas Elyot.) Finally Eliot accepted 'arras', but the loss of this link with the past still 'rankled' with him.[336] Hayward suggested the English spelling 'wainscot' for the American 'wainscoat' and 'recipe' for the American 'receipt'. As a stickler for factual accuracy he questioned the notion of fieldmice coming into the house. Eliot replied that they did get into his New England childhood home and the line stayed. 'Dawn points and the star fades and another day / Prepares for heat and silence' met with disapproval probably because Hayward noted that the morning star does not fade at dawn. Eliot replied, '*Star fades.* You are right.' The line became 'Dawn points, and another day / Prepares for heat and silence.' Hayward also hated repetition. He underlined and put a cross in the margin of the line about the houses which 'Are removed, destroyed, replaced, or in their place / Is an open field'. Eliot substituted 'restored' for 'replaced'.

Hayward disliked the line, adapted from Sir Thomas Elyot's 'The Governour', which originally read, 'A most dignified and commodious sacrifice' and ended the verse paragraph. He put a cross against 'most' and objected to the word 'dignified'. Eliot deleted 'most' and moved the whole line back to line 30 with the rest of the Elyot. This also had the advantage of ending the paragraph with the peasants' dance: 'Feet rising and falling / Eating and drinking. Dung and death.' Eliot found difficulty in getting the right word in the quatrain beginning 'Our only health is the disease ...' He began with '... to be restored, our suffering must grow worse', and then changed the noun to 'malady'. Hayward suggested 'sickness' and the line became, '... to be restored, our sickness must grow worse.' Eliot wrote on 27 February 1940 a note of thanks saying that he was 'primarily grateful to you for encouraging me to believe that the poem is worth the trouble'. In Tarantula's next despatch to Morley, no. xii, Hayward wrote:

> Well, the old master, Tom, polished off his poem more quickly than he expected or led me to expect, and a copy reached me for comment yesterday. He says 'You might keep it to yourself', but I don't think this applies to you, who, for this purpose, I count as myself. So, I will tell you that I think that this poem – 'East Coker' – is prodigiously fine. Just over 200 lines in five sections. It has moved me a good deal more deeply than 'Burnt Norton' (of which it is a kind of sequel), one explanation of this being, perhaps, the outstanding beauty of the lyrical verses. It is also poignantly self-revealing – such confessions, for example, as: 'So here I am, in the middle way, having had twenty years – / Twenty years, largely wasted, the years of *l'entre deux guerres* ...'

When 'East Coker' was published its arrival delighted Hayward, as he told Frank Morley: 'Tom's pome "East Coker" suddenly appeared in print this morning as a supplement to the *New English Weekly*, issue of March 21, and reads very fine notwithstanding murky paper and mouldy type.' It was unenthusiastically reviewed – 'How low *The Times Literary Supplement* has sunk since the good old days of Sir Bruce and the Spider!' he lamented. But from the first the poem sold well and had to be reprinted in May and again in June. Hayward felt that this major poem should have much more publicity, especially as it was reminder that warfare could not crush the creative spirit; Eliot, as usual, was nervous about popular success. 'Tom's "East Coker" has been received with the greatest possible applause by the few people who knew, or who were told that it could be found in that obscure weekly in which Tom is interested. I wish it could be given a wider circulation without delay – that the world should not have to wait until it is incorporated in a new edition of his collected Poems.'[337] His suggestion was implemented after his energetic intervention with the Book Committee in September when Faber's published it as a pamphlet at the cost of one shilling, quickly selling nearly 12,000 copies. It was a poem of its moment, celebrating the enduring qualities of English culture just when they seemed most under threat: its arrival coincided with the retreat to Dunkirk in May 1940 and the fall of France, looking forward to the autumn when the Blitz began in earnest. Many of Eliot's readers who knew the wrecked and burning houses of London's East End or of Liverpool must have felt that the opening of 'East Coker', with its evocation of houses rising and falling and old timber being reduced by fire to ashes, spoke directly to their own experience. 'The clock has stopped and I see little hope of it being set back in our time. This is what "East Coker" says,' wrote Hayward.[338]

It was not the only wartime poem the two men were discussing. Eliot had been commissioned in early 1940 by the Ministry of Information to write a piece to go round the walls of the exhibition of war photographs at the British Pavilion at the New York World Fair.[339] 'Defense of the Islands' was Eliot's 'sole contribution to wartime propaganda', wrote Hayward. Eliot, as was now his habit, wrote a draft and sent it to Hayward to comment on. He was especially anxious about the final lines: '... we took up / our positions, in obedience to instructions' and asked nervously, 'Is it too much like the epitaph of the Lacedemonians after Thermopylae?'[340] ('Go tell the Spartans / Passerby, / That here, obedient to their laws, / We lie.') Hayward reassured him, and the line was published unchanged, with its clear message that the British were heroically holding the hot gates at tremendous sacrifice while they waited for the American forces to turn up.

In May 1940 many feared that a German invasion was only a matter of time 'One waits for the blow to fall, as one waits for the first distant thunder at the end of a hot and breathless day ... To-morrow may bring us all, whether in town or in the fields, face to face with the enemy. We live from day to day in great jeopardy and imminent peril.'[341] The regular droning of aeroplanes over Cambridge signalled the end of the Bluff Krieg. Even the blue skies of a perfect May morning were full of aircraft.

On a rare trip away from Cambridge to visit the economist Roy Harrod at Elsworth, Hayward noticed how all the signposts had disappeared and rusty coils of barbed wire were piled up at every crossroads. He reported to Eliot that the best minds in the country had turned their attention to foiling the invaders by stretching string across the roads or by covering deep pits with bracken. Then, on 8 June, the war finally came to Cambridge. Hayward was roused by the banshee wailing of the siren and spent two hours in the shelter as German raiders flew overhead. He lay uneasily awake, listening to 'a slightly batty cuckoo' talking in its sleep as he waited for the raid. Increasingly often in his daily calendar he began to mark in neat black letters '**arw**' – air-raid warning. On the 18th and 19th German bombers, 'these loathsome nightbirds', attacked the east of England. A row of houses in Cambridge just a mile from the Hall was destroyed, killing nine, including women and children. The rapid thuds of explosions were followed by the loud detonations of an anti-aircraft gun mounted on a lorry 400 yards from the Hall.

Meanwhile, in London, Eliot listened anxiously to the news bulletins wondering whether 'a market town in the fen district' or 'an East Anglian town' that had been hit by enemy bombers could be Cambridge, and what might have happened to his friend.[342] The situation in London was bad too. If the wind was from the south, distant rumblings of the barrage could be heard in Cambridge. Information was scarce and worryingly hard to decode. Hayward was disturbed that he had had no news from Eliot, especially as it was rumoured that Faber's had been bombed and two houses in Bina Gardens laid completely flat. He also heard (wrongly) that Swan Court had been badly hit during one of the raids on Chelsea and now resigned himself to the 'total loss of that small corner of the warren where you and I spent many happy Sunday evenings'.[343] Large areas of slumland in the East End and elsewhere were destroyed and the wholesale destruction of property would, he feared, eventually rot the social fabric. As the Blitz worsened Eliot decided that London was becoming too difficult and dangerous and, like Hayward, retreated from the capital. He became a paying guest at Shamley Green ('the Shamblies'), near Guild-ford. It was a spot Hayward knew from childhood when he had trun-dled round 'the Surrey Highlands' in a two-horse brake before the 'Southern Electric had made Surrey safe for pluto-democracy'.[344] Eliot stayed with Mrs Mirrlees, mother of the novelist Hope, her sister and the eccentric lesbian Margaret Behrens.There he was surrounded by five pekinese dogs – 'unpleasant little animals' – a parrot, numerous cats and some female paying guests. He nicknamed Mrs Mirrlees the 'Field Marshal' because of her manner with dogs and people. Here, in the 'Catticombes', he too was petted and looked after, his socks darned and his clothes carefully packed and unpacked. The cook and house-maids made sure he had little to do. Now, he wrote, he shared with Hayward the problems of being homeless, adding, 'I seem to be depen-dent on a place where I can go and be ill from time to time.'[345] He still returned to London every week for the Wednesday book committee and his fire-watching duties; but back in the 'Catticombes', even if the atmosphere seemed sometimes fussily geriatric, he grew very fond of the kind old ladies.

Hayward felt that 'while the storm howls round one's ears' it was the duty of literary men to support the war in whatever way they could. He himself proposed a scheme for supplying the Swedish market with English books. It was part of the propaganda vital to keeping British culture alive in such an important neutral country. He also reviewed for the British Council's propaganda service, wrote a weekly cable on recently published books for the Ministry of Information for the troops in Finland and fortnightly 'jolly letters', cablegrams to the *World Press Review* in Cairo for the forces in in the Middle East. Initially he had applauded Eliot's decision to go to Italy to lecture on British culture, but felt its dangers too. What if he were incarcerated or, even worse, had to spend the whole duration of the war locked up with 'old Ezra'?[346]

After the trip had to be cancelled Hayward was relieved, but encour-aged Eliot to visit America to speak against the nation's ostrich-like stance. He also urged Morley to use all means possible to change Amer-ican isolationist attitudes. Even Eliot's edition of Kipling's verse was praised 'as a contribution to the war effort'.[347] On the other hand,

Hayward commented bitterly on the anti-British propaganda of the Pétain government, telling Morley not to believe a word of it. Ever the Francophile, he wrote that the best way of supporting the Free French was by circulating, publishing or even printing French literature. Even the boring tasks of supervising the staff, spring cleaning, and household repairs at Merton became more tolerable by 'regarding them in a way as war work'.[348] In October he told Morley 'We are all on active service, even those who only stand, or as I do, sit and wait from one hour to the next.' As he wrote, a bomb fell nearby, making the whole Hall shiver. In November Hayward was summoned to the Cambridge recruiting centre to explain his non-combatant status. 'Next Saturday I have to offer to take up arms for my country and explain why I cannot take up my legs as well.'[349] Once he got there he speculated whether a mechanised unit might be suitable for him and suggested to the surprised officer in charge that the 11th Hussars (Bath Chair Div.) would be just right.

In late 1940 Geoffrey Faber asked Hayward to edit a small volume of about 30,000 words of Eliot's prose. The aim was to introduce people so far unacquainted with his writing to get a taste for more – or in Hayward's eyes for the publisher to get the 'cokernuts' he wanted. 'I'm proud to be asked to do it, and trust that I shall justify your confidence,' Hayward replied and asked Eliot to recommend 'confidentially' what he would like included.[350] Modestly, Eliot demurred and added, perhaps thinking of Hayward's father, that he was 'entirely in favour of select extracts cut out by the expert surgeon'.[351] Eliot was very apologetic about his American lectures, *After Strange Gods*, which he said were potboilers, 'largely drivel', written under the pressure of bankruptcy. He could not face looking at them again, but was not, however, against Hayward's exhuming nuggets from them. Eliot also turned down the suggestion that the editor should remain anonymous or appear under a pseudonym, arguing that the book will 'have a different and superior status if the choice is known to have been made by you'.[352] As the Prefatory Note stated, 'This selection of T. S. Eliot's critical writings has been made and edited, with the author's approval, by John Hayward.'[353]

Points of View was a kind of prose manifesto, beginning with Eliot's claim from 'The Use of Poetry and the Use of Criticism' that 'From time to time, every hundred years or so, it is desirable that some critic shall appear to review the past of our literature, and set the poems and the poets in a new order. The task is not one of revolution but of readjustment.'[354] Hayward cut essays down to single paragraphs and supplied titles. Eliot wrote to his editor urging him to put his name on the cover. Naturally Hayward was flattered and delighted by the 'cogent and flattering views' Eliot expressed, but he said he was much more concerned about the title which might be imposed on the work by Faber's. He warned of the possible dangers of 'SWEET BREVITIES or PICK AND CHOOSE or, CULLED FLOWERS I HAVE LOVED, THE SHELTERER'S VADE MECUM'. In January he sent off to Faber's the manuscript of 'Choyse Droppings: Worldly & Divine, Artfully Collected into a Fragrant Bucket from the Entire Workes of Thos. E...t, Doctor in the University, by J. H., Gent.'[355] He got his way with the title when *Points of View* was published in July 1941 in an edition of 4,000 copies – but his name did not appear on either the cover or the title page.

Having lost a good deal of his income, Hayward hoped to cash in on the popularity of anthologies. Duckworth's had assured him that people in wartime liked reading about love and offered him a tempting advance of 100 guineas. While he was acting as Eliot's 'creative critick' for what was to become *Four Quartets* he began to choose poems for his anthology and canvassed his friends about what to include. He told the poet Anne Ridler that Barbara Rothschild had suggested

> A Turkish cigarette with lipstick's traces,
> An Air Line ticket to Romantic Places ...
> These foolish things ...
> Ree-mind me of U![356]

Hayward was amused, but left it out. There were some problems with choosing a title, but finally he settled on *Love's Helicon,* because, as he explained to Eliot, it was an allusion to the Elizabethan *England's Helicon* and also hinted at the *mons veneris* – a hint few of its readers probably picked up. The central idea was to allow the poems to speak to each other, to reveal themselves in new ways by putting them in unusual contexts. Hayward boldly set out his extracts without chronological order or any interference of dates or authors to obscure his theme: the progress of love. He allowed himself considerable latitude – a surprising freedom in one normally so hostile to any laxity with the text. Ruthlessly he cut poems up, often reducing them to one or two lines, and even supplied or altered titles. Snatches of dramatic verse were included too, from Shakespeare and his favourite Jacobeans, Webster and

Tourneur. In this way *Love's Helicon* was a considerable departure from the conventional anthology.

Published by Gerald Duckworth, the anthology was well received and reprinted once in 1941 and twice in 1942. By 1943 it had sold more than 5,000 copies, bringing Hayward both popular notice and some welcome cash. To his chagrin and surprise, the owner of the Cambridge bookshop Heffers told him it was very popular with the men – but the ladies all bought Rupert Brooke. ('Rupert Brooke poems. 10/6 with a panel of soughing pine trees blind-stamped on the cover. Ugh!')[357] Eliot wrote with his congratulations on a notable piece of work.[358] He suggested that a limp cover would have been better, 'not as a symbol, but as an incentive to the purchaser to slip the book into his tunic'. He especially enjoyed the introduction and approved ending with poems by Yeats and Hardy, but was pulling the editorial leg when he praised Hayward for 'preserving the doubted reading of 169', and added that 'the variant of 227 might have been enshrined in a footnote'. (227 was in fact a one-liner from a play by Ford.) Eliot also wrote that he felt some aspects of love had been omitted such as, 'A little of what you fancy does you good'. Even more surprisingly he suggested a section on 'Lovers' Quarrels' which might include verse such as

> One day Columbo and the Queen
> They fell into a quarrel:
> Columbo showed his disrespect
> By farting in a barrel …

'In short, a notable piece of work,' Eliot summed it up. He would bring a copy with him to Cambridge to get the author to sign it.

Hayward noted the peculiar quality of English attitudes to love and found in these the reason for the particular tradition of poetry he was celebrating. English poets were more likely to write sonnets in praise of their mistresses' eyebrows than to praise them to their face. It was, he argued, this refusal to see sexual relationships as natural that led Englishmen to be 'inhibited and maladroit in the art of making love',[359] but nourished a tradition of love poetry which elevated love into a mystery. 'A consequent predisposition to exalt passion, in fear and trembling and ignorance of its effects, into a remote, romantic and almost sacred experience, goes far to explain why the condition of being in love has always been such an intense source of inspiration for English poets.'[360] The treatment of love in his anthology also had a much more personal edge. His affair with Elaine was long past and Joséfa had remarried in 1936. During the cold winter of 1940 there was plenty of time at Merton Hall to brood over his lost loves. He wrote in his Preface: 'Just as we learn by experience that the course of true love never did run smooth, so experience teaches us that the passion of love cools – alters at the best into some lesser thing – and finally grows cold.' Unusually for Hayward there was no dedication: the selection begins and ends with an anonymous early medieval lyric:

> Western Wind, when wilt thou blow,
> The small rain down can rain?
> Christ, if my love were in my arms,
> And I in my bed again!

All the varying moods of love are enclosed within this cry of loneliness.

As Hayward became a familiar figure in Cambridge his daily calendar began to fill up again. As usual there gathered round him a group of sympathetic women who pushed his chair, admired his wit, discussed poetry and confided in him. Rosamond Lehmann was a most welcome visitor. Hayward had known her from her undergraduate days at Cambridge – when he went up she was in her final year at Girton College. With large almond-shaped eyes, pale skin and a tall slender figure, she possessed 'a magnetic sexuality'.[361] She was one of the beauties of her generation and well aware of the devastating effect of her looks – she sometimes frightened herself by the power she wielded and the 'frightful jealousy' that men's wives often felt towards her. Eliot said that she was the most beautiful woman he had ever seen and Hayward, always ready to be impressed, was equally struck. She looked on Hayward as literary adviser as well as friend, and her letters to him were full of questions about her latest novels. Soon, however, she turned to personal matters and the problems of her marriage to Wogan Philipps. 'I *knew* you were the one person to help me.' When Wogan returned from Spain in 1941 she found herself deserted. She was near to breakdown and once again decided to call on Hayward for help. His sympathetic words helped bring her back from despair – later he was to perform the same role for both Eliot and Kathleen Raine. When Rosamond visited him again in October 1942, with another new lover, the handsome poet Cecil Day Lewis, she remembered how much he had helped her: 'You were so kind, I was so grateful. But when you said I would be put together again one day, I thought how kind you were, but

I *knew* it would never be so. I thought I was done for: and so I was for months, months, months.'[362] A year later she was still recalling how he had restored her, writing letters in her flowing hand on her characteristic royal-blue writing paper, peppered with endearments such as 'John darling', and 'Darling John I long to see you'.

> John, you are neither straw nor shadow, but a solid ripe shock of wheat garnered in gentle perpetual sunshine. You'll never know what a hope you gave me that I wasn't some kind of monster ... I trusted you because you didn't give me any false comfort at a time when most people were getting it wrong one way or another![363]

Behind the blunt honesty of his comments there was, as his confidantes knew, real sympathy.

Not only beautiful young women such as Rosamond Lehmann and, later, Kathleen Raine confided in him and and beat their way to his door. Through Victor, Hayward got to know his sister the naturalist Miriam Rothschild, who lived not far away at Ashton Wold near Oundle. She recalled meeting him frequently and how he swished into the Common Room at the Hall in his wheelchair, with his elongated face typical of spinal illness, his academic way of talking and his donnish wit. They discussed poetry, and especially *Love's Helicon*, and she broke up the monotony of his Cambridge life with invitations to her home. Gabriele Annan, the wife of Noel Annan, the Provost of King's, was a close friend who loved to tease him; Vera Birch, the wife of another King's don, was a regular and kind pusher. Paradoxically, the man who revelled in gossip and scandal was entirely discreet in his dealings with his women friends. Graham Greene had a dream that amounted to an erotic fantasy, or perhaps a nightmare, that Hayward was carefully keeping notes of all these shared intimacies ready for publication – but in fact, of course, no such memoir existed.

After the publication of *Love's Helicon* Hayward was in a low state as he faced another winter at the Hall and felt the responsibilities of his housekeeper role weighing heavily upon him. Throughout the spring and summer of 1940 he had waited impatiently for the 'third poem in the trilogy' from Eliot. In its place he had received in June five early drafts of 'East Coker' which Eliot had found and mailed for the Archives: 'I may as well send you the lot,' he wrote. Eliot clearly wanted his manuscripts and drafts kept as his memorial and had chosen Hayward as the custodian of his reputation. In August Hayward explained Eliot's delay: 'ARP duties have kept him at the stirrup pump after office hours.'[364] But by November Hayward felt that it was 'extremely unlikely' that anything could be produced by the New Year. In fact Eliot did start work on the third poem as *Points of View* was being edited in December 1940, but he sympathised with Hayward's gloom and frustration: 'I am also in a low mood ... working on a poem to follow "East Coker" and at this stage it seems to be very unpromising ... but I am still more depressed by the growing isolation of your Cambridge life ...'[365] For the last entry in his 1940 calendar Hayward wrote simply: 'So ends a year of sorrow.'

Poetry and War

When icicles hang by the wall,
And Tom the typist blows his nail,
O then comes in the sweet o' the year
With the stirrup pump in the frozen pail ...[366]

So Eliot wrote in midwinter 1941 from the 'Shamblies' in Surrey. There
was no hot water and in this weather 'every house becomes either a sink
or a sieve'. It was just as bleak in Cambridge as Hayward endured the
second winter of his exile. Both men felt the cold acutely. 'It is enough
to make the bittern boom, grumbled Hayward to Anne Ridler.'[367] The
fingers of his left hand turned numb and blue. Eliot advised him to wear
a pair of mittens when he typed, like Geoffrey Faber. To try to keep
warm he designed his own garment of Harris tweed, a kind of 'moujik's
blouson', buttoning at the neck with five huge buttons down the front
and blouse-like sleeves tight at the wrist. He thought it made him look
a bit like a cartoon version of Uncle Joe Stalin. From his windows he
looked out onto a desolate scene: 'a white blanket of lawn fringed with
black skeletons of trees in which the birds sit and shiver all day long'.[368]

Then, just at this bleak point, came the news that he had been hoping
for for so long: 'The best possible beginning of another year was
marked by the arrival on January 1st of the typescript of the first draft
of the third poem of Tom's trilogy' – 'The Dry Salvages':

No warning that it was even begun – which confirms what I said
about the Master's ability to strike quickly once the iron is hot. It
is a superb piece – finer, I think, than its predecessors. I attribute
its excellence to the beauty of the marine imagery, which provides
a haunting background to the recurrent 'Time Past – Time
Present' theme. And you know, probably better than I do, with
what nostalgic longing the sea affects Tom's sensibility ...[369]

This was the first chance that he had had to be involved in the editorial
work in *Four Quartets* from the earliest stage; he had seen 'Burnt

Norton' only in the final form for the printer, and he had not seen or commented on 'East Coker' until its third draft. He could reassure the ever-doubtful Eliot of the worth of his poem as it developed – as Eliot became less and less confident, Hayward felt even more sure that each piece was better than the last.

They worked on 'The Dry Salvages' at speed. By 4 January, only three days after seeing the draft for the first time, Eliot had already received Hayward's comments and was responding to his suggestions:

> Thank you very much for your helpful letter, and its promptitude: I was surprised at hearing from you so soon. There are some, perhaps most of your suggestions which I accept at once; some which I must think about; some which my first impulse is to reject. That is the normal and proper mixture.

To Eliot Hayward was the arbiter of English correctness: as an American by birth, Eliot relied on his friend's scholarship and knowledge of English idiom and grammar. Part of Hayward's role was to act as a representative British reader and filter out any Americanisms that might be unclear or confusing. Work started with the title; Hayward wondered whether 'dry salvages' was a phrase he did not know. Was there perhaps a half-remembered distinction between dry salvage and wet salvage, he asked. (The Dry Salvages are, in fact, dangerous rocks off the coast of Massachusetts where Eliot sailed as a boy.) Eliot replied that he was concerned by his friend's ignorance of American geography: 'It doesn't matter that it should be obscure, but if it is going to lead people quite on the wrong track, then something must be done ... please advise.' Although Eliot disliked the idea of a note of explanation he added it under the the title. Hayward next questioned what a 'groaner' could be, having failed to find it in his dictionary. Eliot told him it was the New England word for a whistling buoy. 'A pretty problem,' he added. But when Hayward suggested 'warning groaner', thinking that the noun could be explained by its epithet, Eliot stood firm. 'Heaving groaner' stayed – but, again, was glossed under the title.

The relationship was often that of two scholars and friends working together to find the solution to a knotty verbal problem. In the final section of the poem Hayward pointed out the error of 'haruspicate with sand'. (The obscure verb 'haruspicate' means to divine using entrails.) Eliot meekly concurred, but suggested, bizarrely, 'haruspicate with guts', which again met with disapproval:

No, I don't think 'with guts' is quite nice! Isn't it a pleonasm anyhow? I should not like to lose the conjunction of horoscope – haruspicate: on the other hand (speaking as a coscinomancer) I should like to keep 'sand' (or sieves). I think you should be able to find a solution without great difficulty. But let me know if the change raises more trouble than I envisage.[370]

'Coscinomancer' was naturally the trump card – and a trump card played with disarming humour. Eliot responded with the word 'scry', which has a primary sense of seeing the future through a crystal, but an older obsolete sense of sifting.[371] Thus the final 'haruspicate or scry' came into being, just about preserving the allusion to sand that Hayward liked.

Secretly Hayward felt that Eliot's verse could be dogmatic and prosy and he tried to remove what his fellow-commentator Geoffrey Faber called 'lecture-stigmata'. He pencilled a query against: 'It seems, as one becomes older, / One has to repeat the same thing in a different way / And risk being tedious.' Eliot changed the lines to read: 'It seems, as one becomes older, / That the past has another pattern ...' After Hayward questioned the wooden clause 'I have suggested also', Eliot substituted, 'I have said before'. Hayward offered 'not merely' for 'I don't mean': Eliot cut the personal pronoun. On 12 February 1941 he wrote that he had made a number of alterations 'incorporating most of your suggestions and some from Geoffrey [Faber]', and announced that 'The Dry Salvages' would be published in ten days' time. It duly appeared in the *New English Weekly* on 27 February 1941 – less than two months after Hayward had seen the first draft. On 5 March he sent his congratulations on 'a most splendid piece' which he found 'a most moving and disturbing and consoling poem'.[372] Later in the year Eliot inscribed Hayward's copy with scrupulous if not entirely generous accuracy: 'For John Hayward whose suggestions somewhat altered this poem. Eliot 10 ix 41.'

For some time Hayward had derived a small but steady income from teaching once a fortnight at Longstowe Hall, a private girls' finishing school set in a mock-Tudor mansion near Cambridge. Soon the girls began to come in ones and twos to the Hall. (The young Shirley Williams was one of his pupils.) He loved teaching the 'pretty scions of the nobility and gentry' – the Brigits, Sonias, Dawns, Dianas, Guineveres, Carolines and Hermiones – just as much as the money he earned. Soon after the publication of *Love's Helicon* he received a note from the Vice Governess – a title Hayward was especially fond of.[373] She wrote that she had decided to terminate his employment, as she could not possibly let her girls have contact with the editor of an anthology that contained 'such a farrago of lascivious obscenity'. Shaken, he put the letter aside until the following morning. When he read it again the handwriting puzzled him. Carefully checking it with previous letters from her, he found they did not match. Then a sudden thought struck. The young Gerald Wellesley, later to become 7th Duke of Wellington, had been billeted to the Hall. Hayward disliked his effete character and his evident homosexuality just as much as he hated his habit of spending long hours giggling at obscene words he had looked up in the dictionary. 'I never feel at ease with a middle-aged pansy with a smutty mind and a strictly cerebral interest in young male bodies,' he wrote to Eliot. Wellesley's enforced companionship was a real trial of Hayward's patience. His distracting presence underlined Eliot's signifi-cant absence.

Hayward compared the handwriting to Wellesley's – and there was a complete match. For a couple of days he did and said nothing. Then a telegram arrived at Merton Hall which read: 'LORD GERALD WELLES-LEY stop AM IN RATHER A FIX stop COMING TO STAY NEXT WEEK stop PADDY BRODIE.' (Brodie was an outrageously dissolute character who served as one of the models for the Hon. Miles Malpractice in Evelyn Waugh's *Vile Bodies*.) His presence at the Hall would be dangerously embarrassing for Wellesley's reputation. After the telegram's arrival there was a knock on Hayward's door. It was Wellesley, who had come to say that, very inconveniently, urgent family business meant that he had to take leave for a week or two. And there the matter rested. When Wellesley returned to the Hall neither ever mentioned the Vice Governess of Longstowe or Paddy Brodie again. A month later, follow-ing an argument with Victor Rothschild about the rent, 'a clash of Bullion against Blood', as Hayward put it, Wellesley left.

Spring 1941 was a difficult time at Merton Hall. The weather contin-ued cold and the Hall freezing. It was impossible to get razor blades, and in his letters Hayward went into extreme and tedious detail about ways of sharpening old blades on a bezoar stone. Cigarettes were very expensive and drink almost unobtainable. As Easter approached he felt more keenly the lack of companionship: 'In other times we should be spending a happy Easter Evening together. I wish them to return for they would bring you with them,' he wrote nostalgically. Then in March came the news that Virginia Woolf had drowned herself in the Ouse: within little more than a year James Joyce, W. B. Yeats and Virginia Woolf had all died. Hayward wrote consolingly to Eliot and lamented his loss of 'an old and dear friend', adding, 'we've all lost something by her death'.[374] Eliot replied that he had in fact not known her writing very well but had felt as if she were part of the family. She was a 'kind of pin' holding together a whole network of people; after her death he faced 'social isolation with the prospect of becoming a ghost in an alien, plebeian and formless society'.[375]

'The times are dark and difficult and disturbing,' wrote Hayward in a letter carefully dated St George's Day. Or, in doggerel:

> This is the most 'orrible world ever made,
> Nuffink but Hairraid after Hairraid:
> Where it's all goin' to finish I simply don't know
> And there's plenty more comin' afore we're through ...[376]

Eliot shared his friend's gloom; the war seemed to be dragging on with no end in sight and he feared civilisation 'was going to pot whatever happens'. But, he added, nothing could be worse than a world run by Germans. The cold weather finally broke in late April, but the onset of summer only pointed the contrast between the brilliance of the blue skies and the darkness of Hayward's mood: 'I lead a futile life ... the soul languishes and I blame myself for allowing this to happen – even though the caged bird cannot always sing to Heaven.'[377] Initially he had welcomed the thought of American intervention in the war, but as the prospect became more likely he confided that he feared a terrible Armageddon: 'I foresee America in the war, as least as a naval belligerent, and then Japan will follow and the whole world will be consumed.'[378] May brought news of a personal loss as Peter Quennell told of the damage that the bombs had done to Swan Court. Now Hayward felt himself truly one of 'the great army of the homeless'. He made a trip to London to see how bad things were and to retrieve some of his belongings. The flat was not as damaged as he had feared but seemed 'lifeless, unreal and somehow like a dead person'. But it was the sight, after nearly two years away, of 'dear old Londinium that stabbed me through the heart'.[379] And then he found out that the bombs had blown away in a single night the entire warehouse stocks of his editions of Donne and Swift, along with *Love's Helicon*.

Eliot came to stay at the Hall for the long weekend of the Whitsun holiday and Hayward continued to worry about his visitor's health:

> He was in bed again last week with his fourth feverish cold of 1940–1941 and I regret to say that he looks with [it] very haggard and washed-out and dispirited. For the last two afternoons he has simply gone to sleep on my bed ... Like you, I wish there was more chance than there seems to be of his new book of poems appearing before the late autumn ... He wants if possible to complete the cycle with a fourth poem – Earth, Air, Water, *Fire* – and has got as far as making a rough, preliminary draft. I take it as a good sign that he is dissatisfied with what he has already done. We discussed all this over the dregs of the inestimable hair-oil, which I had husbanded against his coming.[380]

'Hair-oil' was Bina Gardens code for the old Kentucky whisky that Morley sent to a few select friends every Christmas. 'At this period almost any form of alcoholic liquid, however nauseating, was priceless.'[381] Perhaps it helped.

In July as 'Little Gidding' began to take shape in his mind, Eliot relied heavily on Hayward to dispel his chronic anxiety. A draft was sent on 7 July with more than the normal high levels of concern. 'You will understand my being worried and diffident and depressed at this writing: I do not want ANY comments at this stage. I want to do more polishing myself before I receive hints from the Critick.' He was unsure a week later, on the 14th: the problem was 'not so much whether it is as good as the others (I am pretty sure it is not) but whether it is good enough to keep company with them to complete the shape'. By the 28th he was even more despairing but still needed Hayward's advice, adding that now he wanted from his critic general impressions as well as detailed comment. Eliot felt that he had improved the poem a little, but 'if it is uninspired as I fear it is, it must just be put away and forgotten'. Hayward, on the other hand, was determined to get the poem published as soon as possible: 'My own view is that in these times the less delay the better in bringing into the world the kind of work that consolidates one's faith in the continuity of thought and sensibility when heaven is falling and the earth's foundations fail.'[382]

Always tactful when dealing with the sensitive business of editing, Hayward began his letter of 1 August with modest self-deprecation. After marking 700 examination scripts he felt that 'whatever critical faculty I possess is momentarily distempered by the work it has [had] to do in the past fortnight. So please bear this [in] mind ...' As usual, however, he was encouraging: 'I need hardly say that it has given me intense satisfaction and pleasure to read it even in its present unfinished condition.' He went on to reassure Eliot that 'Little Gidding' was just as good as the rest of the poem and that the only problems lay with the first paragraph of Part iii, and the very brief Part iv, which 'seems to me to break down'. All that was needed was limited revision and perhaps some rewriting.[383] He concluded, 'You *must not* discard it' – adding that Eliot's misgivings about the poem were 'doubtless exacerbated by the miserable time you have had with your teeth'. He signed the letter 'Love from yr. old creating critick: John.' But now, despite all Hayward's efforts, Eliot finally lost confidence in 'Little Gidding' as he had done with 'The Dry Salvages'. He was exhausted and strained by the Blitz in London and sleepless nights fire-watching – letters to Hayward often read like medical bulletins. He was also busy preparing an edition of Kipling and lacked the strength and the will to continue. Hayward confided to Frank Morley later in the year that Tom 'fears it is uninspired and mechanically repetitive of the earlier poems in the group'.[384] Hayward himself was still bracingly confident: 'There are, I think, weaknesses in sections of the poem which could be remedied without much labour. As a whole it seems to me to [be] a fine confirmation of the old tag – *finis coronat opus*.'[385] Nevertheless, he had to wait for nearly a year before he heard any more news of the poem.

The situation at the Hall was not improved by the arrival in October 1941 of Barbara Rothschild's mother, Mary Hutchinson, her sick husband St John ('Jack') Hutchinson and a nurse. Jack Hutchinson had had an illustrious career as a barrister, but now a stroke had left him incapacitated and unable to read. Together with all their furniture and pictures, they had to be installed and all this added to the pressure on Hayward. He felt momentary despair about the whole situation. As he wrote to Eliot, 'I have no privacy, people just bursting in on me whether I'm dressing or pissing! ... these are the occasions *entre nous* when I feel my helplessness, my relative powerlessness to escape (even for a cleansing walk) most keenly.'[386] It was at this moment that John Gielgud, giving ENSA shows at nearby RAF bases with Beatrice Lillie, went to King's to hear the organist Boris Ord give a recital. While he waited for the music to begin, in the chapel lit by a single candle, a man in a wheelchair was wheeled up the aisle and parked opposite his pew. Gielgud immediately recognised his prep school friend and fellow cricket-scorer from twenty years back. He spoke a few embarrassed words to him. After the concert, as he left, he turned and saw Hayward's chair wheels getting caught in the step of the chapel and its occupant being tipped out on to the ground. He was shocked to see the 'dreadful curve of his misshapen back and shoulders' as Hayward was helped back into his chair, cursing furiously. The next day, by chance, Gielgud visited Merton Hall to see Mary Hutchinson's daughter-in-law Peggy Ashcroft and was surprised to find that Hayward was staying there. Peggy told Gielgud that his schoolfriend was extremely randy and likely to make passes at any pretty girl who took him out in his chair. When they met in Hayward's flat they reminisced about Hillside, but Gielgud found his friend terribly changed; he had become 'bitter and rancid'.[387] He saw Hayward now as 'a tragic and brilliant creature'.

There was one other correspondent to whom Hayward wrote regularly during the first years of the war: Anne Ridler. He had got to know her through Faber's where she had worked as a secretary and then as assistant to Eliot, when she had presented him with an immaculate typescript of *Noctes*. He had fallen so deeply for the silver-tongued voice he heard over the telephone that he began to ring Museum 9543, the familiar Faber number, just to hear it. In 1940 she had left with her husband Vivian to live in Oxford and write poetry. Hayward had actually met her only once, but throughout the war he retained an image of her as an almost angelic figure: 'a very radiant gentle-eyed creature with a nice large mouth', wearing a long surtout of cloth of gold. His wartime letters to her are not spiced with witty anecdotes and the male humour he shared with Eliot and Morley, but are more intimate and honest. With her he could discuss marriage and sex, his feelings of ageing, his loneliness and religion and even his disability. He was able to confide his deepest unhappiness.

Hayward's knowledge that Anne was happily married gave him licence to write such personal and loving letters; he felt she was a wonderful correspondent who put his own efforts into the shade. Soon she began to send him her poetry which he became genuinely enthusiastic about: 'There is Eliot, then Auden, then YOO!' He learned some of his favourites, including 'Remember Him', about her fears for her soldier-husband. Inevitably, he became her editor and began to send back his usual perceptive, discreet commentaries. She dedicated 'Exile' to him. It was a continuation of their letter-writing – the title itself was a word he used constantly about his time in Cambridge: 'Exile you say is a sympathetic theme,' the poem begins. She reminds him of their long silence: 'You and I have not exchanged a spoken syllable thirty months and more' – before writing about the Dark Ages of the past into which they had fallen. But she goes on to argue that he is not really a sad exile at all, but at the heart of things.

> You, no doubt of it, live at the centre
> And with the sensations of darkness, work
> The effects of light, by bitter practice. [388]

Furthermore, because he has been used to pain, he is able not merely to survive, but also to make best use of hardship. The reference to his muscular dystrophy is tactful and sympathetic; the patient transformed into the critic wielding the surgeon's knife.

> Deprivation to the patient skilful
> Is a means to make new.
> This was a lesson you had by heart,
> Long ago, I suppose,
> And long learnt in what respects
> Writing may gain on speech: worked with
> Wit and warmth with scorn a sharp knife …[389]

Her natural kindness was something that Hayward lacked and needed in the long blacked-out evenings at Merton Hall. When he reached what he called 'the middle of the path', his thirty-fifth birthday, his only card came from Anne Ridler. 'You've done more, truly, than anyone at a distance to solace and sweeten and inspire during my long exile,' he wrote.[390] For the first time he began to think about the single state that seemed to be his destiny. Marriage was the ideal to which he aspired. He held up examples of the two spinster secretaries, Miss Swann at Faber's and Miss Flack at the Hall, as awful warnings and described the pull of marriage.[391] The 'craving not to be left on one's lonely branch' did not have its ultimate source in a wish to avoid illicit sex, or the desire for a bedfellow or children, or even to find a helpmate. The real impulse was 'the search for Plato's other half' which made a human complete. It was, he explained, a kind of return to childhood with its re-creation of a world of security, sympathy, forgiveness and intimacy. Even the best friendship could not match these. On one issue, however, they could not agree. Anne Ridler was a devout Christian:

Hayward was an equally devout atheist. 'I have no faith and I am not troubled by the lack of it,' he wrote to her and went on to quote his favourite Rochester's dying words to Bishop Burnet: 'They are happy that believed, for it is not in every man's power.'[392] But he went on to say, in the rarest of confessional moods, 'I suppose my inexplicable disability may have something to do with the failure of belief.'

In autumn 1941 Hayward met, and fell for, a very different kind of woman – 'one of those tantalisingly beautiful American brunettes with a poise that would make a performing sea-lion jealous'.[393] She was Catherine Walston, an American friend of Barbara Rothschild. With her Lauren Bacall profile, high cheekbones and dark auburn hair, she had the kind of looks that turned men's heads in the street – 'sans merci but so belle', according to Malcolm Muggeridge. She was married to the landowner, farmer and, later, Labour peer Harry Walston, and lived, according to Evelyn Waugh, at Newton Hall near Cambridge 'in great magnificence with a domestic chaplain, butlers in black coats and groaning tables of delicatessen'.[394] Hayward's letters to her are larded with statements of slavish devotion and reflect a playful love affair. He addressed her as 'my darling' and peppered his correspondence with sentimental flattery. 'I love you dearly ...' 'You write the most enchanting love letters ...' On writing paper headed 'Ambassade de France', he began, 'The indiscreeter the paper on which we correspond – the better: our love must never be proclaimed ...'[395] Behind the joking he was deeply attracted. He implored her to visit more often, was upset when she seemed to have forgotten him and charmed by the way in which she seemed at once personal and detached. He loved it too when she squatted barefoot on his floor at Merton Hall and gazed quizzically up at him. 'I feel very secure and cosy in your affection,' he wrote to her after the war.[396] She was a younger, seductive version of Ottoline – and indeed he addressed her 'my dear patroness'. However, if Hayward played the game of being the courtly lover, her 'très loyal serviteur', Graham Greene, was the real thing. He got to know Catherine in 1946 when she wrote asking if he would be her godfather when she was received into the Catholic Church. He accepted and very soon godfather and goddaughter began an affair that lasted for four and a half years, linking their shared devotion to sex and Catholicism in an unusual challenge to 'commit adultery behind every high altar in Italy'.[397]

12

Exile

The Cambridge of Hayward's undergraduate days had vanished. Now it seemed to him like an armed camp and he felt like a ghostly intruder in the streets and colleges of the city he remembered from nearly twenty years before. The population had doubled since the war began. Despatch riders rushed about on their errands – *Vogue* magazine remarked that you were more likely to be knocked down in Trumpington Street by a jeep than by a bicycle. The stained glass of the Chapel had been removed and windows blacked out. Camouflaged lorries, sandbags and barbed wire clogged the streets. The Divinity Schools had become the Army Recruiting Centre, the lawns of Emmanuel College had been dug up for Victory and Ridley's Walk bordered with cabbages. The Pitt Club had given up gastronomy for a few rich undergraduates to become a British Restaurant feeding 900 people a day in the dog days of August Hayward liked to lie reading by the Backs and was distracted by pretty bare-thighed '*jeunes sportives*' and by 'Rabelaisian scenes' of coupling around him.

New faces turned up on the streets and in the colleges. Some seventeen-year-olds came up for a year's study before going off to join the Forces. Shops took advantage of the reappearance of youth by hopefully dusting off their prewar stock; stationers' windows once again displayed engraved cards and crested college notepaper; tobacco jars and hookahs filled the tobacconists' windows and striped college blazers brightened up the outfitters. Snobbishly Hayward was appalled by the way Cambridge had been taken over by the barbarians. Now the quiet courts of the colleges were full of '2000 spotty faces besides much cattle from LSE, Bedford College, along with larking tommies, ogling misses and broad-bottomed saucy amazons in blue and khaki uniforms'.[398] 'Bare and hairy-legged' Civil Service typists gossiped and shouted from college windows, smirking at him while keeping up 'an incessant aimless twitter'. 'The great seat of Learning is given over to the readers of Penguins and Pelicans and to the shameless pranks of the Wuggas and the Wux-Ho-s.'[399] ('Wux' was the name of two gods in

Eliot's fantasy kingdom of King Bolo and became a running joke between Hayward and Eliot. The correct response to the greeting 'Wux-ho!' was, Eliot wrote, 'Arse-ho!')

At Merton Hall, as the constant stream of servants and workmen were released for war service, their replacements had to be interviewed and appointed by an increasingly frustrated Hayward. 'Plumbers, boiler-makers, electricians, billeting officers, new gardeners, new chars, removal men, picture hangers, coke deliverers, gas inspectors and fire wardens' – all had to be seen and given orders. He was annoyed by the absence of Victor Rothschild and the total lack of interest he and his wife seemed to show in what was happening at the Hall. To add to his concerns the surveyor for Merton College told him that the concussive effect of bombing would certainly destroy the ancient building. He was also frustrated by wartime Cambridge, by the complacency of university dons and by 'scoundrel' taxi drivers who always overcharged him.

When, like most people in Britain, Hayward tuned in to the nine o'clock news on the wireless to listen to tantalisingly vague accounts of attacks and counter-attacks, he could not understand what was going on and was frustrated by the war's lack of progress. Increasingly the clichés of wartime broadcasting annoyed him: 'There has never been a time of such catchpenny phrases.'[400] He grew tired of hearing of the Liberty that was Dearer than Life itself, of the Voice of Democracy, the Common Effort, the War Effort and of Finally Attaining the Ultimate Victory. He was saddened when 'raiders in the vicinity' prevented him from hearing Eliot broadcast on the wireless, and very much missed hearing the familiar tones – 'the modulated croak of the Possum being one of my favourite ethereal voices'.[401]

After the raids of the previous autumn, there came in 1942 an eerie period of suspended animation in Cambridge. Hayward wrote to his friend Lord Kinross, 'We're going through a bad patch – like 1917 in the last war when the old way of life has gone for good and a new way, with all that it should promise and inspire one to toil for, has not yet become plain.'[402] There was worrying news too from the Far East. On 15 February in Singapore, the British force of 60,000 troops surrendered to the Japanese. 'I write in mid-February, the dykes full of snow-water as the heart is full of tears – Singapore fallen and the German battle-cruisers triumphant,' Hayward wrote to Morley.[403] He was especially fearful as his sister Diana, her husband and their four-month-old twins were there. In fact she and the children had managed to get on one of the last boats to leave the island, but her husband was taken prisoner by the Japanese. She wrote her brother a letter enclosing a poem expressing her fears: 'Far East'.

> So far away;
> A thousand oceans, a thousand days and nights,
> A thousand bitter nights.
> No word or sign; nothing to measure the long hours;
> The distant shore.
> O God keep warm his heart;
> Sharper than death was this which parted love
> Before its time,
> And left a silence full of sad surmise.[404]

Sometimes Hayward was able to view events in Cambridge as comic opera: 'The two following nights we put up a barrage. Such larks! The sky lit up by large tomato-coloured petards and much popping and rattling behind the house.'[405] A raid later in August, however, came uncomfortably close when 'bombs fell by night killing three people (including the inevitable poor widow huddling in her basement), blowing my barber's geraniums and windows into Jesus Lane, blasting the Union and the ADC [Theatre] …'[406] In Sussex, meanwhile, Eliot was very concerned about the bombing raids over Cambridge and Hayward 'sticking them out in that very feeble old house'.[407]

King's became the HQ of the 51 Division, its courts filled with American soldiers, its lawns strung with telephone wires and field wireless posts covered with branches. Day and night the streets were full of hordes of 'lascivious-eyed' Americans who flirted with the girls and drank the pubs dry within an hour of opening time. The British soldiery was no better. Hayward loathed the way that members of the BEF ('Being Extremely Forward') propositioned women in the streets and dark alleys of Cambridge, but wrote that 'soldiering and fucking had always gone hand in hand'.[408] Even the site of the ordinary British Tommy with a well-thumbed Penguin in his hand made Hayward fear for the future: 'The sixpenny Penguin edition is a serious menace to the livelihoods of authors, publishers and booksellers alike,'[409] he thought. (It was a view he had to reconsider later when he himself became a best-selling Penguin author.) He was dismayed, too, as he wrote later to Eliot, by the literary scene, which he dismissed as 'a rather threadbare and grubby group of young men and women – foreigners, invalids, conscientious objectors and similar scourings of a wartime intelligentsia ... who together form a somewhat seedy avant-garde of literature and the arts who publish small brochures called new leanings ahead, or VIGOUR, or PIFFLE'.[410] Their fault, it seemed to him, was less to do with their writing and more to do with the fact that they were floating around Cambridge looking as if they did not know the war was happening.

Visits from the novelist and poet Stevie Smith were welcome interruptions. Like so many of his friendships, this one had started with a book. When her *Novel on Yellow Paper* was published in 1936 she was almost unknown. Hayward had written an enthusiastic review in the *New York Sun* and a personal note to the young author, thanking her for 'the intense and continuous pleasure' she had given him. 'Your praise encourages me to go on,'[411] she had replied and soon they arranged to meet at Jonathan Cape's. In January 1942 she confided that she was 'really in an awful stew' about the book she was preparing for publication. She felt like sending all her poems and an envelope full of drawings for him to sort out before she visited him. In April more advice was needed when she asked whether an 'obscene' poem she had written should go in – 'I don't want to be an obscene poet though the word thrills me to death ...'[412] He advised against. In August she was in Cambridge visiting the Rothschild exhibition that Hayward had organised. She wrote to say how very impressed she was with the sherry and the 'glossy' good looks of Lord Rothschild.

By that time she was embarked on her next novel *The Holiday* in which she was including all her friends' conversations, and looked forward to seeing Hayward, 'so that I can put some of yours in, heigh ho'. Meanwhile she wanted help with a highbrow piece she was commissioned to write as a Christmas article. Gradually letters between them became much more playful, beginning, 'Well John Dear'. She told him she was consumed with envy of the 'Oyls' daughters' he taught and threatened to let her hair down and join his class: 'I can't pretend my Pop was an Oyl ... Would you take me, I'm unlettered, but ambitious. I do think your handwriting is beautiful.'[413] When he could not meet her he sent 'Peevy' as an apology:

> Oh dear I feel ever so grievy –
> Have to lunch elsewhere and can't meet Stevie!
> (No wonder they only provide a fork,
> The cutting edge, of course, will be Stevie's tork!).[414]

All this badinage, however, could not disguise Hayward's longing for old friends and his nostalgia for the city that he felt was home: London: 'In these canicular days I have a Londoner's nostalgia for the smell of hot pavements cooling down at midnight; even more perhaps for that puff of hot wind which greeted one in the banlieu after motoring in from the country.'[415]

Eliot's friends were concerned about his lack of progress with 'Little Gidding'; it was nearly a year since they had heard anything. Hayward confided to Morley in July that despite some tactful feelers about the poem's progress he had heard nothing and feared Eliot would 'not get down to it again before the autumn'. Still worried that he might only produce an 'elegant parody' of the earlier poems, Eliot needed more time to allow the material to 'ferment and mature'.[416] So it was with delight and surprise that Hayward opened Eliot's letter of 17 August 1942 announcing a reworking of Part ii, the 'centre of weakness' of the poem. As usual Eliot was full of self-doubt, arguing that if that section was not good enough 'the poem must simply be allowed to disintegrate'. He therefore submitted it 'with some trepidation'. Hayward replied reassuringly on the 20th in a letter that gave 'great satisfaction'. A week later Eliot sent another revision of Parts ii and iii, noting that 'in several cases I have followed your advice negatively if not positively'. He ended: 'Humbly awaiting your further advice and thanking you for various favours. T. P.' ['Tom Possum']. The nicknames helped to take the sting out of Hayward's criticism: it became much less of a personal critique and much more of an ironic game, played to strict rules, between an eighteenth-century 'critick' and the Noble Possum.

   In September and October letters flew between the two men as the poem took shape. Eliot acknowledged the help on 2 September. 'According to my figures, I have altered nine passages according to your suggestions, rejected six suggestions and remained uncertain about two others.' He wrote further to Hayward about the poem five times, on 3rd, 7th and 19th of September, and on 10th and 20th of October. When he sent the 'final' version he was still unsure: 'I am still unsatisfied ... But I think there is a point beyond which one cannot go without sacrifice of meaning to euphony, and I think I have reached it ... to spend much more time on this poem might be dangerous.' He was uncharacteristically effusive: 'I cannot find words to express a proper manifestation of my gratitude for your invaluable assistance.' But even after the poem had been printed in the *New English Weekly* he still hesitated: 'But are you still assured that is proper to speak of a hindrance <u>between</u> two termini? I have definitely accepted your THAT. If you notice any other blemishes in the printed text please communicate your views.'[417] (As a stickler for grammar Hayward had picked up Eliot's technically incorrect use of the relative pronoun 'which'.) The final change came in the very last line of the poem. The draft read, 'And the fire and the rose are the same'. Hayward suggested 'as one'. 'Very well then, "And the fire and the rose are one",' Eliot replied on 7 September, but crucially dropping 'as'. His deference to Hayward's suggestion made a fitting end to their labour. Hayward literally had the last word of the poem – but Eliot modified it.

Hayward had helped to shape 'Little Gidding' in a more detailed and substantive way than he had the other three poems. Even the title emerged from their discussions: Eliot had suggested 'Kensington Quartets', linking it to the 'Gloucester Road Period' in the 1930s when he was staying in his hide-out with Father Cheetham. Hayward rejected this as too private a reference. 'I see your objection to Kensington,' conceded Eliot. (After all the fuss about the title, he was amused by a French reviewer who decided 'Little Gidding' 'doit être le nom d'un petit garçon très cher à M. Eliot ...')[418] Eliot had to justify and sometimes explain his meaning in the face of the keenest scrutiny. Hayward's loyal support for the poem continued after it was published when a luke-warm review upset Eliot. 'I have long ago despaired of *The Times Literary Supplement*'s ability to review anything well except books about fly-fishing,' Hayward condoled.[419]

Just as Eliot had turned to Ezra Pound to help him edit *The Waste Land*, so he now turned to another friend. Of course, Hayward's comments did not alter *Four Quartets* in the radical way that Pound's altered *The Waste Land*, but they made Eliot rethink and rework the poem – if Pound was the surgeon, performing, as he called it, 'the caesarian operation', Hayward was the candid friend. His suggestions were always made in tactful pencil, often merely a line or a small cross, and his comments in their letters are made with disarming humour within the context of encouragement and praise. Schoolboy puns lightened their discussions and lowered the temperature of Eliot's anxiety and made it easier for him to accept corrections to 'Dry Sandwiches' and 'West Croaker'. Without that *Four Quartets* might well not have seen the light of day: 'One thing in particular was most gratifying to

Tom: the taste and skill with which Hayward criticised his work as it was being composed,' wrote Sencourt.[420] According to Mary Trevelyan, Eliot depended on him as his literary critic 'and seldom felt quite easy in his mind about anything he had written unless John approved'.[421]

Hayward had little truck with Eliot's ideas of impersonality in poetry. He read *Four Quartets* as an autobiographical poem, just as he had read *The Waste Land* as a topographical poem based on London. He remembered how Emily Hale had come to England in 1934 and how Eliot and she had visited the manor house and its rose garden at Burnt Norton in the Cotswolds just before he met her at Bina Gardens. Hayward felt that 'Burnt Norton' reflected Eliot's newly-revived relationship. The sea imagery in 'The Dry Salvages' were memories of happy summer holidays he had spent as a boy sailing on the coast of Maine. The speaker in 'Little Gidding' patrolling the London streets in 1940 was Eliot the fire warden waiting for the all-clear to sound after an enemy air-raid. The passage about the mostly wasted twenty years 'entre deux guerres' reflected all the frustrations of his time in Kensington and the break-up of his marriage to Vivienne. And, as for the struggle to find the exactly right, but unpedantic, word – that was exactly what they were discussing together in letter after letter.

As soon as he opened his copy of the American edition Hayward read the prefatory note acknowledging 'a particular debt to Mr John Hayward for general criticism and specific suggestions during the composition of these poems'. Immediately he replied: 'I am more pleased and touched by your note of acknowledgement than I can say. It is by far the biggest compliment that I've ever had paid me and I am correspondingly delighted.'[422] Naturally, this did not prevent him from savaging the book as a disgraceful example of the art of the printer:

> The most wretchedly printed book produced by a firm with all the resources of modern typography I've seen ... The choice of type on cover and for the text is deplorable. The inking is bad. The layout is contemptible ... the imposition appalling ... However, these faults cannot abate my pleasure in having a copy of a wollum I've looked forward to for so long – or my gratitude to you for associating me with it ...[423]

Hayward's strictures proved accurate and in fact most of the copies had to be destroyed.

Of the poetry itself, however, Hayward had no doubt. 'I do not think there can be any doubt that they are the outstanding poems of the last decade,' he declared, hoping some copies 'could cross the dangerous seas' to his Swedish readers.[424] The apparent failure of the Auden/Spender group and the death of Yeats 'made T. S. E. Chief Bard'. And, he might have added, himself the closest friend, editor and critic. He told Helen Gardner, whose 'neat moustache was appropriate to her academic rank', that, of all his activities, his share in bringing *Four Quartets* to its conclusion gave him the most satisfaction.[425]

The winter of 1942/3 was the 'longest, coldest, and most dispiriting winter' Hayward could remember. As usual Christmas was a time for him to reflect and tot up his yearly accounts. There was little cheer in them. His difficulties with 'Beechingstoke', along with a feeling of his youth slowly draining away, led him to write to Anne Ridler on Christmas Eve that he was in 'a low state, aware of encroaching age and a kind of sorrowing dullness of spirit that comes over me when I think of how I have achieved nothing that has pleased me and that now I never shall'.[426] The mistletoe that the cook hung kindly over his desk was a sad reminder of what he was missing.

In early 1943 Stephen Spender posted Hayward a sequence of sonnets, written in the character of a monk. In June these '6 sketches for the kind consideration of John Hayward' arrived at Merton Hall. Spender intended to call them 'Spiritual Exercises' – a title Hayward thought pretentious. 'Only saints go in for spiritual exercises,' he said and suggested 'Explorations' as a better title.[427] (It eventually appeared as *Spiritual Explorations*.) He thought Spender's poems worthy, 'with a hard core of goodness in them', but sloppily written: 'Oh, how careless he is with words! And how often ignorant of their connotation! And how often he's stumped for the right word!'[428] The detailed work, or 'carpentry' as he liked to call it, Hayward found very troublesome. Nevertheless, he showed his usual tact in offering comments, his customary forensic analysis and his good ear for the sound of verse. Spender wrote to thank him for his 'invaluable suggestions'. 'No one has ever helped me so much, & so lucidly,' he added.[429] He came to rely on Hayward's judgement and in 1946 sent the typescript of his new collection, 'Poems of Dedication'. Despite the hard editorial task, Hayward liked Spender very much and saw him as 'a very patient victim of my pedantic criticism'.[430] Five years later Spender took his autobiography *World Within World* to his mentor. The comments caused him to scrap it and start all over again. When the book was finally published Spender inscribed the dedication copy: 'To John with love for this book and with gratitude for the book I scrapped as for his help and kindness always.'[431]

London was on Hayward's mind as he wrestled with 'Beechingstoke'.[432] He had written and revised about 30,000 words. The novel started with a panoramic view of the city and hoped that through a satiric gallery of characters it would dissect London life in all its complexity between the wars. Eliot had cast Hayward as its 'definitive social chronicler'.[433] He began with potted biographies of his leading aristocratic characters, the Baron Beechingstoke and his family, but soon became too tied down by tedious details of their family life. The satirical scenes were stronger. When the young hero Julian Carr Ransome goes to an embassy party he finds Baronne Falaise D'Anvers bearing down upon him, mangling Eliot …

> 'I am reading since yesterday,' she continued, beaming rapturously at a complete stranger who had momentarily got wedged between her and Julian, 'some poèmes which are quite wonderful.'
> Julian noticed with alarm signs of a recitation.
> 'April is a so cruel month
> Breeding pale lilacs out of the waste land …'[434]

She goes on to propose a party for Julian, 'the wonderful man Mr Eliot', and a few special *invités* and suggests that Julian can design the programme for the party with a cover of pale lilacs. This *femme de lettres* then asks 'Dee-ah Julian do you find the April so cruel?' to which he replies, 'Well it rather depends on what one means by cruel, doesn't it? It is certainly not as cold as it might be …' The portrait of the talentless poet Alwyn Twimble hits its target. He has published one slim volume printed on tinted paper, in Paris. Half in English, half in French, it is called 'Mon Coeur Ralenti'. Hayward's presentation of typists and lonely spinsters living in their London bed-sitter wasteland is much more sympathetic:

> Surplus women still eager with the hopes and desires of their age and sex, living in expectation of the hour that would never strike for them, and meanwhile working long hours in shops and offices, making small meals on gas rings, ironing and darning on Sunday

mornings ... always for them the cheaper seat at the cinema, the 'bargain' blouse, the silk stocking 'slightly faulty manufacture', the last bus rather than a taxi, the one often-refashioned evening dress, the full heart still unsatisfied ... In a thousand suites, flatlets and bed-sitting rooms they are turning in for the night ...[435]

Hayward continued to wrestle with 'Beechingstoke', but he found writing it very hard going. He had given his reason for this in a reply to one of Eliot's letters urging him to hurry up. It was the dilemma of the over-critical intellectual: 'By circumstance, I'm a pedant and a whale for accuracy and I can't decide whether to allow this training to help or hinder such inspiration as I possess. O Golly!'[436] He knew too that he would be judged without mercy by the highest of standards and felt the pressure of feminine competition: 'Timeo Virginia atque Dorothy Richardson.'[437] The chaos of wartime and life at the Hall made writing difficult for him, but he began to have serious doubts about his own ability. He promised to go on 'until I recognize an absolute failure of talent in myself' as he did not want to add any more rubbish to the "Great Literary Midden". By the end of 1942, however, Hayward's hopes for his *magnum opus* had, perhaps fortunately, come to nothing and he had to abandon it. He knew that 'Beechingstoke' was just not good enough and he was not the great writer he and his closest friends thought that he might become. 'If I had genius I should write at all costs. But I am a plodder caught in the toils of Diurnity.'[438] This was a sad moment of self-recognition. It was left to Anthony Powell to write the chronicle of the Thirties in his sequence *A Dance to the Music of Time* and, later, to include a portrait of Hayward as the dictatorial wheelchair-bound figure in *The Fisher King*.

Hayward was becoming an institution in Cambridge. When British *Vogue* – or 'Brogue' as it was known – decided to do a feature on the city he was picked out as one of its most well-known characters, 'running a salon' in his room at Merton Hall.[439] He met and was immediately impressed by the photographer, the startlingly beautiful Lee Miller in her uniform of war correspondent with the US Forces, and enjoyed being pictured with two attractive Newnham girls pushing his chair along the Backs. His social calendar began to fill with concerts at King's, with the London Philharmonic Orchestra, with pantomimes, visits to Arts Theatre films, including *Citizen Kane*, the first talkie he had seen, poetry readings and exhibitions of modern paintings at the

---

Fitzwilliam, followed by dinners with the Keeper of the Gallery. There were dances at the Young Ladies' Academy at Longstowe Hall, where he flirted with 'the bulk of the survivors of Tewkesbury and Flodden Field'. A university statute was rescinded to allow him the right to roam 'in his chariot or curricle' through college gardens. As an honorary guest he was taken glumly to see wartime propaganda films in Luton as part of the programme of the recently-founded CEMA (the Committee for the Encouragement of Music and the Arts) under the leadership of Maynard Keynes. George Kinnaird, who was in charge of Army Recreation, became a good friend and loyal pram-pusher.

Hayward also loved meeting the local aristocracy and relished their eccentricities. Through his 'new chum' George he got to know the FANY (First Aid Nursing Yeomanry) Diana 'Dasher' Heathcote of the Cottesmore, who kept her favourite hunter in her kitchen during the winter and serenaded it in the evening on the grand piano. After attending a godchild's wedding he visited Hinchinbrooke, the Huntingdonshire family home of the Earls of Sandwich since the time of Pepys, for a cup of tea. There he had 'the interesting experience of talking to a Sandwich and eating one at the same time'. Captain Jack Bambridge of Wimpole Hall, High Sheriff of Cambridgeshire and the husband of Rudyard Kipling's daughter, saw himself as an eighteenth-century squire and throughout the war, according to Hayward, kept two footmen dressed in buff livery and white gloves. The Captain was taken off his guard 'when I enquired, quite naturally, whether he kept a cold venison pasty in the high pew of his private chapel'. To Anne Ridler however, Hayward wrote that he lived a Cinderella-like existence, but promised that 'I like being alone and wrapped up in myself but really I'm not a selfish crusted bachelor.'[440]

Sir Edward 'Eddie' Marsh was a welcome newcomer to Cambridge in 1943. A close friend of Rupert Brooke, he had been Winston Churchill's private secretary for over twenty years and had edited *Georgian Poetry* from 1912 to 1922.[441] The septuagenarian scholar became a regular tea-time visitor to Merton Hall. Hayward, of course, was hostile to Georgian poetry and had written very critically of it. Now he seized the chance to convert Marsh to Eliot and modern verse by reading the opening section of 'The Dry Salvages' to him. As he read, he was pleased to see tears beginning to form in the old man's eyes. Eddie Marsh very much wanted to be useful and, as typists were unavailable, Hayward began to rely on him to write by hand the printer's copy of *Seventeenth Century Poetry*, an anthology he had been asked to do by Chatto and Windus. Through Marsh Hayward also got to know the poet Frances Cornford, the granddaughter of Charles Darwin, who soon began to bring drafts of her poetry for his comments. He also became friendly with the First World War poet Robert Nichols, whose brief moment of fame rested on verse that had been compared to Rupert Brooke's. Hayward listened to the 'effusions of Nichols, dressed in poetic garb in his yellow shirt and petunia velvet breeks', who spoke with pride of his contributions to 'English Poesy'. When 'Owd Bob' threatened to visit the Hall and bring his new play to read aloud, Hayward wrote to Eliot, 'As yet I have seen only the line for which he has rejected forty six variants. It is not a good line.'

In early 1943 came the long-awaited visit from Eliot. With childlike excitement Hayward carefully drew a map of the Hall so that his friend might make a secret entrance through the private side. The official reason for his visit was a student production of *The Family Reunion*, directed by Dadie Rylands. The play had disappointed at its West End opening in 1939 and closed after only six weeks; this was Eliot's first chance to see it again. So, despite dreading the fenland winter chills, on Saturday 13 February Eliot arrived in Cambridge. He joined Hayward, Mary Hutchinson, Helen Low and the handsome 'Ace of Bomber Command Pathfinders', Patrick Trench, in a party to see the revival at the Arts Theatre. A green light at the side of the stage shone during the performance to indicate the all-clear. If it changed to red the programme told everyone to go straight to the Cambridge Union shelter. Eliot immediately took to Trench who 'radiated charm and had women buzzing around him like mosquitoes' – but felt there was a strange sense of doom about him.

After the solemn London performance Eliot was surprised and delighted by the loud laughter of the student audience. Despite only three weeks of rehearsal and a young undergraduate cast, the production was a success. For Hayward, though, the real point of the weekend was the opportunity to meet Eliot again on his own. The reunion that he had anticipated so keenly, and for so long, did not disappoint: it was an evening, he wrote, 'as happy as any I have spent in exile'.[442] They slipped easily into the old Sunday night mood of prewar days and as they talked they revived the thought of living together after the war was over.

Hayward's happiness was short-lived. Three weeks later, in early

March, the news came to the Hall that Trench had disappeared whilst leading a bomber raid over Nuremberg. He and Hayward had dined together only the night before his last sortie. The following morning Hayward rang the airbase to find out more information, and was told Trench was classified as missing, but that there was no one more likely than he was to get out alive. In the afternoon a distraught Helen Low turned up and for four hours Hayward tried to comfort her. A few days later the news of Trench's death, aged twenty-five, was confirmed. Hayward preserved his memory in the dedication of *Seventeenth Century Poetry*: 'In Memoriam / Sodalis dilecti Patricii Trench.'[443] ('In memory of a special friend'.)

More bad news followed in the autumn. Every afternoon Hayward read to Jack Hutchinson and gradually became very fond of the old man, who seemed to be making a good recovery from his stroke. In late October Jack and his wife Mary spent a happy week away in London. When they returned he complained to Hayward of feeling 'liverish' but seemed otherwise fine. On Thursday his condition became much worse and a doctor was called. Another stroke followed and he lapsed into unconsciousness and died at 3 o'clock the following morning. 'It has been a distressing, distracting week and I still feel thrown out of gear,' wrote Hayward. Now the central office of the CEMA was installed in Jack's old rooms and Merton Hall became the base for this parent of the Arts Council which, to begin with, was run in amateur fashion. Hayward at first viewed it all as a silly nuisance and resented the idea of having to answer the telephone to 'elderly female visitors asking if arrangements had been made to rehearse sea-shanties in the Women's Institute at Helion Bumpstead'. He laughed at the prospect of every villager in the kingdom humming Beethoven's late quartets and detected something deeply patronising about schemes to provide music and poetry entertainment 'for the lower orders'.[444]

In public Hayward remained discreetly silent about the bitter quarrels at the Hall. From the beginning of the marriage Dadie Rylands had noted that there was scarcely a meal 'when tears were not shed with the soup'. There was talk of a separation in which Barbara would stay on at Merton and Victor in London. This would mean Hayward's eviction and the difficulties of finding another suitable place to live. He sent Eliot his sombre greeting: 'I share your desire for a quiet Christmas and wish you all the joy you may find within. I look for no joy without.'[445] Even the pleasures of traditional pantomime, which Hayward loved, could not be enjoyed that year. Dadie Rylands had composed a more highbrow Bloomsbury concoction of *Romeo and Juliet*, *Comus* and the Ballet Rambert. Hayward regretted the loss of traditional red-flannel knickers, sentimental songs and bawdy jokes, as did most of the town. Instead of taking the wholesome medicine of high culture, Hayward wore a false moustache and an opera hat that he borrowed from Victor and went to a fancy dress party as 'a Performing-Seal-Trainer en retraite'. But when he came to write his New Year message to Eliot he was a little more cheerful, looking forward to the last year of his exile and 'the beginning, perhaps of our domestic association'.[446] He was so excited he scarcely believed it could happen. 'I shall treasure all these things in my heart and not allow myself to place too much expectation in their fulfilment,' he wrote.[447]

Although Hayward hoped that the war would end in 1944, the future remained clouded. Victory, he thought, would only come at the cost of an enormous loss of life: 'I fear that great terrors and disasters await us in the New Year if ... the War in Europe is to be finished within another twelvemonth,'[448] he wrote. The heavy bombing of London frightened him as did the prospect of the invasion of France that he thought would begin soon after Easter. By April the incessant roar of aircraft by day and night was an 'unnerving reminder that the great and terrible embarkment must be near'.[449] The advent of the V bombs, or 'engines', as Hayward called them, added to his fears. Hitler, he was sure, doomed and cornered, would cause as much devastation as he possibly could. He hoped that Eliot would not be in London for these last desperate raids. Then in June came the news that the offices of Faber's had been hit and severely damaged by a buzz bomb which fell in the middle of Russell Square. The ceilings were down, windows broken and doors blown open, and the building, like the rest of the Square was in a horrible mess, but, luckily, no one was killed. Eliot told Hayward that he was not as frightened as most people there, but more struck by the 'nightmare of evil'.

The wet autumn found both men depressed about the future. Hayward looked gloomily from the Hall windows as the wind drove rain down in cold slanting showers and the last ragged flowers sprawled in the herbaceous borders.

I can only share your despondent prognosis of continuing distress, conflicting policies, and civil war. The future could hardly be less reassuring. My return out of exile will be no easy journey; my ultimate homecoming seems at present fearfully remote. But the cold dull days of November are perhaps no time to look forward. It is sufficient if one manages to keep warm while the sap runs down and survives a sixth hibernation.[450]

But there were encouraging signs. At last the blackout was lifting, and he was cheered by the company of lit windows 'which gave a pleasant reminder that people do live in houses after dark'.

University politics too suddenly became more interesting. Robert Nichols wrote to Eliot to canvass support for Hayward's being offered the King Edward VII Professorship of English at Cambridge to succeed Sir Arthur Quiller-Couch and spoke to Hayward full of enthusiasm: 'Can't you see, old boy, what a whacking great thing we've got hold of. Eliot the greatest poet of the moment and I the greatest poet of the Old Gang – a bit out of the picture *pro tem* but that won't last forever – getting together and bringing our combined weight on all the old mugs – my dear fellow, it would be irresistible.' Eliot agreed to offer his whole-hearted support but, perhaps tactfully, suggested that the metropolis would suit Hayward better. Flattering though the suggestion was, Hayward had no doubt that it was unrealistic: 'Regius Professors are not drawn from the obscurest garrets of Grub Street,' he commented, adding that he was not even a member of a college and that his literary reputation was negligible. Bill Empson wrote to Eliot asking him if he had a chance of the Professorship and Eliot referred him back to Hayward who, of course, loved gossiping about the appointment. He told Empson that he felt C. S. Lewis and J. B. Priestley were the favourites.[451]

Then, out of the blue, on 24 November, came a letter from Edith Sitwell. 'I have long wanted to tell you that I feel towards you exactly as if there had never been any interruption of the friendship.' [452] The ten-year-long silence that she had imposed was now over. Osbert joined with her in suggesting that the whole episode should be completely forgotten and treated as if it had never existed. 'I think it would be one of the nicest things that could happen,' she added. Hayward immediately replied in his most courtly style and said that he hoped that they could pick up everything where it had been left. In dramatic banner headline form he gave the news to Eliot: 'GRAND RECONCILIATION AND REHABILITATION.'[453]

'Christmas which is as much a physical and mental disturbance of the body as illness, needs to be spent in one's *own* home,' wrote Hayward[454], but Christmas Day 1944 found both Eliot and Hayward isolated from friends and families in their lodgings. Eliot was at Shamley Green, surrounded by his old ladies; Hayward had Merton Hall to himself as the Rothschild family spent Christmas in London at the Savoy. After five years of exile he fretted, waiting for an end to the war and his return to London: 'Another spring renews the soldier's toil / But finds me vacant in the rural cave.'[455] Geoffrey Faber sent a rhyming letter, acknowledging some coloured cartoons Hayward had given him, and urged him back:

> O H-yw-rd! Leave thy enervating fen!
> London's the place for an ambitious Crayon
> And I will stand thee, every now and then,
> A Thimbleful of Whiskey to get gay on.[456]

And then, on Tuesday 1 May 1945, the long-awaited moment finally came. Hayward's calendar entry read: 'Hitler dies. Mary Fyffe to tea.' Six days later Germany surrendered unconditionally and on 8 May Cambridge celebrated VE Day with a huge municipal bonfire on Midsummer Common; a crowd of many thousands turned out, children sang and a display of searchlights flashed through the night sky. The city itself was bedecked with flags and Merton Hall was draped in the large red banners of the USSR.

Despite his relief, the uncertainty of his future made Hayward unable to share in the general rejoicing. He even found it strangely disorientating that he could no longer find German stations on any waveband of his wireless. At this time his friendship with Eliot was at its most intense. In his letters he signed off with 'Your devoted friend', or 'Your ancient and devoted', or 'Your affectionate and faithful'. So when Eliot planned another visit in late spring the prospect thrilled Hayward with as much delight as his appearance two years earlier had done. As he had scarcely got away from the Hall for weeks he looked forward to 'a sunny ramble' with his friend: 'My time is entirely at your disposal and the more of it I can spend with you the happier I shall be.'[457] The whole trip took on the excitement of a cloak-and-dagger exploit. He assured Eliot he had told absolutely no one about his arrival and drew him another map so that he could make a private entry by 'La Route Des Amis', a back route to his rooms known only to 'particular intimates'. 'Friday Night shall be Wux-Ho Reunion Night,' he promised. Now the two homeless men could at last talk realistically about setting up together. It was not easy to find a suitable place. Eliot favoured 'a small house with a cosy couple', a room with no northerly exposure and conditions where he could be easily looked after for a few days in bed – a house and nursing home combined. Hayward liked the idea of a flat 'with a grand horizon'. By July Hayward had discovered through his 'network of Ladies' a promising third-floor flat at 19 Carlyle Mansions, just off Cheyne Walk in Chelsea. He went to London to view it and excitedly described the accommodation to Eliot. The rent of £300 a year was high, but within their means. Finally, Eliot agreed to the arrangement that Hayward had dreamed of for the past twelve years. 'Nothing has delighted me more,' wrote his father, 'than the most opportune and friendly offer of Mr Eliot to set up a joint abode with you in town after the war. You are tried friends, know each other's moods and idiosyncrasies, are entirely sympathetic in interests and outlook on life, and I imagine at heart have very much the same foundations of belief – religious and philosophic. What could be better?'[458] He did not know – or perhaps had forgotten – that his son was an atheist. At any rate it was an immense relief, releasing Dr Hayward from 'a last and unnatural anxiety'.[459]

In October a letter arrived at Merton Hall from the young poet Kathleen Raine. It was an invitation from the British Council, for whom she worked as General Editor for publications, to write a long essay on wartime prose. The fee was an attractive sixty guineas. As Hayward brooded, halfway between the world of war and the world of peace, and halfway between Merton Hall and a flat in London, he could sum up his thoughts on the experience of the past five years. By 11 January 1946 he had completed a draft and suggested the illustrations he needed. The list was that of the literary aristocracy as he saw it: Eliot at Stockholm; Maurice Bowra at Wadham College, Oxford; David Cecil at Hatfield; Osbert Sitwell at Renishaw and 'CHARLES MORGAN looking phoney (but not otherwise)'. The poet and novelist Charles Morgan wrote a wartime column as 'Menander' for *The Times Literary Supplement*, and was detested as a fraud by Hayward and Eliot. Kathleen Raine immediately endeared herself by replying that she thought that his picture as specified was probably the easiest to find.

Prose Literature since 1939 duly came out in 1946. Hayward now saw the war as part of the 'moral regeneration' of a nation as it escaped the evasions of the past; he looked back on the crisis of 1940 after the retreat from Dunkirk, when Britain and the Commonwealth stood alone against Hitler, with a sense of pride. That year 'added an illustrious but sombre passage to English history, comparable in kind, though immeasurably greater in degree, with the emergency created by Napoleon's threat of invasion'.⁴⁶⁰ This new and different kind of 'total war' demanded that writers should play their part by fighting, by writing or by broadcasting, but in its very nature, Hayward argued, was hostile to the calm reflection a writer needed:

> For five years, the energies, mental and spiritual no less than physical, of the whole nation were conscripted for one end; and the activities and interests of every man and woman were directed if not actually prescribed, by the overriding needs of the state.⁴⁶¹

A constant preoccupation was the effect of the war on books. There was a lack of skilled labour in the printing and publishing worlds. Materially, the paper shortage reduced the supply to 40% of prewar levels. The problem was exacerbated by the wholesale destruction of publishers' stocks in the raids on London. It was not just the meagre supply of paper that Hayward noted; he also bemoaned the poor quality of wartime 'grey blotting paper', and the lack of skilled typography. 'We have got used to bad paper, cramped type and flimsy bindings which gape,' he lamented.⁴⁶² With limited options, publishers often played safe and relied on the classics. It was therefore very hard for an unpublished writer to get his work into print. The little reviews offered the best chance and *Penguin New Writing*, edited by John Lehmann, stood out like a beacon. Yet Hayward felt one positive benefit of the conflict was the growth of reading. A public faced with nightly blackouts, theatres and cinemas often shut, newspapers a quarter of their prewar size, together with enforced leisure in the evenings, had rediscovered the pleasures of the book.

The main theme for prose writers from 1939 to 1945 was naturally the war itself. Hayward noted how combat in the air had caught the readers' imagination and especially admired Richard Hillary's best-selling account of the life of a Spitfire pilot in *The Last Enemy*. But for him the central figure in the literature of the time was unquestionably Eliot.

> His influence is paramount on his own generation, on its immediate successor – the generation of such writers as Auden, Spender,

MacNeice, Day-Lewis and Empson – and on the young. No
English writer living is more revered by his admirers or, it may be
added, more respected by his critics. None, in his writing, has
done more to create the climate of thought and sensibility which
has conditioned the form and content of English literature in the
past quarter of a century.[463]

The rest of the pamphlet is a broad account of wartime books on biography, science, philosophy and history, spiced with irony. There were
notable exceptions to the general fairness, however, when Hayward
settled old scores. Charles Morgan was dismissed as 'the literary pontiff
and spiritual director of studies of the conventional reading public'.
Aldous Huxley and Christopher Isherwood were in the firing line for
their personal cult of 'neo-Brahminism', which was 'a good deal easier
to practise on the sunny hillsides of the golden west than in Britain's
grey industrial north'. The old enemy, Leavis, was 'the cold intellectual
leader of a minority group of Cambridge critics' – a destructive
Cromwell in the world of English letters.

Rather surprisingly Hayward included the *Beveridge Report* (1944)
as a sign of the emergence of a developing social conscience and foresaw the 'coming years of social revolution'. In the face of this, literature
had to avoid the ivory tower, but also had to steer clear of the opposite
danger, political engagement – he had seen enough of the literature of
the public platform in the Thirties. He was very suspicious too about
the growing influence of broadcasting: 'It is as well to remember that
among the more alarming possibilities of misapplied science is the mass
production of the moron.'[464] The writer had to resist all the blandish-
ments of cheap journalism and calls to provide 'reading matter' for the
lowest common denominator. In future, only an 'attitude of absolute
intransigence to the philistine and all his works' could preserve a
writer's integrity and his value to society:

> Not only in the immediate postwar era, but during the years of
> man's painful spiritual recovery which lie ahead, such an attitude
> must be preserved, if out of disintegration a scheme of values is to
> arise, and out of disillusionment a dynamic faith in the power of
> the printed word to express the finest operations of human
> thought and sensibility.[465]

Hayward's six years in Merton Hall had been a kindness which he never forgot. In Victor Rothschild he had found a true friend. In September 1945, partly as a tribute to his host, Hayward used his collection of Swift's manuscripts and printed books – 'unsurpassed by any library in this country or abroad' – to mount an exhibition to commemorate the 200th Anniversary of Swift's death. He selected the exhibits and borrowed some Queen Anne chairs from Wimpole Hall, which Swift had once visited. Original busts of eighteenth-century men of letters recreated the atmosphere of the home of the famous Harleian Library. Hayward persuaded G. M. Trevelyan, the Master of Trinity College, to inaugurate the exhibition in the East Room of the Old Schools. There were many unique copies in the finest collection of Swift's works ever to be shown in public, every one of the eighty five exhibits had been carefully chosen to illustrate a particular literary or biographical point. Ten years on one reviewer, still dazzled by the stars of this 'high spot collecting', remembered the 'superlative' uncut, large paper *Gulliver* and other 'transcendent specimens' which had 'an uncanny luxuriance about them, like giant vegetables at a village flower show'.[466] *Gulliver's Travels* was followed by a unique run of *The Penny London Post* in which it was first serially printed. Hayward organised everything from the posters to the guest list for the grand opening; the catalogue he compiled was a model of its kind.[467] As he looked towards his new life in London the praise that the exhibition earned seemed to open up new possibilities for its curator.

Long after the war, every year, as Christmas approached, he devoted some time to considering special presents for his wartime protector, often well-chosen books, including the anonymous *Discourse on Free Thinking for the Use of the Poor*. Victor Rothschild, in return, was imaginative in giving his guest an early television set which, he warned, might only produce 'sheet lightning on its screen'.[468] Many years later, first among the legacies in Hayward's will, was a gift of five hundred pounds to buy 'some piece of silver as a memento of our friendship'.

Another kind of memento of his stay is the poem that Hayward wrote for the young Sarah Rothschild called 'In Love with Every Month: Poem for a Child' in a style that is hard not to call 'Georgian'.

> I name the twelve months of the year
> And choose from each one thing I love;
> Twelve sights or sounds to see or hear,
> Which joy or beauty's presence prove.

Exile

In January a frosted bough
Still in the snow-grey evening light;
In February a horse-drawn plough
Or the wind-shaken aconite.

In March to lie curled up in bed
So snug beneath the counterpane,
While the wind rumbles overhead,
And dream that Spring has come again.

April sun and April shower
Stirring life in last year's leaves;
May time with every tree in flower;
Flutter of wings about the eaves.

Shadow of cloud on waving grass,
The first plump strawberries of June;
July – warm rock-pools calm as glass;
Ribbed sand beneath an August moon.

Lark-song above the sun-baked corn
In soft September's milky sky;
Wood-smoke at dusk, white mist at dawn
That on October hedgerows lie.

November firelight on the ceiling;
Cockcrow at day break far yet clear;
And in December midnights wheeling
The seven bright shiners of the Bear.

So from memory I recall
From every month one cherished thing;
Some loveliness perennial
Of Summer, Autumn, Winter, Spring.[469]

Just before he left he wrote to Catherine Walston, 'Exile is a strange experience and now I have been rooted in it for more than six years. Somewhere in the middle of it I lost my youth. As I haven't yet found my middle-age I don't know quite where I am.'[470] It was time to move on.

13
Carlyle Mansions

'I am coming home at last,' Hayward told Elaine. At 8 am on 14 March 1946 he left Merton Hall to travel to London. The car drew up in Cheyne Walk and parked outside Carlyle Mansions. He was greeted by the elderly porter and pushed through the elaborate Italianate portico for the first time. Then he took the rackety old fashioned lift up to the third floor and number 19 where he was greeted by the housekeeper who organised his belongings and packed away his clothes. Eliot, already installed, returned at six o'clock after work. Then the two friends ate their first dinner together in the new flat which they were to share for the next eleven years.

They might have preferred something more central, but to Hayward Chelsea was still 'a charming village, full of small period houses'. Carlyle Mansions itself was a substantial and imposingly solid red-brick building of six storeys built in High Victorian style in an equally imposing row of buildings. This was an area full of literary echoes. Apart from Thomas Carlyle himself, who had lived just around the corner in Cheyne Row, Hayward was pleased to note that 'the immediate neighbourhood was once familiar to Sir Thomas More and Donne, to Swift and Smollett, to Leigh Hunt and George Eliot, to Rossetti, Morris, Swinburne and Henry James'.[471] Henry James had in fact lived in the flat directly above Hayward's, and died almost exactly thirty years earlier in the room above Eliot's bedroom. Hayward sometimes called Eliot 'The Master' after James's own nickname. Cyril Connolly lived nearby, as did Kathleen Raine in Paulton's Square. Cheyne Walk was quite a contrast to the grim respectability of Bina Gardens.

Looking across Cheyne Walk and a small grassed area to the Embankment, the flat had a good view along the tree-lined river. Hayward had finally got what he had always wanted: 'The view from my riverside bay window is enchanting at any hour of the day or night.'[472] Later, when he had his portrait painted, he chose to portray himself staring out from from his flat with the Thames in the background and the chimneys of Battersea Power Station in the distance. An added attraction was the view of the legs of pretty typists and secretaries as they sat on the wooden park bench in the grassed area in front of his window taking their lunch break. Sometimes a considerable time would pass without any attractive sight. He would then ring Oliver Low, Stephen Spender's brother-in-law, to 'deplore the evil days'. Low would simply inquire, 'Bench trouble, John?' and 'Hayward would sigh assent'.[473] He was much upset when 'some vandal, nihilist or foreign agent' had moved it. Low took pity and concreted it to its original base.

'The accommodation allows for the swinging of several Practical Cats,'[474] Hayward had promised Eliot and the pleasant roominess of the flat compensated for its rather ugly façade. There were also the advantages of a resident porter, a regular supply of hot water and space for a living-in housekeeper. The accommodation for the two flatmates was generous: a shared dining room, a large front room and three bedrooms reached through a long, book-lined corridor. Eliot dismissed the idea of having the big room, so Hayward took it for himself, lining its walls with bookcases and painting them a soft green with gold pilasters. Beneath them he placed a statuette of a classical Greek *kore* which visitors were often asked to move so that he could appreciate her from another angle. He reassembled his furniture from Bina Gardens and re-created its drawing room in prewar style. He brought with him bed linen, china, cutlery, rugs and curtains and had the seventeenth-century portrait of his favourite, Rochester, languidly playing with his pet monkey, hung from a wall of the dark corridor. Eliot brought with him his clothes and two cases of books. Special arrangements obviously had had to be made for Hayward's disability. He had written to Eliot giving a precise account of how the lavatory should be modified. The bowl needed to be lowered to eighteen inches above floor level: 'I should wish to be able to push myself unaided to the Throne. This, I need hardly say, is simply a matter of personal pride, arising from my stubborn desire to dispense, as far as possible, with assistance.'[475]

They agreed to employ a housekeeper who sometimes acted as cook, and a cleaner. Their first was Ellen Cross. She was Irish, very pretty and soon left to get married – much to Hayward's regret. The second was more serious and strait-laced. Strangely, both housekeepers refused to concede that Eliot might be a famous writer. '"No, no," Ellen would say, "I've known many a writing man, and he's no writing man, Mr Eliot. He's a very holy man ... it'll be playing patience I've only seen him doing."'Apparently no argument could disturb her view and she would finally say to Hayward, 'It'll be you that's using his name in your writings.' ('A born Baconian,' commented Christopher Sykes.) The two were followed by a Frenchwoman, Madame Amory, who accepted that Eliot was a writer, but had limited English and could not pronounce his name. She called him, simply, 'Monsieur le Professeur'. After she retired Hayward needed more physical help and employed a capable and loyal manservant, an ex-army batman, Askwith, on whom he grew to depend more and more.[476]

The atmosphere had a powerful effect on the young bibliographer Nicolas Barker when he came to visit:

> Once inside his room, with its peculiar slightly bitter stuffy smell, the green book-case, the green bed and the comfortable but some-how uncomfortable sofa became the world and the dim hootings outside became not less real but less important than John's world.[477]

In the evening a dozen lamps cast green and gold shadows that made one visitor think it had a 'mysterious quality like the bottom of the sea'.[478] In this 'gilded birdcage' amidst his books and some French furniture, Hayward set his desk where he wrote during the day. Beneath the untidy glass surface he kept pictures of classical female nudes and saucy seaside postcards from Graham Greene, sent from all over the world. In a typical one a doctor is speaking to a nurse holding a large pair of scissors above the hapless patient: 'But, nurse, I said remove his *spectacles*.'[479] The big room also served as a place in which to entertain, and Hayward's gregarious nature ensured that it was full of guests for tea, for cocktails, or for dinner. He was the host at all the parties even when the 'lodger' was there. His Siamese cat, Mimi, lay curled up on the window sill and apparently never went out.[480] Eliot's two small and sunless rooms, by contrast, were at the rear of the house overlooking the 'well' that divided the house from its neighbour. The bedroom's only window faced a brick wall and reminded Peter Quennell of the chill study of a nineteenth-century parson. When Madame Amory showed Anthony Hobson round the flat she opened Eliot's door: 'Venez avec moi. C'est le bureau de M. Eliot. Il est un saint.' An ebony crucifix hung over the single bed and a few pictures in 'Oxford' frames with strips of wood forming little crosses at each corner decorated the walls. Robert Sencourt described it as 'furnished in a spartan, almost monas-tic taste, with a 60-watt bulb to emit the only electric light in the room

– and not even a lampshade to protect him from the glare'. When the considerable royalties from *The Cocktail Party* started rolling in,[481] Hayward suggested that they might do something about the room. After some thought, according to Tom Matthews, Eliot replaced the 60-watt bulb with a 100-watt one.[482]

It was clearly an enormous practical help for Hayward to have Eliot as a lodger but it was a good arrangement for Eliot too. Paying £3 a week out of the total rent of £300 a year he could keep his annual living expenses down to less than £1,000 and save a substantial sum, to be invested by his stockbroker brother-in-law, Maurice Haigh-Wood. Hayward had told Robert Sencourt that his aim was to take Eliot 'away from all those parsons',[483] but the move also meant that he could relish the position of being Eliot's landlord. Very soon 'the Bard' became 'my Lodger'. Hayward liked to be in a dominant position as editor, stage-manager or landlord but he knew he was ultimately not the most important person in Carlyle Mansions. On the other hand Eliot as tenant could slip quietly into the background, happy for his landlord to steal the limelight.[484] Both men carefully observed the thresholds and the boundaries of sharing a flat. Eliot would always knock before entering Hayward's side, as Hayward would before entering Eliot's. Hayward was in charge of the telephone and would answer it; Eliot, who went through an agony of indecision before ringing anyone up, very rarely did. (Miss Swann, the secretary at Faber's, would deal with all his calls at work; Mary Trevelyan was always amazed if he managed to ring her.) Only those 'in the know' could reach him. Hayward was the gatekeeper, the host and the telephone operator.

Appointments, too, were made to see them separately. 'It was not DONE to visit both of them them at the same time'[485] – although sometimes Eliot put in a surprise appearance. Visiting Carlyle Mansions, wrote Frances Partridge, 'was the high spot in my own personal life. They really are congenial souls ... seeing them *does* cheer one up'. She got on with Hayward like 'a house on fire', but on one occasion was shocked by Eliot's sudden arrival in the sitting room 'in a bathrobe, utterly distracted and Strindbergian and perhaps dead drunk'.[486] When J. M. Brinnin, the Director of the New York Poetry Center and friend of Dylan Thomas, came to call, hoping to persuade Eliot to give a talk, he was greeted by Hayward who offered to show him round, aiming his wheelchair towards a closed door which he pushed open with his stick:

'His,' said Hayward, indicating the room we had entered. Its walls looked as if they'd been uniformly stained with nicotine. There was one bare bulb on a chain, an ebony crucifix over the single bed. The wardrobe closet was open: crow-black silk ties on a rod, a scarlet water-silk sash, three glen plaid suits, others in shades of gray and black; a Prince Albert hanging by itself. 'The confessional,' said Hayward, 'here we have our bedtime chats. He tells me *everything*.'[487]

The tone is ironic but possessive: Hayward relished his role as Eliot's confidant. When they returned to the sitting room Hayward pointed out Eliot's straight-backed chair, the bowl of sixpences and shillings for the bus beside his favourite 'giant umbrella' lying on the table. Surprisingly, according to Bunny Garnett's son Richard, 'It was John who was the literary lion in Cheyne Walk whom these brilliant visitors came to see, not T. S. Eliot, a shadowy figure, flitting past a doorway, hardly doing more than pass the time of day.'[488]

The flatmates' taste in clothes was just as revealing as their taste in furnishing. Eliot's clothes were an expression of the outward correctness he cultivated. His wardrobe was based on different kinds of uniform: the morning suits of different weights to suit the season, the banker's city pin-stripes, stiff collars and bowler hat; the anonymous black for Faber's and the country tweeds. It all expressed his desire for social anonymity. Hayward, on the other hand, was a dandy. Meticulous about his dress, as about every area of his life, he wore ties from Charvet and Lanvin, socks from Italy and needlepoint slippers. He was especially fond of colourful checked suits, floral waistcoats, silk bowties and cummerbunds. He got his tailor to make him a 'cerise taffeta weskit with four paste buttons and a pearl grey satin lining'. 'I shall wear, I think, my admirable red velvet waistcoat to your party,' he promised his American friend and fellow book collector Mary Hyde.

Hayward's extraordinary appearance when seated at his desk, dressed in dark coat, 'his shrunken little legs in pepper and salt trousers', kept one visitor in 'a mixed and alert state of sympathy and alarm'.[489] To others he looked more like Mr Toad with his withered legs and broad chest.[490] When outside, the whole dramatic ensemble might be enhanced by a cloak, buckled at the neck and topped by the familiar black hat. He carefully chose clothes to attract attention and perhaps also to distract it from his 'rigid torso and twisted limbs'.[491] He was a man of some personal vanity: just after the end of the war Christopher Isherwood was surprised to hear him say, 'Well at least you and I can congratulate ourselves that we have kept our figures.'

The flatmates' lives were shaped by daily rituals: Eliot's habit of mind made it just as necessary for him to follow a fixed daily pattern as Hayward's immobility made it for him. Each morning Eliot left Carlyle Mansions at 6.30 for early mass at St Stephen's and knelt, winter and summer, in prayer on the cold stone floor. He then returned home, ate a large breakfast, did the *Times* crossword and said good morning to Hayward. At noon he would set off for Faber's, taking the number 9 bus or the Sloane Square tube, leaving Hayward working at his big desk. There Hayward read and wrote all day if he was not invited out to lunch, while Eliot worked until 6 pm. Eliot took Thursday afternoons off and returned to Carlyle Mansions. If possible he avoided all invitations to tea – one of the few English traditions he could never see the point of. It was Hayward's task to ward off such invitations whenever he could. If he had no evening commitment Eliot returned to the flat. Often he took his frugal supper on a tray in the isolation of his room and Hayward, 'an inveterate diner out',[492] went off for dinner with friends. Sometimes they took supper together, or Hayward persuaded Eliot to eat at a favourite spot such as The Good Intent in the King's Road or L' Etoile in Soho. Brown's Hotel in Mayfair was another regular destination after meetings of the Bibliographical Society in Burlington Square and entailed Eliot pushing the chair and weaving his way towards Bond Street 'past gaggles of platinum blonde whores who were still allowed in those days to ensnare elderly poets and chair-borne critics'.[493]

The weekend routine was for Eliot to wheel Hayward out for a walk, often with Christopher Sykes:

One day he and Eliot and I were in Chelsea Hospital Gardens on a wintry day. It came on to drizzle. A football match was in progress and its only spectator was a melancholy old man in a heavy overcoat and cap. A notice informed us that the match was between (as far as I remember) the Marylebone Dustmen and a team from the Chelsea Municipal Maintenance Staff. We approached the match and the solitary spectator could be heard raising his voice in a slow and melancholy chant, 'Come ... on ... the ... Maintenance!' This forlorn London scene fascinated Eliot, and in spite of the cold and the drizzle he stayed and watched for several minutes.[494]

Eliot's enthusiasm was infectious and soon a trip to the Royal Hospital Garden or across Albert Bridge to Battersea Park became a regular entertainment. In the summer they took to watching cricket and, almost by accident, the flatmates became an unlikely pair of sports spectators. The distinctive figure of Hayward being wheeled along by the stooping Eliot became a familiar sight to their Chelsea neighbours. One Sunday the cartoonist Osbert Lancaster watched a circus procession passing through Battersea. The last vehicle, an animal cage on a float, passed by, then, looking exactly as if it was 'the final promenading spectacle of the show', there followed Hayward's wheelchair being pushed by Eliot.[495]

At Carlyle Mansions Hayward picked up the pieces of his prewar existence. He carried on with his *Letters from London* and once again began to write reviews. London's literary life resumed almost as if the war had not happened – the same cast of characters still held the stage, partied, drank cocktails, had affairs, married, divorced and gossiped – and yet there was a sense of unease. Cyril Connolly observed the scene through the eyes of a fictional American novelist, Harold Bisbee, in London for the first time. At his first cocktail party he took stock and noted four impressions of English writers: 'They are not young, they are not rich, they are even positively shabby; on the other hand they seem kind and look distinguished.'

> The Sitwells are generally in the country but Mr Eliot will probably be there accompanied by Mr John Hayward (Dr Johnson disguised as Boswell) and they already convey an atmosphere particularly English to the gathering (not Angels but Anglicans, as Gregory said). Towering over the rest are Stephen Spender and Mr John Lehmann ... About nine inches below them come the rank and file: Mr Roger Senhouse, Mr Raymond Mortimer, Mr V. S. Pritchett, Miss Rose Macaulay, Miss Elizabeth Bowen, Quennell, Pryce-Jones, Connolly, we are all there.[496]

Bisbee is surprised to find that there is no one under thirty at the party: Dylan Thomas is the youngest of them. Where, he wonders, as did Hayward, is the literary avant-garde? Evelyn Waugh wrote that Connolly had been offered $1,500 for an article on the theme of 'Young writers swing right'. 'His mouth watered but he couldn't find one writer under 35 right, left or swinging.'⁴⁹⁷

The Cresset Press was a survivor of prewar days. Founded by Dennis Cohen in 1927, it had produced *éditions de luxe* until the book market collapsed in the slump. It followed the pioneering Nonesuch Press in employing the best printers and binders. Hayward felt that it never produced a shoddy volume and demonstrated 'how pleasant a book can be with a little trouble and taste'.⁴⁹⁸ The owner, Dennis Cohen, belonged to the school of gentleman publishing. A man of Edwardian style, he drove a green Rolls-Royce convertible and dressed in a tweed ulster. 'By profession a publisher and by nature a connoisseur', he lived nearby in Old Church Street and often dropped in to discuss his plans for the firm. In 1945 he invited Hayward to become literary adviser and general editor of the Cresset Library. Hayward was delighted to accept, attracted by the idea of a selection of reprints from the classics. He quickly broadened it to explore some of the by-roads of European and English literature. Often enlisting the help of his friends, he picked just the right editor to write a preface for each volume: Eddie Sackville-West for De Quincey's *Opium Eater*; Edmund Blunden for *The Life of George Crabbe,* Eddie Marsh for Eugène Fromentin's *Dominique,* and Anthony Powell for Aubrey's *Brief Lives.* Hayward recycled his own earlier work for Swift's *Selected Prose.* His major coup was to cajole Eliot into writing the introduction to the Cresset edition of *Huckleberry Finn.* Faber's, Eliot remarked, now had to pick up any literary scraps they could find that fell from the Cresset table.

Kathleen Raine, 'shy, intense and vulnerable', was another near neighbour. She began to take Hayward around in his wheelchair to go shopping and invite him to neighbourly tea parties at her house in Paulton's Square – although she still wrote to him formally as 'Mr Hayward'. Soon after becoming one of his regular 'pushers' she somehow tipped him out of his chair onto the pavement in Chelsea. He fell awkwardly, his face badly cut, and he had to be taken to the local hospital to be sewn up. ('Chair accident! Atomic Bomb Test', read his calendar entry for Sunday 30 June.) Embarrassed and shocked, Kathleen Raine had nightmares about the calamity at least twice a week. 'I dare not now suggest I take you to Battersea Park or Peter Jones or elsewhere,' she wrote.⁴⁹⁹ Yet despite the accident the friendship developed. Her letters were progressively signed 'Yours sincerely', 'Yours ever', 'with respectful love', then 'with love as ever'. Soon Hayward became a regular visitor for dinner or tea. She confided in him her fear of his flat-mate: 'Mr Eliot intimidates me into an absurd kind of paralysis.'

Events followed their usual pattern when she began to send her poems for comment, a habit she maintained until he died. She implored him to 'criticise them and not to spare me'. He also became her counsellor when her complicated love affairs became difficult. When she was breaking up painfully with the writer Gavin Maxwell, it was to Hayward she turned. 'It was kind of you to give me a good talking-to, and I shall try to pull myself together and stop being a trial to everyone,' a chastened Kathleen wrote on Christmas Day 1946. The friendship was not a relationship of equals – she was always deferential towards a man she felt was much older than she was, although in fact, born in 1908, she was only three years younger. There was a certain bond of shared weaknesses too – Hayward's physical and Kathleen Raine's emotional. 'I lack the courage', she wrote, 'to resume life in which the price of every unguarded love or happiness is vulnerability to some new wound, which is, of course, why we all build around ourselves these hard shells that we would much rather not have.' Both had to construct social masks as protection from the world. With delight she recalled Hayward's barbed remarks and said, admiringly, 'He was the most malicious man I ever met.'

The Poets' Reading at the Wigmore Hall on 14 May 1946 was a glittering occasion. The guests of honour were Queen Elizabeth, and the two royal princesses, Elizabeth and Margaret. The poetic establishment was there in force: readers included the Poet Laureate John Masefield, Walter de la Mare, Eliot, Edith Sitwell and Dylan Thomas. Establishment figures shared a platform with Fitzrovia. The evening began dangerously when Dylan Thomas's attractive young wife Caitlin somehow contrived to meet the Queen without formal introduction. 'I can't hear a bloody thing, can you? I'm going to ask for my money back,' she said – before flicking cigarette ash down the Queen's dress.[500] After the reading there followed a private dinner party at Edith Sitwell's club. This ladies' establishment, the Sesame, Lyceum and Imperial Pioneer Club at 49 Grosvenor Street W1, was an old-fashioned place where, behind a narrow frontage flanked by marble pillars, back windows looked onto a flowery garden and a fountain. As Edith Sitwell recalled, 'Its corridors seemed haunted by dowdy peculiar ladies with inquisitive eyes, wandering about clutching glasses of sherry.'[501] Before the party started a drunken Dylan Thomas berated Eliot: 'Why does a poet like you publish such *awful* poetry? *You know* it's bad.' At this point Edith Sitwell's sister-in-law Georgia came in and announced to the company at large: 'There is a woman in the cloak-room more *roaringly* drunk than anyone I have ever seen in my life.' 'That will be my wife,' said Dylan.

Caitlin Thomas finally took her seat at the dinner party and fastened, as if fixated, upon her neighbour, Hayward. When the pudding arrived she spilt some ice-cream on her bare arm and ordered him to lick it off. He refused. Caitlin insisted. 'He said he would lick it off any other part of her body anywhere else but *not* in the dining room of the Sesame.'⁵⁰² '"Mother of God!" she replied, turning on him, "The insults of men! You great pansy. What for are [*sic*] you sitting in that throne and twisting your arms like that!!!"'⁵⁰³ As Hayward prided himself on being the 'least homosexual man in London', as he said afterwards, the gibe missed its target. Then she began to stroke his wrist affectionately as if she had taken a fancy to him and repeatedly call him 'Old Ugly'. Caitlin was eventually helped from the dining room. But if the unshockable Hayward was unperturbed, Rosamond Lehmann felt furious about such a macabre attack and pity for 'poor John for a sad and tragic reason unable to move'. Edith Sitwell was appalled: neither she nor the Sesame Club had ever seen anything like this. She wrote to him condolingly: 'I have never spent such an evening in my life, & when I die the date will be found on my heart as Calais was inscribed on the heart of Bloody Mary.'⁵⁰⁴ More coolly, Eliot remarked later that he had reason to know that Mrs Thomas 'sometimes takes occasion to show her Irish character'.⁵⁰⁵

Very early on the morning of 22 January 1947 the telephone rang at Carlyle Mansions. Hayward, as usual, answered it. The call was from Maurice Haigh-Wood, Vivienne's brother. He reported that Vivienne had died unexpectedly in the night at Northumberland House mental hospital in Stoke Newington. Hayward was given the task of telling Eliot that his wife was dead. The news came as a complete and devastating surprise. 'Oh God! Oh God!' Eliot cried as he buried his face in his hands. His grief, no doubt compounded with guilt, was profound. 'Through his tears he said, "I've not a single second of happiness to look back on, and that makes it worse."'⁵⁰⁶ He fell into a state close to despair. His natural tendency was to retire into himself and hide from the world, but it was now that he turned to Hayward for comfort. Friends acknowledged it was Hayward's sympathy and tact at this time that helped Eliot compose himself, meet people and avoid another mental breakdown. 'It was John more than anyone else who persuaded him to meet new people and to live a natural life again,' wrote Christopher Sykes.[507] Trying out his flatmate's typewriter in March, two months after Vivienne's death, Eliot wrote:

–ou may not be so perfect
–n a lot of ways is true,
–t when it comes to brothers
–d take one just like you.[508]

14

Fame Is the Spur

'I never imagined that I should ever sit freezing & unlighted in the capital city of the greatest Empire in history,' wrote Hayward to Catherine Walston in February 1947.[509] The streets were still blacked-out, bread was rationed, potatoes unobtainable and the Siberian winter seemed to him like Russia's revenge for its wartime suffering. At this time, following his success with the Swift exhibition, he was busy organising 'the most comprehensive and valuable loan collection of first and early editions of English poetry ever shown in public'[510] on behalf of The National Book League at their Mayfair headquarters at 7 Albemarle Street. It was an enormous undertaking for anyone, let alone a man confined to his wheelchair.

The exhibition was a celebration of the survival of five centuries of English poetry and represented the major landmarks of English literature. On view were 346 items representing 250 poets. Using his encyclopaedic knowledge of private collections, Hayward had personally hunted down the copies he needed and had written to each lender, detailing what he wanted and discussing all the particulars of insurance, transport arrangements and so on. Owners had to be cajoled and reassured to part with the treasures of their libraries. 'Certainly: but for God's sake, don't lose the damned thing,' said Earl Fitzwilliam when asked to loan Caxton's edition of *The Canterbury Tales*, the only surviving copy in private hands in England and, at £10,000, the most heavily insured book. The famously fastidious collector Richard Jennings, fearing the worst, gave his permission 'with a despairing groan'. The list of lenders that prefaced the catalogue began with King George VI himself, who lent presentation copies by two poets laureate, Tennyson and Walter de la Mare, and then, descending in due order of rank from the Duke of Norfolk, through four more dukes to two marquesses, two earls, two viscounts and half a dozen lords. If almost half the list came from the peerage, the other half came from friends whose generosity Hayward could call on – Cyril Connolly, Rupert Hart-Davis, Richard Jennings, Geoffrey

Keynes, Simon Nowell-Smith, Kathleen Raine, Stephen Spender, and John Sparrow.

First editions of Chaucer, Spenser, Shakespeare, Donne, Pope, Wordsworth, Tennyson, Yeats, Eliot and Auden were at the heart of the collection. It started with Earl Fitzwilliam's copy of Chaucer's *Canterbury Tales*, printed by William Caxton in 1478, which 'may justly be claimed to be the first substantial book of poetry to be printed in the English language'.[511] In the catalogue's introduction Hayward stated his aim to recapture the excitement of the book's first reader. It certainly worked for the *Times* reviewer who noted how the immaculate page of print had defied the effects of time and caught the thrill when 'we encounter the man who first bought a Chaucer from CAXTON, and opened it for the first time to read what was in effect the first line of English Poetry'. The exhibition also showed how important the book as a physical object, and the study of its making, were to a literary critic. There could be no better or clearer statement of the purpose of book collecting, as Hayward saw it, than the final remarks he made in his Preface to the Catalogue:

> Those to whom it is a matter of indifference whether a book is a 'first edition' or not, and who hardly distinguish between the bibliophile, the bibliographer, and the bibliomaniac, may yet feel some interest, if not emotion, on reflecting that almost every one of the books in this Collection was, for its original owner and its earliest readers, the first intimation of the emergence of a new poet. It was, in fact, by means of these first folios, quartos, and octavos, that the genius of English poetry, in its incomparable variety and appeal, found its way into print and so became accessible to a poet's contemporaries; and, with the help of scholars, bibliographers, and all those whose business is with the transmission of texts, to later generations of readers. The survival of English poetry, indeed, ultimately derives from the existence and preservation of these primary printed sources.[512]

Hayward knew that this would be his only chance to put together such a collection: many of the volumes on show were the last copies in private hands in Great Britain. The exhibition celebrated victory and the future, but also gave an elegiac look back at the world of the hushed private libraries of the great houses Hayward had loved to visit. It sounded the knell of aristocratic patronage and perhaps also the private collector.

It is unlikely that an opportunity will come again for arranging an exhibition on a similar scale in this country. With the progressive breaking-up of old libraries, and their forced sale to liquidate death-duties, together with the keen acquisitiveness of American libraries and collectors, it would seem to be only a matter of a few years before a large number of books described in this Catalogue will no longer be seen outside our grand national collections and other corporate libraries ...

Fifty years ago, it would not have been difficult to form a collection at least as fine and as comprehensive as the present one, and almost certainly more completely representative. At the beginning of the century, for example, the treasuries of English poetry books in the famous Hoe, Huth and Britwell libraries, which have since enriched the great libraries of the U.S.A., were still intact; and in many undisturbed and not yet impoverished country-houses there were still rare volumes to be found which their owners had not contemplated sending to the auction rooms in Bond Street and Chancery Lane.[513]

Not only did Hayward have an exact idea of the titles he needed, he also knew the particular copy that he wanted. His catalogue was itself to acquire incomparable status: 'Hayward 47' became a byword in bibliographical circles, not only because of the depth of knowledge that informed it, but also because each book had its own individuality and its own story to tell. The entries brought each one to life almost as if it were an old friend. Of Barnabe Barnes's *Parthenophil and Parthenophe* Hayward noted that: 'This single copy stood alone between Barnes and oblivion. Its survival has preserved a minor poet of considerable merit, possessed of a finer frenzy than most of the Elizabethan sonneteers.'[514] The catalogue was also full of obscure titbits of information. Hayward's inspection of Fulke Greville's *Works* led him to discover a slip of inscribed paper: 'Judging from the discoloration, this slip was almost certainly intended to be placed between the leaves of the book so as to project from the fore-edge and thus identify it when it was customary to arrange volumes on a shelf with their spines to the wall.'[515] Of George Keate's poem *The Alps* he noted that the poet 'was one of the earliest writers to admire, without terror, the sublimities of alpine scenery'[516], adding that the poem was written a quarter of a century before the first ascent of Mont Blanc in 1786. No detail escaped his eye. He wrote of Hardy's signature in his *Satires of Circumstance* that 'Inscriptions by Hardy are uncommon, and it may be noted that he always added a full-stop to his signature.'[517]

Hayward loved bibliographical byways and curious oddities. It is easy to imagine his delight in finding a copy of *Reeds Shaken by the Wind* by Robert Hawker with an old newspaper cutting pasted inside the cover: 'A rare little volume by the eccentric parson-poet who usually conducted his services with high-legged sea boots showing to his knees.'[518] The first edition of Kipling's *Departmental Ditties* was another fascinating curio:

> The book is a bibliographical freak. There is no title page, the title being printed on the upper cover, which is designed to represent an official envelope, addressed in the poet's facsimile script to 'All Heads of Depa [*the remaining letters overlaid by the title in an ornamental frame*] and all Anglo-Indians.' At the top left-hand corner of the 'envelope': 'No.1 of 1866 ...'[519]

Books, like people, gained interest and character through their associations. The copy of Walter de la Mare's *The Listeners and Other Poems* was the one 'which Hardy read on his death bed', and Tennyson's *Ode on the Death of the Duke of Wellington* was lent by the Duke of Wellington whose company Hayward had so much disliked at Merton Hall. John Masefield's *Reynard the Fox* was lent by King George V: 'This book was illustrated for me by the Poet Laureate himself. G.R.I.'[520] Hayward especially liked comments and inscriptions. Rupert Brooke's first poem, 'The Bastille', was lovingly prefaced by his mother, 'by Rupert Brooke at 16 yrs 6ms, awarded an extra prize as being so nearly equal to the prize winner'. Hayward prized the inscription in Auden's first poetry collection, privately printed by hand by Stephen Spender in 1928: 'From the young author to the younger printer with youthful love. Wystan Auden. Oct. 1929.'[521] The exhibition included two volumes of Eliot's: *Prufrock and Other Observations* and *The Waste Land*, both lent by Hayward himself. His description of *Prufrock* ended: 'Presentation copy, inscribed on the half-title: "John Hayward from his friend T. S. Eliot."'[522]

Hayward spent the Wednesday afternoon before the exhibition

opened showing Queen Mary around, explaining and discussing the exhibits; he found her well-read and anxious to know more about contemporary poetry. On 10 April it opened to the public with a speech by John Masefield. Hayward sat on the platform immediately to his right, relishing the limelight. On the new BBC Third Programme four days later, he discussed the exhibition. It was to run for two months and attract great attention and even a visit from the King. *The Times*'s leading article was full of praise for 'a remarkable exercise of perseverance and learning' and included a photograph of 'T. S. Eliot's knees and my bald pate'.[523] The *Daily Telegraph* congratulated Hayward on 'the most complete collection of first and early edition poets from Chaucer to the present day that has ever been shown in public'. Nicolas Barker felt that the famous catalogue represented 'the most individual and permanent single monument of his work'.[524] The publisher Hamish Hamilton wrote, 'As an orator you are a spell-binder; as an exhibitor a genius.'

But public success was soon followed by personal disappointment. As he was preparing the exhibition Hayward had met an attractive Swedish woman called Lena Wickman. Twelve years younger than he, she worked for Bonniers as a publishers' scout. Soon she began to pay regular visits to Carlyle Mansions. One Sunday in August the following year she took over the kitchen when the cook had her night off, and made omelettes. Hayward marked the date with a star in his calendar – a sure sign of erotic interest. Gradually he began to introduce her to his friends and sensed romance was in the offing. But when he made an advance she suddenly rebuffed him. What he had thought was the start of an affair was for her no more than a flirtation. It was a misunderstanding that was as embarrassing as it was hurtful, and made him think about 'M', Elaine, Joséfa and all the other relationships in his life that had come to nothing:

> My failure has always been to have loved in a false way, although at the time I can't see where I'm going wrong – except that I tend too easily and foolishly to forget to take into account the physical disability which is bound in the end to set me apart from the course of true love. Given the slightest encouragement to believe that I am loved (as I was in this case) I respond too gratefully and I daresay too exactingly.[525]

He confessed that one side of him felt all this was very silly – but he just could not help it: 'the heart goes on thumping away and won't listen to boring old reason.' He confided his bitter disappointment only to Anne Ridler. Lena Wickman never visited him again and there was no other young woman to follow her.

Eliot's sixtieth birthday in 1948 was marked by the Order of Merit from George VI. In September, when asked to do a celebratory broadcast on the Third Programme to mark the event, Hayward recounted how it was Eliot who had opened his eyes and the eyes of the world to a new kind of poetry. Then, in November, came another award – the Nobel Prize for Literature. Since Eliot was in America at the time the news was relayed to Hayward by a 'coded message'. He then told their housekeeper:

> She received the news with no trace of emotion but merely remarked that she had known a girl in the West Country who was given the Nobel Prize for watercolours. John said that he rather doubted whether a Nobel Prize was awarded for watercolours ... The severe lady drew herself up, 'I've known the family for many years,' she declared in awful tones, 'and if you don't believe me you can make enquiries at their home in Paignton.' With this she swept out of the room and shut the door with a bang. Eliot's prize was not discussed further.[526]

On Eliot's return from America Cyril Connolly hosted a party for seventy guests in the grand Regency house in Sussex Place he had just bought. Connolly was pleased with Hayward for putting in a good word on his behalf to Eliot. The supply of champagne was generous and by the end of the evening Connolly and Hayward were doing a double act reciting *Sweeney Todd*. Eliot 'surprised everyone when he responded with a lively rendition of a song from *Sweeney Agonistes*',

> Under the bamboo
> Bamboo bamboo
> Under the bamboo tree
> Two live as one
> One live as two
> Two live as three
> Under the bam
> Under the boo
> Under the bamboo tree. [527]

For Hayward and Eliot it was Bina Gardens revisited.

In May there came an invitation for Hayward to lecture in Dublin as part of the celebrations to mark the bicentenary of the founding of St Patrick's Hospital by Jonathan Swift: 'He gave the little wealth he had / To build a house for fools and mad, / And showed by one satiric touch / No nation needed it so much.' This was an opportunity to follow in Eliot's 1940 footsteps when he had visited Ireland to give the first Annual Yeats Lecture. It was also a chance to escape from the drabness of postwar London and to take his first flight in an aeroplane. At 11 am on 10 May he took off from Northolt. Sitting on a green plush seat and looking through a little round window as the 'flying machine' cruised over Blenheim Palace and Oxford at 275 miles per hour he waved down to where he imagined Anne Ridler lived. At the airport his old friend Bryan Guinness, now Lord Moyne, greeted him and drove him to the family castle, Knockmaroon, just beyond Phoenix Park.

At the grand opening of the Swift exhibition Hayward was introduced to the President of Ireland. The following day Lord Moyne gave him a tour round the Guinness factory and in the afternoon Hayward spoke to the Royal Irish Academy on 'The Psychology of Swift'. Then he lectured to the Royal College of Physicians. His chosen title was: 'What was wrong with Swift?' The problem he put to his medical audience was the mystery of Swift's character: much was known about his life, but little understood. Hayward began to answer his own question by dismissing wilder speculations about Swift's possible sexual neuroses, syphilis or impotence. He granted that Swift suffered from inner frustration, but 'there is nothing singular in this, for, in a sense, frustration in one form or another, is the condition of civilized existence … Living, we know, is largely an act of compromise.' The crucial fact was that from the age of thirty-two, Swift suffered from Ménière's disease, which led to deafness and loss of balance. The key to understanding his difficult and sometimes indecipherable character was to be found in the conflicts the disease caused: 'a sense that life was in some way thwarting his strongest instincts and desires'. He faced his difficulties with an indomitable will. 'It is a terrible thing when some disabling circumstance forces a man to regard his own body, not as an ally, but as his own worst enemy, ready at any moment and without warning to interrupt or restrict his intellectual and emotional activities.'[528] Even more pointedly Hayward continued: 'Perhaps only those who have been struck by an incurable disability, which still enables them to play a normal part in social life, will understand Swift's fear of giddiness that will make him fall in public.' This fear grew progressively more acute as he grew older and caused 'peevishness and moroseness; the shadows cast by despair; a tendency to scorn and contempt; the fear of physical dependence; the tendency also to establish self-confidence and exercise power by giving advice and holding forth in company; and above all the fear of emotional entanglement'.[529] He quoted Swift's harrowing resolution from 'Polite Conversation', 'Not to be fond of Children, or let them come near me hardly'.[530] Children, Hayward remarked, might remind him too poignantly of the possibilities of happiness from which his disease had alienated him. As Hayward delivered his speech from his wheelchair, few of his audience could have failed to see the sad irony of his portrait.

The lecture was lauded in the Dublin press as 'an epoch-making address'. The general praise was marred only by the hostile reaction Hayward received for his typically outspoken remark that 'Swift loathed the Irish'. The visit continued with garden parties, drinks and dinners and a reception at the Vice-Regal Lodge. On 13 May there was an interview on Radio Eireann on 'Dublin, the city of Swift as seen by you'. The next day Hayward launched an Irish exhibition of early editions of the English poets by giving another lecture to the friends of Trinity College: 'On the Rarity of First Editions of English Poetry'. The visit to the College Library that followed was a special treat. After having been cooped up in Cambridge and London, Hayward was delighted to escape to a city where bright lights shone at night and luxuries of all kinds were available in the shops. He thought it ravishingly beautiful, built with eighteenth-century elegance and the impeccable sense of design that he admired most in King's Lynn, Edinburgh and Bristol, but here bathed in an 'attractive aquatint hue'. It represented a way of life fast disappearing in England: 'I don't say I don't regret the decay of the aristocratic way of life; with all its faults of omission and commission it has contributed more than any other to civilized values.'[531] Above all, Dublin breathed literary associations; he was delighted to stay in the city of Swift, Yeats and Joyce. The next three days he spent with his friend the poet Sheila Wingfield in Powerscourt, a magnificent but comfortless house overlooking the Wicklow Mountains. Totally lacking in amenities, it appeared to him to contain nothing but 'vast pieces of baroque furniture, stuffed elephants' turds and monumental statuary'.[532] From there he was driven through the spring countryside and introduced to notables such as the painter Jack

Yeats. He returned to Dublin where he enjoyed shopping for some Donegal tweed before the Tuesday afternoon flight took him back to Northolt, London and work.

While Hayward was enjoying his Irish trip Dr Leavis was preparing an attack on the sick state of postwar literature and criticism, which duly appeared in *Scrutiny* of December 1948.[533] 'The Progress of Poesy' was a diatribe against all that he found most poisonous. It began by castigating the *Times Literary Supplement* reviewer for his praise of Auden and moved on to attack Cyril Connolly's *Horizon* for devoting an issue to honour the Sitwells. Both Auden and the Sitwells had symbolic values for *Scrutiny*. Auden represented Wasted Talent and the Sitwells Talentless Aristocracy. When Hayward praised Maurice Bowra, Warden of Wadham College, Oxford, who in turn praised Edith Sitwell, Leavis sensed the usual closed backslapping circle and denounced the destructive influence of this self-satisfied coterie. *Scrutiny* stood on its lonely eminence against them and what Leavis saw as the house journal of the Establishment, *The Times Literary Supplement*.

The essay then went on to deal with Hayward's pamphlet for the British Council, *Prose Literature since 1939*. Leavis quoted Hayward's description of himself in it as 'the cold intellectual leader of a minority group of Cambridge critics whose methodical and uncompromising destruction of reputations periodically enlivens the pages of their hypercritical but bracing magazine *Scrutiny*', before going on the attack:

> It would of course be hypercritical to suggest ... that nothing could be worse for the prestige and the influence of British letters abroad than Mr Hayward's presentment of the currency values of Metropolitan literary society and the associated University milieux as the distinctions and achievements of contemporary England.[534]

Hayward's pamphlet had closed with a sarcastic barb against the cold intellectualism of *Scrutiny*. In return Leavis accused Hayward of leading 'an array of warm British intellectuals', and noted finally: 'The warm intellectual is not, like the cold kind, offensively highbrow: however intransigent, he promotes cosiness.'[535]

Hayward was stung by the direct attack. His sense of the literary divide was clear in the table he drew up in 1949. Beneath the title '*SCRUTINY* Winter 1949' he drew two columns: Pro and Anti.[536] The first column comprised those who were favoured by *Scrutiny,* and the second those who emphatically were not. On the pro-side was the unlikely collection of Henry James, Conrad, Yeats, T. Powys, Lawrence, Joyce, Eliot, Forster, Pound and Edward Thomas. This literary team faced their opponents of Graham Greene, Shaw, Auden, Spender, Dylan Thomas, Sir Kenneth Clark, Edith Sitwell, Norman Nicholson, Cyril Connolly, Max Beerbohm, Robert Bridges and Lawrence Binyon. Hayward weighed in with nineteen antis as if to suggest a victory by force of numbers rather than by literary quality, but what he was really underlining was the narrowness and distaste for the modern that he saw in Dr Leavis and his scrutineers. Under his list he wrote: 'Lit. is meant to be enjoyed. Do they ever enjoy it? Louse upon the locks of literature.' Edith Sitwell was even more outspoken. 'Dr Leavis wants an immediate massacre of all poets, critics, scholars – in fact all men of letters, leaving Dr Leavis in sole possession of the world.'[537]

Leavis was right in seeing how closely linked many literary figures of the period were. They shared a public school background in which Etonians figured disproportionately: Cyril Connolly, Anthony Powell, Henry Green, George Orwell and John Lehmann were all at Eton together; Aldous Huxley was there a little earlier. Auden and Hayward were at Gresham's, Empson at Winchester, Isherwood at Repton, Graham Greene at Berkhamsted – and so on. They all left their public schools to go to Oxford or Cambridge. They knew each other well, reviewed each other's works, and met regularly at London parties and weekends in the country. An anecdote of early 1950 tells of the cocktail party celebrating fifty years of *The Times Literary Supplement,* held at Printing House Square. The anonymous reviewers all got their invitations and duly met – only to discover that they were all old friends and acquaintances. The surprise is that they were surprised. Dr Leavis would certainly not have been. He saw that Hayward's metropolitan network was the basis of postwar writing, publishing and reviewing. But he was not entirely right. He tended to describe his foes as if they were a united force, whereas in fact there was little sympathy between those whom he lumped together: between the Auden/Spender 'group' and Eliot or Hayward, for example, there was almost no common ground about politics and poetry. The 'currency values' Leavis discussed did not reflect at all the left-wing politics of many of the so-called 'group' – Orwell, Spender and Auden had leant towards Communism at the time of the Spanish Civil War and had gone to Spain to oppose General Franco. In emphasising their background Leavis failed to account for their work. There was more than a whiff of paranoia about his sense of conspiracy.

The argument did, however, reflect deep fissures between some Cambridge-based academics and metropolitan writers and critics. Hayward was Leavis's natural foe, symbolising all that was wrong with English culture. If Leavis wanted to attack a literary network, Tarantula was his obvious target: They were well-matched enemies. Hayward numbered among his friends Auden, Spender, the Sitwells and Cyril Connolly – all linked in Leavis's mind with smart commercialism. He also regularly reviewed for the enemy – *The Times Literary Supplement*. His whole approach to literature, with its emphasis on pleasure, seemed hopelessly out of date and frivolous. Leavis felt that his attack was so important that he chose to reprint it as the last essay in *The Common Pursuit* and explained that he gave it 'the salience of the final place' in the volume to counteract 'the formidable menace' of Establishment views on literature. 'What particularly characterises our time in England is the almost complete triumph of the "social" (or the "associational") values over those which are the business of the critic.'[538] Naturally Edith Sitwell was quick and eager to leap to Hayward's defence: 'What *have* you been up to? What have been your errors, heresies, crimes against Good Taste, Sensitivity and Adult Awareness? When did you fail to wince at, or condone, an ill-placed comma? Really, what an impossible man he is!'[539] It was only a matter of time before Dr Leavis would have to 'retreat into the shade of a Lunatic Asylum, driven there by mingled conceit and thwarted ambition'.

Never one to shirk a challenge, as a member of the Advisory Council of the recently-formed Institute of Contemporary Arts, Hayward decided to write to Leavis to invite him to defend his views at the Institute's Dover Street headquarters. He agreed and in July 1952 the two antagonists debated. As neither was prepared to give ground the meeting must have been a contentious one. Nevertheless, afterwards, Leavis wrote to Hayward to thank him for the opportunity of promoting *The Common Pursuit* (which, of course, was the opposite of the reason for the invitation), saying how much he had enjoyed the evening, with just a hint of an apology, followed by an attack:

If I made so much play with the British Council illustration it was because (in spite of what seems to be generally believed of me) I hate personalities. I am very much aware too that self-righteousness is odious. But what is one to do in a world in which what was once the Sitwell Circus has become a constellation of genii and Spender has been a major writer for 20 years and Desmond MacCarthy writing up his friends ... is a great critic and Cyril Connolly is credited with both critical and creative gifts.[540]

All the names singled out for abuse were of course, as he well knew, Hayward's friends.

It was difficult for Hayward to get out of London but one favourite refuge was Thriplow, near Cambridge, where he was welcomed by the Walstons and Graham Greene, when he was there. They sent their yellow convertible Rolls-Royce to pick him up and their chauffeur to help him in and out of the car. In a house where Picassos on sliding panels opened to reveal the vista of the Cambridgeshire countryside, paddocks, stables and stallions, the Walstons looked after Hayward. The task of having him to stay was not simple. In his thank-you letter after the visit he thanked Catherine for 'sock-pulling, tie-straightening, pot-handling, knee-pushing, heave-hoeing, etc etc', for tucking him in at night and providing four volumes of the *Catholic Encyclopaedia* to support his po.[541] Evelyn Waugh noted how she 'tenderly and candidly petted him'.[542] Graham Greene too proved to be an admirable valet to Hayward on his visits to Thriplow. It was not everyone who had the greatest living novelist to 'pot' him, he remarked. On his return he was chauffeured back to Carlyle Mansions in the Rolls stacked high with fresh eggs, chickens and pheasants – produce that was nearly unobtainable under rationing.

The visit was so successful that it was repeated for the next four years. This gave Hayward confidence to travel further. He had always wondered what happened to people in London in August when they seemed to vanish, leaving him alone in Carlyle Mansions. The overcast wet weather did not add to his cheer. So he did what many fellow Londoners did – he took a day trip to Brighton. He found he could just squeeze into the guard's van of a Pullman carriage and whisk there in an hour, but was out of sympathy with his fellow holiday makers whom he watched with appalled fascination: 'I sunned myself on the pier in the company of the New Rich – the uglies from the London suburbs, hideously apparelled & richly appointed, all licking "sugar-floss" or "choc-blocs" or sucking things through straws out of small bottles. It was very enjoyable in a low, carnal way.'[543] Much more to his taste was a trip just down the road to the nearby Hurlingham Club to watch old gents playing croquet and young ladies bathing.

Many men were envious of the gaggle of attractive women who seemed always to surround Hayward at Bina Gardens, at Merton Hall and later at Carlyle Mansions. He delighted in trying to shock them by his sexual frankness or by doodling erotic coloured sketches as he talked. 'How you ladies could stand it I don't know,' his manservant Askwith wondered to the musician Griselda Kentner. On the other hand the worldly Graham Greene felt that Hayward's scandalous talk was an attraction: 'Young women loved him for his frank delight in their beauty and the directness of its expression – he would think nothing of reading aloud to them at first meeting from Rochester's "The Imperfect Enjoyment",' a poem about premature ejaculation ... 'Any "girl friend of a friend" was always sure of welcome and friendship,' Greene continued, recalling how unlikely 'lovelies', such as the pretty French trapeze *artiste* he met at Carlyle Mansions, would gather at Hayward's feet.[544] According to the critic and novelist Elias Canetti, there was a vogue among the pretty girls of Chelsea to compete to pick him up at Carlyle Mansions, escort his wheelchair down the lift and push him along the Embankment. At parties women stood in a line waiting to be introduced. Indulged by this attention, he became a compulsive flirt. When his nephew Henry Oakeley took a girl friend round, he was surprised to find that his uncle had taken advantage of his absence for a moment to ask the girl for a date. After she left he asked the surprised young man, 'Have you enjoyed carnal relations?'

Sometimes he pushed his luck too far. A keen young undergraduate from Newnham College made careful arrangements to meet Hayward to discuss her poetry. She arrived nervously at Hayward's flat. When he asked her to undress completely before he would look at her work she fled. It was an open question to some of his friends as to whether he could have sex. Christopher Isherwood reported the rumours that he was a ladies' man, heartlessly jilting his girlfriends one after another. 'It was supposed that he managed to fuck them somehow,'[545] he concluded. In fact, Hayward was not a serial jilter but he may well have still been able to enjoy sex with some of his admirers. The record is silent on any details.

Not all of Hayward's female friends were impressed by the frankness of his language: Natasha Spender visited him with her friend Peggy Ashcroft. When he started to embark on 'panty talk', Peggy, still managing to smile nicely, burst out with, 'I'm awfully sorry, John, I can't bear it,' and fled, leaving Natasha Spender to calm him down.[546] She understood that these outbursts were the result of pent-up frustration. As he grew older he gradually became locked in a body that meant that he could not fulfil his strong sexual desires. The affairs of his youth gave way to aggressive challenges, risqué stories, and a collection of literary pornography and erotica that he shared with his friend Oliver Low.[547] The flesh was made word. Often even the ribaldry itself was more a teasing promise than the real thing: Richard Garnett never got to hear him recite the story of the mass rape of a troop of schoolgirls on an outing by train to Margate that Hayward had volunteered for the railway anthology Garnett was editing – at this point adolescent fantasy, as unreal in its way as the dream world of P. G. Wodehouse, begins to sound like something much more nasty and sadistic.

After moving to Carlyle Mansions, Hayward rarely saw his parents, who were now comfortably retired in Eynsham, near Oxford. In a poem he had written to commemorate his mother's eightieth birthday in 1946 he wrote as her 'ugly duckling boy' to express his sense of her still-powerful presence:

> With fond and filial love I write,
> Remembering, though far away,
> That fourscore years ago to-day
> At Oxford, you first saw the light.
>
> Still, though my years are now two score,
> Your mind is clear, hand firm, eye keen,
> I see you as you've always been,
> This day the same as heretofore.
>
> Still, without doubt, your eagle eyes
> Intimidate the lingering dust
> And looks of ill-concealed disgust
> Th' unwelcome bore still terrorize!
>
> I do not doubt, that as of old,
> The fearful scourings still proceed,
> And that with undiminished speed
> You make things do what they are told!

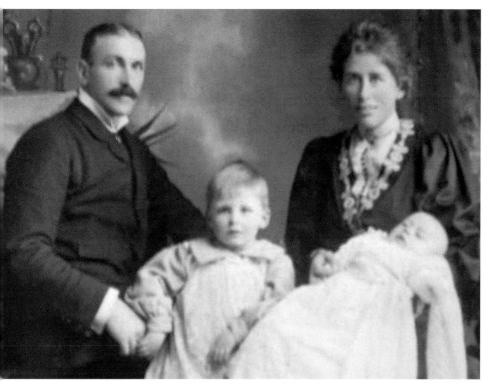

Dr and Mrs Hayward with George (left) and John

John (centre) with brother George and sister Rose Mary

Uniformed encounter: Mrs Hayward and Douglas Haig

Woodlands House, Gresham's: performance of *The Rivals*, with Hayward (facing) and his brother acting as seconds

Hayward as a prefect, Woodlands House, Gresham's

Elaine Finlay and the young Richard Garnett observed by Hayward from the car

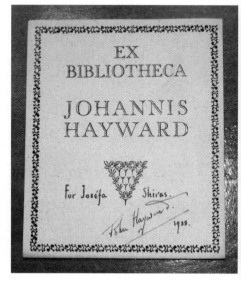

LEFT Joséfa Shiras RIGHT Hayward's bookplate inscribed to her

At work at Faber's: Eliot left, Geoffrey Faber centre

LEFT Eliot by Hayward RIGHT One of Hayward's suggestions for Possum

LEFT Outside King's with Lord Rothschild's butler RIGHT A choice of direction

Carlyle Mansions

Hayward at Carlyle Mansions

Queen Mary with Hayward, previewing incunabula for the Le Livre Français exhibition

In the face of what he had learnt from his own generation's experience he no longer had the confidence to dismiss the Victorianism of his parents that had annoyed him so much as a young man:

> When now, as grandmother, you cross
> With foot less swift those paths again,
> How much do you account as gain
> In all this change, how much as loss?
>
> Do you discern across that span
> Some slender stock of hidden good,
> Which notwithstanding has withstood
> The trampling of 'progressive' man?
>
> And, looking back across the years,
> Believe, despite the evidence,
> That he aspires to common sense
> Through blood and toil and sweat and tears?
>
> Child of the great Victorian age,
> How happily, it seems, you fared,
> When with your youth I have compared
> My generation's blotted page! [548]

In 1947 Hayward had written a companion poem for his father's eightieth birthday in mock-heroic style ('An Epistle in Verse Addressed to the Most Worthy Doctor of Physic & Amiable Gent. John Arthur Hayward ... on the Occasion of his Eightieth Birthday'). In Augustan style he painted a picture of his father as a country gentleman, possessing every civic virtue.

> Recall his prowess with the feathered hook,
> Skilfully cast upon the glassy brook,
> That brought the foolish finny tribe to book ...
> But most of all pay tribute to his skill
> When anyone at any time was ill ...[549]

He stressed his father's good health and his ability able to enter on his eighty-first year 'with foot less quick / Though not dependent yet upon a stick'. When he wrote these lines John Hayward had been in a wheelchair for more than twelve years. In his tributes to them he saw his parents as belonging to other ages – his father a model eighteenth-century squire and his mother a high Victorian matron.

But in March 1949 there came worrying signs about Dr Hayward's health. For some time there had been concerns about his heart; Mrs Hayward wrote that he was stubbornly ignoring orders to rest. He sent his son a sad and worried letter in which 'he hinted that he felt his days were numbered'.[550] The following Friday he tried to take a bath and was found by the nurse wandering about in a dazed condition. She got him back to bed with difficulty. A week later the family doctor rang to say that his patient was seriously ill and under morphia. Later in the day came the news that Dr Hayward had died quietly in his sleep at 4.30 in the afternoon. Hayward wrote to tell his sister and to reassure her that their father had suffered no pain. He sent his mother a letter of condolence armour-plated with politeness. She would understand, he said, that it was impossible for him to make the journey for the funeral – a strange show of weakness from a man who had only the previous year returned from a four-day lecturing tour in Ireland and was about to embark on a trip to Paris. The warmth of his relationship with his father after his adolescent squabbles makes it all the more surprising. Perhaps it was his mother he could not face. In fact, none of Dr Hayward's four children attended the funeral: Rose Mary had died in 1931; George had cut himself off; Diana was abroad and John pleaded disability. Dr Hayward's ashes were taken to be buried at Beechingstoke alongside Rose Mary's.

In the absence of George, Hayward took on the role of the head of the family in looking after his mother. Although she had borne the shock of her husband's death well, she was in a very weak state. She too was now disabled and needed a housekeeper and a nurse to stay with her and dreaded the prospect of having to go into a nursing home. Hayward promised that she could stay on at the family home in Eynsham until the end of her life and warned Diana: 'There is no doubt, I'm afraid, that she is gradually failing and we must be prepared for her death.' Given his mother's helpless condition, he added that this could be seen as a welcome release from her misery. The language of this letter is once again lacking in warmth, suggesting more the dutiful than the grieving son.

Nineteen months after her husband, on 1 October 1950, Mrs Hayward died, at the age of eighty-four. Eliot wrote sympathetically saying how he had felt 'a sudden loneliness, almost panic' when his own mother had died and 'an awareness of being irreparably middle-aged'.[551] After a funeral service at Eynsham on Saturday 7 October her ashes were interred along with her husband's in Beechingstoke church-yard. Neither of her sons was present.

15
London Life

Hayward was relishing his return to London. '*Everyone* wanted to know John Hayward,' wrote Lady Violet Bonham Carter. 'No London literary party of any consequence for many years was complete without him,' added his Cambridge contemporary, the publisher Ian Parsons. Hayward's mantelpiece was littered with invitations and the flat telephone rang incessantly. This was the happiest time of his life, thought his old friend Denys King-Farlow – it was certainly one of the busiest. In breathlessly gossipy style Hayward detailed a typical week from his hectic social calendar:

> I have attended the wedding of the older Miss Colquhoun; a party at the Redfern Gallery; the Picasso exhibition; a dinner given by the editor of the *Sunday Times* to meet Anthony Nutting MP whose wife is a kleptomaniac; a dinner party of the Huttons to meet Cyril [Connolly] and his new wife, a dumb blonde cast-off mistress of Quennell's and Sutro's. He ate and drank too much and had to spend most of the evening in the cloakroom; a luncheon of Cecil Beaton's where I met another Princess Bevar, daughter-in-law of the Nizam who came to tea a few days ago with Princess Zaid ...[552]

At parties his wheelchair was often waltzed around the dance floor and its occupant was keen to stay as long as possible – his stamina surprised even those who knew him well. Eliot stood directly behind, almost standing to attention. The moment when he took hold of the chair was often the signal for the party to end and guests to disappear. As Hayward's last secretary, Catherine Porteous, noted, 'He talked for his life.'[553] Like Dr Johnson's, his bons mots and scathing dismissals were enjoyed and feared. 'I know of no one more vitalising to talk to, whether seriously or in fun,' said Edith Sitwell.[554] He had no Boswell to record his words and most of them are lost, but his wit was remembered by those who met him: a man in a wheelchair, gesticulating with a cigarette, surrounded by pretty women, scandal and explosive laughter. Anthony Powell saw a more sinister side to this performance:

> In dealing with well-wishers of both sexes (men would push his chair or otherwise attend to his physical needs) Hayward whose temperament was at once nervous and dominating, could at times approach the positively tyrannical. Indeed, holding court at a party, he had much about him of Ham, the seated autocrat of Samuel Beckett's *End Game*, regal yet immobile, continually dispensing a rich flow of comment, imperious, erudite, malicious.[555]

Work was just as busy but had to be fitted in somehow. According to the writer J. E. Morpurgo, Hayward and John Lehmann were the two most important literary editors in London at this time.[556] In May 1950 he described to his mother how he was writing an introduction to Turgenev for the Cresset Press, correcting proofs for his Penguin *Donne*, doing biographical notes and blurbs, broadcasting on the Third Programme about books and book collecting, entertaining two 'sawdust' publishers, drafting an article on Henry Green, attending committee meetings of the Group Theatre, the Advisory Council of the ICA and the *Sunday Times* Book Prize Committee and discussing some 'ill-written proofs' with their authors.

Throughout his life Hayward loved meeting the aristocracy and the famous. Does this make him a snob? Christopher Sykes was sure that he was not: 'His judgement of people was never in the least affected by the rank of his acquaintance, but he liked the glamour of ancient titles and great names, and he indulged the taste openly, without inhibition, and with all his sense of humour and frequent self-mockery.'[557] So when Sykes asked him to dinner, Hayward wanted to know who his fellow guests were: 'I hope there'll be some guests with handles to their names for me to boast about after,' he commented. He continued to brag about his own pedigree, descended, as he thought, from Haywards of the Middle Ages who were Wardens of Scarborough Castle when Sykes's own family was 'unmentioned and unmentionable'. Sykes asked him how he was so sure that he was of the same family as those Scarborough Haywards. 'Don't ask such blasphemous questions,' came the reply.[558]

It is disingenuous, however, to think that because he treated it with irony, class did not matter to him. Even Lady Ottoline Morrell worried that he sometimes seemed more interested in her rank than her. Ian Parsons, like many of Hayward's enemies, was sure that he was both an intellectual and a social snob – 'Hayward had no use for "the middle classes" and could often be heard railing against them to some aristocratic litterateur.'[559] Hayward regularly used the language of snobbery – his domestic arrangements turned all too often on a 'slut' and a 'char'. When Betty Carr visited Carlyle Mansions for tea as part of her research for a civilian history of the war both flatmates asked her about the civil servants she was working with. She mentioned Sir Norman Brook,[560] Sir Edward Bridges, Lord Hurcomb and Sir Gilmore Jenkins. Hayward and Eliot immediately looked up their names in *Who's Who* and found that only one of them had been to a public school. Norman Brook's entry also showed that he lived in the fashionable St James's Terrace. 'Why, he's almost one of us,' they agreed. Gilmore Jenkins came in for the worst of it: 'Little Puddlington School and London University'. But when they came across the entry 'MC & Bar', all the jeering stopped at once.[561] Hayward's 'snobbery' was part of his veneration for the past and a fascination for what he saw as a doomed aristocratic way of life. He looked back fondly to a world of feudal loyalties and titles and was out of touch and out of sympathy with the growing egalitarianism of his century. It was buttressed by a sense, shared with modernist writers such as Eliot and Virginia Woolf, of belonging to an intellectual élite. He certainly thought that culture was to be appreciated and defended by a small group of educated people – 'the mandarinate', as he and Cyril Connolly called it. It was up to them to remain true to their standards when under threat. By today's standards he would certainly be seen as a snob, but his attitudes to class were very much those of his time.

The arrangement with Eliot seemed to be working very well. They took pleasure in each other's company and shared a taste for jokes and mutual teasing. When Eliot said that he had never eaten anything blue Hayward asked their cook if she could put this right. Noel Blakiston, an old friend from Cambridge days, came round to Carlyle Mansions and was taken to the kitchen to admire the result. On the table sat, completely untouched, a large sky-blue blancmange. *Time* magazine of 6 March 1950 drew a picture of the cosy domesticity of flat-sharing, with Eliot emerging into the parlour wearing a Sherlock Holmes dressing gown and slippers, addressing his startled friend, 'My dear Hayward, I am put in mind of the incident in Bosnia, at the time of our struggle with the Professor over the Crown Prince's jewels ...'

As Hayward was enjoying London parties and his flatmate's company, a new woman entered Eliot's life. Mary Trevelyan was quite a contrast to the unstable but talented Vivienne and the formal Bostonian Emily Hale. Tall and dark, with a low throaty laugh, she was a likeable witty woman who enjoyed male company, with an easy manner that made her just as at home with the humblest students as she was with ambassadors and statesmen. She loved music, played the piano and had taught at various schools. Her clear sense of Christian duty led her to devote her life to the cause of the welfare of foreign students, for which much later she received the CBE. From a distinguished intellectual background, Mary was related to the historian George Babington Macaulay; G. M. Trevelyan was a cousin; her brother-in-law was the Bishop of Oxford. This was an English family that was a match for the Eliots of Harvard.

Eliot and she had first met in 1938. Then forty-one, she ran the Student Movement House in Gower Street. She was asked to look after Eliot when he was invited to lecture at a Christian conference for young people at Swanwick in Derbyshire. Eliot went to fulfil his duty with reluctance and a head cold. Although he was not a success with the students – they were too gauche and 'the Poet looked terrified' – she found, to her surprise, that afterwards he melted in the face of her teasing. She joked about his stiff-necked reading and he began to laugh. Mary, like Hayward, found it easy to penetrate his reserve. Four years after meeting him, she confessed that, just like Vivienne and Emily Hale before her, she had fallen in love.

In her unpublished memoir, which she entitled 'The Pope of Russell Square, 1938–1958',[562] she told the story of how their relationship developed. Both High Anglicans, they worshipped regularly at Eliot's church, St Stephen's, Kensington. There High Church ceremonial was presided over by Father Cheetham. On Sunday mornings Eliot and Mary Trevelyan met outside St Stephen's and then enjoyed the ritual celebration of the church year, the choral singing, and the sense of theatre that Father Cheetham, always something of a showman, brought with him. They especially relished the drama of the Maundy Thursday Service of Tenebrae, 'that great, dark, magnificent service' as Mary called it, where, one by one, the candles were put out until the church was in total darkness and silence. The stillness was finally broken by a mysterious and tremendous crashing sound from behind the congregation – which made Mary jump – leaving everyone to depart in complete silence. Morning service was often followed by a drive around favourite spots in London. They discussed theology and history at the Garrick Club where Eliot sometimes invited her to dinner. 'Did you remember to pray for Richard III?' he asked her – Eliot always wore a white rose in memory of King Richard III on the anniversary of the Battle of Bosworth and a red tie for Charles King and Martyr. In the evening they drank sherry or gin together in Eliot's flat and enjoyed suppers of bacon and eggs before settling down to listening to Schubert or Mozart on the gramophone or, on a less elevated plane, to championship boxing between Randolph Turpin and George Angelo on the wireless.

Mary worried about Eliot's bronchial illnesses, his cold flat at Carlyle Mansions, his chilly office, and his loneliness. He enjoyed her company and gave her regular and generous presents, including a car as an acknowledgement of all the chauffeuring she had done for him, and a rosary that had been blessed at his audience with Pope Pius XII. She gave him a huge crucifix rescued from a devastated town in Germany, which he hung over his bed. Sometimes he held her hand for what she felt was 'an embarrassingly long time'. Every night they prayed for each other; but whereas she was falling in love with him, his feelings were much less straightforward. Privately, he told Hayward that 'this indefatigable woman' was bossy and 'hearty' in a very English way. He did, however, share with her his anguish about his marriage to Vivienne. He told her that he had never truly loved his wife; that they had married very young and had never been happy together. There were dreadful nights when she would say she ought never to have married him and that she was 'uselesss and better dead', before bursting into floods of tears. He recalled the 'terrible experience of watching a mind slipping from the real world into the world of imagination'.[563] After Vivienne's death in January 1947 he felt 'more disintegrated than I would have expected'. It was, he told Mary, if anything worse now for him than it had been before because of the 'diminution of resolution' that went with ageing.

Yet often after a meeting in which he had confided in her, he would suddenly, Macavity-like, stage one of his disappearing tricks and Mary would hear nothing from him for days or sometimes weeks. He imposed a rule, which she could never understand, and he rarely kept, that they should never meet more than once a week – and less frequently in Lent. Undaunted, she proposed marriage in a long letter in April 1949, two years after Vivienne's death. Eliot, taken aback, took nine days to respond. 'Oh dear Oh dear, I haven't been so distressed since a catastrophe I can't tell anyone about,' began his disheartening reply. He told her that he wanted friendship but as 'a burnt-out case' could not offer love. 'A haunted man' could do no more. The five or six years of agony before the war had 'exhausted and crippled' him. Hence the thought of sharing his life with anyone was 'a nightmare'.[564] Despite this refusal she proposed again in May the following year. 'Why should we both be lonely?' she asked. This time his reply was different: 'I have never wanted to marry anyone except this one person,' he wrote.[565] He had been very much in love with someone and would have sacrificed everything for the possibility of marrying her. In July that year Emily Hale visited England and was formally introduced to John Hayward. Mary realised immediately that she was indeed 'THE lady'. 'Here was the truth at last!' she exclaimed in her journal.[566] But now that Eliot was free he knew that he had been deluding himself. He still loved Emily, but as an ideal figure from his past, not the real, older woman she now was. He had rejected both of them.

Hayward was still deeply involved with Eliot's plays. They had sat together in the front row of the studio to watch the BBC televise *The Family Reunion* in February 1950 – during which a lady sitting in the second row poked Eliot in the back and told him not to talk. Eliot's acknowledgement before *The Cocktail Party* (1950) thanked Martin Browne, the producer, for his advice on the dramatic structure of the play, and Hayward for 'continuous criticism and correction of vocabulary, idiom and manners'.[567] He added that his debt to both these 'censors could only be understood only by comparison of the successive drafts of the play with the first draft'. Hayward performed the same kind of editorial function for Eliot's plays as he did for his poetry. The London first night of *The Cocktail Party* on 3 May 1950 was tense. Eliot had been on the committee in America that had awarded Ezra Pound the Bollingen Prize for poetry. Pound had been imprisoned in Italy during the war for his his fascist views. The news was greeted by the *New York Times* with the headline: 'Pound in Mental Clinic, Wins Prize for Poetry Written in Prison Cell.' As a result Eliot was excoriated as anti-American and treated as an accomplice to neo-fascism. After this he was especially worried about the success of his newest play. The general director, Henry Sherek, left cellophane-wrapped baskets of gardenias and carnations for Hayward and Eliot in the small box which they shared, tucked discreetly at the side of the dress circle.

Resplendent in his flowered waistcoat, Hayward reported the play to be 'a *great* success', with an appreciative audience laughing at all the right points. Immediately after he had listened to Eliot's modest, almost inaudible curtain speech, he hurried off to the Savoy Hotel for the celebration first night party he had organised. There were champagne cocktails and a candlelit meal in a private dining room. Hayward had carefully arranged the seating plan the night before. Eliot occupied pride of place at the central table, sitting with Rex Harrison and Margaret Leighton. Martin Browne sat to his left with Mary Trevelyan; Hayward was at his right with the French ambassador and Sir Kenneth Clark and his wife. The famous acting couple Dulcie Gray and Michael Denison were there, as were the Swedish, Italian and Burmese ambassadors. Afterwards Hayward wrote to his mother about the 'astonishing pulchritude of the ladies' and the operatic ice cream desserts that flamed like miniature Mount Etnas. Eliot and Hayward returned by taxi to Carlyle Mansions at 2 am tired, overwrought and excited.

In *The Cocktail Party* the tangled affairs of the main characters are sorted out by two mysterious angel-like figures, Julia and Sir Henry Harcourt-Reilly. There is a toast to 'the Guardians' at the end of the second scene of the first act; Celia Coplestone wonders explicitly if Julia 'is my guardian'. The second act closes with a kind of 'libation' to the gods and a prayer. At the party that followed the performance Hayward said to Mary, 'I look on you as part of the family.' Mary recognised parts of her own character in Julia who conceals her control behind the mask of amiable dottiness. In her memoir entry of 5 June she recalled saying to Eliot she wanted him to know that she was certain that there was something between them that could not be killed: 'Here was one person who loved him and that from now on he had better adopt her as one of the family.' When they next met he gave her a beaming smile and said, 'I'll give you a toast – TO THE GUARDIANS': Mary herself and John Hayward. 'So we drank to our guardians of our future,' she added, perhaps still half hoping that they were toasting angelic guardians to bless her romance. It was, of course, a rejection; Eliot was happy to change Mary's role from suitor to guardian. From Mary's point of view, if she could not be Eliot's wife she could at least be welcomed as a kind of tutelary spirit. So this strangely-assorted group came into being around Eliot: an unmarried woman full of unrequited love and a physical cripple, looking after a poet who called himself a burnt-out case. Or, perhaps, an angel, a sinner and a prospective saint.[568]

Hayward's Penguin edition *John Donne* appeared in 1950, based on the text he had prepared twenty years before for Nonesuch. In his Introduction he argued that 'Donne's poetry, more than that of any of his contemporaries, not excepting even Shakespeare's, seems to satisfy, or at least assuage, the appetencies peculiar to the intelligence and sensibility of our own time'.[569] Donne did for seventeenth-century poetry what Eliot and Auden did for poetry in the 1920s and responded to a time of crisis by breaking the mould of poetic convention.

> To an older generation, brought up on the sonnets and blank verse of Wyatt and Lord Surrey – themselves innovators less than fifty years before – Donne's uncouthness must have seemed as reprehensible or at least as unsympathetic as Hardy's peculiar ruggedness did to a generation accustomed to the mellifluous flow of Tennyson's or Swinburne's verse, or as the rhythms of *The Waste Land* to the admirers of Rupert Brooke and Flecker.[570]

Here he was not only tracing the intellectual current of his age but also his own progress from the schoolboy admirer of Brooke and Flecker to the undergraduate whose discovery of *The Love Song of J. Alfred Prufrock* changed his view of poetry for ever. Hayward noted with pleasure that the number of copies of the first issue of his Penguin *Donne* was vastly greater than all the other copies of all of the previously printed editions put together.

Meanwhile Hayward was working with Eliot on a strange publishing project surrounded with secrecy. For this Hayward dealt with his old Swedish friends at Bonniers who had published his 'Letter from London'. He impressed upon them the need for complete discretion. The firm itself was so worried that it could not 'command an absolute assurance of loyalty' from within that in April 1950 it suggested abandoning the plan. Nevertheless the private edition went ahead, strictly limited to twelve copies, each one personally numbered by Georg Svensson, a director of Bonniers. No copies were to be sent to the Royal Library in Stockholm or to the three Swedish universities, even though Swedish law required this. The firm would hang on to four copies, sealed up in the basement of Bonniers, just in case the news got out. If they had to be sent to libraries they would become 'secret deposits' to be kept in a strongbox. Eliot's *Poems Written in Early Youth*, printed and bound on very fine rag paper, eventually saw the light of day in December 1950. Rumours of all kinds about the book and its possible contents were widespread. The clandestine method of publication naturally provoked the very gossip and curiosity it was designed to prevent. (In fact so much interest was aroused that in 1967 Valerie Eliot published a reprint of *Poems Written in Early Youth* for Faber's 'as a corrective to the inaccurate, pirated versions'.)[571]

This scheme for publishing a collection of Eliot's earliest poems had been long planned. There were poems from his schooldays at Smith Academy, St Louis, along with some he had written at Harvard that had been published without permisssion in the *Harvard Advocate* together with the unpublished 'Death of Saint Narcissus'. The collection of just fourteen poems was made up of all the surviving material written by Eliot as a schoolboy and undergraduate between the age of sixteen and twenty-two. Eliot had handed on to Hayward the original draft of 'the first poem I ever wrote to be shown to other eyes', beginning 'If Time and Space, as Sages say, / Are things that cannot be ...' Reading them now it is hard to know what all the fuss was about – the poems were in no way obscene as rumour had it, but gave insight into Eliot's development. The most likely explanation for the secrecy was that Eliot was, as usual, averse to printing anything he was not entirely satisfied by, and opposed to the kind of biographical and personal interest the collection might provoke. Hayward, on the other hand, wanted to celebrate their friendship through a literary collaboration. Eliot's giving way to his friend's wishes is an indicator of their closeness at the time – and, perhaps, of the power of Hayward's will. There was also a welcome element of skulduggery too about the whole enterprise.

More and more Hayward's life began to revolve around the world of bibliography, book collectors and book collecting. He was elected Vice-President of the Bibliographical Society and was a regular participant at its dining offshoot the Colophon Club, but it was with the unnamed club known as the Biblios which met periodically at the Garrick Club where he really shone. Contacts with America multiplied. In 1955 he was elected as Honorary Foreign Corresponding Member of the Grolier Club of New York and became closely associated with Paul Mellon and the Bollingen Foundation which he had founded. Hayward was fascinated by Americans and their directness; many of his closest friends were American – but professional academics were another matter. When the Oxford don Helen Gardner went to Los Angeles he asked for a report on 'those immensely earnest people in oatmeal coloured suitings, rimless dodecahedron specs, cravats (or black knitted silk tie and tyrelene [*sic*] shirt) with their filing cabinets and typewriters fitted with six kinds of brackets and their appalling Ree-search Projects'.[572] He thought that, in their scientific gadget-ridden approach, like Dr Leavis, they seemed to have forgotten that the point of literature was to give pleasure.

Hayward's friendship with Mary Hyde began when he met her lawyer husband Donald on a book-buying trip to London. Mary and Donald lived in colonial style at Four Oaks Farm in New Jersey where they housed their books and she ran a farm with a milking herd. The couple of bibliophiles were beginning to put together what was to become the finest collection of Dr Johnson's works. Soon the correspondence between John Hayward and Mary developed into a close friendship. Their annual visits to England in the spring to buy books and meet friends became fixed points in Hayward's calendar.

Mary was a scholar whose first interest was Elizabethan drama. She was 'rich, very intelligent, highly cultivated, generous, hospitable, and a delightful and faithful friend'.[573] She was also stylish and elegant. Unsurprisingly, Hayward was entranced. She was his dark-haired 'New Jersey Lily', or 'Pomona' bringing summer back to to his life. He wrote that he dreamed of her wearing an embroidered blouse and a powder blue skirt as they went together to watch trains at the local station. He often thought of her in a longing sort of way – and hastily rephrased it as 'longing to see you'. They played hilarious games of Scrabble in his flat. During the mid-1950s they began to discuss together the plan which they called 'THE GREAT PLOT'. Since the beginning of war he had hoped to visit the United States. Full of enthusiasm, he wrote to her, 'I hope to go to all my favourite libraries and outstay my welcome.'[574]

An American book collector of a very different kind to Mary and Donald Hyde was the American Dr Jake Schwartz, doctor of dentistry from a mid-western university. Well known as an inveterate haggler, and something of a parasite, he tried to get his bargains by any possible means. He persuaded Eliot to sign several of his books, on the grounds that they were a charity offering for his alma mater. When Hayward told the story to another New York book dealer, Mr Cohn, known as 'the Captain', he exclaimed, 'Alma mater! Alma mater! Jakie Schwartz hasn't even got an alma pater!'[575] On another occcasion he suddenly accosted Hayward in the lift of Carlyle Mansions and offered 'stunning prices for my Eliot book'. 'Turn out your pockets, Jakie Schwartz,' said Hayward – with which he vanished 'to the sound of widows and orphans in distress – and with a strong smell of brimstone'.[576]

Hayward broadcast on the Third Programme a talk 'Why First Editions?' on Saturday 17 June 1950.[577] It was one of a series of four talks and the first time that book collecting and bibliography had received any attention on the air. He granted that part of a collector's motive might well be financial or simply the desire to own a rarity – but this was not the major reason for collecting first editions. The main point was to help the literary scholar establish 'the canon and the text of an author's writing'.[578] Sometimes bibliographers, by dint of painstaking analysis of the printed book, could help to establish which was the first edition and therefore the best copy text. He next spoke of his personal addiction. He loved the book for 'its sensuous appeal', its paper, its binding, its typography and its design. Although he felt all these strongly, they were not sufficient in themselves. 'The pleasure of collecting first editions comes from a collation of these physical factors with the literary and historical qualities, and technical features, which the scholar and bibliographer cherish.'[579] What had started for him with a dog-eared Rochester bought from Old David's market stall became an obsessive desire to possess a copy of every seventeenth- and eighteenth-century edition of his poems. When, twenty-five years later, Hayward had managed to buy another rare 'Antwerp' edition he had built up the best collection of Rochester's first and early editions and was finally satisfied. He also had fine collections of the writers he loved best: Donne, Swift and Saint Evrémond. His interests in modern literature were closely bound up with his friendships: he had nearly all the first editions of Graham Greene, Ian Fleming and P. G. Wodehouse. The most personal statement of his lifelong love-affair with the book came at the end of his talk.

> We treasure what we love – to the heartwhole the raptures of a passionate collector may appear as fond, as foolish and even as ridiculous as those of a passionate lover – and what I, for one, treasure in a first edition is its association with the moment in time in which its author lived and in which his work first saw the light.

To own a copy of a first edition is to share, with an author's first readers, the experience of realizing how his words originally appeared in print. It is indeed a moving experience to open one of the books I have mentioned and to find oneself reading, as it were through the eyes of a contemporary:

'When the Funerall pyre was out, and the last valediction over ...'
or: 'It is an ancyent Marinere, And he stoppeth one of thre ...'
or: 'O saisons, O châteaux , Quel âme est sans défauts ...'
or finally: 'Longtemps je me suis couché de bonne heure ...[*sic*]'[580]

Early in 1950 the publisher Rupert Hart-Davis was asked by his old friend Allan Wade if he would publish his bibliography of Yeats, based on more than fifty years of dedicated collecting. Hart-Davis's fellow 'Biblioboys' John Carter and John Hayward were immediately enthusiastic about the scheme and the first of the 'Soho Bibliographies' emerged in 1951. It was a most unusual and daring enterprise for a commercial rather than a university publisher. Original in approach, it contained 'a full bibliographical description of all Yeats's separately printed works, with further entries for books to which he had contributed, translations, periodical contributions and critical writings, all in chronological order'.[581] Hayward formally joined the Advisory Board in 1952, and took upon himself the tasks of 'checking typescripts and the instruction of neophytes'.[582] The meticulous love of, and attention to detail that marked all of his work made him just the man for the job.

For fifteen years Hayward was in almost daily telephone contact with Rupert Hart-Davis. Meetings were held in the flat above his offices at Soho Square or at Carlyle Mansions where Hart-Davis, Carter, and Munby thrashed out common policy and enjoyed 'ribald gossip'. 'He and Jake and I worked together so harmoniously and so closely for so long that it is difficult to remember exactly who was responsible for this and that, and that if these words of mine are more about the Soho Bibliographies than about John, that is because he was so completely and inextricably identified with them,' Hart-Davis wrote.[583] Wade's Yeats was followed the following year by two more bibliographies, based on the same pattern, on A. E. Housman, and on Max Beerbohm. Volumes on James Joyce, Norman Douglas, Frederick Rolfe, Baron Corvo, Henry James, Oscar Wilde, Virginia Woolf, Rupert Brooke and many others followed at roughly yearly intervals. The format evolved as mistakes were made and the editors learned from experience, but the basis of the famous 'Soho formula' was established. Hart-Davis called his team 'amateur bibliography publishers'. Amateur or not, the 'Soho Formula' had a lasting success. 'Distinguished, even remarkable for their care and accuracy, they are one of the great projects of modern literary scholarship,' wrote Charles Burkhart,[584] but others, such as Simon Nowell-Smith, were critical of the lack of uniformity and consistency in the series. In 1970, after nearly twenty years of indepependent existence, the Soho Bibliographies were taken over by the Oxford University Press.

Such was Hayward's prominence as a man of letters that it was natural for him to be the 'general provider of material for all manner of celebrations' for the Festival of Britain in 1951. *Literary Britain*[585] was a collection of some one hundred evocative black and white plates of buildings and landscape by Bill Brandt. Hayward wrote the accompanying text. He also organised an exhibition of books and manuscripts at the Victoria and Albert Museum and provided the quotations and references for an illustrated literary map of the British Isles. What turned out to be a much more controversial task was to judge the poetry competition. The Arts Council of Great Britain, together with the Festival of Britain organisers, had decided to award prizes totalling £1,100. Hayward was one of the six judges; he was also asked to edit and introduce the volume of the prize winners. The panel was made up of predictably middle-aged Oxbridge establishment figures: Sir Kenneth Clark as Chairman, Professor Maurice Bowra, Lord David Cecil, Dadie Rylands, and Professor Basil Willey. No list could have been calculated to annoy Dr Leavis more. When the names had been announced in 1949 he immediately drew a damning set of portraits of the panel in *Scrutiny*.[586] None of the judges, he felt, had any right to award the prize. Of the chairman Leavis wrote that he had never before been known as a critic of poetry, apart from 'an appreciation, in its vulgar sense, of Edith Sitwell'. Leavis's Cambridge colleague Dadie Rylands was 'an actor-producer of Elizabethan drama' and Lord David Cecil a biographer. The character assassinations varied in style from sarcasm and innuendo to direct attack. Hayward's was a mixture of all three:

> Mr John Hayward is known as a specialist scholar who has done some editing. He wrote the British Council Booklet ... *Prose Literature since 1939* in which, to quote our own comment, 'he

presented the currency values of Metropolitan literary society and the associated university milieux as the distinctions and achievements of contemporary England'.[587]

Leavis would have been on stronger ground if he had criticised the panel for not containing a single poet, but that was not his point. He felt that once again criticism had been taken over by the insider club. This 'coterie' elected itself onto committees and took control of 'the institutions of taste and cultural authority'. Ultimately the club principle meant that a magazine such as *Scrutiny* was never mentioned in the pages of *The Times Literary Supplement*. It seemed to Leavis that only *Scrutiny* had stood out for the past seventeen years maintaining 'a strenuous and lonely pre-eminence in the language as representing the function of criticism'. A year later he returned to the subject of the poetry prizes in a *Scrutiny* review, 'Keynes, Spender, and Currency-values'.[588] Here he analysed more closely how these insiders had grown from the 'Axis Eton-King's-Bloomsbury' to redefine themselves in the 1930s to include 'the Gang' of Auden, Spender, and MacNeice. 'Today the triumph of the social-personal (or "club" we may now call it) is complete. The club is not narrowly exclusive, but you must belong (and keep the rules) if you are to be recognised to exist.'[589] Leavis noted with satisfaction the predictable disappointment of the Festival Poetry competition. He added that even respectable newspapers like the *Manchester Guardian* had apparently been dismayed by the results and begun to question how the panel had been selected. The failure of the committee to choose any worthwhile winners seemed to Dr Leavis a vindication of his views.

Hayward agreed in private that the standard was terribly low. He nicknamed it 'The Festival of Britain Piffle Competition' and wrote to Edith Sitwell about the 'appalling experience' of having to look at more than 1,000 of the 2,080 entries. 'Does everyone in the kingdom secrete this horrible stuff?' he asked.[590] At least, however, some of the entries made him laugh and he made a collection of the best ones. He told her that he had not awarded the prize to the lady from Paignton who had written a 2,000-page epic or the 'Lady of Title' from Scotland who addressed a lyric to the concrete rabbit in her garden, 'The pansy lying by thy side / Is happier far than me ...' He duly sent her the most unpromising titles: 'Mother', 'Sea Fever', 'Warbleswick Revisited', 'Springtide of Love', 'Forsythia', 'Hiker's Song' and 'The Gnomes'

Wedding'. He was also amused by the bizarre presentation of the poems: some on cardboard in coloured chalk; some on vellum written in illuminated letters; others bound with loving care, leather thongs or silk ties. The poets themselves were a bizarre mixture of 'the eccentrics and the moonstruck, bemused and halting followers of Blake or Smart, with their obscure cosmic visions and their fearful prophecies of imminent damnation underscored in blood-red ink'.[591] A real concern was that the average age of the winners was over forty and the average age of the committee over fifty. Was this, he wondered, a sign of a second lost generation of English writers?

The winners were published by Penguin in *Poems 1951*: Hayward contributed an introduction in which he surveyed the prospects for poetry. Inflation and the perennial difficulty of publishing a first volume meant that 'the future of English poetry is darker than it has ever been'. Too many books, too little literature was his diagnosis. Old-style aristocratic patronage was long gone and even Auden and Eliot could not live off their earnings as poets. This all left a gap which an enlightened state ought to fill. He applauded the efforts of the Arts Council in awarding the prizes and hoped that it would continue to support poetry as it did other art forms. Publication in the Penguin edition guaranteed the largest possible readership: 'In the end poetry cannot survive unless the public can be induced to read it.'[592] Only bodies such as the Arts Council could keep poetry alive: otherwise, the outlook was bleak indeed. This was quite a reversal from his wartime snobbery about Penguins and the CEMA. A much more significant and long-lasting legacy than the competition was the creation of the Poetry Book Society. Hayward played an important role in setting it up. He interested Eliot in the scheme and urged him to sit on the board of management and act as its figurehead. That was a virtual guarantee of success. Together with Edwin Muir and Janet Adam Smith, Hayward formed the first team of 'selectors' who chose the poetry for the magazine. 'It was largely due to the high critical standards they set that the society got off to such a good start. When his time as a selector was over, he continued to sit on the board offering wise advice and trenchant criticism.'[593]

As part of the Festival celebrations Hayward also took a major role in planning an exhibition of 'Le Livre Anglais' held at the Bibliothèque Nationale in Paris in 1951.[594] Through his auspices Eliot had been invited to inaugurate the exhibition. It had been the Queen's idea: after enjoying 'A Thousand Years of French Books' at the National Book League in London she had suggested a 'return match'. Both the President of the French Republic and the King acted as patrons. Hayward was an obvious choice to be on the committee that chose the exhibits as he had an intimate knowledge of the contents of other people's libraries, an insatiable curiosity about them and an exact memory for who owned what. Flicking through his 'mental card index' he would say, 'I think that Lady X has the original draft of that; I will get onto her about it.'[595] There was a price, however, for having him on the committee. Charles Morgan, who enjoyed a considerably higher reputation as a novelist in France than in England, had presented an autograph manuscript of his 'Ode to France' which the Bibliothèque Nationale was very keen to include. However, the mere name of Charles Morgan was enough to make Hayward see red. In one particularly acrimonious committee meeting he stated flatly, 'If Charles Morgan is included in this exhibition, I will see to it that my lodger does not come to Paris.' He was not – and his lodger did. 'Few of the distinguished guests at the opening ceremony could have guessed how touch and go Eliot's participation had been,' remarked Sencourt.[596]

On 16 November the President of France and the British Ambassador attended the opening in the Galerie Mazarine. With its rich gilt ceiling and ornate chandeliers, built by 'the great Cardinal bibliophile himself',[597] it was a suitably splendid setting for the 782 treasures on show which were arranged in fourteen aisles. There were five sections: manuscripts, first editions, printing, binding and portraits. On arrival the visitor was greeted into the ante-room by some twenty-five of the finest examples of medieval art. Manuscripts started with the tenth-century 'Benedictional of St Aethelwold', a masterpiece of Anglo-Saxon illumination which had crossed the Channel in a 'specially-made reliquary in a reserved *coupé*, in the anxious charge of the then keeper of the Manuscripts at the British Museum'.[598] Exhibits included the only known manuscript of the *Morte d'Arthur*, a fifteenth-century illustrated *Canterbury Tales,* the only known copy of Shakespeare's *Venus and Adonis* and first quartos of *Romeo and Juliet* and *Hamlet*. There were eighty-five examples of English binding, including the earliest leather binding in Europe: the Stonyhurst Gospel of about 695, bound for St Cuthbert. Printing exhibits began with Caxton. The exhibition ended with autograph manuscripts of Virginia Woolf, Graham Greene and Evelyn Waugh. According to *The Times* it was 'the choicest and most comprehensive display of British books and manuscripts ever organised' and Desmond Flower called it 'the greatest assemblage of the treasures of our literature and book-production that has ever been brought together'.[599]

Eliot began his inaugural address in characteristically apologetic fashion. A writer, he said, should only be heard by the sound of his typewriter. Then he spoke of how he depended upon the scholar's care for textual accuracy, continuing:

> I am no bibliographer but only a man of letters. Those whose primary concern is the soul of literature owe a good deal to the scholars who preserve its physical body from corruption; the bibliographer is a man whom I regard with gratitude, and even with a certain awe. I have the benefit of numbering several distinguished bibliographers among my acquaintance.[600]

He went on to examine the importance of the book as a physical object, quoting the words of 'a preface written by a distinguished bibliographer who should have been present today': 'The survival of English poetry, indeed, ultimately derives from the existence and preservation of these primary printed sources ... ' Many of the guests would have appreciated Eliot's compliment to Hayward for those are the very words which ended his 'Preface to the Exhibition of English Poetry' that he had arranged four years earlier.[601] Finally Eliot stressed how important it was for the continuation of culture that works of genius should be handed down accurately, preserving the integrity of the text. 'Such was Eliot's tribute to Hayward,' wrote Sencourt, for every word of Eliot's address smacked of his friend's views and style. 'If further proof were required of the nature of Eliot's relation with Hayward, it is surely here: far from their companionship being a mere arrangement of convenience or the gregarious instinct of two lonely and ageing men, it was a deep communion of interests in which each side contributed faithfully to the other.'[602]

In the early 1950s Hayward was busy preparing catalogues for the Cambridge University Press for two important private libraries and two 'high-spot' collectors. Sir Louis Sterling, American by birth, was a self-made millionaire who became Chairman of EMI.[603] Over fifty years of 'ambitious and well-advised collecting'[604] he put together a library of more than 4,000 rare and early books, including the four Shakespeare folios, a Caxton, Herrick's *Hesperides*, 1648, and Shelley's *Adonais*, 1821, amongst many other treasures. Hayward admired the library, but felt that Sterling himself knew next to nothing about books. When Sterling decided to decided to present his collection to London University as the basis of a Rare Book Department, he chose Hayward as the expert bibliographer in charge of the team of librarians who catalogued the library at Sterling's home. It was said to be the most generous gift ever from a private individual to a British library and was installed in a specially designed galleried chamber and formally opened on 30 October 1956 by Queen Elizabeth the Queen Mother. Hayward, proudly wearing his CBE with its pink ribbon, was there to greet her along with the other dignitaries. The 600-page catalogue itself followed the pattern of Hayward's 1947 work, and 'does ample justice to a lordly project'. Its design was 'wholly admirable' and the indexing and cross-referencing very clear and useful.[605] The other private library was also the collection of a millionaire and one that Hayward knew exceptionally well: Lord Rothschild. Hayward's wartime hours in the library at Merton Hall and his exhibition at Cambridge all came to fruition with the publication of this lavish two-volume catalogue, illustrated with sixty collotypes.[606] Its scope was strictly limited to books and manuscripts published between 1700 and 1800, and Swift was at its centre. In his introduction Lord Rothschild listed all the distinguished advisers he had called upon to advise him, but Hayward was the ultimate arbiter 'who planned the catalogue and supervised it at every stage of its production'.[607] No doubt Hayward was delighted to print David Holland's flattering comments about his exhibition and his catalogue in *The Book Collector*: 'a beautifully balanced bibliograpical tool … often improving on published bibliographies and its general method and design owe a good deal to the successful principles we have come to associate with Mr John Hayward.'[608]

When Hayward looked back on the first half of the century he saw how the various literary movements each had figures who acted as their spearheads: Yeats had inspired the lyric, Pound the Imagists and Auden the political writers. Eliot had expressed the spiritual yearning of a generation. Now there was a terrible gap: 'For the first time in living memory there is no avant-garde' and the future for English poetry 'is darker than it has ever been'.[609] The situation, Hayward thought, was not only one of lack of talent; it was also a problem of a changing culture. He noted that the prewar writers had come from similar backgrounds; they were middle-class, public school, Oxbridge, metropolitan. That was the 'central literary culture' to which he himself and many others belonged. Where could the avant-garde come from now, he wondered, when writers had buried themselves unpromisingly in 'redbrick universities' and schools scattered all over the country? By contrast to their predecessors, the postwar young writers seemed to him to be both 'unambitious' and 'parochial'. It was this failure to accept or understand the social and literary changes of the 1950s that led him to be increasingly out of touch. He met and dismissed Jean Paul Sartre as a melodramatic villain. 'It was not an experience I would wish to have on a dark night,' he confided to Eliot, 'he has a fearful ball-eye which rolls in an alarming syncopated fashion while the other glares with a sinister and phosphorescent glow.'[610] He had little to say about the Faber poets of the time. To his distaste, 'The Movement' poets such as Philip Larkin, Thom Gunn and John Wain turned their backs on modernism and documented the ordinary and the humdrum. Ted Hughes and Sylvia Plath came too late for him to notice them. He had no sympathy for the provincial realism of novels such as Kingsley Amis's *Lucky Jim* and John Braine's *Room at the Top*. In 1956 *Look Back in Anger* effectively killed off the poetic drama that he had been so involved with in the 1930s. In the mid-1950s the avant-garde had not ceased to exist: he had just completely lost sight of it.

In the general bleakness he saw one light of hope. When Dylan Thomas's *Collected Poems* appeared in 1953 Hayward recalled an early visit to Bina Gardens:

> I met him for the first time in 1935, a year before his marriage to a wild and beautiful Irish girl. He was brought to my flat by Emily Coleman, an American friend of Djuna Barnes ... He presented himself characteristically, each of his jacket pockets weighed down and bulging with a quart bottle of beer, and a similar bottle tucked under each arm – all of which he drank with enormous relish while Miss Coleman and I toyed delicately with glasses of Madeira. His capacity for drink then, as now, is gargantuan and is not the only trait he shares with Rabelais' jovial character. In appearance he seems to me to have changed hardly at all during the eighteen years since that first encounter: stouter in build perhaps, but with his rather puffy pigling face,

looking as always like a cherub in a massive group of baroque sculpture – a cherub with interests and duties in this world rather than in Heaven.[611]

He admired Thomas partly because he had refused to join any political or social movement in the 1930s. Hayward saw him as the inheritor of a very different tradition of poetry – the Celtic: 'He is first and foremost an inspired singer … playing on the sensibilities of his readers rather than their intelligence.' His appetite for drink and women showed that he followed the best romantic traditions of excess. Part of Hayward admired and approved of Thomas as an irrepressible natural force, a geyser spouting unstoppably out of the earth. His Augustan side criticised Thomas for the 'intoxicating effect of his exuberant and heady poetic vocabulary'. Thomas could be a slapdash writer too and 'the substitution of a syntax of associative sounds for a grammatical syntax' meant that he often sounded as if his poetry was 'mere shouting' – nevertheless he seemed to Hayward the most promising young poet of his time, offering prospects of a revival of romantic verse. Hayward also admired his success in commanding sales only Eliot and Auden could match.

Just as he believed in the importance of little reviews and periodicals run on enthusiasm and a shoestring, so Hayward believed in the small independent publishing house. His experience with the Nonesuch Press and his friendship with Francis Meynell had been the starting points for this long love affair. 'The cultural history of our time would commemorate John Lehmann and Gerald Duckworth and Martin Secker and Leonard Woolf … who with meagre resources, but with faith and enthusiasm, between them launched most of the writers who have made a significant contribution to English literature in the past forty years or so.'[612] Their existence was now threatened by commercial pressures as never before. What happened to John Lehmann was an example of this process. During the war Lehmann had edited *Penguin New Writing* and afterwards he ran his own firm which established standards of excellence in book production. The beauty of the decorations on page and jacket was a bright contrast to the drab wrappings of wartime Penguins. Lehmann also saw it as his job as editor and publisher to bring on young writers. It was he, for example, who encouraged Laurie Lee to write *Cider with Rosie*. Elizabeth's David's *A Book of Mediterranean Food* arrived in 1950 as a grubby typescript from an unknown writer, but its colourful recipes spelt the end of austerity and the beginning of a more sun-blessed diet. In November 1952 he was dismissed from his own company. To Hayward and many of his friends the collapse of this small publishing house came as a complete shock. It was, they felt, nothing short of a disaster. The sacking made front-page news in the *Evening Standard*. Rose Macaulay organised a letter of protest to *The Times*, signed by Graham Greene, Stephen Spender, Angus Wilson, Arthur Koestler and Hayward, stating that the loss to the world of books was enormous. Hayward summed it up: 'John Lehmann lost his job because he was determined to publish literature and not merely "reading matter" which is what the large-scale publisher is principally engaged in purveying.'

The state of the world of postwar publishing was both a symptom and a cause of the dearth of new talent. Hayward quoted Eliot approvingly: 'The value of the "little reviews" for my generation was very great ... they helped to keep literature alive ... they lived under sentence of death; and they always died.' Hayward wrote that 'the little reviews have always been, and will always be, the mouthpiece through which youth makes its voice heard'. But so grave was the situation that these 'valuable testing grounds' could no longer keep afloat financially.[613] With the end of Cyril Connolly's *Horizon* in 1950 Eliot and Hayward agreed there was now no magazine left in England of any standing. This state of affairs had to be put right.

For many years Cecil King, the editor and Grand Panjandrum[614] of the *Daily Mirror* and the *Sunday Pictorial* had been a friend. He was a near-neighbour in Chelsea and a frequent visitor to Carlyle Mansions. In September 1952, to his surprise, Hayward finally managed to persuade King to telephone Lehmann to discuss starting a new periodical and to canvass the possibility of him becoming its editor. King hesitated, but in the Coronation excitement of 1953 he finally agreed to back the magazine. Hayward was proud to boast that after six months' persistence he had persuaded the newspaper magnate to support a 'high-brow' publication from the profits of the four-million-a-day sales of the *Daily Mirror*. The editorial board of the new magazine consisted of Elizabeth Bowen, the historian Veronica Wedgwood, Rex Warner, William Plomer and Hayward himself. He had masterminded the whole scheme and, as it neared fruition, became caught up in the excitement. There was one unexpected hitch. The arrival of a competitor took the board of the new venture completely by surprise when in September 1953 the first issue of Stephen Spender's monthly magazine, *Encounter*, emerged. King was extremely worried that this upstart rival might pre-empt his own publication and rang up Lehmann 'in a state of some agitation'. Lehmann reassured the tycoon that all was still well and urged him to ring Hayward for confirmation. 'Well, I do ring him up,' the great man replied, 'but he always says he's too busy to speak to me. Well I'm a busy man too.' The first lunch of the editorial board took place in the newly-painted red and gold dining room of Lehmann's elegant town house, 31 Egerton Crescent, South Kensington. Thus the *London Magazine* was born.

Its character was unlike its American-sponsored rival. Whereas *Encounter* had a clear political stance and political funding, the *London Magazine* set out to be non-ideological. Hayward persuaded Eliot to add an encouraging introductory word to the first issue, which he modestly called a 'message of goodwill from an elderly man of letters who is also a retired editor … whose years of experience qualify him to write affirming my belief in the importance of the Literary Review'.

> It is undoubtedly a scandal that we have had in London, since the end of the war, no literary magazine to compare with those which have sprung up in other countries … The type of magazine from the lack of which we suffer is neither that which provides a vehicle of expression for those occupying university posts nor that which elevates the Public Taste. What we need is a magazine which will boldly assume the existence of a public interested in serious literature, and eager to be kept in touch with current literature and with criticism of that literature by the most exacting standards …
>
> The first function of a literary magazine, surely, is to introduce the work of little known writers of talent. The second is to provide critical valuation of the work of living authors, both famous and unknown. The third is to be in the best sense *international* … [615]

Or, in other words, a new version of *The Criterion*. He urged all those with a serious interest in literature to support this new venture. Many did so, and the magazine was an immediate success; the first four numbers sold an extraordinary 30,000 copies when the publishers had hoped for a sale of 2,000. (*The Criterion* had never sold more than 1,000.) King was delighted: he had expected, he told Hayward, that it would be so highbrow that it would be totally unintelligible – and a commercial flop.

Despite the success, the relationship between Hayward and Lehmann became tense and difficult. Amidst the general delight with the first number, Hayward, in his most pedantic style, 'devoted a long telephone conversation to unearthing minute misprints' and complaining that the first number was dated 19 February whereas it actually appeared on 15 January.[616] 'Hayward thinks ... of everything within the literary world in terms of intrigue and influence,' Lehmann confided to his diary. He was 'totally unscrupulous about the way he damns people he wants to eliminate or score off'.[617] He felt that Hayward's obsession with the idea that nothing goes on unless he initiates it was the result of a mania 'to control and dominate'.[618] Perhaps the two natural autocrats were too alike to get on, but despite this clash of personalities, the *London Magazine* continued to flourish under Lehmann's editorship for the next seven years.

Queen Elizabeth's first Coronation List in June 1953 marked the hope of a second Elizabethan Age, a celebration of the new reign and a tribute to those who had helped to organise events for the Festival of Britain two years earlier. As 'broadcaster, editor and critic' John Hayward was awarded a CBE – he was especially pleased to have been cited as a critic and so 'differentiated from icerinkistes, jockeys and those who perform public services at Aston-sub-Edge'. The cricketer Jack Hobbs, champion jockey Gordon Richards and John Gielgud all received knighthoods; the cartoonist Osbert Lancaster, the poet Edwin Muir and film director David Lean were also honoured. For services to French literature Hayward had already become a Chevalier de la Légion d'Honneur and had received the honour in March from his old friend the Ambassador. He felt enormously surprised like 'the guilty thing in ye old play by Shagsbag'[619] when he heard the news that he was also to receive a CBE. What unknown political uncle had been behind it all, he wondered to Christopher Sykes. Was the award really meant for Hayward's the furriers in Bethnal Green Road? He remembered the story that Winston Churchill had entertained I. Berlin for a whole evening, believing that that I stood for 'Irving' not 'Isaiah'. Had they got the wrong man?

The Investiture was held at Buckingham Palace on 14 July. Arrangements for receiving his CBE were complicated by the fact that Hayward was confined to his wheelchair. The Secretary of the Central Chancery of the Orders of Knighthood had written telling him the protocol:

I note that you will be brought to the Palace *in your own wheel-chair,* and I should be grateful if, when you arrive at the entrance hall there, you will inform the State-Porters on duty at the door that you are attending as a recipient of the CBE. They will then arrange for you, accompanied by Mr. Eliot, to be taken *in your chair* to the Ball-room, where the Investiture is to be held and where it will be possible for you to remain until your turn comes to go forward to the Queen. As it is not customary for a guest to do so on these occasions, one of the Pages on duty will push your chair forward to the Queen so that you may be invested with your CBE and Mr. Eliot will be able to join you immediately after you have been invested. [620]

The small boy who had hidden behind *Punch* in his parents' attic was now forty-eight years old. Slightly stout, hair tinged with grey, bright red lower lip swollen, around his neck he proudly wore the silver cross of the Légion d'Honneur, which he had been granted special permission to wear. As the others bowed to receive their awards he sat in a wheelchair with solid rubber wheels and a rattan back that had evidently seen better days. He was glad that there were no mishaps and that 'the pink ribbon did not get caught in my ears and the cross did not fall into my mouth'. Behind him was the stooping figure of T. S. Eliot.

Another of Hayward's friends, the writer Janet Adam Smith, invited him to celebrate Coronation Day, 3 June 1953, on a steamboat junketing down the Thames to see the fireworks at Westminster.[621] The party also turned out to be a celebration of Hayward's CBE, which was announced in the Honours List on the same day. It was a cold and overcast night. Their boat was moored alongside many others. As Hayward's chair could not be lowered into the cabin, his hostess found a corner near the gangway for him. He remained on deck surrounded by a dozen or so noisy children rushing furiously around and up and down eating ice creams. Although he was wrapped up in his long black cloak and 'villain's hat', Janet Adam Smith feared he would freeze to death. In fact he was carefully, and typically, keeping a tally of the ice creams the children ate – 'Johnny, you're on your tenth,' he was heard to say. From the shadows, in his wheelchair, he watched the searchlights cutting the night sky and a blazing firework display that he compared with the Coronation Day of 1937 and perhaps even the

Coronation of 1911. Below deck the dancing and drinking of the party went on without him.

Hayward was overwhelmed by 140 letters and more than 50 telephone calls of congratulation from his 'old pals and palaces'. He grumbled that the whole routine of his life had been turned upside down. 'It is a fearful thing to fall into the hands of the Living God. The next worst thing is to command the British Empire.'[622] He now knew, he wrote, what having a heavy cross to bear meant – but beneath it all he was delighted, and always wore the medal when he could. The *Evening Standard* picked him out as an outstanding CBE. Under the heading 'This is inadequate' the paper looked forward to a knighthood in the near future. 'He is a man of the highest intellectual judgement and his honour is well deserved,' declared its columnist. In the *Daily Telegraph*, *Atticus* called him 'the outstanding *belle-lettriste* of his generation' and linked his name with Benjamin Britten and Auden. Notes of congratulations and good wishes flowed in. Edith Sitwell took him to lunch at the Sesame Club. Lord Beaverbrook said he had given a lead in criticism and agreed that 'the leader of the critics should be singled out for recognition'. He invited Hayward to dinner at Cherkley Court, his Surrey country house, and sent 'a big motor with a big door' to pick him up.[623] Bunny Garnett imagined his wearing his decoration whilst 'surrounded by the greatest beauties our age can produce'. Gabriele Annan implored him as a well-known dashing dresser to '*Please* wear that pretty salmon pink ribbon next time I come and see you. Perhaps you will have to order a special waist coat to tone, as they say in Marshall and Snelgrove.' Scholars, publishers, librarians and bibliophiles all sent their congratulations. The Secretary General of the Arts Council, W. E. Williams, praised Hayward's achievement:

No one has done more for English Literature, in my lifetime, than you have – and these are carefully weighed words. A great deal of your contribution ... has been through the fearless quality of your conversations about books and writers, and I can recall half a dozen social occasions when you took the right bull by both horns. To hear you again is to remember how mealy-mouthed so many of us have become in our judgements. Then again you are the most scrupulous of editors, yet with the capacity to rouse an interest in people to whom literature had not previously been an exciting discovery.[624]

The chorus of approval was not universal: Hayward made enemies as naturally as he made friends. Helen Gardner warned him to expect 'a broadside in the next *Scrutiny* unless your soft answers have turned away Dr Leavis's wrath'. Nevertheless, it seemed that the Indian summer of 1953 was just the beginning of Hayward's success and that he was about to gain the fame he had dreamed of as a little boy.

16

Round the Prickly Pear

In 1954 Hayward had his photograph taken by Douglas Glass for the *Sunday Times*. No longer the handsome, thin-faced young intellectual of the 1930s; his whole frame has filled out in middle age. He sits in his ancient wheelchair, neatly arranged bookshelves behind him, fixing the the viewer with his penetrating grey-eyed gaze. Immaculately dressed in double-breasted suit with silk pocket handkerchief and bow tie, he has a high domed forehead; his lips are full and sensual. In his left hand he grips a cigarette; there is a knotty tension in his fingers.

As a young student at the Chelsea College of Art, Ann Baer had first met Hayward in the 1930s when she painted his bookcases in Bina Gardens to earn some pocket money. In the middle 1950s she met him again at one of the *Sunday Times*'s Book Fairs, and was shocked by how much he had altered. 'The disease had progressed horribly, his body in the wheelchair was more contorted, his hand movements jerky, his features changed and out of proportion, but he was talking as volubly as ever.'[625] The once handsome face had become distorted. An American visitor gave an idea of how potentially menacing he could look and sound:

> His face was heavy and oblong, the face of a cruel clown; his eyebrows nearly met, and behind his black-rimmed spectacles his eyes moved as watchfully as an auctioneer's. His lips were gross, almost swollen (an effect of his disease) and hung open, giving him a voluptuous look. His voice was harsh. He was adept at raising a laugh, usually at someone else's expense. It must be said to his great credit he was without self-consciousness and apparently without self-pity; he had evidently come to terms with his fate, and with traditional British gallantry could now pretend to ignore it and enable others to ignore it as well, though neither they nor he could ever really forget that it was daily devouring him.[626]

To friends like Graham Greene, however, Hayward's appearance was not at all off-putting:

I remember being 'warned' that I would find his physical appearance ugly – an extraordinary misapprehension. That powerful head ugly? that twist of the half paralysed arm, as the agile hand seized a cup or procured itself a cigarette? A cripple, yes, but there are few men I can remember with greater vitality and with a greater appreciation of physical love.[627]

When as a schoolboy Hayward was editing *The Gresham*, he wrote about how much could be learnt from studying pupils' choice of library books and what surprises an inspection of the borrowing book could shed on their characters. Thirty years later, in one of his 'Letters from London', he drew a literary self-portrait.[628] He began by picturing himself as a small boy in his parents' attic in Wimbledon, full of ambition, surrounded by bound volumes of *Punch* and piles of books, and playing with ink and paper inside the breastwork of his literary castle. He compared this with his writer's desk in middle age as he sat in his room at Carlyle Mansions. There was still the same clutter of paper, books and writing materials – even if the hope of becoming a famous writer had gone. Dictionaries and works of reference sat permanently amongst the changing piles of manuscripts and books to be worked on and cleared away. On the left side of his desk lay a novel in galley proof that had arrived an hour ago awaiting a blurb. On top of this was today's correspondence – with the poet George Barker, with the editor of *The Book Collector* about advertising, and with the Society of Herbalists, turning down an invitation to speak. On top of three 'spotless' eighteenth-century volumes, bought from Richard Jennings, was the first edition of Dylan Thomas's latest volume of poetry, *In Country Sleep*; proofs of the catalogue of the library of Sir Louis Sterling which he was to present to the University of London and a *de luxe* edition of Saint Evrémond, for which Hayward was commissioned to write the introduction. On the right side of the desk lay the first draft of Eliot's new play which, Hayward revealed to his readers, was to be called *The Confidential Clerk*, adding chattily that Eliot hoped to finish it next year. There was also a very untidy pile of the papers of Evelyn Waugh which had been submitted with a view to a collected edition. Autographed typescripts, booksellers' catalogues, lectures, bills, and estimates for work filled almost every other space, allowing him only just enough room for that most vital tool of his trade: the telephone. The sheer amount of material suggests the daunting task that Hayward undertook every day as he sat down to work. He presented himself to his readers as the learned guide to all matters literary, as the friend and confidant of famous writers, as collector, editor and publisher. A friend helping to tidy some of the drawers filled with ancient rubber bands and pencils found a small book. 'What's *Lyrical Ballads* doing here?' she asked. 'Oh, do be careful,' came the reply, 'that's Coleridge's copy.'

A trip to see Hayward, and possibly Eliot as well, became a necessary part of a visit to London for literary men and women from all over the world. They came by appointment and Hayward tried to ensure that they did not overlap. Brinnin's account of the experience gives a good idea of the procedure. He had been told not to come unannounced, and duly wrote a letter of self-introduction. He was finally invited to Carlyle Mansions to meet Hayward on a grey London Sunday. Nervously he pressed on the bell 'which looked like a belly button set in brass' and was summoned upstairs to be greeted by an intimidating sight, 'a Quasimodo figure in a wheelchair'.

> Grotesquely bent, he had a big head, thick lips the colour of raw liver. 'You'll have to get used to me,' he said, 'just like everybody else.' The hand he offered hung like a broken wing. 'Make yourself a drink.' He pointed to a table on wheels. 'And one for me, some whisky and a little water. You can have ice, if you insist.'
>
> His head was as shaggy as Beethoven's, his back curved like a sea-lion's.[629]

Knowing of Brinnin's close connection with Dylan Thomas, Hayward asked him what it was like to be a friend of the poet: 'Sit where I can see you he said ... Over here everyone's his friend ... at least everyone thinks he is. Poor Dylan. Isn't his idea of a friend anyone who can lend him a pint of bitter and a packet of Woodbines?' Brinnin was then given the tour of the house including Eliot's bedroom and Hayward's own 'pig-sty bedsit'. And then it was time for the next caller, an earnest young man from Toronto, an expert on the Pre-Raphaelites. He was quickly followed by 'Hilary' – sometimes the appointments system did not work – who ignored the other two with a stream of literary gossip and told Hayward not to bother with the new Hemingway (*The Old Man and the Sea*) – 'unless he happened to be bonkers for big fish, and brave little boys'.[630] By now Brinnin had overstayed his time and he was shown to the door by his host. Hayward's parting shot was, 'As you see, Hilary's full of himself. Come back. I want to hear about

Dylan's American woman. It's serious this time. Won't there be hell to pay?'[631]

Brinnin duly visited again and was surprised to be asked for tea at the early hour of three o' clock: 'I had still not caught on to the fact that John Hayward was the most indefatigable and, in the eyes of some people, the most malicious gossip in the parishes of literary London.'[632] 'I understand there's bloody hell to pay, Dylan's liaison has been discovered,' Hayward began. Thomas apparently did not know that Caitlin opened all of his letters. Unable to prise any more gossip from his guest, Hayward then moved on to ask Brinnin about his recent stay in Ireland with Elizabeth Bowen, whose husband, Alan, was an invalid: 'Is Elizabeth still devoting body and soul to that hopeless old blimp?' he demanded. After ordering his guest to help himself from a wicker caddy full of cakes and sandwiches, the questioning continued: 'The story goes that she took him to Ireland to keep him out of sight as if he were an idiot nephew. Is he – out of sight?'[633] At this point they were once again interrupted – this time by the arrival of Eliot and one of his elderly Bostonian lady relatives. 'Mind you outstay her,' Hayward commanded Brinnin, warning him that 'she'll tell what Tom's nephew said to Tom's niece when they saw cousin True or Charity – those sort of names they have – riding her bum down the steps of the Church of the Advent on Pentecost Sunday.'[634] After Eliot had shown her to the door, Hayward suggested three hefty whiskies: '*Bon voyage* to the world's nicer types,' adding in a stage whisper, '*Au revoir* from the scrofulous.'[635]

When Brinnin made his final call – in 1953 – he found Hayward 'heavier, more painfully twisted in his movements, more slurred in speech' – but still trying to lure him into some scandalous story and then cap it with 'some acid' of his own. Once again he was up to date with the tittle-tattle about Dylan Thomas:

> So you've survived another visit to the Thomases. They still playing rugby on the bedroom floor? Dylan lost his trousers, Tom tells me, on the way to a reading for the Queen Mum, had to take the podium wearing Louis MacNeice's. Then they sent him back to John Davenport's flat wrapped in some poor soul's mac he nipped from the cloakroom on the way out.[636]

These vignettes show how Hayward made theatre out of life. His presence dominated his guests who were treated to an act of pure bravura. Each performance was carefully prepared and lasted a certain amount of time. To begin with he would take centre stage as host by leading the tour of the flat, or organising the whiskies, or the cakes – and then the witty demolition, the gossip and the anecdotes would flow. Normally he spoke with assurance, but when he wanted to shock or outrage he would hesitate slightly, as if embarrassed. Using his strong bass voice with all the dramatic timing that he had learnt at school and with the Marlowe Society in Cambridge, he fixed his gaze attentively on his listener in a way that could be intimidating. When he shared a particularly tasty piece of gossip he rolled his eyes dramatically with a 'gleeful conspiratorial gleam'. In repose he held his head well back and steady; in conversation he would often jerk it backwards and then swing it round in a gently circular motion. Some wondered if this was the nearest he could get to nodding. As soon as one audience was shuffled out another was waiting eagerly in the wings. The moment the door closed on you, your character was fair game and you could expect little mercy from the host.[637] And so the circus went on.

Why did people put up with this treatment? Kathleen Raine argued that Hayward was not mean-spirited or malicious at heart: his sardonic comments were in part a defence against his affliction. (His written work is in fact almost without trace of personal venom.) There was a splendid impartiality about his attacks and anecdotes. No one was spared. To accuse Hayward of petty malice is to miss the point. The real answer lies in what is missing from Brinnin's account – delight in Hayward's bracing wit; gossip as an art form. Visitors enjoyed the gusto and style of the performance. Either sitting in a chair holding court at Carlyle Mansions, or at the centre of a party, in his favourite scarlet cummerbund, gesticulating with his cigarette, surrounded by guests waiting to hear wilder flights of malicious gossip, the latest *bon mot*, or the scandal of the moment, Hayward loved to entertain, was rarely worsted, could not be embarrassed and feared no one. There were times, of course, when victims of his barbed remarks did take offence – especially when they counted themselves among Hayward's closest friends. When the *Sunday Times* published a flattering profile of Edith Sitwell which delighted her, he said, 'The whole of London is saying *Osbert* must have written it, because no one else would!!!' Naturally enough, she was extremely hurt: 'I had never been anything but nice to J. H. Are not people incredibly envious and spiteful?' she concluded.[638]

The bibliographer and surgeon Geoffrey Keynes was another close friend. He always wrote in a rather affected reddish-brown ink. 'Why do you always write letters in your patients' blood?' asked Hayward. Keynes was so annoyed that he did not speak to him again for several months.[639] Hayward's life was littered with more serious rows, fallings-out and angry splits with his parents, and friends as different as David Garnett, Edith Sitwell, William Plomer, Grisella Kentner, Geoffrey Keynes, John Lehmann, Cecil King, Stevie Smith, Noel Blakiston, John Carter and Kathleen Raine. The poet Roy Fuller recalled how he had to plead a hernia to avoid having to haul Hayward's chair and its owner up the steps of the Arts Council premises. 'John's personality', he wrote, 'was such that only service seemed to confer neutrality let alone benevolence.'[640] Hayward could take on an aggressive, intimidating tone. Gwen, the wife of the Faber poet Vernon Watkins, was a shyly attractive twenty-one-year-old when she was introduced to Hayward at a party as a witty woman. '"Be witty", he commanded through bulbous lips.'[641] The next time they met he grabbed hold of her hand and with a convulsive movement leant over to grasp her. 'Will you give me a kiss?' he asked.

This acerbity could also have disappointing consequences. For some time Evelyn Waugh had wanted to meet Eliot, whom he much admired. He approached Christopher Sykes to make an introduction to 'this close companion of yours, Eliot, a poet almost as famous as Stephen Spender I believe'.[642] Waugh recalled having met Hayward before the war at le Mortier where he had been most impressed by his learning and asked Sykes to reacquaint him with 'the cripple'. 'Rarely have I regretted a fulfilled promise more,' admitted Sykes.[643] For no sooner had he made the introduction than Hayward put in 'an uncannily well-placed remark' about religion to annoy the irascible Waugh. This resulted in a violently angry response and, Sykes felt, 'an explosive outpouring of religious polemics, wholly unsuited to the occasion and grossly insulting'. After this embarrassing public row, trying to make amends, Waugh began a correspondence with Hayward adding many amusing references to Eliot in the hope that he would repeat them to his flatmate and a meeting would follow. But the damage was done; Eliot hated scenes – and no doubt Hayward had told the story in the blackest colours. As a result Eliot and Waugh never met. Sykes summed up his view of his friend's behaviour: 'As with many cripples, the effect of his infirmity on his character was not wholly agreeable. If he was one of the most courageous men I have ever known, John Hayward was also one of the most treacherous and mischief-making.'[644]

Despite being confined to his wheelchair Hayward managed to get around London with energy, enthusiasm and the help of a select group of pushers. Hayward was at the centre of fashionable literary London society. When he arrived at a Kensington party with Eliot, it took four men to heave his chair upstairs while, 'like a hulking overweight coxswain', he shouted the orders to the crew. 'By the time we had got him ensconced we were puffed but he was talking sixteen to the dozen.'[646] The evening did not continue well: Hayward talked constantly and Eliot was mum. It seemed that he was artificially trying to 'show Eliot off', or to 'produce' him. If so, he finally succeeded by stating that his flatmate was so familiar with Sherlock Holmes stories that he could recall whole paragraphs from memory. That did the trick. Eliot began to recite quietly, almost to himself, and the ice was broken.

Visits outside London were harder but not impossible. The painter and writer Roland Penrose was one of Hayward's oldest friends. He was married to the photographer, model and surrealist muse Lee Miller, whom Hayward had met at Merton Hall when she worked for *Vogue*. Hayward was a frequent weekend visitor to their Sussex home, Farley Farm. It was one of the few places that enjoyed 'AHC' (All Hayward Conveniences) as he told his host. Among the Picassos, the surrealist paintings and Lee Miller's photographs he could relax. Her photograph of him sitting solemnly black-hatted next to a bare-breasted ship's figurehead captures the surreal spirit of their weekends. Another photograph shows the rears of Penrose, Sonia Orwell and Hayward as they peer through the slot machines on Brighton pier at 'After the Bath', 'Parisienne Can Can' and 'What the Butler Saw'. Penrose especially admired the way his friend was able to joke about his disability. When Penrose suggested that he might drive him back to London rather than take the train, Hayward airily dismissed the idea. 'Why not put me on the train in the guard's van. After all I'm no more than a trunk.'[647]

Eliot's ill-health was a constant concern to both Hayward and Mary Trevelyan. Heavy smoking had left him with bronchitis and a dry cough which attacked him in winter; he often looked white-faced and exhausted from asthma. He was a hypochondriac addicted to the tranquilliser Nembutal and, according to Herbert Read, dependent on numerous pills and potions, a good supply of which he carried in his waistcoat pocket. From his youth he had had to wear a surgical truss. He consulted a laryngologist for throat problems and was given a cocaine spray; he took anti-cold injections and homeopathic treatments for rheumatism and had a course of massages with a lady who told him that he had been starved of sugar for a lifetime. He feared contact with colds and sneezes, described Geoffrey Faber's nose as a 'germ centre' and suffered regularly from 'topical flux' and low blood pressure. Many of his symptoms seemed to belong to a nervous highly-strung disposition: fear of catching cold in north-facing rooms; fear of getting on the wrong train; fear of losing luggage; fear of strangers and perhaps even his terror of dying. If Eliot's illnesses were often neurotic, Hayward's were all too visible.

As Eliot's health worsened and he became increasingly ill-tempered and dogmatic, Hayward and Mary Trevelyan found their roles as guardians much more demanding. Both felt that Eliot often used his ill-health for his own purposes and that he tended to malinger – 'it's a delightful excuse for not seeing ANYBODY' complained Mary. In her memoir she recalled that in April 1952 she paid an illuminating visit to Hayward, who felt hurt and concerned about the way his flatmate behaved, often 'snapping his head off' in front of other people and when they were alone. The two made common cause against their moody poet and 'cheered themselves up by comparing notes'. When Mary had asked Eliot if he would visit her in hospital he replied, 'Not unless it's really necessary.' She felt that this lack of sympathy was exactly Eliot's weakness as a dramatist: he drew puppets rather than real characters because, although he seemed to know a lot about human nature, 'In other ways he seems quite blind – perhaps because he does not love them.'[648] Eliot responded, 'You mustn't want to know too much about people.' The problems were also made clear in the letter he wrote in December 1952, which accused her of hinting that he was hurting his guardians. If that were the case, he added brutally, he would just have to sever all connections with both of them.[649]

Stress of another kind came when an American magazine 'practically accusing him of homosexuality' mentioned John Hayward's name.[650] In July the Canadian critic John Peter published an article in *Essays in Criticism*[651] which examined the theme of homosexuality in *The Waste Land*, arguing that the central figure of the poem had fallen irretrievably in love with a young man who had then drowned. The linkage with Eliot himself was clear and Peter revealed in a later article that the lover was in fact Jean Verdenal to whom the poem was dedicated. Eliot, who had asked Hayward to act as his literary executor precisely in order that this kind of scandalous talk and rumour should be quashed, threatened to sue writer and journal. Hayward told Bill Empson that Eliot was under pressure from his publishers to sue and was the slave of his lawyer. Empson wondered if it was simply loyalty that made Hayward argue this or just his characteristic way of making social comedy from the Bard. At any rate the article was withdrawn. The whole incident continued to disturb Eliot and added to the tensions in Carlyle Mansions.

Meanwhile Eliot began working on what was to become his next to last play, a metaphysical drawing-room comedy, *The Confidential Clerk*. It was based on the central figure of Sir Claude Mulhammer and his wife Elizabeth and their children, legitimate and illegitimate, adopted, lost and found. Eliot depended more than ever on his two closest advisers, Hayward and Martin Browne, to help him: he told Mary that now Hayward had 'passed' the rewritten Act 1 he could feel 'quite happy about it'.[652] But by the time Hayward had begun to look at *The Confidential Clerk* his wartime deference to the Master had gone. In the typescript of twenty-five detailed suggestions he gave to Eliot he commented much more boldly on the draft's shortcomings.[653] Eliot indicated that he had dealt with each of Hayward's points by striking a blue pencil through them. Hayward, of course, still retained his role as commentator on English social mores. A maid would never knock twice; a visit at dinner-time would be 'a curious hour to choose' and 'the confidential clerk' of the title, Eggerson, would not call his mistress both 'Lady Elizabeth' and 'your ladyship'. Sir Claude would not call his daughter 'Miss Angel'. No English person would say 'stake me'. Hayward worried too that he 'could not place Slingsby, renamed Colby by Eliott, socially' and thought it unlikely that the suburban clerk Eggerson would have 'week-end guests'. When he suggested that some of the audience would be unfamiliar with the role of verger that the Colby Simpkins finally takes on, Eliot immediately made him an organist.

Hayward's influence was, however, now much more wide-ranging. He felt that the dramatic structure was wrong and found the scene divisions irritatingly short and distracting. He suggested conflating them. There was much to criticise too in terms of characterisation and in the revelations that came at the end of the play. They were too sudden and implausible. He argued that Sir Claude's confession in the first act that he was in fact the father of Colby 'is far too abrupt – should be led up to via implication, more cunningly and gradually. S's [Simpkins] immediate reaction unconvincing. Might be better if S. began by humouring Sir C and trying to laugh it off.'⁶⁵⁴ Other parts of the play he found 'curious', and 'very ingenious but very complicated'. Hayward's comments on the resolution of the plot are in the same vein: 'The whole intrigue gets too hurriedly knit up. S's decision to become a verger is too sudden. I don't approve of L. [Lucasta] and B. K's [Barnabas Kaghan] engagement.'

Eliot responded by revising his draft radically. He removed all the short scene divisions. He softened Lucasta's announcement to Colby that Sir Claude was her father in just the way Hayward had suggested and again followed Hayward's advice by having Sir Claude's revelation occur before the action of the play started. But he also sometimes stuck to his guns. Lucasta's engagement to Barnabas Kaghan stayed – but instead of its being a neat romantic comedy ending to the play, the audience are told that they are engaged at the beginning of Act 1. Hayward's comment that she ought to marry Colby Simpkins and his puzzlement about the name⁶⁵⁵ show that he had not understood that Colby, like Eggerson, is one of those almost invisible saintly figures in Eliot's plays who disappear from worldly notice. Eliot naturally ignored Hayward's suggestions on this point. Although Hayward disliked the complicated ending – 'I don't find the dead sister and the changeling device plausible enough' – that too remained. Hayward's suggestions all tended to make the play more naturalistic whereas Eliot wanted to explore the extraordinary and mysterious patterns of life.

The Confidential Clerk was premièred at the Edinburgh Festival on 30 August 1953, directed by Martin Browne, with a programme 'blurb' written by him and 'passed' by Hayward. It summed up the dilemmas of life in Carlyle Mansions as well as the play. 'There is no easy way of reconciliation between a man's desires and his obligations, between what he wants of life and what life demands of him.' In his Preface Eliot generously recorded that 'the evolution of this play from the earliest draft to the final text has been influenced at every stage by the suggestions offered and by objections raised by Mr E. Martin Browne and Mr John Hayward to both of whom I wish to make grateful acknowledgement'. Inside the copy he gave to Hayward in March 1954 he wrote:

'Inscribed to John Hayward, the clerk's most kind nurse', a revealing image of their 'hypochondriacal collaboration'.[656] Hayward had indeed helped to nurse Eliot through the winter and also to bring the play to life. When Mrs Beck, their cleaner, saw the play on television she confided to Hayward, 'Fancy (giggle) fancy Mr Eliot writing a play about illegitimates!'[657] As Hayward read the lines of Sir Claude Mulhammer describing his relationship with his wife, in Valerie Fletcher's meticulous typescript, it is hard not to wonder if he had any sense of how relevant they were to the flat-dwellers at Carlyle Mansions:

> There's always something one's ignorant of
> About anyone, however well one knows them;
> And that may be something of the greatest importance.
> It's when you're sure you understand a person
> That you're liable to make the worst mistake about him.[658]

In March 1953 Penguin Books published Eliot's *Selected Prose* in an edition of 40,000 copies – evidently not a book for Wuggas and Wux-hos – and the beginning of an association for Hayward which would lead from *Donne* to *Herrick* and to the *Penguin Book of English Verse*. The selection was heavily indebted to his earlier *Points of View* and recycled many of the same extracts, but Penguin had asked for a wider coverage and longer passages. Once again he was guided by Eliot's advice and the edition boasted that it had his approval. He collected material from the often obscure publications and journals which Eliot liked to use. His edition became the most accessible collection of Eliot's prose and it was through its pages that for more than fifty years many readers first got to know Eliot's writing.

In his introduction Hayward began by placing Eliot in the line of critics from Dryden and Johnson to Coleridge and Arnold. As a 'master of criticism' he had helped a generation of readers to re-evaluate their literature, giving more prominence to the poetry of Donne and his school and 'our early poetic drama'.[659] He had also changed the critical perception of Milton and had brought Baudelaire, Valéry and the symbolists to critical attention. Hayward saw Eliot's work as emblematic of the social and artistic upheaval just after the First World War. It spelt the end of the Victorianism that Hayward felt his father and mother epitomised but, more broadly, he had changed the way that literature was read and understood by his generation. As the key for understanding Eliot's critical standpoint Hayward took his famous statement that he was 'classicist in literature, royalist in politics, and anglo-catholic in religion',[660] and explained that this was 'a triple affirmation of a single belief – belief in the value of Tradition'. This was not a simple veneration of the past but a sense of how tradition informs the present, just as the present is bound up in the future. Eliot's Christianity was naturally relevant. At this point Hayward began to suggest some tentative criticism, only to withdraw partially from it: 'Thus if he is occasionally pontifical, or seemingly condescending, it is not from arrogance or complacency; for he is without intellectual pride or vanity, and in print, at least, more tolerant than most moralists of human folly and frailty.'[661] There is a sting in the tail of the words 'at least'. In private – and out of print – Hayward and Mary were discussing how they could manage the prickly and dogmatic character 'The Pope of Russell Square' had become.

Yellow London smogs added to Eliot's bronchial trouble; winter colds weakened him and there were concerns too about a racing pulse and tachycardia. In late 1953 his doctor advised him to escape the English winter and prescribed relaxation and a cruise. While Hayward supervised the repainting of the two front rooms and 'the offices' and developed an allergy to fresh paint that made him feel slightly ill all the time, Eliot enjoyed South Africa for ten weeks. Soon after he returned, in March 1954, however, there were alarms about his heart again and he was taken to the London Clinic under strict orders to rest. Hayward was deluged with calls, cables and letters inquiring about his flatmate's health. He visited the Clinic and was surprised to find Eliot propped up against his pillows looking remarkably cheery and comfortable – 'like a cat which has eaten several canaries and surrounded by a large part of the Chelsea Flower Show'.[662] Hayward was able to reassure callers that there was never anything organically wrong – just an inexplicable acceleration of the pulse. He was sure that with some peace and quiet Eliot would be restored to normal. In January the following year, however, he had another spell of six weeks in the London Clinic. When he returned to Carlyle Mansions, his secretary Valerie Fletcher came at 5 o'clock four times a week to take dictation.

More and more often Eliot had spells in the London Clinic. The guardians now regularly consulted about his health and, when necessary, wrote reassuring bulletins to his American relatives. Mary suggested that they should appoint another guardian. 'He has no close friends except us,' replied Hayward. The tension came to a climax at the Easter weekend of 1955. On Good Friday both Hayward and Madame Amory were irritated that Eliot did not make an appearance. He even missed his customary visit to St Stephen's and Mary rang her fellow guardian in the evening to ask what was wrong. Hayward told her he was becoming infuriated by Eliot's difficult moods and invisibility. He had little patience with what he saw as Eliot using his ill-health to manipulate others. Mary found it 'disturbing' that Hayward did not dare to go into Eliot's room to sort the matter out. So, finally, Hayward plucked up courage and told his flatmate that he was developing a damaging reputation for hypochondria and he should stop it.

On the evening of Easter Sunday Mary received an 'agitated' phone call from Hayward to say that Tom had not been in to see him all day – his daily visit was another rigidly observed custom. He asked if Mary knew whether he had upset Eliot in any way. She was aware that for some time the two men had not been taking meals together and recalled a remark of Eliot's: 'John and I know less and less of what each other is doing.' She could understand Hayward's hurt and alarm. 'He hasn't even wished me a Happy Easter,' he told her, 'which seems unchristian.' 'He can't help hurting us sometimes,' she replied. Hayward agreed that Eliot had 'a streak of sadism which he fights against'.[663] Finally they agreed that Tom had probably simply forgotten – although Mary added in her memoir that 'personally I doubt it very much'.

The following morning Hayward, in desperation, sent for Eliot and asked him frankly why he had hidden himself away and what had caused his ill-temper. Eliot replied that he felt that Hayward was responsible for spreading rumours about his health and gossiping about it to friends. An incident of the previous week still rankled too. Eliot had said 'Both Picasso and Dior are good window-dressers.' Hayward had dismissed the remark with some scorn – he admired Picasso and one of his closest friends was the Picasso expert Roland Penrose. Eliot rather pompously admitted, 'I didn't like the *tone* of your criticism of my remarks.' He then discussed his rages, adding, 'I am very *slow* in my reactions. I often remain angry for some time.' After this, the air was cleared.

The reconciliation did not last long. Hayward was upset that he now saw so little of Eliot. In Carlyle Mansions Eliot had become the secret sharer, hidden from view. Mary noted how often she now had to endure Tom's 'FURY' and how 'difficult and dogmatic' he could be. A lady in slacks cleaning her car outside Carlyle Mansions on a Sunday morning was enough to upset him: 'What distresses *me* is that people like that should live in the same block as I do.' Thomas Hardy, Lord Halifax and the Oxford don Enid Starkie were frequent targets for his venom, but Mary felt he hardly ever spoke well of anybody now. As she was driving him around Kensington he turned to her and asked, 'WHY should I have been cursed with such mediocre contemporaries?'⁶⁶⁴ He described the whole Bloomsbury set as 'black beetles' and was scornful of all living poets apart from Auden. On 'Education Sunday' in October 1955 an evangelical vicar led the prayers at Chelsea Old Church and asked the congregation to pray for the educational system. 'I cannot *pray* for a framework,' said Tom peevishly.⁶⁶⁵ Even though Mary was still deeply in love with him she could not bear the rudeness and moodiness he sometimes showed both to her and to John. Her letter to Hayward headed '<u>Oh VERY PRIVATE</u>', revealed how touchy the relationships had become. Part of the problem, she felt, was that Eliot suffered from the fame of being 'a classic writer in one's own lifetime'.⁶⁶⁶ Nevertheless, when Hayward, with uncharacteristic timidity, wrote to her suggesting that even he had to be very careful to 'cover' any hint of criticism so as not to enrage his flatmate, she urged him to speak his mind:

> <u>ONLY YOU</u> can say things to him that must sometimes be said – nobody else would dare. I have noticed of late his immense *indignation* with anyone who disagrees with him (never you) … it is practically your mission to tell him what you think. Tom needs honesty. Besides he doesn't admit criticism from anyone else because he refuses to admit their views have any importance.⁶⁶⁷

Hayward telephoned Mary on 24 January 1956 to say that his flatmate had been taken to the London Clinic by ambulance, but felt it was nothing worse than a cold in the head. Perhaps his apparent lack of concern sprang, he said, from remembering that the last visit had been for a ten-day stay to deal with athlete's foot. 'It's becoming a danger to him, this Clinic,' Hayward told Mary.⁶⁶⁸ The news grew more worrying when, at the beginning of February, Eliot's pulse began once again to race. Even Hayward was agitated and the guardians sent a bulletin to the family in America. Soon Eliot improved enough to have visitors, but when Mary visited him on 24 February she found him in a terribly anxious state. Hayward was expected to telephone and the thought of bringing his two friends together disturbed his sense of their separate existence. As it happened, the call came through just as she was leaving. 'Yes, John, the visitors are just going – now there's nobody in the room,' said a much-relieved Eliot. 'Well I never!' wrote Mary, desperately hurt, but his behaviour brought about just what he feared, in that the two people he had chosen to look after him became more like conspirators, sharing their discontents behind his back. He left for America in March. On the return journey, looking 'stricken' and 'cadaverous', he had to be carried off the *Queen Mary* on a stretcher. In June he saw a specialist about his chest pains. Abnormal heart lesions were diagnosed. Although they were not serious, 'the sensation of the patient was of the imminence of death'. By September he was back once again in the Clinic. There he told Hayward, 'I find, as I grow older, that I have hardly any real friends.'

Eliot increasingly felt used and resented the way in which Hayward 'farmed him out for favours', furious that he was being dangled as a kind of reward. He began to scrutinise the legal settlement by which each man had promised the other a year's rent if he were the first to leave. Perhaps suffering under the burden of concealing feelings from his closest friends, he began to act 'like one demented'.[669] The differences between the two came to a head as Hayward examined what was to be Eliot's last play, *The Elder Statesman*. Hayward felt that the draft that he was shown was not up to the standard of the earlier work. No longer the 'très loyal serviteur' that he had dubbed himself in happier times, he did not mince his words. He told Eliot he felt it was 'a poor imitation of *The Confidential Clerk*' and that he ought to start again.[670] According to the American novelist Djuna Barnes, Hayward gave Eliot such a 'lashing' that it reduced him to tears, 'saying he'd never write another word'.[671] Thinking about the play now gave Eliot shivers down his spine. The plot turns on guilty secrets. Its hero, the elderly and distinguished Lord Claverton, has to confront his past, including a death in a motor accident that he failed to report, and a broken promise of marriage. He is redeemed by facing up to his ghosts and baring his truthful soul to his daughter. Although only 'a beginner in the practice of loving', by the end of the play he can say, 'I have been brushed by the wing of happiness.' The play ends with an almost operatic love duet between Lord Claverton's daughter

Monica and her fiancée. 'Not even death can dismay or amaze me / Fixed in the certainty of love unchanging.' Did Hayward, as he went about his business of attacking the script, have any sense of how proleptic these words were to prove?

'I have read the whole of English poetry, *twice*,' Hayward claimed 'with justifiable pride' to Kathleen Raine, adding that his anthologies 'contained most that was worth reading at all'.[672] When Penguin wanted to produce an anthology of English verse Hayward was the obvious man to choose for the job and in Eliot and Auden he also had the benefit of the best of advisers. As he assiduously collated all the original texts he could find, it became an arduous task. In 1956 the *Penguin Book of English Verse* was published in an initial run of 50,000 copies costing 4s 6d. The 484-page anthology spanned four centuries, beginning with *Songes and Sonettes* of 1557 and ending around the year 1940. This decision cut out Chaucer and medieval literature but allowed 'a kind of royal progress' of four hundred years of poetry from the reign of Elizabeth I to that of Elizabeth II. The omission of all Scots writers, including Burns, may have been influenced by Eliot's hostility – he had roundly declared that no good poetry had been written there except for one poem of William Dunbar.[673] It was certainly a notable exclusion. By contrast and again perhaps influenced by Eliot, Hayward included in the canon the work of American poets such as Emerson, Longfellow, Whitman and Frost. The anthology included one hundred and fifty poets, some represented by a single work but most by a selection. (Shakespeare gets twenty-four entries.) Each section is a vignette of a whole career, the final poem coming as an appropriate close. Shakespeare ends with the song from *Cymbeline*, 'Fear no more the heat o' the sun', and Milton with the epilogue from *Samson Agonistes*: 'Calm of mind all passion spent'. Hayward's art as an anthologist is shown especially in the way he inlays poem with poem to reflect and contrast.

A comparison with the *Oxford Book of English Verse* shows startling differences between the two anthologies. The first editor, 'Q' (Sir Arthur Quiller-Couch), was especially fond of choice nuggets of verse. Hence long poems such as *Paradise Lost* or *The Prelude* found no place in his selection. This stress on brief lyrics meant that only two of Donne's religious poems were included and Herrick was the second most generously represented poet. Hayward, as a student of

Donne, saw the seventeenth century in a totally different light. The age was not exclusively concerned with 'rosy cheeks and daffodils and the instability of human affection', but sceptical, doubting, satiric. He therefore gave the poetry of Donne, Jonson and the Metaphysicals much more weight, and put more stress on Pope and the eighteenth century and less on the Romantics.

Q was also cavalier about making texts fit his scheme: Donne's 'The Ecstasy', for example, was reduced to a quarter of its original length, a mere twenty lines. His editorial method was completely at odds with Hayward's practice:

> I have sometimes thought it consistent with the aim of the book to prefer the more beautiful to the better attested reading. I have often excised weak or superfluous stanzas when sure that excision would improve; and have not hesitated to extract a few stanzas from a long poem when persuaded that they could stand alone as a lyric.[674]

This kind of textual liberty was exactly the way in which Hayward had set about *Love's Helicon*, but it was absolutely inappropriate to a more scholarly anthology. He prefaced the *Penguin Book of English Verse* with a typically scrupulous 'Note on the Text' stating his editorial stance of generally using as his copy text the earliest text, but sometimes later versions if they had been revised by the poet. He would certainly never try to 'improve' a text or prefer a subjective choice of the 'more beautiful'.[675]

Even though it emerged five years after the Festival of Britain had ended, the *Penguin Book of English Verse* was Hayward's final contribution to it. His anthology met with immediate acclaim and became a runaway success, going through twenty-six reprints in its first thirty years; it displaced Q's *Oxford Book of English Verse* as the best-selling anthology of its time. The enormous popular readership also ensured that for half a century it helped shape the idea of what constituted English poetry. 'You really *have* an *extraordinary* gift for making poems shine at their finest. It is a strange gift, and hardly any editor has it,' wrote Edith Sitwell. It was a fine compliment from one anthologist to another. 'My word it is good,' she added.[676] He was on the whole delighted with the result and Penguin's efforts: 'a great work, excellent typography, though a bad paper'. There was only one dissenting voice: he noted the *Daily Worker* disapproved of the total neglect of 'people's poetry' and wrote to Edith Sitwell to warn her to include in her next anthology 'some of Swinburne's well-known drinking songs, some of Browning's "Factory Fancies" and a selection of Morris's neglected revolutionary limericks' – or to face the wrath of the *Daily Worker*.[677] He added that her opinion and Eliot's approval meant more to him than all that the press could write.

As a sixteen-year-old Yorkshire schoolgirl, Valerie Fletcher had listened intently in an English lesson to a gramophone record of John Gielgud reading 'The Journey of the Magi'. She was bowled over. At the end of the lesson she went up to her teacher, Miss Bartholomew, and asked, 'Who wrote that poem?' Miss Bartholomew told her it that it was T. S. Eliot. 'I shall marry that man,' her pupil said immediately. After a moment's pause, she mused, 'But how shall I meet him?' Without thinking anything of it, Miss Bartholomew replied, 'You could become his secretary, I suppose.'[678]

After leaving school she went to train as a secretary in London. By a strange coincidence, her first job was with the critic both Hayward and Eliot disliked most: Charles Morgan. Then through a friend she heard that Eliot needed a secretary at Faber's. In 1949, after a nervous interview with a chain-smoking Eliot, she finally got the job that she had wanted so much. Five years later Hayward, 'who had eyes and ears everywhere',[679] began to sense that something was going on between the secretary and her boss. Four months before Eliot 'sneaked out' to marry Valerie, he told J. M. Brinnin that Eliot had contracted emphysema and apparently needed a nurse more than he himself did. He added: 'I have an informed suspicion that the ever-adoring Miss Fletcher is ready to assume the role ... There's somewhat more to that flower of the Yorkshire marches than meets the eye. The perfect secretary has begun to see herself as the lady with the lamp.'[680] What Hayward absolutely failed to see was that Eliot would prove to be a more than willing patient. 'What are you giving your secretary for Christmas?' he asked Eliot disingenuously. Eliot replied that he had not thought about it. 'You mean old thing. Get her the biggest bottle of scent you can possibly buy,' he urged. Eliot did more than that.[681]

At 6.30 in the darkness of the morning of Thursday 10 January 1957 Thomas Stearns Eliot married Esmé Valerie Fletcher in St Barnabas Church, Kensington. They had obtained a special licence from the

Archbishop of Canterbury to marry at such an early hour and in a church outside the parishes where they both lived. He was sixty-eight years old and Valerie was thirty but he felt, he told Djuna Barnes, 'as spry as a spider'. His solicitor acted as his best man and the only guests were the bride's parents. The wedding was Eliot's best-kept secret: he had not confided his intentions to any of his friends, apart from John Hayward.

The story of Eliot's departure from Carlyle Mansions, according to Eliot's biographer Tom Matthews, is the one vouched for by Valerie: Eliot had met Hayward two days before the wedding and they had a long talk in Hayward's room while Valerie waited nervously outside. It was not true, as rumour had it, that a doctor was with her in case the strain of the meeting damaged Eliot's fragile health although Eliot had consulted his doctor about the meeting. He had advised getting it over as quickly as possible and leaving the flat immediately. Hayward apparently took the news extremely well and a financial settlement was agreed. 'TSE leaves 11-15' is Hayward's brief calendar entry for 8 January. Later he wrote a rather different story to Helen Gardner, confirming what had happened. 'The Bard's elopement was a stunning surprise. I knew nothing and suspected nothing until he handed me a letter to read as he was leaving – literally leaving – the flat, to spend the night with his lawyer before the 6.15 am 25 guineas ceremony.'[682] The announcement was made at the last possible moment.

On the afternoon of the marriage, at about 3.30, John Hayward's sister, Diana, was visiting her brother along with her son Henry and four other children for a Christmas tea party: 'We were shown straight into John's room and Madame (John's housekeeper) followed us in to take our coats. John swizzled round in his revolving chair and exclaimed, "you will never guess what has happened! Mr Eliot has eloped with his secretary."' When she asked how he had heard, Hayward replied, 'after a slight hesitation', that he had heard by telephone at one o'clock. She assumed it was that same day. The conversation then went as follows:

> 'What did you say?'
> 'I said "I'm delighted but why did you not tell me?"'
> 'What did he say?'
> 'Well, John, I thought you would be so cross!'[683]

She added that Eliot had told her brother of his intention by letter on the night before.

> This so well remembered dialogue rings true, and it seems a natural thing for Mr Eliot to slip away after the wedding and to let John know before the Press. It would be good to find the letter which Mr Eliot put into John's hand as he was 'literally leaving' the flat on the eve of the wedding ... Madame was not suspicious until Mr Eliot came to say goodbye to her before he left on what she thought was a holiday. This is what she told us 'Je lui dit [*sic*] 'Monsieur! Pourquoi n'avez-vous dites adieu?' – (instead of 'au revoir') to which Mr. Eliot made no reply. Madame then left us to shoo away a reporter who was ringing the doorbell.[684]

Diana and her family left just after half-past six and elbowed their way through the gaggle of reporters who had gathered outside Carlyle Mansions. On the Embankment she bought an evening paper. There she read a small stop press announcement of the marriage.

Her brother, of course, kept the brief letter, which was 'put into his hand', and preserved it for the archives. Onto the envelope he carefully pencilled, 'the letter TSE handed me to read in his presence, announcing his secret marriage to his secretary'. Eliot began by saying that as he was leaving on Tuesday rather than Thursday it was easiest to say what he had to say in writing. He asked Hayward to treat the contents of the letter as highly confidential. Then came the stunning news:

> On Thursday morning Valerie Fletcher and I are getting married. We shall leave for Menton immediately and shall be away for three weeks. On our return we shall stop in a hotel until we find some permanent place in which to live.[685]

This change in his life would cause several difficult problems, none of which concerned him more than 'the future of 19, Carlyle Mansions in connection with yourself'. It would, he wrote, distress him deeply if his flatmate had to leave, and he proposed generous terms of compensation: he would pay £300 out of the total rent of £470 for the next three years or the whole rent for two and a half years. Eliot added that he wanted 'at this juncture' to avoid any kind of discussion, particularly retrospective discussion of these matters. He made no mention of their long friendship and their parting was treated as a simple financial matter of honouring a contract. This most unaffectionate of brief letters was signed 'Affectionately yours, Tom'.

Diana's story can square with her brother's. Hayward hesitated to tell about the time because he had first heard by letter two nights before of Eliot's planned marriage. What may or may not have been said after he read the letter is a matter of dispute. Eliot also rang him up at one o'clock after the ceremony. A brief telephone call as he 'slipped away' after the wedding would have been the obvious time to give his flatmate a forwarding address. So Hayward probably heard twice, once before by letter, and once afterwards by phone. Later on, as resentment took hold, he added dramatic colour to his story to enlist sympathy. Crucially, he altered the time of Eliot's departure from two evenings before the wedding to Wednesday night or even the early hours of Thursday morning. Gwen Watkins recalled that he told her that when Eliot did not return from church as usual he was so worried that he thought of calling the police. Then he said to her in a most uncharacteristic manner: 'What do you think that bastard did? He just walked out before I was up. He left me a note saying he wouldn't be coming back. And he never did.'[686] According to Tom Matthews, Hayward told Christopher Sykes another different and expanded version of events in which Eliot thrust a letter into his hands very early on the morning of the wedding, saying that he had to go, but wanted Hayward to read the letter that very instant. Somewhat reluctantly Hayward read it and then said, 'Well, that's fine but why didn't you tell me?' 'Oh, because I thought you might be angry,' Eliot said. Hayward replied:

'My dear old Tom, I couldn't be angry with you.' Then Eliot leaned forward, and put his arm around him and kissed him, saying, 'Oh, I knew I could always rely on you.' Hayward said later, with a resigned grin, 'Since I am the most un-homosexual man in London, I found this a most offensive gesture.'[687]

This is an embellished version of the story he had told his sister; the pain of the parting transformed into a whiff of sex and a witty riposte. Still another variant came from H. G. Wells's mistress the Russian countess and spy Moura Budberg, nicknamed 'Bedbug' by John Betjeman: Eliot could not face the task of telling his old friend about his forthcoming marriage and his departure and therefore told him on the telephone afterwards.[688] Hayward was so shocked he hung up without a word. Other accounts stated that Eliot came to see Hayward immediately after his marriage or, more fancifully, that he learnt of Eliot's leaving through a note left on his pillow.[689]

What is indisputably true is that he was kept in the dark at least till just before the event and that the manner of the telling was not that of an old and trusted friend. Diana's account ended:

> I have never heard of the 'canard' that John first heard the news from the press. I agree that John did not seem greatly upset by Mr Eliot's actual departure, but rather in the manner of his going. Afterwards there were difficulties, I believe, and he told me he was not going to the funeral of his old friend.[690]

On the morning of the wedding Hayward cabled Margaret Behrens with a note of goodwill and congratulations for the couple. After the war she had moved from Shamley Green to fashionable Menton in the Alpes Maritimes. There she had played an active part in bringing Eliot and Valerie together, inviting them to stay with her – although, in fact, Eliot slept at a nearby hotel. He had managed to smuggle a letter of proposal (another letter!) into Valerie's typing and they had secretly become engaged.[691] When Margaret met the plane at Nice airport she thrust the cable into Eliot's hands: 'You'd have been glad if you'd seen it when you saw the pleasure it gave them – it was such a charming message – and I think it just put the final touch of happiness upon their day,' she wrote back to Hayward.[692] Both Eliot and his bride looked radiant. Nevertheless the secrecy of the whole affair puzzled her – 'It's not as if Tom were marrying a Hottentot or something,' she added. Eliot replied to Hayward with the customary postcard. He described his wedding arrangements as 'a complete success & the press *baffled*', and thanked him for his good wishes. 'On arrival met by *M.B.* who gave me your telegram – a masterpiece of J. H. wit and gallantry which gave immense pleasure. Nearly every day sunny.' It was signed 'Much love, Tom.'[693] The relief is palpable: he had got away with it. Whatever was happening to their relationship seemed not immediately to be felt and, on the surface at least, all was well.

Far from the brilliant winter sunshine and the blue skies of Menton, wild stories and rumours began to circulate when the news came out that the elderly ascetic Eliot had married his young blonde secretary. Eliot wrote to Mary Trevelyan telling her of his marriage in a letter dated 9 January: 'I have now told John and one of the reasons for not telling you sooner is that I wanted to be able honestly to say to him that I was telling him before anyone else.' She was dumbfounded. She had seen Eliot three times over Christmas at the Russell Hotel and they had met a week before the wedding where they drank Tio Pepe sherry and discussed Vivienne. All the carefully preserved rituals of friendship were going on just as normal. As they had parted, he held her hand with the words, 'As you know I always mention you in my prayers.'[694] And now, without any hint or warning, he had married a secretary half his age.

Immediately she rang her fellow guardian to try to make sense of the news. Although she thought that he had 'gone out of his mind', Mary immediately sent her congratulations – only to find that Eliot had given her a false address in France. She wrote again to his office but there was still no reply. A third letter assured him that her 'affection would not change'. This time Eliot did reply; he was furiously angry. He accused her of 'gross impertinence' and the newly married couple cut her off completely. 'He has gone into a strange world into which I cannot follow him,'[695] the baffled Mary wrote. She tried to explain it to herself. She listed the various factors that might have led to his 'startling change of personality'. He always had a hypochondriac's terror of death and was now panicking about his future. The devoted admiration of his secretary posed no threat to a man who had become less and less able to take any criticism of his views. For a long time he had 'deliberately frustrated' strong sexual feelings which could now be released.

In her memoir she noted how Hayward, 'Eliot's literary executor, advisor and friend',[696] had also been abandoned just as abruptly. He who 'had vetted every line of Tom's plays' and had already worked on the first act of the new one had been just as suddenly dropped. Tom Possum had done another of his disappearing tricks – 'He has always been a great runner-away,' wrote Mary, and both guardians came to feel as if their friendship had never existed. In the opening to her journal, she mused sadly: 'I do not know if he was ever in love with me – John Hayward maintains that he was.'[697] It was not the marriage that caused the division between Eliot and his two guardians: it was the surgical way in which he had removed them from his life. Just as Eliot had told Vivienne of the end of their marriage through a solicitor's letter, so it was by letter that he told Hayward and Mary Trevelyan of his second marriage. On the other side of the Atlantic, Emily Hale, hearing the news of the wedding, suffered a breakdown and was admitted to the Massachusetts General Hospital in Boston.

Behind his polite exterior Hayward was numb: 'I am completely baffled and feel as if Harry had suddenly turned up at Wishwood with a typist in tow and the explanation that he could not face all that thirst in the desert business.'[698] ('Harry' is Lord Monchensey, the hero of *The Family Reunion* who leaves the family home to renounce all human contact to follow a spiritual quest in the desert.) Hayward could readily have understood such a parting from Eliot, but his actual course seemed inexplicable: the aristocrat going off with the typist; the missionary renouncing his call. 'I am still, like Othello, puzzled in the extreme. I feel, after eleven years, as if Tom had suddenly died – at least to me; and I can only hope and pray he has done wisely and well and that he has found the happiness life has hitherto denied him.'[699] But when it became apparent that Eliot had systematically and secretly been removing his clothes and belongings, the stealth of his departure left Hayward more and more resentful: 'Think of the treacherousness of a man taking all his shirts and all his ties, little by little.' No doubt he touched up the colours of the story to suit his audience. 'John was not averse to making a good story for us about what had happened' – as Helen Gardner put it – but Eliot's treatment of him was heartless. At first he responded with the wit that was his protection from the hurt and with gallantly polite postcards to the couple, but he became increasingly bitter. He no longer referred to himself as Tarantula and took on the name of another sort of spider – 'the Widow'.

Hayward's friends rallied round to condemn Eliot's behaviour towards his old companion. According to Mary Trevelyan, most of them sent him to Coventry. Edith Sitwell had clearly heard the story of the morning betrayal. Fiercely loyal to Hayward, she was outraged: 'Oh! What a *beast* Tom is!!!' she wrote to John Lehmann on 19 January 1957:

You wait! I'll take it out of that young woman! I'll frighten her out of her wits before I've done … It makes me quite sick to think of the pain John has endured – that waking up at 5.30 in the morning or 5.45, to be told that his greatest friend, on whom he depended in his unspeakable physical helplessness and humiliation, had done him this sly, crawling, lethal cruelty. I feel I never want to see Tom again![700]

When the dramatist Michael Hastings met her in New York later on in the year, she was still seething about the wedding and how 'Tom had done something absolutely beastly to John Hayward, a paraplegic with whom he shared rooms'.[701] Graham Greene thought Hayward was behaving with splendid courage and had every right to acid remarks and stories about the couple. 'Towards the end of his life he suffered a deep wound from a great friend – an unintentional wound inflicted with the moral cowardice of a sensitive man, and I for one was glad to see John fight back, without self-pity, with his sharp weapon of ridicule. He was certainly not a saint, but he was the bravest man I have ever known.'[702] Kathleen Raine, too, felt that the ending was a dreadful blow: with Eliot's departure and separation 'the whole purpose of John Hayward's life was undermined'.[703]

There were a few others, such as Christopher Sykes, who took a very different view.

> It is sad that the story of their friendship did not end happily. The fault was on John's side. I think this was the only time in John's life that his affliction got the better of him in a psychological sense. Living alone, I suppose, after Eliot had gone, he felt his helplessness anew. He developed delusions that Eliot had behaved very badly towards him. This was untrue, and at the time of the marriage John recognised that Eliot had behaved strangely (as he often did) but generously and honourably ... But then, slowly, horrible fancies took hold of his mind. I would rather have not mentioned this, but the episode gave rise to libels, which persist, on Eliot's character, and which I know to be nonsense.[704]

Presumably these 'libels' contained details of Eliot's moments in 'the confessional' with Hayward who became now the very source of the rumours about homosexuality and cruelty to his first wife that Eliot had asked his literary executor to silence.

For five months Eliot made little attempt to keep up their friendship. Hayward reported to Mary Hyde that his 'Distinguished Lodger' and secretary had 'made a nest behind Barker's emporium in darkest Kensington', but that he had not been invited to inspect it. 'I intend to continue here in a dignified state of widowhood – or am I only a poor cuckold?'[705] In May 1957 he was invited to lunch at 3 Kensington Court Gardens with Robert Frost and Rosamond Lehmann. The meal was not a success. Out of politeness, as he left, he said, 'You must come to tea some day', but he had no heart to pursue it. Some months later Valerie rang to say that they were still waiting for a proper invitation. Soon afterwards the Eliots finally came to Carlyle Mansions, but Hayward found the tea party both 'embarrassing and depressing'. A year later, in September 1958, Eliot booked a box for Hayward, having checked with Sherek that it was suitable, as he had done in the past, for the first London night of *The Elder Statesman* at the Cambridge Theatre. In his Preface he also thanked Hayward for the criticism that led to the reconstruction of the first act, as if nothing had changed between them. Other invitations were recorded in Hayward's calendar, but they were often crossed out as one or the other could not make the date. Gradually even these disappeared as mutual bitterness took hold. Eliot did his best to avoid meeting Hayward in public, just as he had tried to avoid Vivienne thirty years before. This made their encounter at Christie's auction rooms in June 1960, at a sale of books and manuscripts in aid of the London Library, a very public and dramatic scene. 'You must come and visit us sometime,' said Valerie: 'I am waiting for the invitation,' replied Hayward.[706] Stalemate.

Hayward continued on the attack, speaking with his usual sarcastic wit about the marriage and Valerie. When wounded, his riposte was snobbish dismissal. Helen Gardner, for example, received a letter which was 'very funny in John's most characteristic manner', a letter which could not be shown to Valerie on account of its references to 'typists and other non-U persons'.[707] Even Kathleen Raine, loyal to Hayward though she was, felt that he was very horrible about Valerie. He was snide about the fact that, in the phrase of the time, 'she did not come out of the top drawer'. Some semblance of a relationship, however, was gradually resumed and polite Christmas cards sent. Hayward finally dined with the Eliots in their new flat in Kensington Court Gardens and wrote to Helen Gardner about their taste in furnishing: 'My dear, the very *best* from Maples.'[708] She felt that for their part the Eliots did try to mend the situation, but did so tactlessly.

After his marriage Eliot seemed a changed man. To the amazement of his old friends he seemed to have moved straight from an ascetic cell to a world of department store soft furnishings; the old man who had seemed so dangerously near to death was now taking lessons in ballroom dancing and attending charity balls. In company he gripped

tightly the hand of his new wife, in an ostentatious display of together-
ness, as if he feared to let her go. 'I'm the luckiest, the very luckiest man
on earth,' he told Djuna Barnes. Mary Trevelyan spoke for Emily Hale,
Edith Sitwell and John Hayward when she wondered: 'I am sure he is
not the person I know – but have I known the real person? Have John
and I known and loved the real man?'[709]

17

The Book Collector

Christopher Isherwood visited Carlyle Mansions every time he came to England from his home in California. In February 1956 Hayward was clearly feeling the passing years. He told Isherwood how much he admired his youthful looks and trim figure and contrasted them with his own increasing fatness and baldness. For his part Isherwood felt that it was uncanny that his host always spoke of himself as an able-bodied person. Twisted in his wheelchair, he made remarks such as: 'You know after bronchitis a morning always comes – though one never can believe that it will – when one wakes up and suddenly one's legs belong to one again and one leaps out of bed like a two year old.'[710] Isherwood wondered, 'Does he say these things from bravado, or to make his hearer uncomfortable, or does he will himself to think like a normal person?' It was, of course, all of a piece with Hayward's refusal to notice what he called his infirmity. When he told a story, for example, he would often begin, 'As I was walking down Bond Street ...' He always used the active 'walk' and never the passive 'was pushed'. In private papers and journals that reveal his innermost thoughts he scarcely ever referred to his creeping paralysis.

But by the 1960s Hayward's features had become further contorted by the effects of age and illness. Christopher Isherwood, was struck by the contrast between his 'rigid torso with its spasmodic puppet-like movements' and the charm and dignity of his manner. For him Hayward's eyes had all the mobility his body lacked: 'His large grey eyes were so intelligent.'[711] Loss of muscular control caused his bright red lower lip to fall and it was this that made him so strikingly ugly, even 'repellent' to some friends such as Humphrey Spender. Elias Canetti noted how his lip's 'red fleshiness gave Hayward's face a coarse animalistic expression quite at variance with the perfectly formed sentences in which he would at all times express himself'.[712] Anthony Powell too was aware of the contrast: 'Suffering had left its grim marks on Hayward's features, turbid lips and an expression of implacable severity, making him look like a portrait of Savonarola.' But he added that, 'In fact nothing could have been less puritanical than Hayward's lively talk, always expressed in carefully chosen phrases, somewhat Augustan in diction.'[713] Even Janet Adam Smith, a friend for many years, wondered if her very young children might take fright at 'his ugly and formidable face, his general look of a wicked godfather in a fairy-tale'. In fact they did not: children were fascinated by him and Hayward himself was always intrigued by them and kept a box of sweets for his young visitors on his mantelpiece.

Roland Penrose, working for the British Council in Paris, tried to cheer up his old friend by inviting him to spend a fortnight with his family in their rented apartment in the Place Vendôme. Here was a chance for Hayward to revisit the places he had known thirty years earlier, and to try to forget the parting from Eliot. He flew from London in September and was installed in his host's penthouse. Then he rocketed around in the taxi that Penrose had organised for him. He was on the go day and night, exhausting his hosts by his energy, 'cramming the six days of the locust with quintessential pleasure'.[714] He lunched at the British Embassy and noted appreciatively 'La Reine de Torrents en gêlée de Chablis'. The sun shone brilliantly as he made the rounds of booksellers, libraries and old friends. He visited Versailles, Saint-Germain and Nogent which he associated with Manet and Monet, Ville d'Avray where Corot lived and Bougival where Turgenev died. At 3 am Hayward surveyed the sleeping city from the terrace of Sacré Coeur.

He insisted on seeing the Epstein's monument to Oscar Wilde at the Père Lachaise cemetery, and demanded that his host take him: 'I was treated to a shower of scorn at the gate when I hesitated to say frankly to the guardian that my friend beside me was an *estropié*. "I am a cripple," Hayward said emphatically.'[715] Penrose thought that he seemed almost to take a pride in his disability. Hayward described to Graham Greene what he noticed about the statue: 'Two holes bored in the balls of the symbolic figure to hold a metal fig-leaf in the event of a pudibond government coming to power.'[716] Later he stared respectfully at the notorious brothel on the rue Chabanais 'where clients were shown the chair specially constructed for Edward VII when he was too stout and too lazy to do it in bed'. 'I wish I had had you as a companion,' he confided to Greene. All in all, the trip was such a success that on his return Hayward wrote in a postcard to Mary Hyde, who was working on the plan for him to visit his American friends, 'Look! This is a big step forward to my reaching you.' And so 'The Great Plot' began to take shape. Plans were made for Hayward's next trip: a schedule of lectures worked out; American taxis carefully measured and importing an English one considered; a friend had a library room, complete with bed, set up, and many others were quick to offer accommodation. All looked promising.

After the loss of friendship remained the consolation of work. In 1952 Hayward had been recruited by Ian Fleming, the creator of James Bond, for the Queen Anne Press, a newly-formed small publishing house.[717] It was not a commercial outfit and initially had to search for 'any discarded material by certain esteemed authors that could be rescued from their waste-paper baskets', as Percy Muir, the dealer in rare books, remembered.[718] Relying on the money that Bond brought in, Ian Fleming ventured to take over an occasional publication *The Book Handbook*, 'an illustrated quarterly for discriminating book lovers', as it called itself. It was renamed *The Book Collector* and was at first produced slowly in an old-fashioned way – the first fourteen numbers were printed on a hand press. But if it still relied on archaic printing methods it was new in its approach and style.

The new board consisted of Ian Fleming, John Hayward and Percy Muir: a book collector, a scholar and a leading antiquarian bookseller. Their range of interests was reflected in the width of the magazine's contents. 'An Announcement' prefaced the first issue: 'We appear henceforward under a new title and with a new Editorial Board. Our aim will continue to be the provision of bibliographical information and entertainment, but we also intend to increase the scope and usefulness of our contents.'[719] It proclaimed its purpose to find a wider readership, promising new material, and a different format. Fleming who, as Hayward noted, owned '49/50ths of the shoestring upon which its existence in the early days depended',[720] was a serious book collector, his interest stemming from the moment in 1929 when he had bought a copy of D. H. Lawrence's poetry collection *Pansies* in a Mayfair bookshop.[721] There he had met – and immediately liked – the urbane bookseller Percy Muir, who soon became his mentor, helping him to make a distinctive collection of 'milestone' books that had changed the world. It was housed in fifty expensive black buckram boxes in his flat, which happened to be two floors above Hayward's in Carlyle Mansions. So *The Book Collector* was masterminded from a building that contained two remarkable collections and two remarkable collectors.

By the summer of 1952 the first number had been 'so warmly

received' that the format was increased to medium octavo size to show off the photographs better.[722] The scholar Philip Gaskell was appointed as editor, but from the start Hayward was the driving force. He introduced items which were to become regular features and cajoled some of the most prominent scholars and collectors of the day to write for him – a task made more difficult as none of the contributors was paid. In a long-running series Howard Nixon, 'the doyen of historians of bookbinding', wrote a series of illustrated articles on famous examples of the art; Anthony Hobson from Sotheby's reported the latest news from the salerooms and soon succeeded his father G. D. Hobson both as a contributor and as a good friend of Hayward; T. J. Brown described 'famous literary holographs' and there was a revival of 'Bibliographical Notes and Queries', which Hayward hoped would provide a forum for readers' contributions. He commissioned some famous names to provide unfamiliar angles on the world of book collecting: he talked his flatmate into printing his 'Address to Members of the London Library'. The food writer André Simon contributed a piece on 'Biblioteca Gastronomica'. Anthony Hobson arranged for Nancy Cunard, daughter of the society hostess Emerald, to write on the Hours Press which she had run before the war in Paris. Percy Muir remembered his own career as a bookman and recalled bookshops such as Elkin Mathews in Mayfair where eccentrics such as Eddie and Robert Gathorne-Hardy presided and customers such as Lytton Strachey or Ottoline Morrell browsed the shelves. This blend of learned articles, reminiscences, up-to-date news, and commentaries spiced with wit remained the pattern of the magazine for the next fifteen years and moved *The Book Collector* well away from its dilettante predecessor.

The magazine never lost its ability to surprise and entertain. There might be an impossibly difficult crossword, a quiz, a spoof on 'Bibliometric Analysis', or an artlicle on almost anything, ranging from collecting early Penguins to an illustrated account of insect pests in books or to seventeenth-century libertine literature. There were pieces too on more obscure libraries and their treasures, including Bamburgh Castle, the Royal Music Library in London, Blickling Hall in Norfolk, Chetham's Library, Manchester, and the town library of King's Lynn. A major scoop in 1955 was an article on the priceless holdings of the Saltykov-Shchedrin state public library in Leningrad, the first report of its kind for forty years to get out from behind the Iron Curtain.[723] The following year Hayward managed to persuade the Director of the

Lenin Library in Moscow to instruct his leading 'scientists' to write for *The Book Collector*. There was a bracing internationalism about the journal which was just as likely to contain articles on Voltaire's library, early printed books in Hungary or collecting Japanese manuscript scrolls as it was to deal with British or American topics. Indeed as the Cold War became icier Hayward was proud to note the part that *The Book Collector* played: 'Bibliophily ... transcends frontiers and other barriers to the free intercourse of kindred minds and spirits and we shall continue to propound its gospel and to play our small part in keeping the lamps in the libraries of the world burning in the prevailing gloom.'[724] Increasingly he came to describe his world of bookmen as his 'sodality', his closest friends in a threatening world.

The pages of *The Book Collector* chronicled the way in which the world of bookselling was changing in Hayward's lifetime. In sale after sale collections were dismantled, auctioned off and often disappeared to the United States. Again and again he noted in his commentaries how the rich universities of Texas and New York amassed their treasured volumes and manuscripts. No longer was the individual collector able to match them and the supply was restricted by the fact that copies never returned to the dealers once the institutions had acquired them. When the manuscripts of Coleridge's 'Christabel' and nine notebooks left the country destined for Toronto University, Hayward wrote to *The Times* suggesting that the public ought to be informed beforehand about the loss of 'their unique literary treasures'.[725] The cry was taken up by the leader writer, who urged a change in the regulations to protect 'our national heritage'.[726] The Tennyson family's collection of manuscripts disappeared to the Houghton library at Harvard in 1955 and Hayward continued his campaign in *The Book Collector*.[727] There was far too little opportunity for raisng money by public subscription. The Board of Trade's decisions seemed whimsical and arbitrary, allowing the export of a 'treasurable portion of England's literary heritage' while preserving works of much less importance. It needed to consult much more broadly before giving or witholding an export licence. Ironically enough, today some of the largest collections of Hayward's own letters have duly made their way to the United States.

Hayward himself wrote few articles, but developed the 'Commentary', which prefaced each issue, into his own personal column. Although 'scrappy at first', it soon gained the authority of his distinctive voice and caustic tone and became the section 'to which every reader always turned first'.[728] He was alert to any error of language or jargon. A catalogue described a book as excessively rare. 'A few may be too rare for words, but they can hardly be *too* rare,' he commented. No correction was too minute: 'Mr Adams should know that the accent on Liège was changed from acute into grave by Royal Decree on 10 September 1946.' He was independent and fearless in his attacks on institutions. Influential American libraries, the British Museum's poor catalogues, the National Trust's hiding away its precious volumes, dealers' rings, or the way in which British law led to so much of the literary heritage crossing the Atlantic – all met with his trenchant criticism. The Distillers' Company earned his wrath when it published an advert showing three bottles of whisky perched disrespectfully on an early nineteenth-century edition of Sir Walter Scott – 'a shocking example to bibliophiles'.[729] Even the Church of England was called to account for 'the unseemly gaps' in the Bible collection at Lambeth Palace. As in his conversation, Hayward never drew back for fear of causing offence. Even his colleagues turned to each new issue 'with fear and trembling'.[730]

There were, however, problems and crises. *The Book Collector* cost £1,000 a year to run and by 1955 the owner, the newspaper proprietor Lord Kemsley, had had enough of the financial drain. Just after the summer 1955 issue the members of the board received a shock. Without any warning a cyclostyled notice came through the post that the journal had come to an end and the balance on all subscriptions would be returned. Hayward and Muir immediately prepared a counter-attack, marshalling all their friends and contacts to appeal for funding. William A. (Bill) Jackson, director of the Houghton Library at Harvard University, offered moral support and other American friends weighed in. Hayward persuaded the millionaire Paul Mellon to help; a cheque for £500 was quickly sent.[731] When Hayward met Arthur Houghton, founder of the Houghton Library, and a great collector himself, Hayward asked nervously if he would conrtribute something about the Houghton Collection to *The Book Collector*. 'That's just what I wanted to ask you about. I hear *The Book Collector* has had a difficult crisis in its affairs and I'd like to know how I can help,' replied Houghton.[732] Hayward told him and the result was an extremely generous cheque. So *The Book Collector* was saved. Lord Kemsley sold the Queen Anne Press and the magazine to Ian Fleming for £50 and a new and sympathetic printer, James Shand, was installed. 'NOW I AM VERY HAPPY,' wrote Hayward to Mary Hyde.[733] From this time he chose to forfeit his salary of £200 a year and worked for nothing.

Ian Fleming was a bibliophile of a more commercial and populist kind than Hayward.[734] As chairman he worried about the money the journal made, or, more accurately, lost. He tried to make it less erudite and specialised. In the editorial offices at Victoria Square he held regular lunches for the board. The meetings were not characterised by gentlemanly agreement. The designer and typographer Robert Harling described them as 'furious hilarious affairs with no holds barred'. Hayward, pinioned in his bath chair, was 'as heroic and formidable a cripple as Roosevelt, sparing no man's reputation and trailing his own with every quip and query'.[735] Hayward dealt with all matters to do with the quarterly with an absolute seriousness which clearly annoyed Fleming. He complained to Percy Muir that Hayward treated the meeting 'as if it were the Annual General Meeting of Imperial Chemicals and is now much put out because I tried to hasten proceedings'. When in 1957 Ian Fleming attacked an issue as 'the most leaden in content we have ever produced'[736] these angry divisions came to a head. On the one side, standing for pure scholarship, were Hayward and John Carter: on the other Ian Fleming and his friend the typographer and designer Robert Harling. Fleming claimed that Hayward's inept editorial leadership led to articles that were 'uniformly leaden, stuffy and unreadable'.[737] Carter, ever loyal, wrote a strong memorandum to the board stating that 'without JH (and let me be clear that would mean without me also) *The Book Collector* would not last two issues'.[738] Its success depended 'on one man only, the present editorial director' – who should be allowed the freedom to edit as he saw fit. If the periodical had served its purpose as a means by which Fleming could write off some tax, it should be sold 'to someone who likes it the way it is'. Ian Fleming took offence at the idea that he had an ulterior financial motive: 'The Company was formed at my personal expense to keep *The Book Collector* under the editorship of John alive and for no other purpose whatsoever.'[739] At this point Hayward called him to order by reminding him that it would not have been 'saved from extinction after you had taken it over from Lord Kemsley without the generous help of a number of guarantors'. Fleming subsided and the magazine continued as before. Disagreements, however strong, never soured their friendship; Fleming planned to leave *The Book Collector* to his friend and

Hayward gradually built up a complete set of presentation copies of James Bond novels.

The best account of Hayward's working methods comes from his secretary Catherine Porteous. In one of his last Commentaries he described himself as 'one who ... is in constant danger of being submerged in a Sargasso Sea of bibliographical *paperasserie* – printed, typewritten, duplicated, xerographic ephemera of every kind'.[740] Catherine Porteous had to arrange all this material within his restricted reach, and faced the added problem that the whole plan of the next issue was never written down, but remained only in Hayward's mind. 'From this chaos, incredibly, *The Book Collector* emerged immaculate each quarter.' She described the way that it was put together and how the material was transformed into an orderly whole:

> There was, of course, a System. It consisted of two large brown envelopes, two very shallow drawers and two wire trays. The envelopes contained reviews, notes and queries, proofs and corrections; the drawers were for articles and their appropriate photographs. Both were ill-suited to the purpose and frequently overflowed, so that no number could ever be made up without a last minute search for some final page. The wire trays housed the unlikely collection of material on which the Commentaries were based: cuttings, catalogues, honours lists and obituaries, mixed up with bills, pills, cross-word puzzles and back numbers of the *TLS*.[741]

Gradually Hayward's hold over the magazine strengthened; in 1956 he announced himself the editorial director and acquired an assistant, Miss Shawyer, who had helped him with the Rothschild Catalogue. Board meetings became more and more irregular. The magazine had become 'the exclusive product of John's brain'.[742] In 1964 underneath the title *The Book Collector* the familiar names of the four-man board were replaced by Hayward's name alone. He was now officially what he had been from the start – the editor of *The Book Collector*.

He ran the quarterly in a style that was, according to John Carter, 'imaginative, dedicated – and autocratic',[743] relentlessly pursuing tardy correspondents with postcards that began, 'I pray and beseech you ...'. Articles were subject to the most exact scrutiny and returned with handwritten corrections. Contributors such as Eva Rosebery recalled him as a hard taskmaster, as she found her work returned, and returned yet again, for still more checking. No one who had his script sent back with Hayward's comments ever forgot the experience. No friend was spared the cool, incisive criticism. Each Commentary took hours of his time; Catherine Porteous remembered him in the last year of his life, exhausted with bronchitis, with a high temperature, still working in his chair at the final changes to a number. 'He was a stern master, demanding of others his own most exacting standards and his own impeccable accuracy' 744 – the obituary that Hayward wrote for his fellow bibliographer and critic W. W. Greg might serve as his own. His achievement was to turn a little-known periodical into a leading international journal. Or, as John Carter called it, 'the best thing in its kind in the history of book collecting'.745

In her passionate nature and troubled love affairs Kathleen Raine resembled Hayward as a young man. Her poetry was romantic and mystical, her heroes Blake and Yeats. Now he had become, outwardly at least, her opposite: an Augustan in taste; an atheist and a believer in reason; his strong feelings hidden beneath a carapace of wit and scholarship. She felt he was not spiritually oriented; he tried to live a life of the mind as a substitute for love. While she stayed in Gavin Maxwell's house, Camusfearna, on the Kyle of Lochalsh, the setting of *Ring of Bright Water*, Kathleen was awed by the grandeur of her surroundings. By comparison with the seascapes of Skye, London seemed unreal. Hayward was one of the few friends whose 'reality does not fade altogether viewed from these islands'. Perhaps he was surprised to receive the gifts she sent of a shell, a common asphodel and later of a few stones from the beach of the loch, but they were love tokens of a sort. Her doomed relationship with Maxwell came to a bitter end and, when he finally married, it came as a shock to all those who knew his homosexual past. Kathleen Raine was distraught and turned to Hayward for consolation. 'You didn't think he'd marry you?' he asked her bluntly. Harsh words were said as they quarrelled and a period of silence between them followed before she wrote an apologetic letter and the rift was healed.

Hayward still hoped to go to America.746 John Malcolm Brinnin also urged him to come to New York and built up his reputation as a maliciously erudite wit. Hayward was amused to note, 'EVERYONE in New York is frightened of me.' The hotel owner and book collector Louis Silver promised that Chicago was at his disposal, 'call girls and all'. But there were enormous difficulties in transporting 'such an inconvenient cargo' as he called himself. And there was no money. He told Mary he could only find $500 to address the Young Men's Jewish Association in New York – not even enough, he said, for the caviare his doctor insisted on him taking each night before going to bed. So the plan had to wait.

When in 1961 Mary Hyde asked Hayward again about the proposed trip across the Atlantic he showed none of his earlier enthusiasm: 'He said there were only three libraries he wanted to see, and even those not very much, catalogues would suffice.'[747] Realising that this was just a pretext, Mary did not press the issue. Travel of any kind was difficult now, but a favourite outing was to the printers, where Hayward loved to chat to editors and compositors. At Cambridge University Press, Graham Greene left him in the Pitt Building to enjoy his conversations until tea time. Greene returned and pushed the chair to the corner of Bridge Street, opposite a tailor's shop. The Walstons' Rolls drew up and he then had the task of getting Hayward into the spare driver's seat in the front:

> To do this, Greene had to put his arms under John's armpits and clasp his hands in the small of John's back. With enormous effort, Greene brought him up, and for a dreadful moment they swayed about on the pavement in a grotesque embrace, with a temporal vein looking as if it was about to burst on Greene's face. Then with a waltzing movement John was swung round and plomped down into the seat.[748]

In March 1962 Hayward accepted an invitation to the French Embassy for a reception to mark the retirement of the Ambassador, Jean Chauvel. Robert Sencourt noted 'the distinctly acidulous' phrase with which Hayward noted the arrival of the Eliots as they 'staged one of their appearances'.[749] Despite this initial hostility the old flat-mates soon fell into deep conversation and, once again, Eliot invited Hayward to visit them in Kensington. 'No,' replied Hayward, 'I made a special exception in this case. It is months since I have been to anyone's house, but I wanted to come and say goodbye to the Ambassador, who has been so kind to me.' This was not enough for Eliot who pressed him about having enough energy to see the Ambassador but not enough to see him. 'No,' was Hayward's final answer, 'I have told you that I am simply going nowhere else.' Still Eliot persevered, 'But what about all the other years when you didn't come?' They were never to meet again.

When the edition of Eliot's *Collected Poems* was published in 1963 the acknowledgement to Hayward that had prefaced *Four Quartets* had vanished. It was the unkindest cut of all. Hayward, however, had the final word. During the war he had suggested that after his death Eliot's papers should go to Magdalene College, Cambridge, where he was an honorary fellow. Eliot, delighted by the thought, said it would be by far the nicest idea. But after their falling out, when he stopped sending Hayward material for the archives, Hayward decided to change his will and left the archive not to Magdalene, but to his own old college, King's, to be called 'The Hayward Bequest'.

Each winter Hayward suffered worse from colds and infections. 'The Big Freeze' of 1963–64 set in after Christmas; Chelsea had seven inches of snow with drifts of two feet and more that lasted for nearly three months. From his bay window he watched as pleasure steamers with handfuls of shivering passengers passed by. The trade union go-slow meant that Hayward's electric fire gave out the power of one candle and he had to huddle beneath a rug as he had done at Merton Hall twenty years earlier. He found it almost impossible to believe that summer would ever come again. The appalling weather, coupled with his own declining health, convinced him that he lived in a 'thoroughly awful bad world'. The Profumo affair and the public scandals that followed added to his gloom. 'I wish the future were less bleak,' he wrote. But there were still some consolations. His social life continued to grow and, if anything, still more visitors came. Large numbers of old friends and American bibliophiles made their pilgrimage to Carlyle Mansions. 'His tea calendar became as full as that of a state personage, and had to be managed as expertly,' wrote Mary Hyde.[750] Transatlantic colleagues were often surprised when he was more up to date with American scandal than they were. Many, on arrival in London, had grown used to looking up from their taxis as they drove along the Embankment to see the familiar light from the window and the bald head bent over his desk: 'Life would be a very displeasing business if it were not for the enchantment of friendship, bibliophily and the view from my window.'[751]

Hayward could no longer travel about in his chair and, like St Evré-mond and Swift before him, became home-bound. Part of the reason for this was an embarrassing one. According to the muscular dystrophy specialist Professor MacKeith, who came to examine him in Carlyle

Mansions, Hayward could no longer take hold of his penis to direct the stream of urine into an appropriate receptacle.[752] His double bed was moved into the big room. It became the centre and the walls the sphere of his life. Every morning Hayward's manservant Askwith lifted him into his favourite chair facing the window where he remained all day until he was carried back to his bed. Even his clothes weighed heavily upon him. Although he had to give up wearing suits he had his tailor make stylishly cut maroon dressing gowns to help him move his arms more easily. Despite this contraction of his physical life, his mind remained as sharp and his comments as biting as ever. When two American visitors stayed till the small hours he asked Simon Nowell-Smith to lift him from chair to bed. The visitors stood in the doorway talking in hushed tones. 'Speak up, can't you! This isn't a bloody church,' he shouted. But, according to his musician friend Griselda Kentner, he had now become a frightening figure – 'a Memento Mori to us all, sitting there with his accusing spectacles'.[753] The deaths of three close friends in the autumn of 1964 – Ian Fleming in August, Bill Jackson in September and Edith Sitwell in December – gave Hayward still more premonitions of mortality, as did news of Eliot's serious illness.

There was still work. Apart from editing *The Book Collector* Hayward was putting the final touches to his last anthology, *The Oxford Book of Nineteenth Century English Verse*. Published in 1964, its purpose was to replace *The Oxford Book of Victorian Verse*, edited by Quiller-Couch and 'the only misguided volume in that treasured series', according to Dadie Rylands. It was indeed an eccentric collection of poets whose names are now as obscure as they are exotic: poems by George Louis Palmella Busson du Maurier, Fitz-Greene Halleck, the Marquess of Crewe, Menella Bute Smedley, and the Hon. Roden Berkeley Wriothesley Noel fill Q's pages. Longer poems were neglected and major poets often represented by their minor work: Tennyson, for example, was reduced to his early lyrics and there is nothing at all from *In Memoriam*. For his anthology Hayward chose more than six hundred poems and extracts from eighty-five poets. In his Preface he outlined how the revolutionary doctrines of the eighteenth century led to Romanticism, which he saw as the major current of thought that ran throughout the nineteenth century. 'It was, one might say, an attitude to life that brought out the best and worst of Keats in every poet of the century,' he wrote.[754] Fidelity to the text was the message he had preached throughout his life. He restated his position, attacking the slackness of editors. The text was 'too seldom treated with respect for authority and accuracy in anthologies'. He went on to criticise the misleading printing of extracts as if they were whole poems. What Hayward found most shocking, however, was unauthorised and unacknowledged cutting. His last words on the responsibility of the editor were:

> In view of the deplorable practice of some anthologists of reprinting poems with lines and even whole stanzas surreptitiously and silently cut out in order to 'improve' them, it may be well to conclude with an assurance that the textual integrity of every poem or passage in this collection has been strictly observed.[755]

Hayward's calendar for 1964 tells its own story of suddenly declining health. In January he recorded a flurry of appointments with Doctor Lovett who visited on the 11th, 13th, 14th, 16th and 25th. There was clearly a serious problem. The entry for Monday 13 January was put in asterisks: 'Crucial date in my medical history.' There follows a complete contrast to the neat, precise entries. In red biro, slashed like a raw wound across the page, is the one word in bold capitals: TRACHEITIS'. This inflammation of the trachea, not normally a cause of grave concern, clearly seemed like a death sentence to the already weakened Hayward. In March a trained nurse, Sister Alice Boff, was hired to live in Carlyle Mansions. In August Graham Greene invited Hayward to the first night of his latest play, *Carving a Statue*, at the Haymarket. 'Alas, alas, the evil days have come nigh and although I can take pleasure in almost any kind of day I can no longer go out,'[756] Hayward replied. It was in fact more than a year since he had left the house. In his calendar the neat handwriting begins to give way to shaky uneven strokes of the pen. By the autumn it is becoming illegible. The last entry for the year is for Monday 28 December: it is written in a big, rounded feminine hand, probably Nurse Boff's. John Hayward could no longer manage his pen.

Eliot had collapsed at home in October and had been rushed to hospital. It was felt that he would not last the night, but he recovered and was able to return home in a wheelchair, 'shouting "Hurrah, Hurrah", as he was carried across the threshold'.[757] He was now too weak to take solid food, but by Christmas appeared to be making a slow recovery. Then his heart began to fail and again he fell into a coma, waking only once to repeat his wife's name. On 4 January 1965 at ten o' clock in the evening Eliot died. Hayward heard of it on the radio on the eleven o'clock news; the announcement was followed by a tribute from W. H. Auden. Kathleen Raine was also listening to the broadcast and immediately wrote:

> I have just heard that T. S. Eliot died an hour ago. I am sure you will already have been beset by all kinds of people, and this is just a note, with my love, to say that I am thinking chiefly of you and of all the complexities of pain you must now be feeling. You were, after all, his closest and truest friend, for longest part of him [*sic*].[758]

She ended, 'God Bless you, dear John, Kathleen.' Hayward was now surrounded by a chorus of lamenting women. 'You gave him so much, and however things turned out, you must be grateful for that,' Janet Adam Smith wrote. Helen Gardner feared he would be very desolate: 'I thought of you last night when I heard of T. S. E.'s death on the radio and thought you must be suffering from many painful and conflicting feelings.' Mary telephoned from the British Embassy in Moscow. 'He was – my – dear friend,' Hayward said haltingly in a voice now hard to decipher. In a letter she described his death as 'a great release for him – and almost for myself, and perhaps you and others of his friends ... I am also thankful as you will understand that I shall not be in England for the funeral – perhaps it's just as well that neither you nor I can be there.'[759]

Meanwhile Hayward had to face being besieged by 'newshounds' outside Carlyle Mansions clamouring for his reaction. Nancy Cunard, now living in the South of France, sent him a three-and-a-half-page poem that she had written on 7 January 'standing up after lunch' after hearing on the radio of Eliot's death. She dedicated it to Hayward: 'It is for you and you only, in the first place,' she wrote.[760] In the poem she described her first meeting with Eliot on a summer night in 1922. As she descended the grand staircase at a society ball in her gold panniered dress she saw him and was immediately seized by his looks; he was like a 'solitary eagle'. Instantaneously she recalled how a lover had given her, as a token, a copy of 'Prufrock'. It seemed like an omen; Eliot and she talked together for two hours and Nancy proposed an assignation for the following night. They met at the favourite Bohemian haunt, the Eiffel Tower Restaurant in Percy Street, Soho, which was just the place for a romantic 'tryst': 'If we ever go to heaven in a group / The Tower must be our ladder,' she had written in her ode to the restaurant. There they truanted from the dinner party given by the Hutchinsons that they had both agreed to attend, and drank gin as they 'cuddled together' by the little gas fire. Now she asked Hayward for his permission to send copies of the poem to two or three friends. Perhaps still safeguarding Eliot's privacy, perhaps embarrassed by the laxity of the verse, he advised against. It was his final act as the censor Eliot had asked him to be some thirty years before. Two months later Nancy Cunard was found wandering around the streets of Paris, having lost her mind and unable to remember her name. She was taken to a charity hospital where she died on 16 March.

Neither Hayward nor Mary Trevelyan went to Eliot's funeral, although Mary did attend the memorial service. The other notable absentee was Emily Hale, the woman who for so long had hoped to marry him. Soon after the funeral Robert Sencourt paid two visits to Hayward. He was preparing a biography which aimed to 'put the record straight' about some of the scandal that surrounded Eliot's life, and they had a long talk about the friendship. To his surprise he found himself 'deeply moved and touched' by Hayward's comments. When Helen Gardner visited Carlyle Mansions soon afterwards he began most uncharacteristically to talk of his own physical suffering and then changed the topic to Eliot. Through almost immobile lips he whispered, 'I can only think of him now as my old dear friend!'

As early as June 1946 Cecil Day Lewis, the Poet Laureate, had been asked to write Eliot's obituary for *The Times*. Now he immediately asked for Hayward's aid: 'I have told them I do not feel able to tackle it without the help of a close friend of his, and they agree I should ask you to collaborate in this melancholy task. Will you? – I'd be immensely grateful and pleased if you could, for I do want to do T. S. E. proud.'[761] Hayward was happy to accept and they decided to split the five guineas fee between them. The main difficulty, it seemed to both of them, was the treatment of the marriage breakdown with Vivienne. Hayward mentioned it briefly in one sentence – Vivienne's 'long, estranging illness was a deep personal sorrow' – and then deleted it. Day Lewis referred explicitly to 'the shuddering distaste, the sense of contagion, the dry despair' and then wrote tentatively: 'I hope you will find my reference to his private tragedy is passable.' He also abbreviated Hayward's draft and, 'patched some of my Utility writing into your beautiful garment, I will not say shroud'.[762]

So it was Hayward who was largely responsible for the *Times* obituary which appeared on 5 January 1965 under the headline, 'The most influential English poet of his time'. The surprising thing about the review is its failure to claim Eliot as the foremost poet of his age, merely the most influential one. Hayward developed a picture of a writer who, despite becoming a British citizen and an Anglican at heart, remained an American. He had shown more dedication to his art than anyone since Wordsworth. *The Waste Land* was 'the poetic gospel of the post-war intelligentsia'. After that he had followed 'a steady line of development towards the positive treatment of religious experience'. This culminated in his finest achievement: *Four Quartets*. More than anyone else, he had represented the idea of the poet and upheld the discipline of writing: he had 'reaffirmed within his own practice the value of poetry'. Hayward also stressed the importance of the revival of the poetic drama which he argued had been 'Eliot's chief preoccupation since the mid-1930s'. His masterly use of the stressed line allowed him to move easily from the cadences of everyday speech to more lyrical and profound expression. Hayward accepted that Eliot's later plays – *The Confidential Clerk* (1953) and *The Elder Statesman* (1957) – represented a disappointing loss in power. Although to some Eliot seemed shy, retiring, and so detached that 'he appeared to have been born middle-aged', he had a mischievous sense of humour and loved 'banter and jokes'. He could, however, become 'dogmatically, even intransigently, conservative', especially when defending his views on ecclesiastical matters, and there was a certain intolerance about his defence of tradition. Despite these allusions to their past differences and arguments, Hayward summed his old companion up with affection. The Eliot he had loved and admired emerges in his last words: 'He was above all a humble man; firm, even stubborn at times, but with no self-importance; quite unspoilt by fame; free from spiritual or intellectual pride.'

In Anthony Powell's view, based on his own experience of Hayward and Eliot, not enough attention has been given to the period between 1946 and 1957: the relationship with Hayward and, especially, their years of flat-sharing revealed the complexity and conflicts of Eliot in his daily life. No man is a hero to his flatmate. At different times Eliot was the joker; the insecure writer; the kind nurse; the sick patient; the difficult friend; 'The Pope of Russell Square'; the elusive Possum – and finally, the deserter ... Their friendship was not, as some saw it, simply one-sided, with the generous-minded Eliot looking after the disabled Hayward. In many ways it was the other way round: the gregarious and social nature of Hayward helping to heal the wounded spirit of his friend. Hayward made sure that social life continued whatever inner anguish remained. Eliot learned to rely on him for emotional support and as the watchdog guarding his need for privacy and silence: his fame helped Hayward to be near the centre of the literary stage in London for thirty years. They complemented each other perfectly. Their relationship was one of literary endeavour and deep affection, mixed with scurrilous jokes and schoolboy laughter, until it was broken by the even stronger force of devoted and unquestioning love.

Kathleen Raine took a different view. She loved and admired Hayward, 'that witty brilliant malicious tragic man who so heroically invented himself',[763] but she was in awe of Eliot, seeing him as wounded, solitary, crippled by personal unhappiness. The relationship of the two men seemed to her more of a 'literary friendship' than an intimate one, a convenience that helped them both to deal with the difficulties of living. She noted their separate lives and that one never called on them together. Eliot, she felt, had always kept his distance and had never been a true friend.[764] She was one of the first to see a growing imbalance in their relationship: as Hayward gradually came to depend more on Eliot, so Eliot came to depend less on him. Eliot's death in 1965 was a loss, but not a separation – that had happened many years earlier.

Regular visitors to Carlyle Mansions began to notice that there was always one thing more that Hayward could not do. As he began to lose muscular control, writing became much more difficult. He had first to twist his fingers into position, then 'gripping a pen in his maimed hand, lifted the limp hand by the forearm until it could be flapped back upon the writing surface, using the forearm instead of the wrist to manoeuvre his pen'. The beauty of the result was a triumph of will over matter. The same growing difficulty in control affected his speech: 'He spoke with a perfection which was slightly thrilling to hear when you realised that he could not move his lips,'[765] William Empson commented. As he found it hard to swallow he did not eat in public and had to be fed by Askwith or by Nurse Boff. He could no longer light his own cigarettes. Saliva began to leak from his mouth: at first he supported his lower lip with his right hand; next he had to prop up that hand as well. Now he could not lift the telephone that had been his lifeline to the world; it had to be mounted on a stand on his desk.

In August 1965 Graham Greene, who had for years sent him scandalous postcards from all the far-flung places he visited, sent Hayward a surprise parcel that for a moment baffled him. At first he thought the enormous quarto volume might be one of Greene's 'super-Entertainments', but as he unwrapped it and turned the pages of *Cowboy Kate*, a collection of Sam Haskins's erotic photos, its nature became obvious. Hayward enjoyed the book, 'hoping, as one always does, that the next opening will reveal something beyond the dreams of carnality'.[766] Although he had some reservations about the photography, 'which makes a girl's thighs look as if they were covered with artificial lizard skin', he still remained excited enough by the pictures of the 'dazzlingly nymph-like and beautiful' women to recall a younger, less damaged self. He thanked Greene for the enormous surprise: 'The foot may be less quick to meet the morning dew as I enter my 60s, but I can still commit adultery in my heart with people like Kate and her kind.'

Hayward began to worry about his stamina for entertaining: 'But how can I see all your compatriots?' he asked Mary in a voice that was weak, but so much the same it seemed impossible he was really sick. 'So many of you coming! What *can* I do?'[767] He talked of it as the 'spring invasion, the summer invasion, and the autumn invasion'. Two old American friends wanted to visit in late September 1965 on their way to an Antiquarian Book Fair in Amsterdam. He never turned any bibliophile away and replied on 1 September:

> I am determined to see you if I possibly can; it's much too flattering for you and Mam to want to pay me a visit, and somehow – God knows how – manage to fit me in with all your other commitments. Could you manage to postpone it until l'heure enchantée du cocktail – that is about 6.15? I can offer you some first-rate firewater! (I take it that you still have that medicine bottle in your pocket?)[768]

Hayward's friend and fellow bookman Nicolas Barker went to see him and took with him his small daughter Emma. Hayward, always the generous host, plied her with chocolate until, covered in it, 'she began to explore the treasured shelf of Eliot's manuscripts: "Careful," said John, "she'll destroy my one claim to immortality."'[769]

Like St Evrémond, Jonathan Swift and great-uncle Abraham,

Hayward thought he had outlived the talents and friendships of his era: Elaine had married and Joséfa was miles away across the Atlantic. Lytton Strachey, Frankie Birrell, Ottoline Morrell, W. B. Yeats, Virginia Woolf, Edith Sitwell, Ian Fleming and now Eliot, were all dead. He told his sister Diana that he now had no friends left and said to Elaine that he knew how long he had got to live. He telephoned his brother George, now living in remotest Pembrokeshire (under the surname Rolleston). It was more than thirty years since they had met. Hayward's niece took the call and was surprised to hear a slurred voice: 'This is your uncle speaking. I feel I am going to die in a few days. I am sorry that things have been so difficult. Goodbye.' It was the first and only time they spoke.

A month after Eliot's death Kathleen Raine, as usual, asked Hayward to look over her latest volume of poetry if it was not too great a burden. 'It would not have seemed right to send in a book of verses which had not passed under your eye, for better or for worse. May I, in my fore-word, thank you for advising me on what to include and omit?'[770] However she did not want to embarrass him by forcing him to defend the work of 'the poet who was and must always remain *your* poet'. She wanted to see him so that they could share bleak views about contemporary writing: 'The literary scene is so depressing I need your reassurance that black is black and not, as they all seem to think, white ... so may I soon come and be reassured by salutary pessimism that all's wrong with the world?'[771] As she was leaving, some lines from Yeats's 'The Gyres' came to her mind and she began to recite 'Conduct and work grow coarse, and coarse the soul ...' 'Go on,' said he, giving her his characteristic listening look, and they recited together Yeats's 'great declamation upon the dark age to which we had come'.[772]

> What matter though numb nightmare ride on top,
> And blood and mire the sensitive body stain?
> What matter? Heave no sigh, let no tear drop,
> A greater, a more gracious time has gone ...

Soon afterwards, after failing to gain entrance to Carlyle Mansions, she left a note: 'Please do get well, we – I – can't do without you at all, by any means.' As a gift she left him a pot of honey – 'that magic food full of the warm south' as she called it – and telephoned to see if there was anything else she could bring or send him. 'A wreath, I think, my dear,' came the reply.[773] On 1 September he wrote his will. He left his collections of St Evrémond, Rochester and his Eliot papers to his old college, along with £200 for installing two glass-fronted mahogany bookcases in which to house them and for the engraving of a 'small book label in Latin' to be inserted in each of the volumes. He wanted the collection to be kept intact and whole in King's College Library, just like Pepys's library in Magdalene.[774] It was to be known as 'The Hayward Bequest' – the nearest a childless atheist book collector could get to immortality.

A fortnight later John Carter visited Hayward and found him 'in very low spirits', suffering from pleurisy. Still Hayward continued to wrestle with *The Book Collector* and rang Nicolas Barker about a knotty problem with the text. Barker's heart sank. He was just on the brink of going away on holiday and Hayward's calls were generally lengthy. Nevertheless, he agreed to go round to 'the familiar, stuffy, book-lined room' that afternoon. There he resolved the difficulty easily and quickly.

> All seemed well, and I made ready to depart. 'And you will see it's all right won't you,' said John. 'Of course I will,' I replied, 'but you'll be here and I'll be in Cambridge – you'll be able to see it yourself.' 'Yes, but I want to be sure that *you* will see it too – all of it.' I was puzzled by his insistence, but gave him the assurance he wanted, said goodbye and left.'[775]

After Barker had gone, Askwith, as usual, carefully lifted Hayward from his chair, helped him to bed and wished him a cheery goodnight.

The next morning, Friday 17 September 1965, Diana decided to visit her brother early, just as some flowers from Mary Hyde arrived. She let herself in and, finding the drawing room empty, looked into the bedroom.

> The lovely flowers arrived a few hours too late for him to see. He had a sudden relapse in the small hours and died peacefully at about 7 am; he looked so wonderfully happy with all signs of suffering gone. His features seemed lit up by an extraordinary nobility and thoughtfulness, his lips had been closed and there was a slight smile at the corners as if he were enjoying something. A few hours later his expression had changed to one of profound sleep and tiredness. I felt his spirit had then gone far far away … we put the flowers near to him.[776]

He was sixty years old. The death certificate listed three causes: a coronary thrombosis, hypertension and muscular dystrophy.

The obituary in *The Times* spoke of his peaceful end 'after a lifetime's disability borne with the utmost fortitude'.777 Graham Greene, like many friends, greeted the news with relief: 'His death seemed to have been really peaceful and in the nick of time. He had lost the use even of his hands ... He was a wonderful friend and a very courageous man,' wrote Greene to Catherine Walston.778 Kathleen Raine thought that the loss of John Hayward marked the end of an era:

> He liked to describe himself as 'a man of letters', regretting that that the phrase could no longer be used (as the French say *homme de lettres*) without its seeming affected; but it is (so with his death we sadly realise) not the word but the thing itself which has almost ceased ... to exist.779

But there was nothing anyone could have done to help her friend endure his tragic life: 'If we are "pilgrims of eternity" one wishes him a better life next time.'780

On 1 October John Hayward's funeral was held at St Luke's, Chelsea, a neo-Gothic church which bore a remarkable resemblance to King's College Chapel. It was a cold grey morning; a light drizzle fell. Mourners arrived, hands deep in their raincoat pockets; John Carter had his hat pulled firmly over his eyes. The church was full. In a list that recalled all the other lists that Hayward made throughout his life *The Times* printed the names of 116 mourners. Old friends and associates – Sir Francis Meynell, Cyril Connolly, Raymond Mortimer, Percy Muir, Roland Penrose, Lee Miller, Dennis Cohen, John Lehmann and many American bibliophiles – were joined by representatives of Faber's, King's College, Cambridge, the National Book League and the British Museum. Kathleen Raine was there, as was Mary Trevelyan. So too was Elaine Finlay. The final name in the list of mourners printed in *The Times* was Mr W. Askwith.

As one of Hayward's closest friends and neighbours in Chelsea, John Carter had helped the family with the choice of hymns and readings. He read 'Death be not proud' from Donne's *Holy Sonnets*, using Hayward's own recension of the text, and Henry Oakeley, John's nephew, read the lesson from St Matthew. From the hymn 'Praise my soul, the King of Heaven' the congregation sang: 'Father-like, He tends and spares us / Well our feeble frame He knows ...' Carter had suggested Psalm CXLII because he felt that its ending was 'very right for John':

> When my spirit was in heaviness thou knewest my path:
> in the way wherein I walked have they privily laid a snare for
>   me...
> Consider my complaint: for I am brought very low.
> O deliver me from my persecutors: for they are too strong for me.
> Bring my soul out of prison, that I may give thanks unto thy
>   Name.

The final hymn chosen was John Bunyan's 'To Be a Pilgrim'.

> Who would true valour see,
> Let him come hither;
> One here will constant be,
> Come wind, come weather.

After the funeral Carter wrote to Diana, recalling her brother's love of parties and gatherings, 'John would be pleased by the turnout on Friday, don't you think?' He put together a celebratory issue of *The Book Collector* which was also published separately as *Some Memories* and invited some twenty of Hayward's friends to contribute. He said that not a single one refused: 'John's masterful command reached beyond the grave.'[781] The 1965 issue was the most fitting of tributes to a man whose creation the magazine had been and who had given up the last years of his life to its success. The Commentary was entitled 'What Next?'[782] It began: 'The loss we have sustained through the death of John Hayward cannot easily be estimated ... his gifts were unique, and to try to continue a formula which was so much the expression of his own personality would invite ridicule and failure.' Hayward's distinctive voice was silenced and could not easily be replaced.

When Hayward's executors started going through his belongings they found a peculiar object in his desk. It was a wooden box containing press clippings: tied around the box was a cord. Carefully attached to it was a card on which there were some lines of poetry written in his most precise hand. Inside the box, neatly cut out from the *Sunday Express* of 1961, was a press clipping from 'Beachcomber'. The gossip columnist quoted 'a friend of Eliot's' who said that after his second marriage Eliot 'never sees any of us now and we have completely lost touch with him. It is a great pity.' Another item in the box was an angry rebuttal of the charge from Eliot in the next week's edition. 'A person quoted as one of my old friends is quoted. I continue to see my friends and the so-called friend deceives himself for no genuine friend would make such an assertion.' The uncharacteristically ugly repetitiveness shows how angry Eliot was. In another extract in the box the *Sunday Express* gave its apologies for Eliot's hurt feelings, but said it stood by its informant as he was someone 'who had considered himself to have been a close friend for over twenty years'. The final clipping was simply a banner headline that Hayward had found somewhere: 'MR HAYWARD GETS CALL TO RETIRE'. On the card tied to the cord around the box he had written two quotations about tears. The first was from a letter of Juliet Drouet to Victor Hugo: 'Dans la rue et dans mon coeur il pleut sans discontinuer.' The second was from Verlaine: 'Il pleut dans la ville comme il pleut dans mon coeur.' The discarded bitter friend was Hayward, but all that remained were his tears. These fragments he shored against his ruins.

A list of 'Papers at Carlyle Mansions' was prepared after Hayward's death. On Valerie's behalf, but without her knowledge, Rupert Hart-Davis wrote to the librarian of King's, A. N. L. Munby, expressing his concern about Eliot's personal papers in the Hayward Archive. He wanted all access to them controlled if they were not burnt. Dr Munby agreed, suggesting that Mrs Eliot should decide 'whether some of the material should not be destroyed, in view of J. H.'s painful break with Eliot'. In addition, he noted, 'There is also an album of press cuttings which should perhaps be destroyed in any case without reference to her.' [783] Perhaps the *Sunday Express* cuttings were among these, and as there is no further record of them, they were probably burnt by Dr Munby. He wrote to Hayward's sister, 'I have also destroyed a lot of very private letters from people of no interest to posterity. John as you know was the recipient of many confidences ...' [784]

Even in death Hayward and Eliot were linked. Eliot had chosen to be cremated and his ashes were interred alongside his English fore-fathers in the little church of St Michael's at East Coker. 'In my end is my beginning' was inscribed on his memorial tablet. Thirty years earlier Hayward had been pleased to tell Eliot how close their West Country origins were. As a young undergraduate he had written an elegiac account in the *Cambridge Mercury* of the Wiltshire village where his father was born and recalled many childhood visits there with him.[785] Many Haywards lay in Beechingstoke churchyard; their family names entered in the solidly-bound parish registers whose pages he had turned:

> One would not regret being buried there among such quiet surroundings; on a summer's afternoon the sun shining through the tall oaks and elms casts a delicate pattern shadow-lace over the grass and gravel pathways; and after the sun has set and for many hours the valley is still warm and full of the scent of dried grass and wild flowers.

By contrast, he wrote, his last sight of the village as he passed nearby after a family holiday in Dorset had been of a poor parishioner's burial service. Through the rain-spattered windows of the railway carriage he saw the vicar struggling to keep his surplice under control in a roaring gale, the few mourners clutching onto their hats and a solitary rook above the elm trees, beating vainly against the wind. It was a desolate scene: 'Seeing how loth one is to leave this life in foul weather when one thinks of wood fires and the companionship of winter evenings – I prayed earnestly that I might be spared for one of those peerless days of early June or late September, such a day of marvellous sunshine as that on which I saw the village of Beechingstoke and its church for the first time many years ago.'

On 24 October 1965 early morning mists gave way to autumn sunlight as John Hayward's ashes were buried beneath the oaks and elms of the churchyard. As he had requested in his will the interment was private and 'conducted with the strictest regard for simplicity and economy of expense without flowers or mourning'. He shared the family vault with his mother, his father and his sister Rose Mary. His gravestone bore the simple inscription: 'A Man of Letters'.

Appendix
The Writing of 'Little Gidding'

In her magisterial *The Composition of 'Four Quartets'*, Helen Gardner deals in detail with the evolution of the text and this appendix is based on her scholarship.[786] Its purpose, however, is slightly different: to put the development of the text in the context of Hayward's friendship with Eliot and to analyse the kinds of ways in which Hayward helped shape the poem. It is based on the numerous letters and drafts that were exchanged between Hayward and Eliot in 1941 and 1942.

Hayward's suggestions and corrections can be seen in the light annotations he made to the manuscript he received on 7 July 1941. He made no comment on the opening ('Midwinter spring is its own season ...') apart from writing to Morley that the description was 'one of the prodigiously fine things in the poem'. He put a cross against the word 'glitters' in the lines, 'Now the hedgerow / Glitters for an hour with transitory blossom ...' suggesting 'Glisters' and 'Whitens'. Eliot took up the suggestion of whiteness and the lines became, brilliantly: 'Now the hedgerow / Is blanched for an hour with transitory blossom / Of snow ...' Hayward became the first of many subsequent critics to be puzzled by what was meant by 'the unimaginable Zero summer', placing a cross in the margin and writing to ask whether it was the absolute zero of physics he had in mind? At any rate he felt the adjective was 'slightly Clevelandish', by which he meant too academic and too obscure.[787] This time Eliot ignored the comment.

Hayward consistently disliked Eliot's use of internal rhymes and the line 'In the may time, the play time of the wakened senses' predictably incurred his disapproval. He compared it with *Baby* and *Maybe*, 'a favourite stand-by in Tin Pan Alley. I should feel happier if this jingle were omitted.' It was: Eliot conceded it was 'too close to the Playbox Annual'. Worse was to follow. Hayward put two crosses against the lines: 'At any time, the day time or the dark time / Or at any season, the dead time or the may time ...' Responding to the tactfully phrased criticism, 'There is just a faint suggestion here, I think, of your parodying yourself', Eliot cancelled the lines. Hayward found a grammatical and logical objection to the phrase, 'this is the nearest ...' 'Nearest to what or to whom?' he asked. Eliot ignored this comment.

Hayward was unhappy too about the second line of the second part: 'Ash on an old man's sleeve / Is all the ash the burnt roses leave.'

> Compared with the other lines in the stanza this one seems to me to have too much weight at the end. The heavy stress on 'burnt' could be lightened by omitting the definite article and this would also lay a shade more stress on 'roses'. As it is, this line takes something from the essential 'airiness' of the stanza – dust, breath, air: the death of air – as if the ash of burnt roses was not an imponderable but a tombstone.[788]

In this case Eliot replied that he too was unhappy with the lines – but left them as they were.

Often suggestion led to counter-suggestion in a process resembling a frank conversation that seemed light-hearted but was ultimately serious. In the second section of the poem Hayward marked the lines:

> The scorched and unemployable soil
> Gapes at the vanity of toil,
> Laughs without mirth.

In the margin he suggested some alternatives and wrote to Eliot outlining his reasons:

> 'unemployable soil': this sounds ugly when read aloud to my ear. (possibilities: acarpous, unavailing, unserviceable) ... 'Laughs without mirth': I should prefer 'smiles'. It is easier, I think, to conceive of a smile without mirth than a laugh without mirth, for all that people speak of a hollow laugh &c. And it's easier and more convincing, I feel, to imagine the soil as smiling than as laughing. An inanimate object can appear to be smiling; it can hardly be thought of as laughing. In any case you can't gape *and* laugh at the same time – I've just tried to in the mirror – and you can gape and smile without mirth at the same time. Perhaps I am being too silly![789]

Eliot stayed with 'laughs', despite Hayward's second suggestion of 'grins'; adopted 'parched', which Hayward had written in the margin, and found the word 'eviscerate'. Thus the final version of these lines became:

> The parched eviscerate soil
> Gapes at the vanity of toil,
> Laughs without mirth.

The second part of Section II went through more revisions than any other part of the poem. The first draft read:

> At the uncertain hour before daybreak
> Toward the ending of interminable night
> At the incredible end of the unending
> After the dark dove with the flickering tongue
> Had made his incomprehensible descension
> While the dead leaves still rattled on like tin …

Hayward, again alert to the sing-song repetition, noted '*end*ing … *int*erminable, *inc*redible … *end* of the un*end*ing' and added that lines 2–3 'seem to me to flag a little … as if the needle of the mind had got stuck into a groove and was faltering. I don't like the mouthful (and earful) "incomprehensible descension".' After more correspondence Eliot reluctantly removed 'descension' and tidied up the opening three lines. He wrote thanking Hayward for his letter of 20 August: 'I hope I have got rid of the unpleasant terminations without any sacrifice of sense.' So the final version read:

> In the uncertain hour before the morning
> Near the ending of interminable night
> At the recurrent end of the unending
> After the dark dove with the flickering tongue
> Had passed below the horizon of his homing
> While the dead leaves still rattled on like tin …

Three lines that caused the most serious problems were, in the draft sent to Hayward,

> And as I scrutinised the downturned face
> With that pointed narrowness of observation
> We turn upon the first-met stranger at dawn …

He marked the lines and put a cross against 'at dawn', objecting to the sound of two stressed monosyllables ending the line. Eliot was unhappy with the verb 'turn' and changed it to 'bear' but Hayward disliked this alteration, as he did the repetition of 'dawn'. Eliot reworked the lines and arrived at:

> And as I bent upon the down-turned face
> That pointed scrutiny with which we challenge
> The first-met stranger in the first faint light …

There was clearly no possibility that Hayward would pass the repetition of 'first', pencilling in the margin 'daybreak'. He also questioned whether one could 'bend' a scrutiny. Eliot replied in a long letter:

> I am glad you objected to 'First Faint' because it calls my attention to that fact that 'light' will not do either, as it comes too close (being terminal) to 'night' a few lines before. It is surprisingly difficult to find words for the shades before morning; we seem to be richer in words and phrases for the end of the day. And I don't want a phrase which might mean *either*. I am inclined to put
>
> > The first-met stranger after lantern-end
>
> unless it seems to you too quaint …[790]

By September, clearly, the moment to stop the revision had arrived: 'This time I accept nearly everything: perhaps it means that my resistance is weakening …' Eliot's solutions to the problem which he had been 'fiddling with' were the rather unlikely alternatives of 'in the antelucan dusk' – a 'lovely word' he had found the previous year in the *Oxford English Dictionary* and wanted to use as soon as possible – or the more homely 'lantern end', 'lantern down' and 'lantern out'. After so many cancellations and emendations, however, he turned back to Hayward's suggestion: 'You will observe that I have accepted "waning dusk" … I cannot find words to express a proper manifestation of my gratitude for your invaluable assistance.'[791] So the lines finally, and much more simply, came to read

> And as I fixed upon the down-turned face
> That pointed scrutiny with which we challenge
> The first-met stranger in the waning dusk …

Hayward's suggestions, even when not adopted, made Eliot think carefully about the precise sense he wanted. A good example of this was Hayward's comment on the word 'pretended' in the lines 'yet the words sufficed / to compel the recognition they pretended …', arguing the word did not mean what Eliot wanted it to mean. He suggested 'portended': Eliot substituted 'preceded' and wrote to the still discontented Hayward on 8 September:

> I am inclined to stick to 'preceded', because the words you suggest convey a different meaning from what I want. I mean, to be aware that it is someone you know (and to be surprised by his being there) before you have identified him. *Recognition* surely is the full identification of the person.

Hayward disliked the conjunction of 'strode' and 'patrol' in the draft line, 'We strode together in a dead patrol' (possibly because of the assonance). Eliot agreed and substituted Hayward's word 'trod', and added the word 'pavement', as 'patrol' seemed to make the word 'together' redundant. Here again the alteration of a single word led to the recasting of a line or more. The same process occurred with the line that initially read, 'But as the passage now is brief and facile …' Hayward marked 'brief' and suggested 'swift'. Eliot rejected this – 'it suggests great rapidity of movement, as if in a car' – and suggested 'quick' and 'soft'. He then altered it to, 'But as the passage presents no barrier …' When Hayward suggested 'hindrance' for 'barrier', Eliot hesitated. At the last possible moment after the poem's first publication in the *New English Weekly* on 15 October 1942 he plumped for Hayward's choice because of his friend's consistency. The line's evolution was complete: 'But, as the passage now presents no hindrance …'

An indication of the closeness of their minds occurred when Hayward objected to the line, 'The final prizes of your lifetime's effort'. He marked the assonance and wrote in the margin 'finis coronat opus' – the same phrase as he had used of 'Little Gidding' to Frank Morley. Eliot inserted Hayward's comment into the poem by adapting the Latin tag to give him a line of gracious finality: 'To set a crown upon your lifetime's effort.' Opposite the lines, '… the rending pain / Of laughter at what ceases to amuse …' Hayward added the phrase 'ulterius cor / lacerare nequit', from the inscription on Swift's tomb. Eliot dismissed 'rending pain' for metrical reasons and Hayward made the 'brilliant' suggestion of 'laceration'. Eliot wrote enthusiastically 'Laceration: yes, I like this.' Hayward's admiration for Swift, as Helen Gardner noticed, added his identity to that of the 'compound ghost'.

Another illustration of how ideas and phrases flowed creatively from one to the other comes in the final lines of the second section which continued to pose problems:

> From ill to worse the exasperated spirit
> Proceeds, unless restored by that refining fire
> Where you must learn to swim, and better nature.
> This you shall learn. Down the dismantled street
> He passed me, with a kind of salutation,
> And vanished on the blowing of the horn.

Unhappy with this, Hayward questioned both 'swim' and 'better nature'. Instead of 'dismantled' he suggested 'demolished'. He preferred 'passed along' and 'vanished with', and added above the line, 'as the sun was near its rising'. He also objected to the word 'salutation'. Eliot, in response, kept the verb 'swim', wanting to stress the spirit's willingness to endure the purgatorial fire ('sound theology and is certainly sound Dante'). Hayward deleted 'better nature', changed 'past me' for 'left me', and substituted 'faded' for 'vanished'. When he argued against 'salutation' on the grounds that there were too many 'on' sounds Eliot insisted that he wanted to preserve the allusion to Hamlet's ghost. Hayward continued to put a cross against 'salutation'. Alongside the final line he wrote: 'vanished (also Hamlet) & fading already / 'Neither budding / nor fading I.' So Eliot replaced 'salutation' with the stronger 'valediction'. He also picked up the word 'fading'. Thus the final lines were arrived at:

> From wrong to wrong the exasperated spirit
> Proceeds, unless restored by that refining fire
> Where you must move in measure, like a dancer.
> The day was breaking. In the disfigured street
> He left me, with a kind of valediction,
> And faded on the blowing of the horn.

Eliot was 'still unsatisfied', but felt that enough was enough: 'To spend much more time over this poem might be dangerous. After a time one loses the original feeling of the impulse, and then it is no longer safe to alter. It is time to close the chapter.'

There was much less difficulty and much less correspondence about Part III but Hayward strongly disliked the opening and was outspoken in his criticism. He wrote against the draft '1 para. Too didactic? / needs fusing', and amplified his point in a frank letter:

The first fifteen lines of Part III – the didactic passage – strike me as being imperfectly resolved into poetry, in fact rather laboured and prosy. I think I appreciate the difficulty of this kind of expository writing. It may be that it is too easy to cast such philosophical and ethical statements into the kind of long, fluid lines you use so ingeniously. But this particular passage does seem to me to drag; to need fusing: possibly to be presented to the reader in a less didactic and uncompromising form.[792]

In fact, Eliot did very little to alter the passage. Tactfully Hayward did not press the point when the next draft arrived virtually unaltered.

Hayward queried the archaism 'behovely' in the lines

> Sin is behovely, but
> All shall be well and
> All manner of thing shall be well.

Eliot explained that these lines were from the medieval mystic, Juliana of Norwich. Hayward asked about inserting quotation marks around the passage. (No, came the answer.) When Hayward suggested capitalisation Eliot initially turned down the idea. 'Too much like headlines: slightly comic', but eventually accepted it in a modified form, capitalising 'Behovely'.

Hayward especially admired the more conventional aspects of *Four Quartets* – the lyrical passages and the personal feelings that he saw reflected in the poem. It was the visionary side of the poem that he found hard to place; hence the problem with Part IV. Different in kind from Part III, it was very brief, three stanzas only when Hayward had seen it first in July 1941. Before Hayward had time to reply Eliot wrote to say he had already cancelled one stanza. Of the two stanzas that remained Hayward wrote in the draft: 'obscure & too little of it non sequiturish?' He made clear he found these stanzas baffling:

> As for Part IV, I can't fit it into the scheme of the poem as a whole … it consists of only two short stanzas and their point has escaped me. This is more than likely due to my own obtuseness. But the point I should like to make is that these two stanzas seem to me scarcely to justify a section to themselves. My own view, for the little that it is worth, is that this section should be extended rather than rewritten … In its present form it has an obfuscating effect –

rather as if you had thrown out a smoke-screen to prepare for the next stage. This, at any rate, is how it affected me.[793]

In his reply Eliot stressed the centrality of this section to the whole poem: 'Some explicit attack on the Descent of the Holy Ghost (which is an undertone throughout) is necessary at this point.' He nevertheless cut one stanza and added another: 'Who then designed the torture? Love …' Hayward maintained an apparently disapproving silence that worried Eliot: 'From your silence on the point am I to infer that you are satisfied with Part IV?' he asked.[794] This time Hayward did not offer the usual reassurance.

By comparison with what had gone before, Part V of 'Little Gidding' was plain sailing. Hayward initially passed the first draft with the terse comment 'All right'. He did suggest 'an inspired improvement'[795] when he substituted 'but unpedantic' for the phrase 'without pedantry'. Thus, 'The formal word precise without pedantry' became 'The formal word precise but not pedantic' – later he was to claim to Kathleen Raine the whole line was his.

References

Abbreviations:

BL   British Library
CFQ   *The Composition of 'Four Quartets'*, Helen Gardner, Faber
        and Faber, 1978
CUL   Cambridge University Library
GA   University of Georgetown, The Graham Greene Papers,
        Special Collections Division, Georgetown University
        Library
GoA   Gowerbank Archive Family Papers, London
Gr A   Gresham's School, Holt, Archive
HB   Hayward Bequest, Modern Archives Centre, King's College
        Cambridge
HL   Houghton Library at Harvard University
HRC   Harry Ransom Centre, University of Texas
JDH   John Hayward
J. Haff John Haffenden
KA   Modern Archives Centre, King's College Cambridge
NYS   *New York Sun.* Copies of Hayward's articles are available as
        part of the HB
PRS   'The Pope of Russell Square, 1938–1958': unpublished TS
        memoir of Mary Trevelyan in the Bodleian Library,
        Oxford
SM   *John Hayward 1904–1965: Some Memories, 1966*, first pub-
        lished in *The Book Collector*, Winter 1965
St Tw   St Twinell's Archive Family Papers, Pembrokeshire
TLS   *The Times Literary Supplement*
TSNS   Tarantula's Special News-Service

References

1 A. S. G. Edwards, 'John Davy Hayward: A List of his Published Writings 1924–1964', in *Analytical & Enumerative Bibliography*, n.s. 8, 1994, pp. 1–53, and 'John Davy Hayward (1905–1965), Scholar, Bibliophile and Man of Letters', *The Book Collector*, vol. 51, no. 3, Autumn 2002.

2 'Recollections of Rushall', *Wiltshire Gazette*, 26 May 1928.

3 This account is based on Antony Chessell's *The Life and Times of Abraham Hayward, Q.C., Victorian Essayist*, Lulu, 2009. *Encyclopaedia Britannica* 1911, (vol. v. 13, p.116), *DNB* 1891, vol. xxv, pp. 308–11 and Phillip Harling's account, *DNB*, Oxford, 2004.

4 J. S. Mill, *Autobiography*, Longman, Green, Reader and Dyer, 1873, p. 89.

5 The Reverend W. Tuckwell, *A. W. Kinglake, A Biographical and Critical Study*, George Bell and Sons, 1902, p. 132.

6 Antony Chessell, p. 57.

7 Henry E. Carlisle, *A Selection from the Correspondence of Abraham Hayward Q.C.*, John Murray ,1886, vol. ii., pp. 310–11.

8 Ibid., vol. I, p. 173.

9 *Encyclopaedia Britannica*, p. 116.

10 *The Times*, 10 May 1873.

11 Ibid., 7 February 1884.

12 I am indebted to Mr and Mrs John Rolleston for these details of 'Aunt Rosie' and her Rolleston/ Davy descent.

13 Ibid.

14 Douglas and Beatrice Norman-Smith, *The Grange Wimbledon: A Centenary Portrait*, K. A. F. Brewin, 1984, p. 31.

15 'Letter from London', *Bonniers Litterara Magasin*, n.d., (1940). The bracketed dates are those inferred from the Letters.

16 The description of The Grange is based on JDH's letters to TSE, especially 'Christmastide 1940', KA.

17 JDH to TSE, 'Christmastide 1940', KA.

18 'Letter from London', 1944.

19 *Cambridge Mercury*, no. 15, 1 November 1924.

20 Tom Faber to J. Haff, HRC.

21 *An Epistle in Verse*, GA.

22 This account of the First World War is based on Mrs Hayward's 'History' that she wrote for her children and Dr Hayward's letters home from France. Both are in St Tw.

23 Julian Huxley (ed.), *Aldous Huxley 1894–1963: A Memorial Volume*, Chatto and Windus, 1965, p. 14.

24 John Gielgud, *Early Stages*, Macmillan, 1939, p. 35.

25 This account owes a great deal to Sheridan Morley, *John Gielgud: The Authorised Biography*, Simon and Schuster, 2002 and to *Early Stages*.

26 John Gielgud to Peter Quennell, 5 October 1982, HRC.
27 JDH to TSE, 3 March 1942, KA.
28 Dr Henry Oakeley's diagnosis quoted in *The Composition of* Four Quartets, Helen Gardner, *Faber and Faber*, 1978, p. 5.
29 JDH to TSE, 3 June 1940, KA.
30 Mrs Hayward's 'History', St Tw.
31 GoA.
32 GoA.
33 JDH to TSE, 29 December 1942, KA.
34 Ibid.
35 Jonathan Croall, *Gielgud: A Theatrical Life*, Methuen, 2000, p.16.
36 The account of Dr Hayward's war years is largely based on the letters he sent to his wife and family. St Tw.
37 These references to Dr Hayward's wartime experience are from http:/www.firstworldwar.com/diaries/casualtyclearingstation.htm, also published in *Everyman at War*, ed. C. D. Purdom, Dutton, 1930.
38 JDH, 'Letter to Mummy', GA.
39 St Tw.
40 JDH to TSE, 'Christmastide 1940', KA.
41 *The Criterion: Collected Edition,* Faber and Faber, 1967, vol. xii, October 1932, p. 131.
42 Robert Medley, *Drawn from the Life: A Memoir,* Faber and Faber, 1983, p. 31.
43 Ibid., p. 32.
44 Edward Mendelson (ed.), *The English Auden,* 'Address for a Prize-day' from *The Orators,* Faber, 1977, p. 61.
45 JDH to TSE, 3 March 1942.
46 *NYS,* 24 April 1937, KA.
47 JDH to TSE, 4 September 1945, KA.
48 'Hayward Bequest', KA.
49 JDH to TSE, 4 September 1945, KA.
50 JDH to Anne Ridler, 10 September 1940, BL.
51 'Notes on Gresham's School', Geoffrey Harber Diggle, p. 10, Gr A.
52 Stephen Spender (ed.), *W. H. Auden: A Tribute,* Weidenfeld and Nicolson, 1974, p. 39.
53 *The Gresham,* 13 December 1919, Gr A.
54 *King's College Annual Report,* November 1965, pp. 30–3.
55 *The Gresham,* 17 June 1922, Gr A.
56 These memories of Trèves are taken from the *The Grasshopper,* 1955, pp. 10–11, Gr A.
57 Ibid.
58 John Hayward, *The Grasshopper,* 1955, p. 10, Gr A.

59 J. M. Richards, *Memories of an Unjust Fella,* Weidenfeld and Nicolson, 1980, p. 36.

60 G. Evelyn Hutchinson, *The Kindly Fruits of the Earth,* Yale, 1979, p. 53.

61 *The Gresham,* 25 February 1922, Gr A.

62 *W. H. Auden: A Tribute,* p. 40.

63 Edward Mendelson (ed.), *W. H. Auden: Collected Poems,* Faber and Faber, 1994, p.110.

64 Charles Osborne, *W. H. Auden: The Life of a Poet,* Eyre Methuen, 1980, p. 23.

65 The evidence is this: Hayward edited *The Gresham* in 1922. He had contact with Auden through the Debating and Literary and Sociological societies. The timing is right. The reference to the young age of the writer points to Auden – there were not so many precocious young poets at Gresham's School at the time! 'A Moment', and 'Dawn', which is undoubtedly by Auden, show remarkable similarities of style and subject. Both use the declamatory 'Lo' or 'behold' and also the poetic word 'vaporous'. Katherine Bucknell notes both poems' indebtedness to the Irish poet A. E. and prints them in her edition of Auden's *Juvenilia, Poems 1922–1928,* Princeton, 1994, with the note, 'probably by Auden' (p. 4).

66 *The Gresham,* 8 April 1922, p. 147, Gr A.

67 *Juvenilia,* p. 4.

68 *The Gresham,* 16 December 1922. The circumstantial evidence for Auden's authorship of this poem is very strong. It is also confirmed by the repetition of 'Hill/mill' rhyme also used in 'California'; the 'twinkling lamps' of that poem become 'the twinkling lights' of 'Evening and Night on Primrose Hill'.

69 'Letter from London', *Bonniers Litterara Magasin* (Stockholm).

70 Ibid.

71 J. H. Clapham to JDH, 19 December 1923, GoA.

72 This account of Hayward's relationships with Sylvia, M and Elaine is based on his 'Commonplace Book', KA.

73 All references to Hayward's stay in France are from his 'Diary', GoA.

74 *NYS,* 28 February 1936.

75 Francis Meynell, *SM,* p.13.

76 David Garnett, *The Familiar Faces* (vol. 2 of *The Golden Echo*), Chatto and Windus, 1962, p. 48.

77 *NYS,* 25 January 1935.

78 Francis Meynell, *My Lives,* The Bodley Head, 1971, p.161.

79 A. N. Wilson, *TLS,* 30 October 1977.

80 Richard Garnett, 'The Nonesuch Press: A Personal View', *Private Library,* Fourth Series, vol. 9, Winter 1996, p. 153.

81 David Garnett, *The Familiar Faces*, p. 17.

82 Ibid., p. 153.

83 Montague Summers, *The Galanty Show*, Cecil Woolf, 1980, p. 184.

84 Ian Parsons to J. Haff, 21 September 1980, HRC.

85 'Letter from London', 3 February 1941.

86 Ibid.

87 JDH to Elaine Finlay, 24 January, HRC.

88 Maurice Bowra's coinage.

89 *A Room of One's Own*, Bloomsbury, 1928, p. 14.

90 George Rylands, *SM*, p. 6. Cecil Beaton's first success as a photographer was the picture, published in *Vogue*, of Rylands standing in his full regalia as the Duchess, 'in the subaqueous light outside the men's lavatory of the Amateur Dramatic Club in Cambridge'.

91 *King's College Annual Report*, p. 31.

92 JDH to TSE, 1 December 1939, KA.

93 Kenneth Rose, *Elusive Rothschild: The Life of Victor, Third Baron*, Weidenfeld and Nicolson 2003, p. 37.

94 Denys King-Farlow to J. Haff, HRC.

95 John Haffenden, *William Empson: Among the Mandarins*, Oxford, 2005.

96 TSE to JDH, 2 October 1925, KA.

97 *King's College Annual Report*, p. 31.

98 John Hayward (ed.), *Collected Works of John Wilmot Earl of Rochester*, Nonesuch Press, 1926.

99 Ibid., p. ix.

100 Ibid., p. xii.

101 Ibid., p. xl.

102 Ibid., p. xix.

103 Ibid., p. 28.

104 Francis Meynell, *SM*, pp. 13–14.

105 *Private Journal*, GA.

106 The *Sunday Times*, 14 February 1946.

107 Graham Greene, *SM*, p. 30.

108 Ibid., p. 30.

109 Donald C. Dickinson, *John Carter: The Taste & Technique of a Bookman*, Oak Knoll Press, 2004, p. 19.

110 John Hayward, *Book Collecting: Four Broadcast Talks*, 'Why First Editions?', Bowes and Bowes, 1950, p. 25.

111 *NYS*, 5 December 1936.

112 B. C. Southam, *A Student's Guide to the Selected Poems of T. S .Eliot*, Faber and Faber, 1968. p. 163, quoting from Hayward's Notes to Pierre Leyris's edition *Poèmes 1910–1930*.

113 *The Nation and The Athenaeum*, 5 January 1926.

114 *The Nation*, 13 December 1930.

115 4 August 1948, HB, KA.

116 John Hayward (ed.), *T. S. Eliot: Selected Prose,* Penguin Books, 1953, 'The Function of Criticism', p. 17.

117 T. S. Matthews, *Great Tom: Notes towards the Definition of T. S. Eliot,* London, 1974, p. 124.

118 Tambimuttu and Richard Marsh, *T. S. Eliot: A Symposium,* Frank and Cass, 1965, p. 37.

119 This account is based on Hayward's article, *The Cambridge Review,* 2 December 1939, lxi, pp. 151–2.

120 'Parting at Morning' from 'Notebook', KA.

121 Michael Davie, *The Diaries of Evelyn Waugh,* Weidenfeld and Nicolson, 1976, p. 263.

122 JDH to Frank Morley, 17 September 1926, KA.

123 *King's College Annual Report*, November 1965, p. 31.

124 JDH to David Garnett, 5 July 1927, HRC.

125 TSE to JDH, 28 September 1928, KA.

126 JDH to Lyn Irvine, St John's College Cambridge Archive, 5 June 1930.

127 This account is based on Denys King-Farlow's letter to J. Haff, HRC.

128 Hayward reviewing *A Garland for John Donne, TLS,* 10 March 1932.

129 *John Donne, Dean of St Paul's, Complete Poems and Selected Prose,* Nonesuch ,1930, p. xvi.

130 *The Criterion*, July 1930, T. O. Beachcroft, p. 747.

131 TSE to JDH, 16 January 1929, KA.

132 TSE to JDH, 7 October 1929, KA.

133 TSE to JDH, 27 April 1930, KA.

134 TSE to JDH, 30 October 1930, KA.

135 John Hayward (ed.), *The Letters of Saint Evrémond,* Charles Marguetel de Saint Denis Seigneur de Saint Evrémond, George Routledge, 1930.

136 Ibid., p. 265.

137 Ibid., p. xxvi.

138 Ibid., p. lv.

139 JDH to David Garnett, 22 December 1931, HRC.

140 'Account Book', GA.

141 A. S. G. Edwards, *The Book Collector,* vol. 51, no. 3, Autumn 2002: 'John Davy Hayward: Scholar, Bibliophile and Man of Letters.' The most authoritative and helpful source on Hayward. Professor Edwards' invaluable article, 'John Davy Hayward: A List of his Published Writings, 1924–1964', *Analytical and Enumerative Bibliography,* n.s. 8 (1994), pp. 1–53, provides the basis for these comments.

142 *The Criterion,* vol. ix, no. 37, July 1930, p. 753.

143 *The Criterion,* vol. xi, no. 44, 1932, p. 521.

144 Ibid., pp. 522–3.

145 JDH to Bunny Garnett, 6 June 1932, HRC.

146 'The Orators: An English Study', *The Criterion,* October 1932, vol. 12, no. 46, pp. 131–4.

147 Ibid., p. 132.

148 Ibid., p. 134.

149 Paul Hendon, *The Poetry of W. H. Auden,* Icon, 2000, p. 63.

150 Ibid., p. 59.

151 *Nineteenth Century Poetry,* Chatto and Windus, 1932, p. vii.

152 HB, KA.

153 John Haffenden, *Selected Letters of William Empson,* O.U.P., 2006, p. 653.

154 Denys King-Farlow to J. Haff, HRC.

155 Peter Quennell, *Customs and Characters: Contemporary Portraits,* Little, Brown and Co., 1982, pp. 114 ff.

156 Denys King-Farlow to J. Haff, HRC.

157 Richard Garnett to J. Haff, HRC.

158 JDH to Lyn Irvine, 7 September 1932, St John's College, Cambridge Archives.

159 TSE to JDH, 2 February 1931, KA.

160 JDH to Elaine, 22 January 1932, HRC.

161 TSE to JDH, 26 December 1932, KA.

162 *NYS,* 10 June 1935.

163 Anne Olivier Bell, *The Diary of Virginia Woolf, vol. 5, 1936 –1941,* Penguin, 1984, p. 71.

164 Ibid., 19 March 1937.

165 Anthony Hobson in conversation.

166 Miranda Seymour, *Ottoline Morrell: Life on the Grand Scale,* Hodder and Stoughton, 1992, p. 389.

167 Sheila Wingfield, *Real People,* The Cresset Press, 1952, p. 96.

168 Ottoline Morrell to JDH, 23 December 1932, KA.

169 Ottoline Morrell to JDH, 12 January 1933, KA.

170 JDH to Elizabeth Bowen, 8 September 1936, HRC.

171 Ottoline Morrell to JDH, 1 February1933, KA.

172 Graham Greene, *SM,* p. 30.

173 Ottoline Morrell to JDH, 2 April 1934, KA.

174 John Dreyfus to J. Haff, HRC.

175 Ottoline Morrell to JDH, 2 December 1932, KA.

176 Ibid.

177 JDH to Ottoline Morrell, 27 November 1932, HRC.

178 JDH to Ottoline Morrell, 21 December 1932, HRC.
179 Ibid.
180 *NYS*, 23 June 1933.
181 'English Literature', *Cambridge University Studies*, pp. 259–94.
182 *NYS*, 23 June 1928.
183 John Hayward, *Charles II*, Duckworth, 1933, p. 38.
184 Ibid., p. 18.
185 Ibid., pp. 79–80.
186 Ibid., pp. 78–9.
187 Hector Bolitho, *Twelve Jews*. Hayward's contribution was 'Benjamin Disraeli, Earl of Beaconsfield', Rich and Cowan, 1934, pp. 41–61.
188 Ibid., p. 44.
189 Ibid., p. 59.
190 Ottoline Morrell to JDH, 31 August 1933, KA.
191 JDH to Ottoline Morrell, 3 September 1933, HRC.
192 Ibid., 14 September 1933, HRC.
193 Ottoline Morrell to JDH, 5 September 1933, HRC.
194 Ibid., 13 September 1933, HRC.
195 JDH to Ottoline Morrell, 20 September 1933, HRC.
196 *Swift: Gulliver's Travels and Selected Writings in Prose and Verse*, Nonesuch, 1934, p. iii.
197 Ibid., p. 2.
198 Ibid., p. xv.
199 *TLS*, 10 January 1935, pp. 13–14.
200 TSE to JDH, 21 August 1936, KA.
201 TSE to JDH, 13 March 1937, KA.
202 TSE to JDH, 26 July 1934, KA.
203 Karen Christensen, *Guardian Review*, 'Dear Mrs Eliot', 29 January 2005.
204 TSE to JDH, 16 June 1938, KA.
205 TSE to JDH, 26 October 1936, KA.
206 TSE to JDH, March 1934, KA.
207 'Letter from London', May 1942.
208 TSE to JDH, 29 January 1937, KA.
209 'T. S. Eliot 1888–1965', collection/ exhibition at King's (1976).
210 Both 'The Country Walk' and 'The Cowlover's Retort' are in HB Eliot (8A and B), KA.
211 A. S. G. Edwards in *The Book Collector*, vol. 51, no. 3, Autumn 2002.
212 'Bovrilber 9th 1939', KA.
213 'Miscellaneous', HB, KA.
214 TSE to JDH, 13 July 1939, KA.
215 TSE to JDH, 2 May 1935, KA.

216 TSE to JDH, 2 January 1936, KA.

217 TSE to JDH, 3 December 1937, KA.

218 Lyndall Gordon, *T. S. Eliot: An Imperfect Life*, Vintage, 1998, p. 300.

219 This account of their meeting is based on Lyndall Gordon, *Eliot's New Life,* Oxford, 1988, pp. 70–72.

220 TSE to JDH, 'Shrove Tuesday' 1936, KA.

221 TSE to JDH, 19 September 1935, KA.

222 TSE to JDH, 14 March 1937, KA.

223 JDH to TSE, 22 June 1937, KA.

224 *TLS,* 12 December 1929.

225 Ibid.

226 This account of Cliveden Court is taken from Hayward's letter to Lyn Irvine, 18 August 1930, St John's College, Cambridge Archives.

227 *NYS,* 12 June 1936.

228 'Letter from London', 1944.

229 *NYS,* June 1933.

230 *NYS,* 23 March 1935.

231 Elizabeth Bowen's phrase.

232 Richard Greene (ed.), *Selected Letters of Edith Sitwell,* Virago, 1997, p. 166.

233 Edith Sitwell, *Aspects of Modern Poetry,* Duckworth, 1934, p. 20.

234 Ibid., p. 31.

235 *Selected Letters of Edith Sitwell,* 13 December 1934.

236 *NYS,* 22 December 1934.

237 *Fisbo or The Looking-Glass Loaned*, William Heinemann, 1934.

238 *Selected Letters of Edith Sitwell*, p. 175.

239 *NYS,* 17 October 1936.

240 *The Observer*, 10 January 1937.

241 Ibid., 30 June 1934.

242 Ibid., 23 November 1934.

243 TSE to JDH, 23 November 1934, KA.

244 Virginia Woolf, *Diary,* vol. 4, p. 260.

245 *NYS,* 8 February 1935.

246 Ibid., 25 June 1935.

247 Ibid., 7 June 1935.

248 Ibid., 19 September 1936.

249 Vera Russell, *SM,* p. 15.

250 *NYS,* 26 October 1934.

251 Ibid., 6 February 1937.

252 David Pryce-Jones, *Cyril Connolly,* Collins, 1983, p. 269.

253 *NYS,* 20 September 1935.

254 *NYS,* 28 March 1936.

References

255 Later published as *Lord Rochester's Monkey*.
256 *NYS*, 25 August 1939.
257 *NYS*, 25 September 1934.
258 *NYS*, 7 September 1934.
259 Virginia Nicolson, *Among the Bohemians*, Viking, 2002, p. 115.
260 *Real People*, p. 94.
261 *NYS*, 25 August 1934, KA.
262 Lyndall Gordon, *T. S. Eliot: An Imperfect Life*, p. 25.
263 TSE to JDH, 13 October 1936, KA.
264 JDH to TSE, 22 October 1944, KA.
265 TSE to JDH, 21 August 1936, KA.
266 *Noctes Binanianae*, privately printed, 1939.
267 TSE to JDH, 19 November 1937, KA.
268 *Noctes Binanianae*, p. 5.
269 Geoffrey Faber to JDH, 11 August 1943, KA.
270 *Noctes Binanianae*, p. 1.
271 Ibid., p. 5.
272 Ibid., pp. 15–16.
273 Ibid., p. 13.
274 Ibid., p. 12.
275 Ibid., p. 7.
276 Ibid., p. 8.
277 Ibid., p. 20.
278 Ibid., pp. 22–3.
279 Ibid., p.25.
280 A. S. G. Edwards, 'T. S. Eliot and Friends: *Noctes Binanianae* (1939)', *The Book Collector*, Winter 2009, p. 505.
281 John Haffenden, *Quarto*, June 1981, p. 4.
282 Carole Seymour-Jones, *Painted Shadow: A Life of Vivienne Eliot*, pp. 524–5.
283 Richard Badenhausen, *T. S. Eliot and the Art of Collaboration*, Cambridge, 2004, pp. 172–4.
284 TSE to JDH, 27 September 1939, KA.
285 HB (Eliot), KA.
286 E. Martin Browne, *The Making of T. S. Eliot's Plays,* Cambridge, 1969, p. 111.
287 *NYS*, 1952.
288 *Cambridge Review*, vol. lxiv, no. 1566, 6 February 1943, p. 179.
289 TSE to JDH 15 February, 1938, KA.
290 *CFQ*, p. 8.
291 JDH to TSE, 7 March 1943, KA.
292 Christopher Sykes, *SM,* p. 33.

293 Donald C. Dickinson, *John Carter: The Taste & Technique of a Book-man*, p. 77.
294 Peter Ackroyd, *T. S. Eliot,* Hamish Hamilton, 1984, p. 234.
295 Mary Hyde, *SM,* p. 41.
296 Humphrey Carpenter, *W. H. Auden: A Biography,* George Allen and Unwin, 1981, p. 233.
297 Robert Medley, *Drawn from the Life,* p.141.
298 JDH to TSE, 8 July 1939, KA. The 'Vans' are Robert Gilbert, 1st Baron Vansittart and his wife. He was made Permanent Under-Secretary for Foreign Affairs in 1930 and vehemently opposed Nazi Germany in the 1930s. Hayward was on friendly terms with his wife, and his daughter whose many personal letters to him were returned after his death.
299 *NYS,* February 1939.
300 'Letter from London', 1939.
301 *The Spectator*, 'P. G. W. and the Edwardians', 8 November 1935, p. 771.
302 *The Book Collector,* vol. 14, no. 4 Winter 1965, pp. 496–7.
303 JDH to Graham Greene, 16 September 1939, Graham Greene Papers, Special Collections Division, Georgetown University Library.
304 JDH to TSE, 14 September 1939, KA.
305 'Letter from London', 1940.
306 'English Letter Writers of the Restoration', Third Programme Talk, 1939, KA.
307 TSE to JDH, 27 December 1939, KA.
308 TSE to JDH, 29 November 1939, KA.
309 'TSNS', 'Memorandum from Frank Morley', 24 August 1967, KA.
310 'TSNS', vii, November 1939
311 TSE to JDH, 23 November 1939, KA.
312 JDH to TSE, 22 November 1939, KA.
313 TSE to JDH, 29 November 1939, KA.
314 'Letter from London', n.d., KA.
315 JDH to TSE, 24 January 1940, KA.
316 *Prose Literature Since 1939,* published for The British Council by Longmans Green, 1947, p. 28
317 JDH to TSE, 30 December 1939, KA.
318 Ibid.
319 JDH to TSE, 19 January 1940, KA.
320 JDH to TSE, 10 March 1940, KA.
321 'TSNS', vii, December 1939, KA.
322 JDH to TSE, 7 February 1940, KA.
323 TSE to JDH, 11 September 1939, KA.
324 JDH to TSE, 24 January 1940, KA.

325 JDH to Graham Greene, 17 March 1940, HRC.
326 JDH to Frank Morley, 10 March 1940, KA.
327 *Elusive Rothschild*, p. 99.
328 Ibid., p. 99.
329 Hayward's story is not consistent. He told Eliot that he had found about thirty leaves inserted and that they were 'modern lithographic facsimiles' (JDH to TSE, 19 March 1940, KA).
330 *Elusive Rothschild*, p.102.
331 'TSNS', xi, February 1940, KA.
332 TSE to JDH, 20 February 1940, KA.
333 JDH to TSE, 20 June 1940, KA.
334 'PRS', 1949, p. 53.
335 The nature of Eliot's collaboration with Hayward and others is the theme of Professor Richard Badenhausen's *Eliot and the Art of Collaboration*.
336 Frank Morley, *Literary Britain: A Reader's Guide to Writers and Landmarks*, Hutchinson, 1980, p. 196.
337 'TSNS', xvi, April 1940, KA.
338 JDH to TSE, 20 June 1940, KA.
339 *The Book Collector*, vol. 14, no. 2, Summer 1965, p. 159.
340 TSE to JDH, June 1940, KA.
341 'TSNS', xvii, May 1940, KA.
342 TSE to JDH, 19 June 1940, KA.
343 JDH to TSE, 16 September 1940, KA.
344 JDH to TSE, 28 October 1940, KA.
345 TSE to JDH, 16 October 1942.
346 JDH to TSE, 19 April 1940, KA.
347 'TSNS', xxxviii, August 1941, KA.
348 'TSNS', xxi, March 1940, KA.
349 JDH to TSE, 9 November 1940, KA.
350 JDH to TSE, 7 December 1940, KA.
351 TSE to JDH, 10 December 1940, KA.
352 Ibid., 3 March 1941, KA.
353 John Hayward (ed.), *Points of View*, Faber and Faber, 1941, p. 5.
354 Ibid., p. 28.
355 JDH to TSE, 25 January 1941, KA.
356 JDH to Anne Ridler, 8 October, 1939, BL.
357 JDH to Anne Ridler, 10 August 1941, BL.
358 TSE to JDH, 24 August 1942, KA.
359 John Hayward, *Love's Helicon*, Gerald Duckworth and Co, 1940, p. 8.
360 Ibid., pp. 8–9.
361 Selina Hastings, *Rosamond Lehmann: A Life*, Vintage, 2003, p. 212.

362 Rosamond Lehmann to JDH, 17 October 1942, KA.
363 Ibid., 7 October 1943.
364 'TSNS', xx, August 1940, KA.
365 TSE to JDH, 10 December 1940, KA.
366 TSE to JDH, 3 January 1941, KA.
367 JDH to Anne Ridler, 8 January 1941, BL.
368 Ibid.
369 'TSNS', xxvii, January 1941, KA.
370 JDH to TSE, 7 January 1941, KA.
371 *CFQ*, p. 143.
372 JDH to TSE, 5 March 1941, KA.
373 This account is based on *To Keep the Ball Rolling: Memoirs of Anthony Powell*, vol. iii, Heinemann, 1980, pp. 127–8.
374 JDH to TSE, Good Friday 1941, KA.
375 TSE to JDH, 21 April 1941, KA.
376 JDH to TSE, 11 April 1941, KA.
377 JDH to Anne Ridler, 1 May 1941, BL.
378 JDH to TSE, 5 May 1941, KA.
379 JDH to Anne Ridler, 9 July 1941, BL.
380 JDH to Frank Morley, June 1941, KA.
381 *CFQ*, p. 22.
382 'TSNS' xxxvii, July 1941, KA.
383 See Appendix.
384 'TSNS', xxxviii, 6 August 1941, KA.
385 Ibid.
386 JDH to TSE, 14 October 1941, KA.
387 Sir John Gielgud to J. Haff, 10 October 1980, HRC.
388 Anne Ridler, *Collected Poems*, Carcanet, 1994, p. 36.
389 Ibid., p. 37
390 JDH to Anne Ridler, 'Holy Innocents' Day', 1944, BL.
391 JDH to Anne Ridler, 10 August 1940, BL.
392 JDH to Anne Ridler, 10 September 1940, BL.
393 JDH to Pilot Officer Lord Kinross, 4 November 1941, HRC.
394 Mark Amory (ed), *The Letters of Evelyn* Waugh, Weidenfeld and Nicolson, 1980, p. 355.
395 JDH to Catherine Walston, 29 April 1948, HRC.
396 JDH to Catherine Walston, 19 June 1948, HRC.
397 Michael Shelden, *Graham Greene: The Man Within,* William Heinemann, 1994, p. 360.
398 JDH to TSE, June 20 1940, KA.
399 JDH to TSE, 12 March 1945, KA.
400 JDH to TSE, 16 October 1940, KA.

401 JDH to TSE, 15 June 1941, KA.
402 JDH to Squadron Leader Lord Kinross, 24 August 1942, HRC.
403 'TSNS', xlix, February 1942, KA.
404 Diana Oakeley, GoA.
405 JDH to TSE, 4 August 1942, KA.
406 JDH to TSE, 4 August 1942, KA.
407 TSE to JDH, 17 August 1942, KA.
408 JDH to TSE, 7 December 1940, KA.
409 'Letter from London', 1944, KA. TSE to JDH, 17 August 1942, KA.
410 JDH to TSE, 27 May 1940, KA.
411 Stevie Smith to JDH, 16 September 1936, KA.
412 Ibid., 9 April 1942, KA.
413 Stevie Smith to JDH, 1 September 1943, HRC.
414 JDH to Stevie Smith, 12 November 1942, KA.
415 JDH to TSE, 23 June 1942, KA. JDH to Stevie Smith, 1 September 1943, HRC.
416 'TSNS', lvii, July 1942, KA.
417 TSE to JDH, 10 October 1942, KA.
418 TSE to JDH, 10 October 1942, KA.
419 JDH to TSE, 29 December 1942, KA. 'PRS', 1949, p. 54.
420 Robert Sencourt, *T.S. Eliot: A Memoir*, Dodd Mead, 1971, p. 152.
421 *Eliot's New Life*, p. 209
422 JDH to TSE, 4 June 1943, KA.
423 Ibid.
424 'Letter from London', 1944.
425 *CFQ*, p. 13.
426 JDH to Anne Ridler, 24 December 1942, BL.
427 John Sutherland, *Stephen Spender: The Authorised Biography*, Viking, 2004, p. 287.
428 JDH to TSE, 15 November 1943, KA.
429 Stephen Spender to JDH, 15 June 1943, HRC.
430 JDH to TSE, 15 November 1943, KA.
431 Sotheby and Co. Catalogue, 12 July 1966, p. 36.
432 Unpublished TS, KA.
433 TSE to JDH, 9 November 1939, KA.
434 'Beechingstoke', unpublished TS, KA.
435 Ibid.
436 JDH to TSE, 1 December 1939, KA.
437 JDH to TSE, 9 November 1940, KA.
438 'TSNS', 8 November 1942, KA.
439 *Vogue*, October 1943.
440 JDH to Anne Ridler, 16 August 1942, BL.

441 This account of Edward Marsh is based on Christopher Hassall's *Edward Marsh, Patron of the Arts,* Longmans, 1959.

442 JDH to TSE, 23 February 1943, KA.

443 *Seventeenth Century Poetry: an Anthology Chosen by John Hayward,* Chatto and Windus, 1961, p. v.

444 JDH to TSE, 12 November 1942, KA.

445 JDH to TSE, 16 December 1943, KA.

446 JDH to TSE, 30 December 1943, KA.

447 JDH to TSE, 7 March 1943, KA.

448 JDH to TSE, 16 December 1943, KA.

449 JDH to TSE, 25 April 1944, KA.

450 JDH to TSE, 18 November 1944, KA.

451 Basil Willey, in fact, became Q's successor.

452 The correspondence between Edith Sitwell and JDH quoted here is at HRC.

453 JDH to TSE, 10 December 1945, KA.

454 JDH to TSE 10 December, 1944, KA.

455 JDH to TSE, 12 March 1945, KA.

456 Geoffrey Faber to JDH, 9 February 1945, KA.

457 JDH to TSE, 24 May 1945, KA.

458 Dr Hayward to JDH, 14 March 1945, GoA.

459 Ibid.

460 *Prose Literature Since 1939,* p. 35.

461 Ibid., p. 9.

462 'Letter from London', n.d., 1945.

463 *Prose Literature Since 1939,* p. 33.

464 Ibid., p. 41.

465 Ibid., p. 45.

466 David Holland, *The Book Collector,* vol. 4, no. 1, Spring 1955.

467 'A Catalogue of Printed Books and Manuscripts by Jonathan Swift DD, exhibited in the Old Schools in the University of Cambridge. To Commemorate 200th Anniversary of his Death.' 1945.

468 *Elusive Rothschild,* p.146.

469 GoA.

470 26 January 1946, HRC.

471 Mark Haworth-Booth (ed.), *Literary Britain,* Hurtwood Press, 1984.

472 JDH to Anne Ridler, 5 April 1946, BL.

473 Humphrey Spender in conversation with the writer.

474 JDH to TSE, 6 July 1945, KA.

475 Ibid.

476 Christopher Sykes, *SM,* p.35.

477 Nicolas Barker, *SM,* p. 21.

478 Catherine Porteous, in conversation with the writer.

479 Michael Shelden, *Graham Greene: The Man Within*, p. 410.

480 This account of Hayward's accommodation owes a good deal to Lyndall Gordon's *T. S. Eliot's New Life* pp. 205–12 and also to Peter Ackroyd's *T. S. Eliot*, pp. 274–9.

481 Eliot told Sencourt he received £29,000 but, to his unspeakable disgust, had to pay £25,000 in tax.

482 T. S. Matthews, *Great Tom: Notes towards the Definition of T. S. Eliot*, p. 158.

483 Robert Sencourt, p. 152.

484 I owe this point to Jim McCue in private correspondence.

485 'PRS', 1949, BL.

486 Frances Partridge, *Julia: A Portrait of Julia Strachey*, Gollancz, 1983, pp. 207–8.

487 J. M. Brinnin, *Sextet: T.S.Eliot and Truman Capote and Others*, André Deutsch, 1981, p. 253.

488 Richard Garnett to J. Haff, 13 April 1980, HRC.

489 John Carswell to JDH, HRC.

490 John Dreyfus to JDH, HRC.

491 See *Eliot's New Life*, p. 210.

492 For more details of Eliot's routines and rituals see Ackroyd, pp. 278–9.

493 Simon Nowell-Smith to J. Haff, HRC.

494 Christopher Sykes, *SM*, p. 33.

495 Anthony Powell, *Journals 1982–1986*, Heinemann, 1995, p. 230.

496 Cyril Connolly, *Ideas and Places*, Harper 1953, p. 205.

497 Mark Amory (ed.), *Letters of Evelyn Waugh*, p. 311.

498 *NYS*, 20 July 1934.

499 Kathleen Raine to JDH, 6 August 1946, KA.

500 As remembered by Lady Natasha Spender.

501 Victoria Glindinning, *Edith Sitwell*, Weidenfeld and Nicolson, 1981, pp. 192–3.

502 John Pearson, *Façades: Edith, Osbert and Sacheverel Sitwell*, Macmillan, 1978, pp. 385–6.

503 *Selected Letters of Edith Sitwell*, p. 282.

504 Edith Sitwell to JDH, 18 March 1946, KA.

505 *Sextet*, p. 261.

506 *Great Tom*, p. 138.

507 Christopher Sykes, *SM*, p. 35.

508 'Trying out typewriter', 12 March 1947, KA.

509 JDH to Catherine Walston, 18 February 1947, HRC.

510 *English Poetry: A Catalogue of First and Early Editions of the Works*

of the English Poets from Chaucer to the Present Day, Cambridge University Press, 1947, p. v.

511 Ibid., p. 1.
512 Ibid., p. vii.
513 Ibid., pp. vi–vii.
514 Ibid., p.16.
515 Ibid., p. 37.
516 Ibid., p. 81.
517 Ibid., p. 122.
518 Ibid., p. 106.
519 Ibid., p. 117.
520 Ibid., p. 130.
521 Ibid., p. 132.
522 Ibid., p.129.
523 JDH to Maurice Craig, 15 April 1947, HRC.
524 Nicolas Barker, *SM*, p. 20.
525 JDH to Anne Ridler, 26 October 1948, BL.
526 Christopher Sykes, *SM*, pp. 34–5.
527 Michael Shelden, *Friends of Promise: Cyril Connolly and the World of Horizon*, Hamish Hamilton, 1989, p. 192.
528 He reprinted a revised version of his talk as the introduction to *Selected Prose Works of Jonathan Swift*, the Cresset Press, 1949, pp. i–xx.
529 Ibid., p. xii.
530 Ibid., pp. xvi–xvii.
531 Transcript of Radio Eirann Broadcast, 1948, KA.
532 JDH to Bryan Guinness, 26 May 1947, HRC.
533 *Scrutiny*, vol. xv, no. 4, December 1948.
534 F. R. Leavis, *The Common Pursuit*, Chatto and Windus, 1965, p. 297.
535 Ibid., p. 298.
536 Hayward's Notebook, GA.
537 Edith Sitwell to JDH, 7 February 1952, HRC.
538 *The Common Pursuit*, p. 297.
539 *Selected Letters of Edith Sitwell*, 7 February 1952, Virago, 1997.
540 F. R. Leavis to JDH, July 1952, KA.
541 JDH to Catherine Walston, 3 June 1954, HRC.
542 Michael Davie (ed.), *The Diaries of Evelyn Waugh*, Weidenfeld and Nicolson, 1976, p. 28.
543 JDH to Catherine Walston, 19 August 1948, HRC.
544 Graham Greene, *SM*, p. 30.
545 Katherine Bucknell (ed.), *Christopher Isherwood Lost Years: A Memoir 1945–1957*, Chatto and Windus, 2000, p. 98.

546 Lady Spender in conversation with the writer.

547 Humphrey Spender in conversation with the writer.

548 'For RGH on her 80th Birthday', GoA.

549 GoA.

550 JDH to Diana Oakeley, 14 March 1949, GA.

551 TSE to JDH, 12 October 1950, KA.

552 JDH to TSE, 16 November 1950, KA.

553 In conversation with the author..

554 Edith Sitwell to JDH, 30 September 1947, KA.

555 Anthony Powell, *Faces in My Time*, Heinemann, 1980, p. 120.

556 J. E. Morpurgo to J. Haff, 9 November 1979, HRC.

557 Christopher Sykes, *SM*, p. 32.

558 Ibid., p. 32.

559 Ian Parsons to J. Haff, HRC.

560 Norman Brook was made a life peer as Lord Normanbrook in 1963.

561 Betty Carr to J. Haff, HRC.

562 'The Pope of Russell Square' unpublished TS in the Bodleian Library Oxford. The relationship between Mary, Hayward and Eliot is very well treated by Gordon pp.190–240 and by Carole Seymour-Jones.

563 Ibid., p.10.

564 Ibid., 27 April 1949.

565 Ibid., 2 June 1950.

566 Ibid.

567 T. S. Eliot, *The Cocktail Party*, Faber and Faber, 1950, p. 5.

568 Cf. *Eliot's New Life*, pp. 213–14.

569 John Hayward (ed.), *John Donne: A Selection of his Poetry*, Penguin, 1950, p. 6.

570 Ibid., p. 11.

571 Valerie Eliot (ed.), *Poems from Early Youth*, Faber and Faber, 1967.

572 JDH to Helen Gardner, 17 April 1954, KA.

573 Anthony Hobson in private correspondence.

574 Mary Hyde, *SM*, p. 43.

575 I owe this story to Anthony Hobson.

576 JDH to Mary Hyde, 21 March 1954, HL.

577 'Why First Editions?' in *Book Collecting: Four Broadcast Talks*, Bowes and Bowes, Cambridge, 1950.

578 Ibid., p. 22.

579 Ibid., p. 24.

580 Ibid., p. 25. Very surprisingly Hayward misquotes Sir Thomas Browne, misses out Rimbaud's circumflexes and writes 'Quel' for 'Quelle'.

581 Nicolas Barker in *The Independent*, 23 June 2007.

582 Rupert Hart-Davis, *SM*, p. 19.
583 Ibid.
584 Charles Burkhart, *Nineteenth Century Fiction*, vol. 27, no. 1.
585 John Hayward (ed.), *Literary Britain*, Cassell and Co., 1951, reprinted 1984.
586 *Scrutiny*, 1949, vol. xvi, no. 4, pp. 333–6.
587 *The Common Pursuit*, p. 298.
588 *Scrutiny*, vol. xviii, no. 1.
589 Ibid., p. 55.
590 JDH to Edith Sitwell, 14 May 1951, HRC.
591 John Hayward (ed.), *Poems 1951*, Penguin, 1951, p. 9.
592 Ibid., p. 13.
593 *The Times*, 21 September 1965.
594 This account is based upon Desmond Flower's 'Le Livre Anglais', *Book Handbook*, vol. 2, no. 4, pp. 163–75.
595 Desmond Flower, *SM*, p. 10.
596 Robert Sencourt, p. 158.
597 Desmond Flower, *SM*, p. 164.
598 *The Book Collector*, vol. 6, no. 1, Spring 1957, p. 334.
599 *Book Handbook*, vol. 2, no. 4, p. 163.
600 T. S. Eliot: 'Inauguration Speech for the exhibition *Le Livre Anglais*, Paris, 16 November 1951', KA.
601 *English Poetry*, p. vii.
602 Robert Sencourt, p. 159.
603 David Holland, *The Book Collector*, vol. 3, no. 3, Autumn 1954, pp. 234–6.
604 *The Book Collector*, vol. 5, no. 4, Winter 1956, p. 313.
605 David Holland p. 236.
606 *The Rothschild Library. A Catalogue of the Collection of Eighteenth-century Printed Books and Manuscripts formed by Lord Rothschild*, Cambridge University Press, 1954.
607 Ibid. p. viii.
608 David Holland, 'Contemporary Collectors IV: the Rothschild Library', *The Book Collector*, vol. 4, no. 1, Spring 1955, pp. 28–33.
609 'Letter from London', 1950.
610 JDH to TSE, 21 July 1947, KA.
611 'Letter from London', 1953.
612 'Letter from London', 1949.
613 'Letter from London', 1951.
614 This account is based on *The Ample Proposition*, vol. iii of John Lehmann's autobiography, Eyre and Spottiswood, 1966, p. 239 ff.
615 Ibid., p. 261.

616 Ibid., p. 259.
617 Adrian Wright, *John Lehmann: A Pagan Adventure*, Duckworth, 1998, p. 199.
618 Ibid. p. 201.
619 JDH to Christopher Sykes, 4 June 1953, GA.
620 The material about Hayward's CBE is at GA.
621 Janet Adam Smith, *SM*, pp. 27–8.
622 JDH to Josephine Baird, 10 June 1953.
623 Lord Beaverbrook to JDH, 13 June 1953, GA.
624 W. E. Williams to JDH, GA.
625 Dr Ann Baer in a letter to the writer, January 2005.
626 *Great Tom*, p. 158.
627 Graham Greene, *SM*, p. 30.
628 'Letter from London', n.d.
629 *Sextet*, p. 253.
630 Ibid., p. 254.
631 Ibid., p. 255.
632 Ibid., p. 264.
633 Ibid., p. 264.
634 Ibid., p. 265.
635 Ibid., p. 266.
636 Ibid., p. 267.
637 Kathleen Raine in conversation with the writer.
638 John Lehmann and Derek Parker, *Edith Sitwell: Selected Letters*, Macmillan and Co., 1970, p. 235.
639 Catherine Porteous in conversation.
640 Roy Fuller, *Spanner and Pen: Post-War Memories*, Sinclair-Stevenson, 1991.
641 Lyndall Gordon, *T.S. Eliot: An Imperfect Life*, p. 460.
642 Humphrey Carpenter, *The Brideshead Generation*, Houghton Miffin, 1989 p. 404.
643 Christopher Sykes, *Evelyn Waugh: a Biography*, Penguin, 1977, pp. 423–5.
644 Ibid., p. 424.
645 They included Eliot, Kathleen Raine, Helen and Oliver Low, Vera Birch, Christopher Sykes and Graham Greene.
646 *Great Tom*, p. 158.
647 Roland Penrose, *Scrapbook 1900–1981*, Thames and Hudson, 1981, pp. 192–3.
648 'PRS.', 26 February 1950.
649 'PRS.', 7 December 1951.
650 'PRS.', 11 November 1952.

651 John Peter, *Essays in Criticism*, July 1952, 'A New Interpretation of *The Waste Land*', pp.140–75.

652 'PRS.', 30 July 1952.

653 HB, (Eliot D11), KA.

654 Ibid.

655 Hayward commented that Eliot's original name 'Slingsby' had been used by Peter Fleming. Eliot changed it to 'Colby Simpkins' suggesting 'simple', and perhaps the idea of the holy fool.

656 Chris Buttram Trumbold's phrase in 'The Bodily Biography of T. S. Eliot', *Yeats Eliot Review*, 15, no. 2, 1997, p. 40.

657 JDH to TSE, 19 August 1955, KA.

658 *The Confidential Clerk*, T. S. Eliot, Faber and Faber, 1954, p. 15.

659 John Hayward (ed.), *Selected Prose*, Penguin 1953, p. 7.

660 *For Lancelot Andrewes*, Faber and Faber, 1928, p. 11.

661 *Selected Prose*, p. 12.

662 JDH to Anne Ridler, 26 April 1954, BL.

663 'PRS', Easter Day April 1955.

664 'PRS', 2 January 1955.

665 'PRS', 23 October 1955.

666 'PRS', 4 October 1955.

667 Mary Trevelyan to JDH, 21 April 1955, KA.

668 'PRS', 4 October 1955.

669 Ibid., p. 285.

670 JDH to Helen Gardner, 5 February 1957, KL.

671 Phillip Herring, *Djuna: The Life and Work of Djuna Barnes*, Viking, 1995, p. 285.

672 Kathleen Raine, *SM*, p. 25.

673 Peter Ackroyd, *T. S. Eliot*, p. 194.

674 Arthur Quiller-Couch (ed.), *The Oxford Book of English Verse 1250–1900*, Clarendon Press, Oxford, 1923, p. viii.

675 John Hayward (ed.), *The Penguin Book of English Verse*, 1956, p. xxiv.

676 Edith Sitwell to JDH, 24 June 1948, KA.

677 JDH to Edith Sitwell, 17 September 1956, HRC.

678 Miss Dorothy Bartholomew in private conversation.

679 Mary Trevelyan's phrase.

680 *Sextet,* p. 274.

681 Lady Spender in conversation with the writer.

682 JDH to Helen Gardner, 5 February 1957, KA.

683 This account is based on Diana Oakeley's letter to Mr Halls, 6 July 1982, GA.

684 Ibid.

685 JDH to Anne Ridler, 3 February 1957, BL.

686 Gwen Watkins in conversation with the writer.
687 *Great Tom*, p. 160.
688 Ibid., p. 160.
689 According to James Stern, quoted in *Djuna: The Life and Work of Djuna Barnes*, p. 285
690 Diana Oakeley, GA.
691 *Painted Shadow*, p. 578.
692 Margaret Behrens to JDH, 12 January 1957, KA.
693 TSE to JDH, January 1957, KA.
694 Lyndall Gordon, *T.S. Eliot: An Imperfect Life*, p. 510.
695 'PRS', Postscript, BL.
696 Ibid.
697 Ibid.
698 JDH to Helen Gardner, 5 February 1957, KA.
699 JDH to Anne Ridler, 3 February 1957, BL.
700 Richard Greene (ed.), *Selected Letters of Edith Sitwell*, Virago, 1997, p. 396.
701 Michael Hastings, *Tom and Viv*, Penguin, 1985, p. xxviii.
702 Graham Greene, *SM*, p. 31.
703 Kathleen Raine in private conversation.
704 Christopher Sykes, *SM*, pp. 35–6.
705 JDH to Mary Hyde, 2 April 1957, HL.
706 Catherine Porteous in private conversation.
707 Helen Gardner to Diana Oakeley, 14 May 1973, GA.
708 Ibid.
709 'PRS', Postscript, p. 169.
710 Katherine Bucknell (ed.), *Christopher Isherwood Diaries*, vol.1, 1939–1960, Methuen, 1996, p. 590.
711 Katherine Bucknell (ed.), *Lost Years: A Memoir, 1945–51*, Christopher Isherwood, p. 98.
712 Elias Canetti, *Party in the Blitz*, The Harvill Press, 2005, p. 50.
713 Anthony Powell, *Faces in Time*, p. 120.
714 JDH to Mary Hyde, 31 May 1957, HL.
715 Roland Penrose, *Scrapbook 1900 –1981*, pp. 192–3.
716 JDH to Graham Greene, 9 June 1957, HRC.
717 This account of *The Book Collector* is based on the contributions of Nicolas Barker, P. H. Muir and Catherine Porteous in *SM*, and conversations with A. S. G. Edwards, Anthony Hobson and Catherine Porteous.
718 P. H. Muir, *SM*, p. 16.
719 *The Book Collector*, vol. 1, no.1, Spring 1952, p.1.
720 Ibid., vol. 13, no. 4, Winter 1964 p. 431.

721 Andrew Lycett, *Ian Fleming,* Phoenix, 1996, p. 43.

722 *The Book Collector*, vol.1, no. 2, Summer p.137.

723 Ibid., vol. 4, no. 2, Summer 1955, pp. 99–109.

724 Ibid., vol. 10, no. 4, Winter 1961, p. 390.

725 *The Times*, January 18 1955.

726 *The Times*, January 29 1955.

727 *The Book Collector*, vol. 4, no. 3, Autumn 1995, pp. 186–7.

728 Nicolas Barker, *SM*, p. 20.

729 *The Book Collector*, vol. 13, no. 4, Winter 1964, p. 446.

730 Percy Muir, *SM*, p. 17.

731 Andrew Lycett, p. 274.

732 JDH to Mary Hyde, 21 October 1955, HL.

733 Ibid.

734 Andrew Lycett. This account of board meetings is taken from pp. 347–8.

735 Ibid., p. 347.

736 Ibid.

737 Donald C. Dickinson, *John Carter: The Taste & Technique of a Bookman*, p. 259.

738 John Carter, 'Memorandum', 19 September 1957, CUL.

739 Ian Fleming to John Carter, 24 September 1957, CUL.

740 Ibid., vol. 14, no. 2, Summer 1965, p. 154.

741 Catherine Porteous, *SM*, p. 22.

742 Nicolas Barker (ed.), *The Pleasures of Bibliophily*, British Library and the Oak Knoll Press, 2003, p. 3.

743 JDH's obituary, The *Sunday Times*, 19 September 1965.

744 *The Book Collector*, vol. 8, no. 2, Summer 1959, p. 124.

745 John Carter, 'Memorandum', 19 September 1953, CUL.

746 Mary Hyde, *SM*, p. 43.

747 Mary Hyde, *SM*, p. 43.

748 John Dreyfus to J. Haff, 22 November 1979, HRC.

749 Robert Sencourt, p. 167.

750 Mary Hyde, *SM*, p. 43.

751 Ibid., p. 44.

752 Dr John Walton to Dr MacKeith, 14 January 1964, HRC.

753 Griselda Kentner to J. Haff, HRC.

754 John Hayward (ed.), *Oxford Book of Nineteenth Century Verse*, 1964, p. v.

755 Ibid., pp. 8–9.

756 JDH to Graham Greene, 18 August 1964, HRC.

757 Peter Ackroyd, *T. S. Eliot*, p. 334.

758 Kathleen Raine to JDH, 4 January 1965, KA.

759 Mary Trevelyan to JDH, 6 January 1965, KA.

760 Nancy Cunard to JDH, January 1965, KA.

761 Sean Day-Lewis, *C. Day-Lewis: An English Literary Life*, Weidenfeld and Nicolson, 1980, p. 162.

762 C. Day Lewis to JDH, 21 June 1946, KA.

763 Kathleen Raine, letter to the writer, 1 October 2001.

764 Kathleen Raine in conversation with the writer.

765 William Empson to J. Haff, HRC.

766 JDH to Graham Greene, 4 August 1965, GA.

767 Mary Hyde, *SM*, p. 44.

768 *Antiquarian Bookman*, 4 October 1965.

769 *The Book Collector,* vol. 28, no. 3, Autumn 1979, p. 415.

770 Kathleen Raine to JDH, February 1965, KA.

771 Ibid.

772 Kathleen Raine, *SM,* p. 27.

773 Ibid.

774 Jim McCue in conversation.

775 Nicolas Barker, *The Pleasures of Bibliophily*.

776 Diana Oakeley to Mary Hyde, 17 September 1965, HL.

777 *The Times*, 18 September 1965.

778 Norman Sherry, *The Life of Graham Greene,* vol. iii, Jonathan Cape, 2004.

779 Kathleen Raine, *SM*, p. 25.

780 Kathleen Raine to the writer, 1 October 2001.

781 Generous, but not quite true. Auden did not write on Gresham's School and Rothschild did not write on the war years. What a pity!

782 *The Book Collector*, vol. 15, no. 1, Spring 1966, p. 7.

783 A. N. L. Munby, 'Papers at Carlyle Mansions', GA.

784 A. N. L. Munby to Mrs Oakeley, 21 February 1966, KA.

785 All references to 'Beechingstoke' are from The *Cambridge Mercury*, no. 15, 1 November 1924.

786 This section is indebted to Helen Gardner's *CFQ* for its textual detail – the essential basis for the study of the evolution of *Four Quartets*.

787 JDH to TSE, 1 August 1941, KA.

788 Ibid.

789 Ibid.

790 TSE to JDH, 7 September 1942, KA.

791 TSE to JDH, 19 September 1942, KA.

792 JDH to TSE, 1 August 1941, KA.

793 Ibid.

794 TSE to JDH, 9 September 1942, KA.

795 *CFQ*, Helen Gardner, p. 223.

Index

To clarify how they would have been known when they appear in the narrative, for those who were knighted or ennobled the relevant date has been included.

Index

Edwards, Professor A. S. G., 130
Eliot, T. S., JDH to TSE on childhood poetry, 30; unknown at Gresham's, 37; JDH invites to talk to Heretics, 49; JDH on *The Waste Land* and 'Prufrock', 52–4; meets JDH, 55; gives Clark Lectures at Cambridge, 55; JDH reviews for *The Criterion* and growing friendship, 70; JDH's version of 'The Hollow Men', 71; shared views on Donne, 72; praises JDH's *Donne*, 73; JDH comments on *Ash-Wednesday*, 73–4; shared liking with JDH for detective fiction, 76; breakdown of first marriage, 82–3; lectures at Harvard, 83–4; visits Bina Gardens, 86; Vivienne disrupts poetry reading, 87; farewell party, 87; JDH and Ottoline Morrell gossip about, 89–90; returns to England, 99; his friendship with JDH resumes, 99–100; brings Emily Hale to Bina Gardens 100–1; shared humour and wordplay with JDH, 101–4, 171–2; lives in Kensington with Father Eric Cheetham, 104; worships at St Stephen's, Kensington, 104; doubts about moving in with JDH, 104–5; correspondence with JDH, 105–6; meets Vivienne again, 106; bachelor festivities, 106–7; kindness to Hayward, 107; Edith Sitwell's view of, 111; and Leavis, 111–12; and the Group Theatre, 113–15; attitude to Spanish Civil War, 116; star of JDH's journalism, 117; attitude to Louis MacNeice, 117; lunch with James Joyce and JDH, 119; as practical joker, 120; attends Ottoline Morrell's tea party, 122; at Bina Gardens salon, 122–4; 133, 198, 220, 252; and Bill Empson, 123; farewell dinner 1936, 124; as Possum, 124; JDH becomes literary executor 132–3; JDH's view of his influence, 136, 188–9; JDH takes 'The Archives' to Cambridge, 139; letters to JDH, 141–3; and politics, 145; marooned in London, 146; hopes sister has a part in JDH's novel, 147; air raid warden, 149–50; fears for JDH's wellbeing, 153–4; leaves London for Shamley Green, 154; and war effort, 154; on *Love's Helicon*, 157; on Rosamond Lehmann, 158; wartime sufferings, 161, 165, 173, 186; death of Virginia Woolf, 165; visits Merton Hall, 166; and Anne Ridler, 168; wireless broadcast, 172; verse mangled, 179; urges JDH on with 'Beechingstoke', 180; goes to Cambridge to see *The Family Reunion*, 182–3; on the bombing of Fabers, 184; on Cambridge professorship, 185; isolation Christmas 1944, 186; plans to share flat with JDH, 186–7; settles in Carlyle Mansions, 192–3; housekeepers' views on, 193, 194; as flatmate, 195, 222–3; wardrobe, 196; daily routines, 197–8; poets' reading at the Wigmore Hall, 200–2; Vivienne's death, 201–2; JDH includes presentation copies of his work at National Book League, 206; receives OM and Nobel Prize for Literature 1948, 208; recites *Sweeney Agonistes* song, 208; condoles with JDH about death of his mother, 218–19; snobbery, 222; friendship with Mary Trevelyan, 223–5; and his 'Guardians', 226–7; deceived by Dr Schwartz, 229; figurehead for Poetry Book Society, 234; inaugurates the exhibition of 'Le Livre Anglais', 234–6; praises JDH as bibliographer, 236; 'little reviews' and the *London Magazine* 240–1; accompanies JDH to investiture of CBE, 242–3; elderly lady relatives visit Carlyle Mansions, 249; Evelyn Waugh on, 251;

Hayward), 227–8; broadcasts on 'Why First Editions?', 230–1; and work on 'Soho Bibliographies', 231–2; writes text for *Literary Britain*, 232; *Poems 1951* (ed. Hayward), 234; prepares catalogues for London University Library Rare Book Department, 236–7; masterminds catalogue of Swift's works, 237; *Penguin Book of English Verse* (ed. Hayward), 261–3; *The Book Collector* (ed. Hayward), 275–81; *Oxford Book of Nineteenth Century English Verse* (ed. Hayward), 284–5

Hayward, Dr John Arthur (JDH's father), marries, 5; sets up house in Wimbledon, 6; takes JDH to Beechingstoke, 9; summoned for Red Cross duties, 10; worried about JDH, 13; in charge of Red Cross aid detachment, 13; Medical Officer, Queen Alexandra Hospital, 14; volunteers as medical officer in France, 20; posting to Boulogne, 21–2; letters from children, 22–3; surgeon at Casualty Clearing Station, Crouay, 23; advances in surgery, 23–4; moves towards Hindenburg Line, 24; returns home and begins to practise medicine, 24–5; sends JDH to Gresham's, 26; worries about JDH's future, 38; holidays in Austria with JDH, 41; hides JDH's *Rochester*, 51; attitude to Elaine, 65–6; son George estranged from, 66; in JDH's visitors' book, 86, 135; delighted by news of flat sharing with TSE, 187; JDH composes 80th birthday poem for, 217–18; illness and death, 218; is buried in family grave, 296

Hayward, Rosamond Grace (née Rolleston, JDH's mother), marries, 5–6; JDH inherits looks from, 6–7; mistress of The Grange, 8; summer

holiday in Dorset, 10; war work with Wimbledon Red Cross, 13–14, 15, 17; her 'History' 15, 16–18; reacts to JDH's schoolboy poem, 16; and food shortages, 17–18; gardening, 19; celebrates news from Western Front, 19–20; final Christmas of war, 20; sees off husband to the Front, 20; tower of strength to family, 22; bicycle holiday with JDH to River Wye, 24; death of Scottish cousin, 27; wartime 'History' ends, 27–8; disapproves of JDH's relationship with Elaine, 65–6, 67; in JDH's visitors' book, 86; JDH's poem on her 80th birthday, 216–17; death, 218–19; is buried in family grave, 296

Hayward, Rose Mary (JDH's sister), 7–9, 14, 218, 296

Heathcote, Diana ('Dasher'), 181

Hervey, Victor, 6th Marquess of Bristol (1960), 140

Hillary, Richard, 188

Hobson, Anthony, 194, 276

Hobson, G. D., 276

Holland, David, 237

Houghton, Arthur, 278

Housman, A. E., 90–1, 231

Howard, Brian, 55, 82, 86, 134, 135

Hughes, Ted, 238

Hutchinson, Mary, 167, 182, 183

Hutchinson, St John ('Jack'), husband of preceding, 167, 183

Huxley, Aldous, 11, 114, 145, 189, 212

Hyde, Mary, 270, 279, 282, 290, correspondence becomes friendship, 229; hatches 'The Great Plot', 274–5; on JDH's busy diary, 283; sends flowers to JDH, 292

Irvine, Lyn, 82, 108

Isherwood, Christopher, 134, 189, 212, 273

Jackson, William A. ('Bill'), 278